Family Therapy

Complementary Frameworks of
Theory and Practice

Family Therapy

Complementary Frameworks of Theory and Practice

edited by

Arnon Bentovim

Gill Gorell Barnes

Alan Cooklin

WITHDRAWN

1987

published for

The Institute of Family Therapy (London)

43 New Cavendish St, London W1

by

ACADEMIC PRESS

London San Diego New York Berkeley

Boston Sydney Tokyo Toronto

ACADEMIC PRESS LIMITED
24/28 Oval Road, London NW1 7DX

United States Edition published by
ACADEMIC PRESS INC.
San Diego, CA 92101

ISBN: 0-12-089355-X

Phototypeset in Great Britain by Dobbie Typesetting Service, Plymouth
Printed in Great Britain by Galliard Printers (Yarmouth) Ltd, Great Yarmouth

Contributors

ARNON BENTOVIM *Department of Psychological Medicine, The Hospital for Sick Children, Department for Children and Parents, The Tavistock Clinic and The Institute of Family Therapy, London*

DORA BLACK *The Royal Free Hospital, The Tavistock Clinic and The Institute of Family Therapy, London*

TERRY BRUCE *St. Bartholomew's Hospital, London*

JOHN BYNG-HALL *Department for Children and Parents, The Tavistock Clinic and The Institute of Family Therapy, London*

ALAN COOKLIN *Marlborough Hospital and The Institute of Family Therapy, London*

MICHAEL CROWE *Bethlem Royal and Maudsley Hospitals and The Institute of Family Therapy, London*

ANNE ELTON *Department of Psychological Medicine, The Hospital for Sick Children and The Institute of Family Therapy, London*

GILL GORELL BARNES *Department for Children and Parents, The Tavistock Clinic and The Institute of Family Therapy, London*

BRYAN LASK *Department of Psychological Medicine, The Hospital for Sick Children*

STUART LIEBERMAN *St. George's Hospital Medical School and The Institute of Family Therapy, London*

WINIFRED ROBERTS *The Institute of Family Therapy, London*

MARGARET ROBINSON *The Institute of Family Therapy, London*

ROBIN SKYNNER *The Institute of Family Therapy, London*

v

Acknowledgements

We would like to thank the many colleagues including secretaries and librarians from our institutions whose assistance has played such an important part in the writing and preparations of the contributions for this book.

Preface

The re-issuing of this book, in an abridged, and we hope therefore more coherent form, in 1987, is a happy celebration of 10 years of the Institute of Family Therapy's development since its formal inception in 1977. As the field has developed, so has the production of literature flourished to proportions which can at times be confusing or even overwhelming to the emergent practitioner.

Thus there are two reasons why we are particularly pleased that this abridged second edition should be issued at this time. First, most of the chapters contained in this edition have been in constant demand, although the price of the two volumes has sometimes been a deterrent to their acquisition. Second, we have been able to select those chapters which we hope will be able to fulfil our two goals for this edition. On the one hand, we believe this volume will provide a thoughtful and sensible guide to help the developing practitioner chart his or her way through the abundance of new ideas, whilst on the other hand we hope we have included some seminal chapters which will continue to be of use to the experienced practitioner and teacher. At the same time, we believe we have retained an essential ingredient of the volumes; that is, the frameworks presented are complementary to each other.

There has been some reorganisation, so the book is now in three parts:

Part I: The Family in Health and Dysfunction
Part II: Practical Issues in the Therapy of the Family
Part III: Intrusions in the Life Cycle and Family Breakdown.

These sections, and the chapters within them, also continue the element of "overlapping frameworks", which featured in the first edition. Thus, in Part I the chapters by Robin Skynner, Alan Cooklin, John Byng-Hall, and Gill Gorell Barnes all to some extent address systemic ways of considering current events, in terms of present influences and influences over time, and all to some extent consider the current observable behaviour in relation to the experiences reported by the members of the family. However the perspectives of the four chapters are quite different, and invite the reader to build up a picture not only based on binocular vision, but recognising the multi-faceted view of reality which the family therapist needs to adopt.

Robin Skynner's chapter (1) helps the reader to form distinctions between the behaviour of an individual, and the behaviour of a set of relationships, between events having a timespan through the generations, and those which can be observed within an observable hour, day or week. He also makes a distinction between what can be observed in the behaviour of the family members, and the inner experiential life of the family. Alan Cooklin's chapter (2), is concerned more with perspectives of therapy, but its focus is to relate the distinct phenomena described by Robin Skynner. To do this he uses the metaphor of various forms of oscillation or vibration as a way of defining sequences of interaction in terms of whether they are short, medium, or long. He relates different therapeutic interventions, as well as different models and their application to these different timespans. John Byng-Hall's chapter (3) covers some of the same issues from the perspective of the symbolic meaning of the family events in terms of each member's experience and the collective experience. Thus he describes graphically the therapist's own experience as a tool for understanding the meaning of the family's behaviour, in the here-and-now, as well as the processes the therapist has to go through to extrapolate this, to an understanding the patterns developing in the family over time.

Gill Gorell Barnes develops a base for continuing to relate these ideas from the research findings of behavioural scientists, ethologists and others. She develops *three* main themes; family patterns, and mutual influence within the family, and uses these as a background for considering interventions in behaviour patterns. Thirdly, she relates such interventions to what has recently been learnt about the processes of learning which occur within families.

Part II: "Practical Issues in the Therapy of the Family" is more in the form of a practice manual for the beginning therapist, particularly in the first three chapters.

Win Roberts' chapter (5) "Presentation of the Referral Network: The Professional and the Family", represents a particularly British contribution to the field as she provides a lucid account of how interventions between the professional network and the family may reduce or maintain dysfunction, and outlines issues which the therapist needs to face in responding to these possibilities.

Gill Gorell Barnes' chapter (6) "Initial Work with the Family", provides a thoughtful and sensible set of principles for the therapist conducting a first interview. However, we've recognised the understandable panic of the therapist who has sweated successfully through a competent first interview and then faces the question "now what do I do"? This is attended to in Anne Elton's chapter (7) "Maintaining Family Motivation during Treatment". Chapters 8 and 10 consider the practical implications of the influence of long-term patterns in the family in treatment, as well as in the family of the therapist. John Byng-Hall's description (8) "Influence of Family Legends", is a unique development of an idea about the growth of legends and their continued influence in the family, utilising history developed over two centuries in his own family. On the other hand, Stuart Lieberman's chapter (10) describes a method for the therapist to review issues in his or her own family as a way of resolving conflicts both in his or her own mind, as well as within the patterns of relationships with the family. He uses this as a form of personal therapy for the therapist, analogous to the training analysis recommended for the practitioners of many individual therapies.

Chapter 9 "The Strengths and Weaknesses in Co-therapy" by Win Roberts, has been included as it remains a controversial practice issue for many new therapists. Co-therapy has all too often been adopted by therapists as a way of "holding hands" in the face of this new and anxiety-provoking therapeutic endeavour. However, Win Roberts provides a lucid account which we believe will help the new practitioner to make a more informed decision.

The last chapter in this section "The Treatment of Marital and Sexual Problems: A Behavioural Approach" by Michael Crowe, is included here for two reasons. Firstly, it is a very lucid account of the thinking and methods of behavioural, marital and sexual therapy, and is refreshing in that it is written by a practitioner who is familiar with, understands, and is sympathetic to an overall systemic framework for viewing such relationships. Secondly, we have been concerned that relevant confrontation with sexual issues is sometimes avoided by family therapists, and within this chapter are illustrations which can help the practitioner to keep sex as part of therapy when it belongs there.

Part III: "Intrusions in the Life-Cycle and Family Breakdown" considers the influence of major disruptions to the family's integrity, and the therapist's approach to these.

Chapter 12 "Loss and Mourning", by Stuart Lieberman and Dora Black provides a systematic review of the processes of mourning as they affect the individual and the family. They then consider common pathological patterns in the family which may develop in relation to loss, and identify therapeutic interventions and foci which are relevant to the problems of bereaved families. The inclusion of Margaret Robinson's chapter (13) "Reconstituted Families: Some Implications for the Family Therapist", is of particular importance when one faces that one in ten children are brought up in single parent families, and that the proportion of reconstituted families will inevitably continue to increase. She includes within her remit adopted families, fostering families, step families, and other alternatives to the two-parent model of family development.

Chapter 14 "Handicap and Family Therapy" by Dora Black, is one of the seminal articles in the field of therapy with the families of handicapped children. She reviews the impact of handicap on the child, the family, and the community and examines the use of crisis intervention as well as longer term therapy with the family of the handicapped child.

Chapter 15 is an amalgamation of Bryan Lask's two chapters "Physical Illness and the Family and Family Therapy in Paediatric Settings". We feel that this amalgamation has added to the usefulness of this chapter, in that he addresses the issues of illness in the family from two distinct but closely related perspectives.

On the one hand he considers models for the influence of family interactional patterns on the development of the illness process, as well as ways of intervening in these; whilst on the other hand he continues to examine the same issues within the context of the primary treatment settings for childhood illness, namely paediatric settings. Any consideration of the two without reference to the other, is in our opinion a deficiency. We think this new chapter provides a very useful guide to both the junior and senior practitioner working with the family in community settings, as well as those working in hospital settings.

Terry Bruce's chapter "Family Work in a Secure Unit" continues the elucidation of some of the institutional issues which the therapist has to face working in different settings. Although this setting of a "secure unit" is unique, the issues he describes have wide application, and are particularly useful to all therapists working with severely disrupted families.

The last chapter "A Family Therapy Approach to Making Decisions in Child Care Cases" by Arnon Bentovim has retained its critical importance. Although child care practices in themselves may be changing in favour of greater use of fostering and adoption, and the greater development of techniques to re-unite families where this is possible, our increasing knowledge of the extent of child physical and sexual abuse, makes a rational framework for thinking about child care decisions essential. The particular value of this chapter is that it combines the principles that have been developed within the child care field with the systemic understanding of the wider implications of those developed by family therapists.

In this preface we have tried to represent the flavour and cohesion of these chapters rather than giving a detailed summary of each. It should be added however that the chapters are all well referenced, and well provided with lucid and interesting clinical examples.

We hope that the re-issuing of this edition will continue to provide a useful contribution to the field.

Alan Cooklin

Contents

Part I

The Family in Health and Dysfunction

Chapter 1

Frameworks for Viewing the Family as a System

R. Skynner

A. THE FAMILY AS A HERE-AND-NOW INTERACTING ENTITY

I. INTRODUCTION: HOMEOSTATIC SYSTEMS

Imagine the situation of primitive man, familiar with fire and able to build a crude hut, who comes upon a modern house, deserted by its occupants, which possesses an efficient central heating system. After exploring the house, the man chooses a room to live in, but finds it a little too cool for his liking. The room is fitted with a fireplace and, recognizing the ashes from previous fires, he gathers sticks, creates a flame by friction between pieces of wood, and lights a fire.

As the flames take hold and throw out heat, he experiences a pleasant warmth. But soon the room is as cool as before. He throws on more wood. Again there is a transient increase in temperature, but away from the direct heat of the fire itself, the room soon feels no warmer. Finally, when the wood is exhausted, the fire dies out. Having found it difficult to generate any warmth in the room even with a large fire, he expects the temperature to drop rapidly now that the fire is no longer providing heat. But even more mysterious, it hardly changes at all!

We know something that he is unaware of: the thermostat in the hall is designed to switch on the central heating boiler at a temperature set on its dial, and to switch off again when the temperature is a few degrees higher. The temperature of the air, at least in the vicinity of the thermostat, will move up and down between those two limits as the boiler is repeatedly switched on and off by the device.

Though the doors and windows to the exterior were shut, the rooms were connected with one another. This being the case, when the visitor lit his fire the warm air in the room gradually passed out into the hallway so that the thermostat exceeded its upper limit and switched the boiler off. Eventually, the more the fire warmed the room, the more the radiators cooled to compensate, keeping the temperature more or less constant. The reverse principle applied when the fire went out.

Here we have a simple, commonly used example of a *system* (in this case a heating system) maintaining *homeostasis* (keeping the temperature more or less constant) through the principle of *negative feedback* (the thermostat informs the

Family Therapy
ISBN: 0-12-089355-X

boiler about the effects of its performance in achieving this task, in such a way that it *resists* change; i.e. it stops the boiler when the air gets too hot, and starts it when it gets too cold, rather than the reverse). It is able to achieve this throughout the house because the house is an *open system* (the doors are open or partly open, so that temperature changes in individual rooms are communicated through the house over a period of time). Had the *boundaries* defining the parts (rooms) of the whole system (house) been more rigid and closed (i.e. if the doors of the rooms had been shut), it would have been possible to change the temperature of separate rooms without affecting the whole house, and without producing the "negative feedback" effect described.

II. SYSTEMS THINKING AND THERAPY

A. From Individual to Families

Though this type of analogy has been used often enough before, we begin with it here because it emphasizes the essential simplicity of the concepts of systems theory, provided they are properly understood rather than employed as a new jargon substituting for thought. The situation of the therapist who attempts to change one individual, without taking into consideration the effects of any success he may have upon the whole family system, is very similar to that of the man who lights the fire in one room of the centrally heated house. Changes may be achieved, to be sure, but they last a short time only, and are mysteriously reversed by influences invisible to all but the trained eye. The patient improves in hospital (subsystem boundary closed = door to rooms shut), but relapses as soon as he is well enough to go home, or perhaps even deteriorates during the visit of a parent (open boundary = doors to rooms open). Not only is it difficult to change him for the "better", while he remains connected with his family; it is also puzzlingly difficult to make him "worse" while he is part of this system. In short, the widening of our perspective from its earlier focus on the individual, to an awareness of family and community systems, has shown us some clear reasons for the extraordinary difficulty everyone has found in changing individuals separately from their family systems; or in changing families separately from the influence of their neighbourhood communities, as long as they remain in close psychological contact with, and so are deeply affected by, these larger structures in which their lives are led.

But the other side of the coin is as encouraging as the first is depressing. If the man who had tried to warm the room with his fire had understood the function of the central heating system, a slight movement of his fingers, taking less than a second and using scarcely any energy at all, would not only have led to a change in temperature of exactly the order he was seeking through his laborious fire-making efforts, but would have maintained temperature at that level until he chose to change it. Similarly, once we begin to understand the feedback systems which govern the behaviour of families by the way they maintain homeostasis in the repetitive patterns of interaction between the members, we have the possibility of finding crucial points of intervention (like the dial on the thermostat in the heating system) where a small intervention can have a maximum affect of the kind we aim for upon the total functioning. Moreover, once achieved, this is likely to be maintained within a new equilibrium without further efforts on our part.

B. Change and Positive Feedback

The example of the central heating system does not help us to explain the idea of *positive* feedback, for though this could be provided by changing the design of the thermostat so that it turned the boiler on just above the temperature setting, and off just below the setting (that is, the *reverse* of the negative feedback condition), this arrangement would quickly lead to the air in the house rapidly reaching either its maximum or its minimum temperature and remaining there, an arrangement which could serve no useful purpose. But even this makes the point that positive feedback produces *change* rather than stability. An example may be seen in a business enterprise, where some proportion of the profits is fed back into the business itself. Then, the more successful the company, the greater the capital investment and the greater the productive capacity. Given an initial success and stable external conditions, the business will steadily grow with time. Similarly, if the business begins to fail, less money is put into capital investment, output diminishes, and the business shrinks at an increasing rate, leading ultimately to bankruptcy. The principle of positive feedback is thus at the root of *changes* in a system, whether in the form of growth or decay, just as negative feedback is concerned with maintaining the system steady.

Biological systems will usually contain a combination of both negative and positive feedback loops of this kind, which together determine the "balance of nature" at a given moment. Positive feedback alone leads to an exponential increase in whatever the positive feedback loop applies to, such as the screaming of a panicking crowd where the *expression* of the panic through screaming constantly magnifies the panic; or in the failure of the control (negative feedback) mechanisms at the Three Mile Island nuclear reactor.

C. Circular Causality

It will be seen that, in moving towards the systems approach, *causality* becomes *circular* rather than simply *linear.* The model of linear causality with which we grew up no longer suffices as an accurate way of construing the world. This may be typified by the image of the movements of balls on a billiards or snooker table, where once we know the speed and velocity of the initial shock, we can in theory predict the movements of all the balls according to the principles of Newtonian mechanics, and can accurately assess the transmission of energy from one ball to the next as they bounce against each other. Once we introduce the ideas of feedback and of circular causality, the individual billiard balls become equipped with self-steering gear or pre-programmed automatic pilots as it were which ensure that they all fall into the pockets no matter what motion the player gives to the first ball, or alternatively that they all avoid ever falling into the pockets; yet again, that they sometimes do and sometimes don't depending upon the state of the game, etc. If these billiard balls are already beginning to resemble living organisms, that is because, as Bateson (1972) constantly points out, such feedback loops are among the most fundamental characteristics of "life".

D. The Need for a General Systems Theory

So far we have presented some of the concepts of systems theory in a manner which is in some ways more typical of a pre-systems, reductionist approach to science. That is, we have given examples of "chunks" of the world, and though we have looked at the relationships within their boundaries, we have treated them as if they can be studied in isolation from the rest of the universe. To some extent we can do this, of course, and all science must be based on approximations of this sort if we are to simplify things sufficiently to be able to think about them at all. As von Bertalanffy (1968, pp.18-19) expressed it:

> the system problem is essentially the problem of limitations of analytical pro-
> cedures in science . . . 'Analytical procedure' means that an entity investigated be
> resolved into and hence can be constituted or reconstituted from, the parts put
> together, these procedures being understood both in their material and conceptual
> sense. This is the basic principle of 'classical' science, which can be circumscribed
> in different ways: a resolution into isolable causal trains, seeking for 'atomic' units
> in the various fields of science, etc. The progress of science has shown that these
> principles of classical science — first enunciated by Galileo and Descartes — are
> highly successful in a wide realm of phenomena.
> Application of the analytical procedure depends on two conditions. The first is that
> interactions between 'parts' be non-existent or weak enough to be neglected for
> certain research purposes. . . . The second condition is that the relations describing
> the behaviour of parts be linear; only then is the condition of summativity given,
> i.e., an equation describing the behaviour of the total is of the same form as the
> equations describing the behaviour of the parts; partial processes can be super-
> imposed to obtain the total process, etc.
>   These conditions are not fulfilled in the entities called systems, i.e., consisting
> of parts 'in interaction'. The prototype of their description is a set of simultaneous
> differential equations . . . which are nonlinear in the general case.

If we take these ideas seriously, we can see that we cannot stop at considering discrete parts of the world one at a time, but that, if these "systems" principles are accepted as applying to any one scale or level of organisation, they must apply at all others and indeed to the whole. In the words of von Bertalanffy (1968) again:

> There appear to exist general system laws which apply to any system of a certain
> type, irrespective of the particular properties of the system and of the elements
> involved.
>   These considerations lead to the postulate of a new scientific discipline which we
> call general system theory. It's subject matter is formulation of principles that are

valid for 'systems' in general whatever the nature of their component elements and the relations or forces between them. (p.37)

Thus, not only can the world be seen as made up of systems, but the systems at any level are parts of larger systems still, in the way that a number of fields are part of a farm, a number of farms in turn may be part of a district, the district a part of a county, and so on. To quote von Bertalanffy (1968) again:

> The above considerations pertain particularly to a concept or complex of concepts which indubitably is fundamental in the general theory of systems: that of *hierarchic order.* We presently 'see' the universe as a tremendous hierarchy, from elementary particles to atomic nuclei, to atoms, molecules, high-molecular compounds, to the wealth of structures, electron and light-microscopic between molecules and cells . . . , to cells, organisms and beyond to supra-individual organisations. (p.27)

If we look at human life from this point of view, we may consider any level of organisation as a system. If we are focusing particularly on an individual, and regard that person as the "system", then the larger system of which he is a part (the family) is termed the *"supra-system,"* and the *parts* of the individual are called *sub-systems* (e.g. the nervous system, the circulatory system, the "unconscious"). However, if we are focussing on the *family* as the system, then the individual is the sub-system (one of its parts), and some higher level of social organization such as the extended family or community, is then the supra-system of which the family is a part. The whole of mankind can then be viewed as a series of concentric circles or "chinese boxes", each circle containing smaller ones contained within larger ones. (We hope that readers familiar with these ideas will bear with us while they are presented. A good grasp of them is essential for understanding modern developments in family therapy, and the difficulty in presenting them is somehow to combine an expression of both their profound simplicity and their profound generality. Emphasis on the generality alone tends to make readers shrink before the vast scale to which the ideas are applied, which suggests a daunting complexity; emphasizing the simplicity alone, however, often has the contrary effect of causing the reader to brush the ideas aside as too trivial and obvious to need emphasis.)

III. THE ELEMENTS OF HUMAN SYSTEMS

A. Boundaries

In our image of concentric circles, the circles themselves would represent the *boundaries* of the system (space) they surround, and in human systems, the boundary can be seen as the dividing line between one system and another on the same level, all marking off the system from its supra-system and defining the sub-systems within itself. Nevertheless, the boundary may be easier to define in spatial terms, like the membrane of a living cell, or the skin of a man. The boundary of a family has more to do with distinctions between the special degree of experience and information sharing among family members when they are compared with outsiders, and also a certain centring of movement or communication in space, in a dynamic rather than a static sense. Similarly, the boundary of a family sub-system such as the parental couple is recognized by the special degrees of physical intimacy, privacy and depth of information exchanged, and the degree and duration of commitment in their relationship, differing from the relationships of the spouses to other family members. "Boundary" denotes a point of transition where *differences* can be observed in structure, function, behaviour etc. on either side. Seen from another view-point, the boundary is defined by the rules as to who may participate in certain kinds of interaction and information sharing, and who may not. In technical terms applicable to all systems, Miller (1965) defines the boundary as that region round the exterior of the system "over which there is less transmission of matter/energy and information than there is within the system or within its environment." (p.214).

B. Decider Subsystems

The other vital part of the system is the *decider subsystem:*

> The essential critical sub-system which controls the entire system, causing its sub-systems and components to co-act, without which there is no system [204] . . . Of (the systems) only the decider is essential, in a sense that a system cannot be parasitic or symbiotic with another system for its deciding. A living system does not exist if the decider is displaced upwardly (to the supra-system), downwardly (to the sub-system) or outwardly (to another system i.e. parasitic or symbiotic). (Miller, 1965 p.222)

On different levels, the "decider" may be the chromosomes in a fertilized egg, the nervous system of an animal, the brain of the nervous system, the queen of a colony of bees, the parents of a family, or the government of a country. The decider has the task of co-ordinating the activities of all the parts of the system in the light of what is required of it by events in the outside environment. The co-ordination must concern the welfare of the whole system, since the decider's fate is bound up with it. The decider is *responsible* for the whole system, in the original sense that it must be able to *respond* appropriately to the situation. And for this to be accomplished, it must receive information about the functioning of all the parts of the system, and of events in the environment.

The decider thus ensures the *integrity* of the system, and its continued *differentiation* from the environment. It has a similar function to the boundary, over which it has a varying degree of control, but they each protect the system's integrity in a different way, which as we shall see, has great relevance to the functioning of families and their treatment. In the case of a nation, for example, a looser structure with more freedom to the sub-systems, may be possible if its boundary is relatively impermeable. Such is the case of Britain's tradition of democratic institutions, which owe much to its sea boundary and past naval power; or the similar case of the United States, divided by oceans and comparable power of potentially predatory neighbours. The democratic traditions of Iceland, even more protected by its inhospitable northern waters, are even older. But a powerful unity and identity may be maintained despite a lack of protective boundaries of this kind, through shared values, information-exchange and clear rules regulating insider/outsider status, as in the case of the Jewish diaspora.

C. Hierarchy

In addition to pointing out that a system cannot exist without its decider, Miller (1965) also notes that "If there are multiple parallel deciders, without a hierarchy that has subordinate and superordinate deciders, there is not one system but multiple ones." (p.218) This is obviously of crucial importance to us in considering the division or sharing of power between father and mother in a family. Unless there is a hierarchy with either mother or father dominant, or some satisfactory system to ensure collaboration between the two parents, perhaps with shared decisions, clearly defined separate roles, or alternating dominance, there will not be one family, but two. Chapter 2 describes a family inter-acting in the present day context to illustrate some these issues.

B. THE FAMILY AS A SYSTEM OVER A PERIOD OF TIME

I. INTRODUCTION

Our discussion of systems ideas has used mechanical/electrical examples to illustrate the principles; or, where living organisms were discussed, has focussed more often on short time-spans than on the life-time of an individual. But the one certain fact of "life" is the fact of death. Living organisms are not only vulnerable to irreversible damage from forces in their environment, including other organisms, but are actually programmed to self-destruct after a variable but limited period of time. Life involves continuance only for the group, not for the separate individual member, and to maintain it, new members must repeatedly be created, to replace those who die.

II. TRANSMISSION OF HUMAN STRUCTURE AND FUNCTION

A. The Family as the Unit of Reproduction

If the continuation even of the group is to have any meaning, some *pattern* regarding the structure and function of the members, both as individuals and as a group, must be transmitted from the existing members to the newly-created ones. Much of this process takes place in, and is the *raison d'être* of, the family, the smallest unit within which this process can be fulfilled. As dysfunction is dealt with in other chapters, the focus here will be on *healthy*, *"optimal"* functioning, the "ideal" rather than the statistically "normal", average or mid-range.

Transmission of the pattern is achieved through a number of routes. The act of sexual intercourse between the parental couple initiates the union of sperm and egg, resulting in a genetic programme different from each parent yet with characteristics of both. Protected at first within the mother's body, and later within the safety of the family boundary, matter/energy is at first absorbed from the mother's blood, then from her milk, later at the high chair and finally the family table. The basic shaping of this material by the chromosomal instructions is further modified by information absorbed by the sense organs from the environment, particularly from other family members. At first the very fact that things exist as they do and where they do; the fact that mother exists, has a certain shape, and gratifies; while at other times seems not to exist, does not gratify, but yet appears again repeatedly; all begin to form within the infant's inner communicational network "a model" or "map" of the outside world. During this early period in particular (say about the first year or so) a certain stability and regularity must obtain in the immediate environment to avoid such a bombardment of new impressions that the infant has no hope of bringing order out of seeming chaos, and is driven to "blinker" itself from the overload. The mother's nurture, both in terms of feeding and of comforting presence, must also be reliable enough to keep *internal* stimulation within manageable limits, avoiding extremes of rage or frustration so that emotional responses may gradually be integrated and mastered. In the early stages, this requires the provision of a protective boundary by the mother while these delicate processes are proceeding, and the mother in turn will need to be looked after herself and to have the family boundary guarded by others, particularly the father or the grandparents, while she gives attention to her immediate task.

B. The Discovery of Boundaries

During this period, the infant will be discovering that *not everything is itself*, that it has an *edge* (boundary), beyond which its wishes and fantasies have less effect than they do within that edge (a task not helped by the fact that it discovers it does not have very much more control even *within* that edge). It is not so much that the infant *thinks* he *is* the world, that he desires to be omnipotent and omnipresent, but rather that there is no reason to be aware that there *is* anything else, anything other than self, until the "not-self" makes its presence felt. The infant is necessarily "all", "everything", indeed "God", until it discovers otherwise. If its needs could be anticipated and met in every detail, it would perhaps have no reason to suspect that it was in any way separate from the rest of the universe. It is the *failure* of the environment to behave as if it is part of the infant's self that shows where the edge or boundary is, thereby providing the beginning sense of identity of self and difference from others (though as already suggested, this failure must be carefully graded to what the infant can tolerate if it is to endure the painful realization that it is *not* God, that indeed it is almost helpless and dependent on another being with a life of her own). Winnicott (1958) has developed this issue particularly clearly.

C. Learning about the Insides and Outsides of the System

Klein (1932) and her followers have emphasized how one aspect of this increasing discrimination between inside and outside, self and other, is an increasing ability to experience feeling-states as contained within that boundary, rather than pervading its view of the external world and distorting the infant's perception of it. And this process is accompanied by a similar integration of perceptions, both internal and external, whereby love and hate, and the gratifying or frustrating behaviour of the care-giving person to which these two states are related, are integrated instead of being kept separate. "Good mother" and "bad mother" become one mother, who is sometimes there and sometimes not. Pure love and pure hate, both overwhelming, become fused to form manageable ambivalence, sufficiently variable through the balance of its positive or negative components to permit management of attachment and rejecting behaviour. The infant is then capable of functioning in what Klein calls the *depressive position*. But poor handling of this developmental process, with excessive frustration in comparison to gratification, does not permit the infant to move beyond the *paranoid-schizoid position*, with consequent failure of integration and discrimination demonstrated by *part-object* relationships (failure to perceive others as separate whole persons) *splitting* (inability to integrate positive and negative aspects of external reality or of internal responses to them) and *projection* (the attribution to persons or events, outside the self, of unacceptable aspects too painful to contain within it). Even where depressive position functioning has been to some extent achieved but is only precariously established, stressful situations, leading to frustration too painful to bear, may cause a regression to paranoid-schizoid position functioning (as with a badly handled hospitalization).

D. The Need for Adequate Parental Boundaries

If these tasks characteristic of the first year of the infant's life are to be accomplished, one requirement which is perhaps not always sufficiently emphasized is that the parental figures should be clear about their own boundaries. If the primary care-giving figure (usually the mother) is not clear and secure about her own personal boundary, she will be unable to help the infant to find its own boundary. Marking the border defining the northern boundary of England, automatically defines the southern edge of Scotland as well. In similar fashion, parents who are clear about their own boundaries, and secure in their identities, will automatically provide relationships through which the child can define itself, even without any conscious attempt to address this problem. Parents who are unclear in this matter tend to attribute feelings to the child which belong to themselves, and vice versa, making the infant's task of self-definition more difficult. Moreover, even the earliest stages of nurture of the infant, when some degree of fusion between mother and child is appropriate through the mother making her boundaries more permeable, empathizing with the infant's experiences (Winnicott's (1958) state of "Primary Maternal Preoccupation") may be rendered impossible if the mother's fragile sense of identity makes her fearful of entering into this kind of relationship, with all its vulnerability. Nevertheless, if all goes well, mother and infant are able at first to enter this symbiotic state, with father and perhaps other relatives protecting them.

As the child grows, the mother is able to re-establish her own boundaries once again, "failing" the child's expectations sufficiently to enable it progressively to define itself. In this she will usually be aided by the father, who not only protects the family boundary at this stage but "holds the life line" permitting the mother to enter safely into this degree of regressive interaction with the infant, and "hauling her back" by stages towards a primary investment in the marital relationship, rather than in the child. It is perhaps this crucial function of the father in assisting the mother and child to grow apart progressively, thereby facilitating self-definition and independence, which makes the presence and active involvement of the father so important in the next stage, comprising roughly the second and third years of life. He needs not only to restore close affectional and sexual bonds with the mother as the child needs her less, but by forming a close and trusting relationship with the child, by nature of the fact that he is inevitably a different person in some respects, he provides another dimension through which the child can find out who he is, as a ship, by taking two bearings on different landmarks, can establish its position. If the first year of the infant's life is concerned more with the taking-in of matter/energy and information, with the establishment of a *base*, then in this second period, the infant ventures out and explores the environment. Increasing maturation of the nervous system brings with it increasing control of movement, freedom of action, and the possibility of impinging actively on the surroundings. The child begins to walk, talk and gain control of its sphincters, and with these new powers comes the possibility of collaborating with, or resisting, the parents.

E.   Parenting and Social Information

It is during this phase therefore, that the foundations are laid for self-control and initiative, the achievement of some compromise between the demands for social conformity and the satisfaction of personal needs, and the development of a sense of identity, difference and separateness from others.

If the child is to accomplish this, the parents and other adult figures must achieve a satisfactory compromise between on the one hand providing freedom and space to try out these new powers, in order to test out the developing will and initiative, and to explore the world, while on the other hand also providing sufficient firmness, limits, controls and requirements that social demands be heeded, in order to enable the child to feel safe in his explorations, and to internalize those social values needed to make satisfactory relationships with others. The prominence of the issue of toilet training during this period led Freud to call it the "anal" phase, though it seems likely that the importance of this issue is due to the fact that it is the first battleground on which the conflict between the desires of the individual and the demands of the society are fought out.

In the second stage, problems may be caused if the parents are uncertain about their own identity or have unresolved conflicts over accepting authority or social demands, as well as where the father is absent or ineffective, or the parents are unable to collaborate over discipline and setting of limits.

F.   Parenting and Sexuality in Childhood

A third phase, reaching its height around 4–5 years of age, is characterized by childhood precursors of adult sexual feeling, by interest in the genitals of the self and others, and in the origin of babies. Something like a love affair with the parent of the opposite sex becomes apparent, together with jealousy of the parent of the same sex.

If the parents are at ease with their own sexuality, have a satisfying sexual relationship themselves, and treat these manifestations with respect and naturalness, the foundations are laid for sexual confidence in later life. The son discovers that mother finds his sexuality pleasurable, but that she belongs to father and is not available; the daughter likewise with her father. The child gets the message that its sexuality is good, but that it cannot marry its parents and must first grow to adulthood and find a partner of its own. Thus, the stage is set for entry into the wider world to learn, to socialize, to join the peer-group from which the eventual mate will have to be selected.

Once again, a balance is needed in the parental response between over-and-under reaction to the child's sexual initiatives. The combination of infantile sexuality, the oedipal conflict and the incest taboo provides, as it were, a powerful motive force towards differentiating from the family (since sex cannot be obtained there) and learning to cope with the wider society (where sex will ultimately be available). Parental prudishness, or complete denial of parental sexual response to the initiatives of the child, removes the carrot from the donkey, as it were. At the other extreme, incest allows the donkey to eat the carrot, but in either case a vital motivation towards differentiation and growth is removed.

As in other periods, several related developmental tasks are being addressed simultaneously, and the achievement of one automatically helps the others. During this third period, the child not only has to accept that the parents are more powerful, but that they have a special relationship with each other and some pleasurable and indeed profoundly exciting activity from which he or she is excluded. The child has to cope with *jealousy* and *exclusion* from relationship. Not only does omnipotence suffer a further necessary reduction; in addition, if this stage is successfully surmounted, the foundations of the capacity for *sharing*, and so for group membership, are soundly laid.

The child is now well prepared to join the peer-group, a capability which may have been enhanced by previous experience of coping with siblings, and the child goes to school. Interest and energy are transferred increasingly from the earlier biological tasks towards learning and socialization. The earlier, more open expression of sexuality appears to go underground, though interest remains active enough, even if confined to discussions or satisfactions of curiosity with peers. Males and females divide into separate groups, and even become antagonistic. Teachers and other adults provide new models, additional landmarks on which children can take their bearings to find their own preferred positions and directions. The parents become less important, though still providing a safe base and refuge.

For the parents, perhaps the main need is to let the children go. Mothers who themselves find it hard to separate and differentiate, and have gratified themselves vicariously during the earlier period, make separation difficult for the child. But in normal circumstances, separation is aided by the fact that the mother is glad to be freed of the burdens of the first five years, and is able to resume her separate interests and activities. Almost all studies of marital satisfaction have shown that during the period between the birth of children and the time they go to school, marital satisfaction reaches its lowest ebb, increasing in general thereafter just as it decreased before.

G. Parenting and Sexuality in Adolescence

The approach of puberty sees a return of the interest in sexual issues which burst into prominence with the hormonal changes at the beginning of adolescence. The child is under biological and social pressures to accept and gratify the emerging sexual needs, and to move away from the primary attachment to the parents and the family towards the loyalties of the peer-group. At the same time, the struggles towards independence alternate with a resurgence of childish dependence, while demands for sexual freedom are counter-balanced by equal fears and a desire that the parents will set limits within which experimentation can be safely attempted. All being well, the responsibilities of adult sexuality are gradually approached, first engaging with the opposite sex in the safety of the same-sex group; then pairing off, but in a crowd; then perhaps in small groups or foursomes; finally in couples.

The task of parents is particularly difficult at this stage, for whatever they do will by definition be "wrong". They will be seen as too restricting at one moment, uncaring at another; prudish kill-joys when they set limits, neglectful and indifferent when they do not.

Parents who are ill at ease with their own sexuality, or whose sexual relationship is unsatisfactory, will find the task more difficult. They may either become over-restrictive out of anxiety, provoking unnecessary rebellion, or avoid the provision of age-appropriate limits through their need to deny the problem. Such difficulties will be all the greater if the sexual relationship between the parents is unsatisfactory and precarious, since their inhibitions, which may not be unsuperable as long as sex is kept in the background as a low-key issue, may be magnified intolerably when they are confronted with the crude directness which can characterize adolescent sexuality.

What is required of the parents at this stage is that they themselves should have completed their own developmental tasks to an adequate degree. They need to be sufficiently at ease with their own sexuality to enable their adolescent child to be at ease too. The sexual relationship between the parents needs to be satisfying and enjoyable, so that it encounters no threat from the powerful sexuality developing in another member of the family. Instead, they can serve as a positive model to the adolescent that sex, within a loving and responsible relationship, can reach its greatest fulfilment. And the parents need to be sufficiently complete in themselves, as well as satisfied with each other, to contemplate the departure of their offspring from the home without being threatened with pain and loneliness, indeed, to anticipate with pleasure the prospect of freedom from child-rearing tasks.

H.   Adulthood and the New Family

As the young person reaches "escape velocity" from the emotional "gravitational field" of the family, the tasks of gaining acceptance by, and finding a responsible place within, the wider society become paramount. The individual learns to work, becomes self-supporting, explores the social and physical environment more extensively, and after "playing the field" to gain more adequate experience of intimate and sexual relationships, is drawn increasingly towards a more permanent liaison, culminating in marriage. All these changes require an increasing ability to see oneself as part of a group, to see others as oneself, to accept a certain discipline and self-sacrifice to permit the performance of a common task, whether the production of goods in work, or collaboration in setting up a home.

The parents, during this time, will be enjoying their new-found freedom, if healthy; or experiencing loneliness and emptiness, behaving as the "interfering in-laws" of the stock music-hall jokes, and anxiously and impatiently awaiting the arrival of grandchildren, if not.

The arrival of the new-generation couple's first child brings profound changes and new stresses. The wife, who is likely to be working, is obliged to give this up, at least temporarily, and to undergo a total change of life-style. Overnight, she loses her former freedom, which may have been greater than she had ever possessed, and must devote most of her attention to serving another person who makes constant demands for attention by night as well as by day. The husband must at least continue to work and support his wife in this task, while much attention and care she formerly devoted to him is now suddenly transferred to the baby. If he shares more fully in the child-rearing activities, as is common nowadays, the change for him is greater still. Even the sexual relationship is disrupted for a period, and may be impaired for months or years through fatigue and distractions. The marriage comes under particular stress for all these reasons, and marital satisfaction reaches its lowest point over the next few years.

At this stage, and particularly around the time of the birth, the calm supportive presence of the original parents (now the grandparents) provides a crucial input. They have been through it all before, and can reassure by the way they take it in their stride. Through their affection and support, they can help to replace the mutual support which the couple formerly gave to each other, and now must give to the child-rearing task. Other relatives can play similarly supportive roles, and it is likely that the larger extended families of previous times sustained young parents through this stage more adequately than is commonly possible today.

I. The Life-cycle Completing

In our description, one cycle is now complete. The original parents, now grand-parents, will continue to play an important part in their children's and grand-children's lives, acting as supports and resources in times of stress and crisis, mediating between the parents and children at times, and providing alternative models. It remains to say something about the later phases of the life cycle, after the children have "left the nest".

The beginning of this later stage will tend to coincide with what is often called "the prime of life". The powers and achievements of the man will often be at their zenith. The woman, too, will still be vigorous and energetic. If she has maintained and developed her own separate life, identity and interests outside the child-ruling tasks, she can now enjoy a period of unprecedented freedom and achievement. Both partners will normally be still sexually vigorous, and if the relationship has been nourished, they may find the sexual relationship more enjoyable at this stage than at any previous time.

As they move beyond this phase towards the 60s physical strength and energy will diminish, and the most active pursuits will begin to be curtailed. If achieve-ment earlier has been adequate, success and recognition will seem increasingly unimportant. Interest and enjoyment turn increasingly inwards, and the satisfaction of these final years will depend on the extent to which an inner life has been preserved and built up through the earlier years. Simple activities and pleasures become increasingly valued, and life becomes easier as unnecessary complications, and meaningless ambitions, drop away. To the extent that this change is possible, and negotiated successfully, retirement becomes something to look forward to, and brings a new and different phase of enjoyment.

The death of the partner is part of this final phase, followed eventually by the death of the one remaining. To the extent that earlier phases have been success-fully surmounted and enjoyed, death will be experienced as a part of life, accepted like the rest.

During this last phase, the caring roles reverse, the parents taking on a caring and managerial role towards the grandparents as the powers of the later fail, even the grandchildren enjoying helping to look after them. By the time the grandparents die, the parents have already been prepared, therefore, for the new responsibility they undertake as they now become of grandparental age them-selves.

This last part of the cycle has been described here in terms of those who manage it well. They will usually be those who have managed earlier phases in the same satisfactory way, so that they have developed satisfactory resources within themselves, and are therefore able to give more willingly, and to demand less. For those who earlier have been deprived and unhappy, looking to each other or to their children to remedy their own deficiencies, the later years are likely to extenuate the feelings of loneliness and misery, so that far from being a support to their children and grandchildren that they become increasingly demanding and burdensome.

J. What makes for Success in the Family

For the process to proceed in a satisfactory, optimum fashion, there should be throughout life a steady decrease in the egocentricity and narcissism of the early infantile stages, counterbalanced by a progressive increase in real skills, interests and internal resources. The meaning and purpose of life must come increasingly to lie in something beyond the individual, ephemeral self, even beyond any one other person, and even ultimately beyond the family. For this to occur, not only must interest extend beyond the self to the family, and beyond the family to the wider community, but as we shall see from the Timberlawn Research, some sense of a transcendent value system is needed which can enable the individual to survive even the death of loved ones without destruction of meaning.

It should be clearly emphasized again, perhaps, that this chapter deals throughout with health in the sense of optimal function, in contrast to dysfunction of varying degree which receives adequate coverage in other chapters. Individuals and families conforming to these criteria are of course rare, as olympic athletes are rare, but we have enough evidence (outlined later in this chapter) to be confident that these high levels of effective function are approached in a small minority of the population. We will not expect to encounter them in our professional work with dysfunctional families, and we will not expect to raise the level of function of families we treat to this optimal level, not least because, as Beavers (1977) has pointed out, mental health professionals are most unlikely to be functioning at that level themselves (and might not be very good at the job, or might not be motivated to take it up, if they were). (See Chapter 2 for further discussion of what makes for a 'healthy' family.)

C.　THE INNER-EXPERIENTIAL LIFE
OF THE FAMILY

I.　INTRODUCTION

In the two preceding sections, we have looked at the functioning of the family and its individual members. First, we considered the family as an interacting system in the present, where we studied its cyclic operations without much reference to its past history. Secondly, we considered the family as a system developing over time, where newer members are being assisted by older ones to transcend a series of developmental stages (in psychoanalytic terms), or (in behavioural language) at age-appropriate times to acquire a series of behaviour patterns, transmitted by learning processes of one kind or another. In both cases, we were viewing the family and its members from outside, from an objective standpoint where the actual behaviour observed would suffice to describe the situation (as those with a behavioural orientation in fact strive to do). If we were confining our studies to central heating systems, steam engines or electronic calculators these approaches would suffice.

II. EXPERIENCING

A. A Human Function

But humans not only go through the motions of interacting and developing. Humans also achieve something called *experiencing* their lives. They can be "conscious" (whatever that means) of some aspects of their surroundings and even of themselves and their relation to others. How much this function is shared with other animals we do not know, and humans appear to have additional abilities, almost certainly not shared by animals, of being *aware of their experience*, of being able to be *aware that they are conscious*, to be critical and analytic towards it, and to communicate and share that second-order (or as in the case of the present communication between writer and reader, *third*-order) consciousness with other members of the species.

These functions *can* be described in behavioural terms and a visitor from space, studying the human race, might have no alternative. But therapists are themselves human, sharing the fact of consciousness and other characteristics of human functioning, so that we are able to *put ourselves in the place of* the different family members to some extent, approaching the problem from inside rather than outside.

It is customary to take these capacities we share for granted, to talk *as if* we do not need to examine or explain them and can safely use them without questioning their nature. This is adequate, when they are functioning effectively, and reflections upon the nature of consciousness can be left to philosophers. But family therapists (and indeed psychotherapists generally) have found their attention drawn particularly to this question because it appears to be precisely in this area of consciousness, communication and control that confusions arise which lead to family systems becoming dysfunctional.

Little or nothing is known, even at the present time, about the *purpose* of consciousness or self-awareness, if by "purpose" we mean the difference it makes to our functioning, the way we would be likely to operate if it did not exist. In his most recent book Bateson (1979) for example states that:

> . . . . the fact of image formation remains almost totally mysterious. How it is done, we know not — nor, indeed, for what purpose. . . . . there is no clear primary reason for using images at all or, indeed, for being *aware* of any part of our mental processes.

Bateson remarks only that

> . . . . speculation suggests that image formation is perhaps a convenient or economical method of passing information across some sort of interface. Notably, where a person must act in a context between two machines, it is convenient to have the machines feed their information to him or her in image form. [p.37] . . . . it will be reasonable to guess that mammals form images because the mental processes of mammals must deal with many interfaces. [p.38]

Bateson does not elaborate this, nor is there at present much help to be found, as far as the present writer is aware, from psychological or philosophical writings so far available. We must resort therefore to "common sense": that is, the writers of this monograph must speak from what they assume to be common among their own experience, and that of their readers. This, as we shall see, is fraught with difficulty, but it is at present the only way to proceed.

B. Consciousness, Insight and Change

For fifty years or more, it was "received wisdom" among most of those engaged in psychotherapy that "insight", that is, consciousness of certain connections between "symptoms" (limited aspects of present behaviour) and present behaviour in a more general sense (e.g. as shown through "transference") or with past experiences or memories, was necessary for change in such undesired behaviour patterns to be possible. *Why* consciousness of these connections should produce this effect was never explained very satisfactorily. The rise of behaviourism, and of behaviour modification techniques of treatment, bypassed the whole issue of consciousness and demonstrated that certain types of symptomatic behaviour, at least, could be altered by submitting the patient to new experiences, according to principles elaborated in learning theories. Later still, adherents of communication theory models, particularly those interested in the pathological and therapeutic effects of "double-binds", claimed that insight *followed* change, rather than the reverse. Yet others have discovered that "prescribing the symptom" (instructing people to try to stay the same, or to get worse) can also paradoxically result in relief of symptoms. And if we go beyond orthodox techniques of psychotherapy, we find that encounter groups emphasize the importance of insight and change, while *est* (Erhardt Seminars Training) claims similar improvements by getting people to accept that there is no need to change at all. Religious conversion experiences under powerful emotional pressures, or the emptying of the mind of its habitual activities in meditation, or concentration on some impossible question such as a Zen Koan, all appear capable of bringing about changes in habitual functioning which are more or less enduring.

It seems as though heightened consciousness or "insight" is *in some way* associated with the kind of changes psychotherapists are interested in bringing about, though the connection is clearly less simple than was at first thought.

C. Pathological Functioning and the Fragmentation of Experiencing

What does seem common to the problems that present to a psychotherapist is a kind of fragmentation of the individual's capacity for experience, whereby he cannot from time to time survey his life as a whole, and is therefore prevented from noting discrepancies which may have arisen between the functioning of different subsystems, upsetting the efficiency of the whole organism. Most human behaviour is carried out automatically or semi-automatically, by learned mechanisms which are outside awareness, even if conscious application is necessary to acquire the skills in the first place. Learning to drive a car, for example, we have for some time to give our full attention to the task to the exclusion of everything else, but it would be a disadvantage if driving continued to need the full range of our conscious attention. It is greatly to our advantage that "lower" centres of the nervous system take over this routine task, leaving our conscious attention free for other purposes (perhaps planning the rest of our day) except when unexpected emergencies alert the higher centres to the need for the maximum available attention.

We may reasonably surmise that many sub-systems develop integrated, efficient performances of this kind, which will not usually enter conscious awareness *unless something goes wrong* and threatens the organism's well-being or integrity. But if we survey the kinds of situation in which individuals or families complain of symptoms or relationship dysfunctions and seek psychological help, we soon discover that *one common feature of all such situations is a discrepancy or discordance between different parts of the total system concerned.* Some piece of behaviour or experience is labelled a "symptom" precisely because it does not appear to have meaning and purpose within the functioning of that individual as a whole; indeed, at first sight it appears *dys*functional, interfering with other functions. Similarly, when a family presents complaining of an individual member, the behaviour of that individual at first appears to be disruptive of the functioning of the whole family, and meaningless in terms of the way they are operating as a unit.

Whatever form of therapy is employed, it usually seems to require the therapist to bridge the fragmentation between the deviant individual and the group, or the deviant sub-system within the individual and the individual as a whole, from a birds-eye-view which not only makes a deeper sense of the discrepancy (even of the fragmentation) but which also discovers a more comprehensive organization in which the deviant sub-system can find a constructive place (once the fragmentation is overcome). Consciousness can then be regarded as something like a "working party" set up to view the functioning of some large organization, the various parts of which may be working effectively, but each of which has grown and changed in such a way as to be out of balance, and so impairs the functioning of the whole. Once the organization is brought into balance and is working effectively again, the working party has served its purpose and its energy can be turned to other tasks.

D.   Consciousness as a Central Function

It is suggested, therefore, that consciousness (in the sense of that self-consciousness to which psychotherapists refer when they use the term "insight") plays some part in bringing subsystems into more harmonious relationship when some form of imbalance or fragmentation has occurred. As Bateson suggests, such consciousness is not an end in itself, but more a sign that the organism is undergoing some temporary period of self-examination and adjustment. When we are functioning most harmoniously, and are most in tune with our surroundings, we may be intensely aware (in the sense of alive and responding) but such "self-consciousness" is at a minimum.

In terms of our present concern, this would imply that healthy families are not, in general, particularly preoccupied with insight, with self-understanding, with self-consciousness in the sense of a self-absorbed, self-improving stance in relation to themselves and each other. We may expect that they will be open, responsive, spontaneous, alive, and that they will show evidence of a vivid and enjoyable inner world, but this is another matter altogether. We may nevertheless expect that they will have this faculty of self-examination readily available, and that they will not be inhibited in using it should some interruption to their fruitful interaction indicate that something is going wrong. They will be insightful in the sense that they will not hesitate to examine themselves and their relationships openly and objectively, as well as in the sense of having much information already available, but once the problem is resolved, we may expect that they will put this capacity for self examination aside until it is needed again, and get on with their lives. Watching the interaction of "optimal" healthy families in the Timberlawn Research Study videotapes one is struck by the openness, spontaneity and relaxed, alive, enjoyable exchange between the members. One is also struck both by their absence of self-preoccupation or morbid unnecessary introspection, as well as by their willingness to look frankly at themselves when this is made necessary to fulfil a task or because some problem has arisen.

E.   Fragmentation as the Root of Conflict

Watching the operation of such healthy families, one is also impressed by the relative absence of persistent, irresolvable conflict, despite the remarkable individuality and difference among the members. Yet conflict and strife seem, much of the time and in most families and social situations, almost as if they are inevitable conditions of human functioning. Freud, among others, certainly took this view of human nature, believing that a constant struggle between the demands of society and the urges of man's animal nature was the price of civilisation.

There have nevertheless been exceptions to this pessimistic view, stemming from both secular and religious sources. It is interesting how Bateson (1972) links the two so naturally in the following quotation from one of his essays:

Aldous Huxley used to say that the central problem for humanity is the quest for *grace*. This word he used in what he thought was the sense in which it is used in the New Testament. He explained the word, however, in his own terms. He argued—like Walt Whitman—that the communication and behaviour of animals has a naïveté, a simplicity, which man has lost. Man's behaviour is corrupted by deceit—even self-deceit—by purpose, and by self-consciousness. As Aldous saw the matter, man has lost the 'grace' which animals still have. I shall argue that the problem of grace is fundamentally a problem of integration and that what is to be integrated is the diverse parts of the mind—especially those multiple levels of which one extreme is called 'consciousness' and the other the 'unconscious'. For the attainment of grace, the reasons of the heart must be integrated with the reasons of the reason (p.128-129)

In his thirteen-part BBC television series, exploring the world's religions, Ronald Eyre (1979) found, despite the diversity of theological views, that the ideas of being *whole*, of being *healthy*, and of being *holy* all had similar meanings, in the sense that Bateson has used above.

Our real dilemma appears to be this: That all man's achievements: the capacity to symbolize, the transmission and storage of knowledge through language, the development of science, technology and all that has stemmed from these, depend in fact on man's capacity to fragment, to isolate, to pursue in his thought and imagination ideas and structures which are *not* bound by his senses, which are not just a reflection of the world he experiences before him at a given moment. He can *abstract* from his experience (Korzybski, 1933) selecting those features of events which interest or attract him, and ignoring others. Having done so, he can play with these as a child plays with bricks, manipulating them and testing out different possible relationships as in logic, mathematics or physics. Then, these experiments with images or abstractions can be tested out and verified or refuted by actual experiment in the real world.

This is the process underlying all scientific discoveries, whereby experiments with inner experience which led to the formula $e = mc^2$ enables us to harness atomic energy. But the same principle underlies all human behaviour, beyond that described by the simplest principles of learning theory. Why is the process sometimes helpful and constructive, and what makes it often harmful and productive of inner and outer conflict? The answer has been expressed in many fashions, but is essentially simple. It seems we are so constructed that our capacity to abstract and isolate parts of our experience readily proceeds past the point where it ceases to be helpful and becomes harmful, this point being the stage at which *we focus our attention and interest on the isolated part to an extent where we forget its origin in the larger whole*. We are then no longer aware of the experience we are focussing on as part of a *system*. We cling to the isolated part, which becomes the "truth", and cease to return to the more profound and complicated source in our total living experience from which this "truth" derived. Moreover, experience is a flux, the world is in motion, we and others are changing constantly; yet, to employ this process of abstraction, to be able to "think", and above all in order to communicate in symbols, we must take static cross-sections of our experience of constant change.

All "truth" arrived at by this process must, for both these reasons, be partial, temporary. As long as we remember this, our abstractions help us to deal with, and adapt to, the real world. But as soon as we forget that ideas, abstractions are isolated, frozen elements of an interacting system, we lose touch with the real world (which is the same for all of us and about which we can hope to agree) and begin to live in different incompatible worlds in our heads (over which we can only argue and struggle).

F. Fragmentation Perpetuated or Healed

The process can be seen at all levels of human interaction. In the individual, such clinging to a past reality explains the fact of "transference", where patterns of response appropriate within the family are carried into later social relationships, including marital interaction and the bringing-up of children. Even within the family, children may retain inappropriate dependent attitudes towards their parents, and their parents may retain infantilising attitudes towards them, though both are physically mature. Families as a whole can similarly fail to learn from experience, but perpetuate unrealistic images of the family, and of the outside world, over generations. Furthermore, whole societies may become arrested in their development through valuing isolated abstractions above the flux of experience from which they were originally derived, as in the Dark Ages when medicine stopped for 1500 years after the work of Galen.

Is there some crucial factor, open to the possibility of our control, influencing the use of our vital capacity for abstraction towards that constructive and creative use which remembers the whole system and does not confuse the part with the whole, rather than towards increasing identification with abstractions, uncontrolled imagination, and finally madness? No question is more important for the survival of mankind, and there is already some suggestive evidence from studies of child development and the functioning of healthy families, which may help us towards at least a partial answer. Studies such as those Bowlby (1969, 1973, 1980) and Winnicott (1958) with human infants, and similar experiments on infant monkeys by Harlow (1966) and others, demonstrate clearly that a certain basic stability, regularity, reliability and consistent support is needed from the mothering figure if the infant is to feel sufficiently secure to venture out into the environment, away from her, to explore and begin to cope with change, unfamiliarity, newness. The "attachment behaviour" described by Bowlby seems essential if the child is to leave the mother and venture increasingly into the strangeness of the surrounding world; the safety of Winnicott's "holding" situation is vital if the child is similarly to engage in the experimental, spontaneous activity of "play".

If this safe situation is not provided, the individual deprived of its security clings to the original mothering figure, or to some substitute for the order and regularity she should have provided, whether in the form of possessions, obsessional activities and routines, recurrent fantasies, or rigid forms of "thought" or belief that must be protected from correction by external reality for fear they may be changed and lost. The individual's development inevitably becomes arrested.

Once this situation exists, it is understandable that the individual concerned seeks contact with others who will not disturb it, or who will at least disturb it as little as possible. People with different views, and above all those who are open to experience, who are constantly learning, growing and revising their ideas, will represent threats to be avoided, and will be seen as aliens if not enemies. It will be safest to keep contact only with family members who share the same rigid beliefs. To the extent that social needs must be met outside the family, friends and acquaintances will be chosen because they hold similar views, rather than for the challenge and stimulation of difference. For the intimacy of marriage (if the individual is able to contemplate this step at all) a partner will be chosen at a similar level of developmental arrest, or in Bowen's (1978) term "degree of differentiation", who will reinforce rather than undermine the frozen belief system. And children, when they arrive, will be indoctrinated into the pattern and prevented from growing, or at least not helped to grow, beyond it. Thus the pattern can perpetuate itself over generations, as Bowen has pointed out and Fisher and Mendel (1956) have demonstrated experimentally.

III. COMMUNICATION AND FRAGMENTATION

A. The Influence of the Different Modes of Communication

In addition to Bateson, others influenced by his work at the Mental Research Institute at Palo Alto in California (Watzlawick *et al.*, 1967; Watzlawick *et al.*, 1972) as well as the Milan Group (Palazzoli-Selvini *et al.*, 1978) have emphasized the vital importance of the different modes of communication in relation to these processes. In the fragment of Bateson's writings quoted earlier, the most crucial phrase is his suggestion, following Aldous Huxley, ". . . that the communication and behaviour of animals has a naïveté, a simplicity, which man has lost. Man's behaviour is corrupted by deceit — even self-deceit . . ." The behaviour of animals, including their simplicity, their completeness, their "grace", has much to do with their limited capacity for communication, as compared with "civilised" human-kind. Though some higher animals show rudimentary capacities for symbolic communication, animals communicate almost entirely through non-verbal, analogic means. They express their relationships to one another, their feelings and intentions, through actual, though partial and incomplete, expression of them. A threat to attack another member of the species, as in competition between males for available females, is communicated by all the bodily preparations for such an attack (posture, gesture, facial expression, growling etc.) which is demonstrated to be a communication and not an actual attack only by the fact that it is inhibited in its development at a certain stage, and stops short of completion. And if the communication is successful (that is, if it intimidates the competitor without the need for an actual fight) the rival will respond with some bodily signs of submission, sufficient to reduce the threatening behaviour of the opponent. The weaker dog presents the jugular vein to its more powerful rival, whose attacking behaviour then ceases.

Such non-symbolic, analogic communication is *similar in form to what it represents;* it is communicative in that *certain relationships present in the event represented are actually reproduced.* The difference between the real thing and the communication about it, is that *a part of the whole is representing the whole.* Even the dance of the honey-bee, indicating to others in which direction nectar may be found, *reproduces* in the pattern of its dance the angle between the direction of the goal and the direction of the sun, and it similarly indicates the distance to be travelled by the speed of its dance, which bears a certain relation to it. The matter does not quite stop here, and Bateson (1979) has clearly demonstrated how the capacity of some higher mammals to engage in *play* is a vital step towards the kind of experimentation that humans can engage in through use of symbols.

In humans, non-verbal, analogic communication continues to play a vital part. It is the only form of communication possible in the earliest years of the infant's life, and probably remains the most important mode of communication mediating social control in small groups, including families. For example, children may ignore the verbal appeals or expressed threats of punishment by parents over a long period, but their behaviour immediately changes the moment they recognize that the parents "really mean it", through information conveyed by the non-verbal channel. The parents' glaring eyes, tight lips, flushed faces, harsh voices and tensed bodies are recognized as "for real" in a way that words may not be, for they *are* real, a part of the developing reality.

The closer humans remain to this non-verbal, analogic mode of communication, then the simpler, more natural, and more "graceful" their social behaviour is likely to be. "Primitive" tribes, or children and relatively uneducated country people in "civilized" societies are likely to retain more of the simplicity and grace of animals, since the nature of this form of communication makes self-deceit difficult. But both man's greatest achievements and his greatest vices are consequences, as we have already suggested, of his capacity for the symbolic, digital mode of communication: the capacity to let one thing *stand for* another in a way which is completely arbitrary (though of course *agreed*), where the symbol bears no relationship whatever to what it symbolizes. This ability to use *symbols* (together, of course, with the abstractions or concepts for which we agree they shall stand) enables us to create an infinite variety of inner worlds, differing in any way we wish from the actual one we inhabit. Among other logical expressions underlying this possibility is the word "not", indicating whether a communication is true or untrue, a communication impossible to make in the non-verbal, analogic mode except by beginning an action and stopping short of completing it (e.g. a threatening fist which does not actually strike) (Watzlawick *et al.*, 1967). "To be or not to be" is now a question which can be asked, of others or oneself.

B. The Dangers of Symbolic Communication

However this development, which makes possible our greatest power, our knowledge, brings with it also the capacity for self-deceit; the ability to create, believe in, live in, a world at variance with the evidence of the senses. Expressed in mythical terms, man has "eaten of the tree of knowledge of good and evil": he has the possibility, which he did not possess before, of choosing between what is and what is not, of inhabiting an inner world at variance with the facts actually encountered. This new-found power brought with it, inevitably, a loss of that innocence, simplicity and "grace" that bound us tightly to the evidence of our senses. Now humans could arrest their development at any point they wished, choosing to maintain an inner world which fitted the facts at one stage of development, but which became increasingly inconsistent with later reality. If one wished, one could remain omnipotent, God, co-existent with the whole universe; where no other individual capable of independent action existed. Alternatively, one could remain a helpless baby to be perpetually looked after, a defiant toddler, or an endlessly competitive child in an Oedipal triangle, and so on. However, this is possible only if the individual restricts communication with others to a degree which prevents the discrepancy between the inner and outer worlds from being exposed. Where the discrepancy is at its most extreme, communication may have to be so completely restricted with others that the individual withdraws from all social contact, and is considered "mad". Where the discrepancy is less extreme, the individual may ally himself or herself only with those members of the family who support the fantasy, rejecting others; may choose friends, or a mate, who do not challenge it; and if there are children, may train them to behave in ways which reinforce rather than challenge the lack of congruence between the inner and outer world. Thus, families as a whole tend to develop shared systems of fantasy, or levels of developmental arrest, with which they collude to preserve from correction. The collusion may extend to communities, even nations, as exemplified in the fairy-tale about "The Emperor's New Clothes".

The real world cannot be got rid of, nevertheless, and maintaining the fiction must inevitably be a constant struggle. Unless a solution of complete social isolation is chosen, someone, sooner or later, may give the game away. The most complete family collusion will be threatened by the fact that children have to go to school, that parents need to meet others in the course of their work, or that members are forced into social contacts through other external pressures. Even within the family, some may find themselves paying a higher price than others to maintain the fantasy, and be more inclined to rebel or escape. In addition, the threat to the fantasy system does not come only from outside. The actual achievements of each individual, in work, in relationships, in sexual attractiveness, etc., somehow have to be reconciled with the fantasy system.

C. Communication, the Maintenance of Dysfunction and its Cure

As a natural result of these constraints, communication becomes extremely complex. Everything an individual says about himself will tend to be influenced by three criteria; or, to put it another way, three simultaneous messages will tend to be contained in every communication:

(1) What is said must somehow not contradict too obviously the inner fantasy-world.
(2) At the same time, it must somehow not be so inconsistent with social expectations that it will actually be challenged by others.
(3) A third message will also be sent (usually non-verbal) exerting emotional pressure on the recipient not to notice any discrepancy between messages 1 and 2, and also not to comment on the inevitable confusion that will have resulted from trying to express two incompatible messages at once.

Needless to say, persons are selected as mates or friends who will obey the non-verbal command and not challenge the contradictions. Those who do challenge them, including children in the family, will be rejected.

The above complexities in communication, which arise quite naturally from the possibility of clinging to a static inner world at variance with the changing outer world, have been much described under the general term "double-bind". However, the explanation given here for this disordered form of communication seems altogether simpler and more understandable than those offered previously. For example, the terrible power struggles, at once immensely destructive though totally denied, seen to characterize the families of schizophrenics by the Milan group (Palazzoli *et al.*, 1978), which they attribute to pride or "hubris", become explicable if each member of the family is in fact seeking to preserve a fantasy that he or she is omnipotent, has no boundaries or limits, is an unchallenged "Lord of Creation". The word "hubris", which indicates a pride which seeks to rival the Gods, is absolutely appropriate. If all family members cling to fantasies of God-like omnipotence, the very *presence* of others, independent beings challenges this fundamental assumption. And since to compete with them openly is to admit that they exist, even competition with such non-existent beings must be denied.

Some of this material will of course be dealt with more fully in later sections dealing with pathology, but it is necessary to mention such matters briefly here for clarity. We can also mention briefly at this point that where nature produces a poison, she usually also provides an antidote. And so it is with the fragmentation described above which forms the source of so many human ills. Though it is made possible by the unique human capacity for symbolic representation of abstractions from sense experience, by the human capacity for digital as well as analogic communication, our ability to use symbols also enables us to overcome some of these difficulties which symbols themselves make possible. For we can use language to speak *about* language, and to study *disorders of language*, if language enables us to step away from reality sufficiently to make independent conceptual thought possible, and so to create science. If it thereby also enables us to lose touch with reality and go mad, by taking a second step we can step outside the problem, stand back from the disorder of language itself, study it and correct it. Should something go wrong with this second order (meta-level) process, the detachment made possible by conceptual thought enables us to stand back from that in turn, and so to observe and correct our errors, indefinitely.

IV.   RESEARCH INTO DIFFERENCES BETWEEN HEALTHY AND DYSFUNCTIONAL FAMILIES

In the preceding pages, we have tried to look at the family from various perspectives as a *system*, and by returning to the simplest first principles we have tried to understand what the concept of *healthy function* would mean in such a system. Let us now turn to a survey of some of the actual research findings available at the time of writing, derived from observation of actual family interaction. Needless to say, in the brief compass possible here, only an outline of the main findings can be given, leaving out many important details which restrict the validity of the results. References are given, however, whereby the reader can explore the subject further.

A.   How much Health and Dysfunction is There?

We might ask first whether healthy function is common or rare. No adequate answer exists to this question as regards the family as a system, but we may judge that truly healthy families are few and far between from existing knowledge regarding the mental health of whole populations. The Midtown Mahattan Study (Srole *et al.*, 1962) for example found 23.4% of a representative sample of the population demonstrating clear psychological dysfunction, and discovered only 18.5% who were definitely well. The results for the Sterling County Study (Leighton *et al.*, 1963), though including a more rural area, found closely similar figures, with 20% clearly dysfunctional and 17% indisputably well. It is important to begin with this kind of information since many existing studies are faulted in that they compare the obviously ill not with the most well, the "optimal" extreme which forms the main focus of this chapter, but with a measure of "normality" based more on the statistical average (that is, the *mid-range* group), comprising about 60% of the population in the studies just mentioned, whose mental health was uncertain.

B.   Unusual Degrees of Health: Research Studies

(1)   Westley and Epstein
Westley and Epstein (1970) examined in detail the families of a group of college students who showed unusual emotional health, and compared these with families of others who were particularly disturbed. The differences observed were checked against a study of a sample of the college population. The main findings were as follows:
1. Regarding the degree of *role differentiation between the parents*, the parents of the healthiest children showed a *balance between separateness and overlap* whereby many of the parental functions were shared, but not to a point where there could be confusion between the male and female identities or paternal and maternal roles and responsibilities. Families where there was greater overlap in the roles and responsibilities of husband and wife, and less differentiation in the sexual roles, produced fewer healthy children, often suffering themselves from role confusion. The "traditional", role-segregated, male-

dominated family, was even worse in its effects, and the degree of ill health in the children was exceeded only in families where the traditional roles were reversed, with the father performing more than half of the "traditionally female" household and child-care tasks.

2. Regarding the issue of *power*, the healthiest families were found to be *father-led*. Next most healthy were those which were *father-dominant*, next *egalitarian* and worst *mother-dominant*.

3. In general, it was found that a *high frequency of sexual intercourse*, together with *increasing sexual satisfaction during the course of the marriage*, appeared related with mental health in the children. But this was not always so, and the existence of a *warm, loving and supportive relationship between the couple* appeared even more vital, compensating considerably for emotional ill health in either husband or wife. Where this was the case parental pathology appeared to be contained and coped with within the marriage, rather than passed on to the children.

Westley and Epstein were studying individual family members rather than family interaction, but in a comparison of matched pairs of families with or without a schizophrenic child, Mischler and Waxler (1968) found similar features. More healthy families showed a strong parental coalition, but with authority exerted through negotiation rather than in a rigid, authoritarian way. Communication was clearer and more direct in the more healthy families, and was either rigid and fearfully-controlled, or confusing and disruptive, in the patient-containing families.

(2) Stabenau, Tupin, Werner and Pollin

A third research study (Stabenau *et al.*, 1965) has already been summarized in some detail in a previous book by the present writer (Skynner, 1976 p.244-246). A comparison of families producing children who are either schizophrenic, delinquent or showing neither of these disorders, showed many features consistent with other studies mentioned here, and

> . . . in the families with a normal control, affect tended to be appropriate, modulated, positive and warm. Interaction featured considerable autonomy, a coping rather than manipulative or controlling pattern in dealing with the family members, and a goal of mutual understanding and satisfaction. Family organisation was flexible with clear role differentiation and expectancy. Empathic awareness with each other's role was evidenced, and the father and mother tended to interact in a complementary manner (p.50).

(3) MacGregor et al.

A fourth study, less scientifically rigorous than the others but reporting the treatment of families containing adolescent members who displayed various degrees of disturbance, (MacGregor *et al.*, 1964) has also been summarized in tabular form in the present writer's previous book (Skynner, 1976). It shows many differences between more healthy and less healthy families, corresponding to those of the other studies. In moving from the description of families of the most disturbed children to families of the least disturbed children, one is struck again

Table I.

Level of function of children	Severe dysfunction	Mid-range function	Healthy function
Types of disorder	"Process" (chronic) schizophrenia Psychopathy (Sociopathy)	Reactive psychosis/Behaviour Disorders/ Neurosis	No evidence of psychiatric disorder; effective functioning
Power-structure	*chaotic* Parent-child coalition (usually between mother and index patient, father ineffective and excluded)	*structured/rigid* Rigid control, little negotiation. Parents either competing for dominance (behaviour disorders) or dominant-submissive relationship (neuroses)	*structured/flexible* Strong, equal-powered parental coalition, but children consulted and decisions through negotiation. Clear hierarchy with mutual respect.
Differentiation	*fusion* Blurred boundaries, unclear identities, shifting roles. Blaming, scapegoating, evasion of responsibility. Invasiveness.	*separateness through distancing* Identities more defined but at cost of emotional distancing, restriction of potential and of spontaneity. Role stereotyping, including male/female.	*clear identity + intimacy* Identities highly defined and secure, permitting also high levels of closeness and intimacy. High individual responsibility.
Communication	Vague, confused, evasive, contradictory. Double-binds. Mystification.	Clearer than in severely dysfunctional, but in rigid, stereotyped way (so often superficially clearer than in healthy).	Open, clear, direct, frank. Lively and spontaneous.
	Imperviousness.	Impervious to new ideas; non-mutual.	Receptive and responsive to new ideas.

	oppositional	oppositional	affiliative
Relationship	*Distrust*, expectation of evil (betrayal, desertion)	Relative *distrust*; human nature seen as basically evil, needing rigid control of self and others. Repression, suppression.	*Trust*; basic expectation of positive response to positive approach. Warm, caring, mutual regard and responsibility.
	Ambivalent feelings unintegrated, swings between extremes; inconsistancy dealt with by denial. Marriage highly unsatisfactory; split by parent/child coalition.	Ambivalence not accepted, dealt with by repression and reaction formation against "bad" impulses. Lack of marital satisfaction; competing or dominant/submissive roles.	Ambivalent feelings accepted as normal. Both sides included and integrated. Mutually satisfying, complementary marital roles; sexuality mutually satisfying also.
Reality-sense	Reality denied; escape into fantasy satisfactions.	Adequate reality sense to function effectively, but with some distortion and incongruent family "myths".	Image of self and family congruent with reality.
Affect	Cynicism; hostility; sadism; hopeless and despair.	Hostility (behaviour disorders) but without the degree of sadism in severely dysfunctional. Subdued, joyless, restricted (neurotic disturbance).	Warmth, enjoyment; humour, wit. Tenderness, empathy.
Attitude to change, loss	Unable to cope with change and loss. Timeless, repetitive quality, with denial of separation and death, escape into fantasy.	Change and loss faced, but with great pain and difficulty. Separation and death not really worked through; substitutes for lost persons and feelings transferred, instead of internalization of lost person.	Change, growth, separation and death all accepted realistically and losses worked through, due to 1. Strong parental coalition (in relation to older and younger generations). 2. Strong, varied relationships outside family. 3. Transcendent value system.

Reproduced by permission from "The Handbook of Family Therapy" 1981, (A. Gurman and D. Kniskern, eds) Brunner/Mazel, New York.

by: the importance, for health, of parental co-operation and collaboration in the matter of authority; a clear inter-generational boundary whereby the children cannot disturb this coalition by forming stronger parent–child coalitions themselves; mutual acceptance and understanding; and an ability of the family as a whole to relate to, and accept help from, the larger community. Once again, moving from the families of the most- to the least-disturbed children, one is impressed by the dominant position of the mother, and exclusion of the father in the former; and the position of increasing leadership taken by the father as the degree or level of disturbance decreases.

(4) Timberlawn Studies

However, even though these studies show much agreement, none of them examined the actual behaviour and interaction of families which ranged from the most dysfunctional to the extreme of health. A first step in this direction has been taken by the group at the Timberlawn Psychiatric Research Foundation (Lewis et al., 1976). Their research, which reports the first successful attempt to find and examine in depth the personalities, relationships and typical interaction found in families at the extremes of health (rather than the mid-range or "average") is of such crucial theoretical and practical importance that the reader is strongly urged to read the published material of the researchers themselves, either in the book just quoted or in the more popular presentation, omitting much of the detail of the research design (Lewis, 1979). In a previous publication (Skynner, 1981), the present writer has attempted to summarize the results in three tables, which have been seen and approved by Lewis, and which should help the reader to grasp their main findings rapidly. (see Table I)

In this first table, the spectrum of level of psychological function is divided into three main categories, for the sake of simplicity. It will be seen at once that in moving our attention from the characteristics of the most severely dysfunctional families, through the mid-range group, to the most healthy families, the change is not simply one of degree, nor is it simply a steady increase or lessening of certain features. Instead, in certain respects, progress towards health appears to take place in a step-wise fashion, by stages.

For example, the chaotic situation in the most severely dysfunctional families, where there is characteristically a parent/child coalition with the father most often ineffective and excluded, gives way at mid-range function to a rigid structure not only with rigid control of the children by the parents, but also a rigid hierarchy with one spouse dominant to the other. But when we come to the most healthy families, this situation is not simply exaggerated, but radically changed. Structure is present, but is sufficiently secure for the children to be consulted and decisions reached through negotiation, and the parental coalition has become equal powered.

Similarly, the fusion of the severely dysfunctional family gives way to individuality and separateness in mid-range function but only at the cost of emotional distancing and role stereotyping, including rigid differences in sexual role. In healthy families this is not taken further, but radically changed. The sense of identity and difference has become so secure that individuals can alternate between intense intimacy, and separateness. A similar transition is seen in regard to communication, where in the mid-range clarity is achieved at the cost of rigidity, while the latter is no longer necessary for healthy families.

As regards relationships, reality sense, and affect, the transition is more continuous. The same is true of the attitude to change, loss, separation and death. The Timberlawn Group found that the capacity to deal with these different aspects of change was an especially crucial and reliable feature in differentiating healthy from less healthy families, affecting physical as well as mental health. This one might expect, of course, in the light of our previous discussion, if "health" is connected with an ability to adapt to the ever changing flux of experience and the challenges posed by the developmental process, by constant change of inner "models" or "knowledge" to fit the new information.

Table I presents the findings in broadest outline. But the Timberlawn Researchers also examined in more detail the families producing healthy children, comparing the six families whose function approximated most closely to mid-range function, to those which showed the functioning of the "healthy" group at its greatest extreme. The former they called "adequate", the latter "optimal", and an outline of the findings regarding this comparison is given in Tables II and III.

Table II needs little explanation and shows that the "optimal" families could be differentiated from the "adequate" on 7 out of 8 criteria, while Table III

Table II.   Main characteristics of "optimal" families, in order of apparent importance

"Optimal" families could be differentiated from "adequate" families on all these characteristics except No. 7 (Initiative) to level of statistical significance. Both produced healthy children, but "adequates" showed many "Mid-range" features.

---

(1) *Affiliative attitude* to human encounter — open, reaching-out, basically trusting (as contrasted with *oppositional* — distrust, withdrawal etc.)

(2) *High respect for separateness, individuality,* autonomy, privacy (as contrasted with expectation of agreement, conformity, "speaking for others").

(3) *Open, clear, frank communication* (as contrasted with confusion, evasion, restriction etc.).

(4) *Firm parental coalition,* egalitarian with shared power between parents (as contrasted with parental splits and parent/child coalitions).

(5) *Control flexible, by negotiation,* within basic parent/child hierarchy (as contrasted with rigid, inflexible control and unchangeable rules).

(6) *Highly spontaneous interaction,* with considerable humour and wit — "three-ring circus, but all under control" (as contrasted with rigid, stereotyped interaction).

(7) *High levels of initiative* (as contrasted to passivity).

(8) *Uniqueness and difference encouraged* and appreciated — liveliness, strong "characters" (as contrasted with bland, stereotyped, conformist types).

Table III.   Differences in marital and sexual function between "adequate" and "optimal" families, all producing healthy children

	Adequate	Optimal
ROLES	Generally traditional gender roles but in rigid, stereotyped, highly role-segregated way.	Generally traditional gender roles but seemingly from choice, with rewarding, mutually pleasurable complementarity and reciprocity.
RELATION-SHIP	*Husbands* successful, agressively work-oriented. More satisfied with lives than wives — distant and providing material but not emotional support.	*Both husbands and wives* express mutual pleasure and enjoyment with relationship and life generally. Husbands involved in work but responsive to wife's needs, supportive and emotionally aware.
	Wives generally unhappy, needy, lonely, feeling isolated from husbands and overwhelmed by children. Tending to obesity, depression and fatigue. Interests outside home limited.	Wives feel appreciated, cherished.
		Many, active interests outside home, though role of mother and wife central and satisfying.
SEXUALITY	Regular, generally similar frequency (about twice-weekly). Mostly satisfying to husbands. Wives generally dissatisfied (too much, too little, unpleasurable etc.)	More variable in frequency between couples (several times weekly to twice a month) but highly, mutually pleasurable and satisfying to both partners. Pattern of long-term marital fidelity.
LEISURE	Limited involvement of couple with community.	More involvement of couple outside the home and family alone.

Both "adequate" and "optimal" families shared very high belief and involvement in the idea of the family, and their children's activities.

Reproduced by permission from "The Handbook of Family Therapy", 1981, (A Gurman and D. Kniskern, eds), Brunner/Mazel, New York.

shows that there were striking differences between the "optimal" and "adequate" families as regards the marital relationships. It is reassuring to see that many couples showing evidence of considerable degrees of mid-range function can nevertheless produce healthy children by dint of hard work, effort and struggle, even at considerable cost. But it is even more reassuring to see that the greatest health and well-being in family function, like the highest development of all other human skills, appears after the basic knowledge and skills are so well established that they no longer require anxious effort, giving space and time to allow spontaneity, playfulness and enjoyment, reminding one of Bateson's use of the word "grace".

REFERENCES

Bateson, G. (1972). "Steps Towards an Ecology of Mind". Chandler, New York.

Bateson, G. (1979). "Mind and Nature", Wildwood House, London.

Beavers, R. (1977). "Psychotherapy and Growth: A Family Systems Perspective", Brunner/Mazel, New York.

Bertalanffy, L. V. (1968). "General System Theory", Brazillier, New York.

Bowen, M. (1978). "Family Therapy in Clinical Practice", Jason Aronson, New York.

Bowlby, J. (1967). "Attachment and Loss. Vol I: Attachment", Hogarth Press, London.

Bowlby, J. (1973). "Attachment and Loss. Vol II. Separation: Anxiety and Anger", Hogarth Press, London.

Bowlby, J. (1980). "Attachment and Loss. Vol III. Sadness and Depression", Hogarth Press, London.

Eyre, R. (1979). "Ronald Eyre on The Long Search", Collins, London.

Fisher, S. and Mendell, D. (1956). The Communication of Neurotic Patterns over Two and Three Generations. *Psychiatry* **19**, 41-46.

Harlow, H. F., Harlow, M. K., Dodsworth, R. O. and Arling, G. L. (1966). Maternal Behaviour of Rhesus Monkeys Deprived of Mothering and Peer Associations in Infancy. *Proceedings of the American Philosophical Society* **110**, 58-66.

Klein, M. (1932). "The Psychoanalysis of Children", Hogarth, London.

Korzybski, A. (1933). "General Semantics", Science Press, Lancaster, Pennsylvania.

Leighton, D., Harding, J. S., Macklin, D. B., Hughes, C. C. and Leighton, A. H. (1963). Psychiatric Findings of the Stirling County Study. *American Journal of Psychiatry*. **119**, 1021-1026.

Lewis, J. M., Beavers, W. R., Gossett, J. T. and Phillips, V. A. (1976). "No Single Thread: Psychological Health in Family Systems", Brunner/Mazel, New York.

Lewis, J. M. (1979). "How's Your Family?" Brunner/Mazel, New York.

MacGregor, R., Ritchie, A. M., Serrano, A. C., Schuster, F. P., McDonald, E. C. and Goolishian, H. A. (1964). "Multiple Impact Therapy with families", McGraw-Hill, New York.

Miller, J. G. (1965). Living Systems, Basic Concepts. *Behavioural Science,* **10**, 193-245.

Mischler, E. and Waxler, N. (1968). "Interaction in Families", Wiley, New York.

Palazzoli-Selvini, M., Boscolo, L., Cecchin, G. and Prata, G. (1978). "Paradox and Counterparadox", Jason Aronson, New York.

Skynner, A. C. R. (1976). "One Flesh: Separate Persons", Constable, London. (US edition entitled "Systems of Family and Marital Psychotherapy", Brunner/Mazel, New York, 1976).

Skynner, A. C. R. (1981). An Open-Systems, Group-Analytic Approach to Family Therapy. *In* "The Handbook of Family Therapy", (A. Gurman and D. Kniskern, eds). Brunner/Mazel, New York.

Srole, L., Langer, T. S., Michael, S. T., Opler, M. K. and Rennie, T. A. C. (1962). "Mental Health in the Metropolis", McGraw-Hill, New York.

Stabenau, J. R., Tupin, J., Werner, M. and Pollin, W. A. (1965). A Comparative Study of Families of Schizophrenics, Delinquents and Normals. *Psychiatry* **28**, 45-59.

Watzlawick, P., Beavin, J. H. and Jackson, D. D. (1967). "Pragmatics of Human Communication", Norton, New York.

Watzlawick, P., Weakland, J. and Fisch, R. (1972). "Change", Norton, New York.

Westley, W. A. and Epstein, N. B. (1969). "The Silent Majority", Jossey-Bass, San Francisco.

Winnicott, D. W. (1958). "Collected Papers; Through Paediatrics to Psychoanalysis", Tavistock, London.

Chapter 2

Change in "Here-and-Now" Systems vs Systems over Time

A. Cooklin

I. INTRODUCTION

Family Therapy may have an in-built predilection to develop controversies about its models of change, if only because its task—to develop a holistic view of the ecological system we call the family—is essentially impossible. Each theory of change can only reflect segments of reality. It may be necessary to stress the boundaries around these theories of change, or segments, in order that each should be sufficiently clear, and readily applicable. However, the relationship between apparently opposing theories needs to be identified if we are to continue the search for a holistic view of what we are about in Family Therapy.

Consider the analogy of the holograph, that surprising phenomenon which has been an off-shoot of laser technology. The laser is a fine, intense beam of "coherent" light. If the beam is split so that part of it falls on a photographic plate, and part of it on to an object from which it rebounds on to the same plate, a recording of light interference patterns is produced. An observer of the developed plate will see a three dimensional image of the object. This image will vary depending on the position from which it is viewed. Furthermore, if the observer smashes the plate into fragments, each fragment will contain an image of the whole object, although from a restricted "telescoped" view-point. The images contained by these fragments can even be of almost opposite views of an object. The fragments of the whole can contain "opposite view-points". The hologram is the most sophisticated image of reality we have so far been able to record photographically, but to understand its process of formation we may have to look at microscopic segments. The purpose of this chapter is to examine the relationship between two now fairly well differentiated segments of family theory: that which considers change in "here-and-now" systems (that is, short segments of time) on the one hand, and that which considers change in "systems over time" (that is, long segments of time) on the other.

I find the analogy of the holograph a useful one, so I shall refer to it from time to time. I shall also make fairly liberal use of other analogies drawn from the natural sciences. This is not intended to present a mechanistic view of human relationships, but to assist in gaining a meta-perspective of the processes of these relationships. The models developed within the natural sciences are somewhat

Family Therapy
ISBN: 0-12-089355-X

clearer precisely because they can more closely approximate a bird's eye view of the total environment. We are much more a part of any human relationship we observe, and therefore the *generalizations* (not necessarily the observations themselves) we can make from our observations are more restricted. However, it must be stressed that these analogies are only used to convey the kind of model, rather than the particular process within the model itself. To do the latter would indeed imply that humans behave like chemical reactions.

A. Practices, Ideas and Belief Systems

In the field of human relations therapy, it is inevitable that there will be a continuous pull towards describing practices (that is, organized sets of events in which a therapist plays a particular part) rather than ideas. This is partly because it is so difficult to establish sets of ideas which are other than temporary constructs about human relations. We cannot make fixed three dimensional models of these as we can with the holograph. Also, the pain and turmoil of some family interactions make such urgent demands on a therapist that he must have *methods* rather than just *theories*. (Haley, 1977; Sluzki, 1978; Treacher and Street, 1980; Street and Treacher, 1980)

Family therapists will sometimes make such statements as:
— The therapist does or does not try to display his or her emotional reactions;
— The therapist makes people stand-up, do this or that task, or does not;
— The therapist asks certain people to talk to each other or relates all questions himself;
— The therapist remains neutral, asks "circular" questions, and "positively connotes" the interactions.

These are sets of behaviour prescribed for therapists which, when clustered in a particular way make up a practice. These sets of therapists' behaviours are a necessary armamentarium not only for survival as an effective therapist in the turmoil of family interactions, but also because it would be quite impracticable to try and base each move on rethinking one's theory from first principles. The therapist would be unable to act. There is, however, a bridge between the ideas and the actions which I shall call "belief systems". They can be found in all therapies. Examples of psychoanalytic beliefs might be that "Change occurs in relation to the reintrojection of object relationships that have become modified in the therapeutic process", or "Change occurs through the medium of the transference relationships from the family members to the therapist".

Other beliefs might include "Change occurs when 'here-and-now' events are influenced actively as they happen", or "Change occurs as the context or significance of events in time is changed". These are the segments of reality which I shall now examine.

II. THE PATTERN OF EVENTS IN HUMAN SYSTEMS

Changes in here-and-now family systems, such as might be sought in Structural Family Therapy, (Minuchin, 1972) and certain forms of Strategic Family

Therapy (Haley, 1977) are in fact changes in *short* sequences of time, and therefore segments of time with a relatively short "wave-length". Changes in family systems over time, such as might be sought by therapists using a psychoanalytic or transgenerational model of family therapy, are changes in relatively long sequences of time which have a long "wave-length". The difference in *quantity* of the two wave-lengths means a difference in the *quality* in the nature of the processes which can be influenced by different methods. Changes in short segments of behaviour may be effected *in vitro* by enacting the actual sequence within the time available for a therapy session. The changes *may* ultimately be *transferred* to the relevant *in vivo* setting. Changes in long sequences (where the length of the sequence may be that of a generation, or even two or more generations) may only be effected by attending to the control processes (sometimes referred to as governing concepts) which maintain the pattern of the sequence (Gorell Barnes, 1981). The nature of these control processes may be found macroscopically by examining the function of family myths (Ferriera, 1963; Byng-Hall, 1973) the Family Group Preoccupation (Cooklin, 1974, 1979) or the Patterning of Intersubjective Meanings (Kinston and Bentovim, 1981). Various techniques may be used either to change these control processes, or "interfere" with their effectiveness.

Some therapies are directed almost entirely to short sequences (particularly structural therapy, and certain kinds of behavioural approaches to family therapy), although in the course of achieving changes in short sequences, they may also effect some changes in the processes which control longer sequences. Some therapies are directed almost exclusively to influencing the longer sequences, such as transgenerational therapy (Lieberman, 1979; Bowen, 1975, 1976) psychoanalytic approaches to therapy (Zinner and Shapiro, 1972, 1974; Box, 1979) and the use of "mourning" techniques (Paul, 1967), while the Milan group (Palazzoli *et al.*, 1980) have attempted to devise interventions which relate current behaviour (short sequences) to the wider system (spatially and in terms of longer sequences). As family therapists have been preoccupied with the relationship between homeostasis and transformation in family systems, it is the thesis of this chapter that it is necessary to develop an understanding of both models of change, and of the relationship between them.

A.   Models of Change and their Mythology

Within family therapy there has long been a concern to distinguish what adherents of a particular method do from what they say they do (Beels and Ferber, 1969). This has been possible as therapeutic secrecy has been dissolved by the use of one-way mirrors and video. Most therapists have been anxious to dissociate themselves from the nosological labelling of the identified patient, but in its extreme form, this concern has sometimes been expressed by an avoidance of all nosology. When this has happened, the description of theories and of their therapeutic practices has often been neglected. In addition, the practices are themselves very hard to define, despite a number of attempts some of which have been quite rigorous (Beels and Ferber, 1969; Cooklin, 1978; Dowling, 1979;

Kinston *et al.*, 1979). Even Epstein's group of experienced researchers in the field have loosely described the techniques employed in one of their studies as "systems-orientated family therapy" (Santa-Barbara *et al.*, 1980). In fact the field is now so complex that for the practitioner beginning work in family therapy, misconceptions and misquotations are almost inevitable. The confusion surrounding such misconceptions has sometimes led to emotional attacks by the representatives of one school on the spectres of another (Treacher and Street, 1980).

The naming of theoretical models has sometimes compounded the problem. For example, in Britain General Systems Theory has been used on the one hand by family therapists to devise Structural and Strategic Interventions in family systems, and on the other hand by workers such as Rice and Miller (1967) to develop a "psychoanalytic" model of organizations which they have applied to industries and other social systems. Psychoanalysts have been seen as being concerned with the past. Yet many British analysts would claim that they were dealing predominantly with what happens here and now, in the present, within the intensified strictures of the analytic situation. Some would even claim that they make little or no reference to the past even in reconstructions.

Within family therapy, controversy has flourished between therapists who observe "behaviour" and those who observe "feelings". Adherents to the communications school have stressed the "black box" approach. They do not need to know what goes on inside the box, but are satisfied to study it's connections. A consequence of this view is that they will only look at the behavioural expressions of feeling, rather than assuming knowledge of the feelings themselves. Thus instead of "Ann is feeling despondent today", they will say "Ann is behaving despondent today". It is interesting that many philosophers of mind would support the latter view, not so much because it is more "true", but because it does not create a false dichotomy between feelings and perceptions on the one hand, and behaviour on the other.

Describing feelings and behaviour separately propagates the "two worlds view"; often represented as the mind on the one hand, and the body on the other (Ryle, 1949). That this is a false dichotomy in neuro-physiological terms has been stressed by Pribam (1971). With this diversity of approaches, there has been an understandable and probably necessary tendency to focus on one or other segment or model. As a result, the particular segment may be coherently illuminated to return to the analogy of the holograph. While this is an essential process in the development of therapeutic methods, it is also important to be reminded that one is only responding to a segment of reality. On the other hand, attempts to achieve some coherence in one's position by attacking the image of another have been unhelpful to the development of coherence in the field, as they have often replaced a satisfactory analysis of the position from which the views are expounded (Treacher and Street, 1980; Wrate, 1980). The real struggle in family therapy is to maintain the observer/therapist's freedom from a perception of "linear causality" (Watzlawick *et al.*, 1969). That is, to replace the perception of events as between victim and aggressor, or from "these events caused what is now happening" with a picture of events and the context or structure within which they occur fitting snugly together and underwriting each other.

Many approaches have been used to try and help the therapist to experience the processes of family interaction in terms other than victim and aggressor. Live supervision techniques, or interviewing methods where the therapist stays "distant" from the family, or even some of the approaches to "working with" the therapist's own family, may all be geared to helping the therapist maintain a circular view of causality. The "schizophrenogenic mother" gave way first to the schizophrenogenic family, and later the "victimized" and "victimizer" gave way to the realization that the "victimizer" is as much a victim of the relationship as is the "victimized". In fact, the move has been from "What causes what?" to "In what way do particular symptoms or symptomatic individuals co-exist more or less comfortably with particular kinds of family structure, and how does each maintain the other?" Conceptually, the models used by the natural sciences may again be of some help. In physics and biology, a different view of the inter-relatedness of events, and the processes which control them, has long replaced the linear view. Not only are energy and matter one, but at the most pragmatic level, the biologist and physicist have been aware of the interrelatedness of electrical, physical, chemical and social influences on any phenomenon, and particularly the feed-back loops which effect a response to change in any one of these. Such an example can be seen in the increasingly complex and circular view which has been developed of glucose metabolism in the body as represented by Kreb's cycle, and the feed-back loops which control this.

So far I have been discussing models of change principally in relation to ideas and belief systems. I have touched on the macroscopic counterpoint of psycho-analysis *vs* systems theory, and the more operational microscopic counterpoint of "feelings" *vs* "behaviour". My purpose in reviewing these ideas is to set a background for the consideration of patterns over short and long sequences of time. When considering questions of causality, natural scientists have also given importance to the time relationship between different events. In a symposium on the philosophy of science, Northrop (1958) points out:

> Two factors in any deductively formulated theory of modern physics must command the focus of one's attention. These two factors are 1) the definition of the state of the system at any given moment of time and 2) the definition of the time relation between states of the system at different times . . .
>
> There is a second possibility with respect to the nature of the time relation between states of an isolated system. The relation may be one of necessary connection characterised by a repetition of constant time relations that hold true not merely for past and present but also for future cases; but it is a relation such that in any first observed instance, given the initial state of the system, one cannot predict the future state until one has observed the present state passing into the future or final state in at least one instance. The physical system in which the initial state is that of the acorn and the final state that of the oak constitutes an example. (p.204)

If this is a valid analogy for events in families, we can not only look at the micro-scopic time relationships between events, but also at the time relationships between events on the level of the life-cycle and beyond.

B. Communication of Meaning through the Ordering of Time

The arrangement of time sequence is what gives meaning to events. If one cleans one's teeth before eating, the event of cleaning one's teeth becomes meaningless in terms of dental hygiene, even though the configuration might have meaning in some other context such as defying parental authority. Also in all language, it is the time relationship which punctuates the meaning of an interaction: "If you do that, then I *will* smack you", rephrased: "I *am* (now) telling you that your action, if in the future you can carry it out (or repeat it), will subsequently be *followed* by my doing to you what I am (now) telling you that I will do". Or to a greater degree of complexity: "If you go on like that you will land up as your father did", reads as "I am *now* defining your behaviour as having consequences in the *future* which *will* need you to be defined by me as I *now* define your father as having been in the *past*". This is only illustrating the obvious, namely, the frequency and potential complexity of the time component in all communication.

The controlling power of time, the fact that in common parlance we usually see it as unidirectional, is a constant preoccupation in family life as in other contexts. We talk of "recapturing the past" (to control it) or of being "haunted by the past" (controlled by it). The fascination of the Dr Who myth, the power to break the rules of the tyranny of the unidirectional nature of time, has always been "present". The prophets and oracles had a limited franchise to read the future as though it were the past. These were only minor infringements in that they only *read* the future. On the other hand, "putting the clock back" as Orpheus tried to do by bringing Euridyce back to life, is breaking rules of a higher order, and risks turning to stone (or timelessness). Again, these examples only point to the obvious human preoccupation with time, in that it punctuates birth, generation and death.

Many have used analogies drawn from relativity theory to give shape to this preoccupation and the way its manifestations are structured. This has either been explicit (Calcroft, 1980) or in terms such as "the curvature of emotional space" (Friedman, 1980). Friedman has illustrated how ceremonies as "Rites of Passage", can give meaning and structure to the periodic wave-like fluctuations over time. As a result, such fluctuations cease to be rigid repetitious two-dimensional oscillations; e.g. son challenges father, father entrenches, son replaces father, grandson challenges son, son entrenches etc.; and are replaced by more three dimensional spirals which lead to new possibilities (Hoffman, 1981). It may be that family therapists' attempts to dissociate from time relationships by talking of "here-and-now" behaviour were partly influenced by the concern to move away from a linear model of causality. Because time is generally seen as going in one direction, prior events are always liable to be "blamed" for "causing" subsequent events. Carter and McGoldrick (1980) have proposed a two dimensional solution to this dilemma by breaking up the in-put to a family into horizontal stressors; life-cycle developmental transitions, and external events on the one hand, and vertical stressors; family patterns, myths, etc. on the other.

C. The Question of Transmission

The question of the transmission of one pattern of events through the family life-cycle and beyond from one generation to another has long preoccupied family therapists. To some extent, it has also been studiously avoided by the "structural" group as it implies some kind of causality. In a paper designed to develop a systemic model from a psychoanalytic framework (Cooklin, 1979), I proposed a model whereby one could see certain patterns of behaviour "leap-frogging" through the generations. On the simplest level, stern parents frequently seem to produce children who in their turn grow up to become more lenient parents, whose children may well return to a model of parenting closer to that used by their grandparents. This was a causal model and it implied some kind of chain reaction going on throughout generations. However it would not explain the way in which certain patterns of behaviours, and familiar attitudes to these, may be passed down through the generations even for hundreds of years as described by Byng-Hall (1982). He gave illustrations of how the court martial and execution of his ancestor Admiral Byng for "cowardice" had laid a pattern on the interpretation of certain sets of events in later generations including that of his own family. He was able to give an elegant demonstration of how recent events in his own family were coded in terms of "cowardice or courage", "innocence or guilt", in a pattern whose form seemed to be isomorphic to the events of 200 years ago.

Bentovim and Kinston (1980) have proposed that a family may process such patterns in three possible ways: (a) by denial, which could be manifested by a kind of superinsensitivity to events which resonate closely with the pattern, e.g. the parents of an immigrant family manifesting unusual insensitivity to a child's difficulties in joining new groups; (b) by repetition without resolution; (c) by reversal, as in Hardy's novel "Tess of the D'Urbervilles", wealth and poverty oscillate with each other in a pattern which codes how the heroine resolves the dilemma of "being owned" vs personal autonomy.

I shall return later to the question of the transmission of sequences of different lengths, and the different processes involved in transmitting a sequence of a few minutes, as opposed to one of a generation or more. But first I want to consider an important building block of transmission: the communication process.

D. The Communication Process

Consider the relationship between digital and analogic communication (Watzlawick et al., 1969). Digital communication refers to verbal, or symbolic communication and includes in it certain formal agreements between the transmitter and the receiver of the communication. For example there is little about the word car which describes the experience of seeing, being in, or being in any other relationship to a car. However the communicator, and receiver of the word car by accepting the formal syntax of language, will have accepted that the sound of the word car, will represent the object car. Because of this communication by labelled symbols, it is possible to distinguish between a digital statement and its opposite. The concept of opposites cannot be communicated analogically. One can say that the word light is the opposite of the word dark. However if one was to communicate about the word light by shining a torch at night, one could only communicate that there was either light or no light. Analogic, or imitative communication requires that the communication in some way directly represents the event about which it communicates. Humans are capable (Watzlawick, 1969) of both analogic and digital communication. With the possible exception of the whale and related mammals, they are the only creatures in the animal kingdom who can use both modalities. Analogic communication is phylogenetically more primitive than digital communication, but different phylogenetic levels of communication can also be distinguished within it. Digital communication is restricted by the formal syntax of language. Therefore although one can use badly written English, or badly spoken English, the actual meaning of the phrases still has to be based on an agreement between the transmitter and receiver of the words about their meaning. Within analogic communication there are more gradations. For example at a sophisticated level, an individual may signify that he wishes to withdraw from some aspect of a relationship by only slightly averting his eyes. At the other extreme, a child may signify a much more total withdrawal by curling into a ball, sucking its thumb, rocking, and being unresponsive to either spoken word or touch.

One important component of analogic or imitative behaviour is that like will respond with like. Some people who talk at length with somebody with a lisp may find themselves using a lisp. Yawns are notoriously infectious. To respond to a smile with a smile is often quite involuntary. Reaching for the natural sciences again, Bateson (1979) has produced a very elegant theory for the self-reproduction of patterns throughout nature. However one only has to look at the phenomena of resonance in physics. One pendulum will initiate oscillation in another close by. Although we can impute transmission of pressure changes through the air for this example, we cannot when looking at the transmission of electro-magnetic waves through space and the way in which they set up analogous waves in instruments which are attuned to them. This is an example of one method of pattern reproduction; i.e. the pattern has implicated in it a different order of pattern for its own reproduction. This is a phenomenon which is being increasingly recognized throughout nature. It is not the DNA in a cell which reproduces the cell, but the DNA/cytoplasm system. This is a different way of conceptualizing transmission from the idea of internal objects being projected and introjected, and it does not slip so easily into our common picture of the universe. Physicists after all were for years searching for the "ether" to explain the transmission of electromagnetic waves. At this stage, one may not need to say more in explanatory terms than that patterns have a tendency to reproduce similar patterns. This phenomenon is given acknowledgement by Minuchin (1972) in the process he calls mimesis. This refers to a communication which a therapist may make, often unconsciously, which is in some way an analogue of a style of communication by some member of the family. It could be that the therapist leans back and stretches his legs soon after the father in the family has done the same, or finds himself adopting a similar tone of voice, or accent, or removing his coat at a similar time. When I had asked one father to tell me about the problem in the family he became very vague and whispered "It is about the one on the left". I asked him to be blunt, to which he responded by leaning forward and telling me earnestly "You know I have not had very much preparation for this interview, you know". When later I saw the video tape, I discovered that I had leant forward in my chair, looked at him earnestly, and said "You know I have not either". Although there was a verbal component to this, I found I was using his tone and accent in a way which was not consciously mocking or ironic. Another example can be found in the powerful pressure people often feel to adopt the local accent or voice pattern when moving to a new locality.

The notion that relationship patterns are transmitted as though like sound waves is represented in current English metaphor;

"We are not on the same wave length"

"We are in step with each other"

"I get strange vibrations from him"

These are metaphors for communicational patterns, and the content suggests a perception of some kind of periodicity. There are other metaphors which portray the periodic nature of much communication and interaction. When we talk of "going round in circles", "vicious circles", "ups and downs", or "coming and going", there is always an implied movement to and from a certain state of affairs. Returning to natural science models, in Fourier's theorem, any pattern can be represented in terms of sine waves. Thus we can see in any apparently continuous event, such as a waterfall, that it is made up of periodic elements, while at the same time the whole event goes through regular changes: the waterfall for example ebbs and flows with the seasons.

Is there any advantage in using the wave motion analogy for human communication? It certainly seems to fit snugly enough for much imitative behaviour, but its importance is that a medium of transmission is unnecessary. That is to say one does not have to ask the question "Who or what caused these events to happen?" It allows one to take a step back and perceive the pattern, rather as one hears the sound instead of each individual wave. While it is interesting to consider individual behaviour in these terms it becomes essential in making sense of the reproduction of patterns in families.

A model of transmission I had previously proposed (Cooklin, 1979) was based on the Object Relations Theory of the personality developed by Fairbairn (1952). In this model, relationship patterns which have been perceived as threatening to the survival of the individual are internalized. Thereafter the individual seeks to be reunited with the aspects of him or herself which have been internalized and seeks others who will play the part of the original "other" in the relationship. In this model, it appeared as though relationship patterns were passed on like quantum packages from one generation to another, in contrast to a "wave" model. It now seems clear to me that this model is too limited. It treats events as though they were sequential, while in reality, any event contains components from all parts of the system simultaneously. A more coherent model for the reproduction of patterns of events would need to include three components;

(1) The sequence of events
(2) The arrangement of the parts at any one time
(3) The wave form of the periodic or episodic nature of the sequence

Let us consider these in terms of a hypothetical short sequence. Such a sequence
might be: Mother is upset, Father responds angrily, Susan responds to Father's
anger by sulking, Johnny responds to these events by placating, Mother joins
with Johnny, Susan joins with Father, the children then fight, the parents unite
to control them. Thus the intensity of interaction in the sequence can be
represented as in Fig. 1.

Six stages are represented here. The pattern must include the configuration of
the relationships in each, the sequential order, and the wave form. Thus it could be

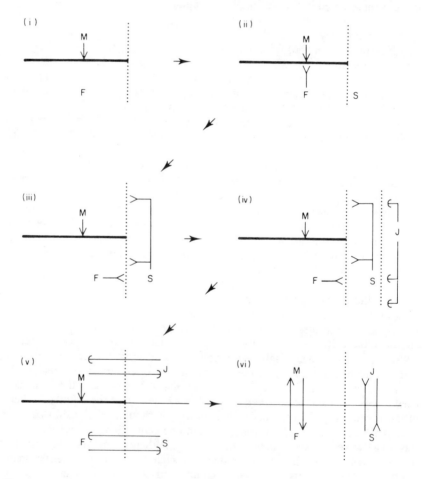

Fig. 1

that the interaction intensifies slowly through stages (i) to (iii), then escalates and is rapidly controlled: Fig. 2. Any other shape would be possible. The intensity could rise slowly and fall slowly (Fig. 3). Also, as shown in Fig. 4, the sequences may occur in rapid succession (a) or with long intervals between them (b). If one asks families to describe a common sequence of this kind, they can nearly always provide more than one. Furthermore each family member can usually predict more or less accurately how a particular sequence will "end", and will often be surprised to find they can do this.

In the view of the communications school, these sequences will in a sense be their own reproducers. In their view it is not necessary to impute either a causal or a transmission link between one sequence and another. Although each sequence may be different in content (the row may not be about mother being upset but perhaps about Susan bullying Johnny), they will nevertheless display the same formal relationships. That is, the overall patterns of interactions will remain the same. A group at the Department of Children and Parents in the Tavistock Clinic led by David Campbell are currently trying to verify the formal pattern in a common sequence observed with certain families (Byng-Hall,

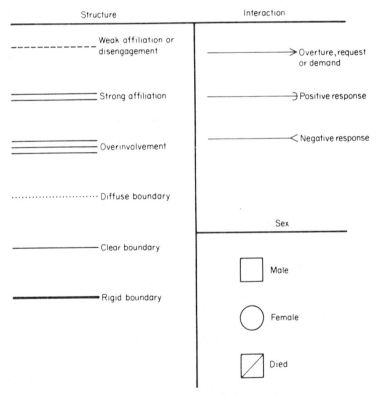

"Key to Fig. 1 and Figs 7-15 (modified after Minuchin, 1974)."

1981). These are families where the identified patient (usually a child) interacts with the parents in such a way that the physical and metaphorical distance between the parents is kept within certain fixed limits (neither too near nor too far).

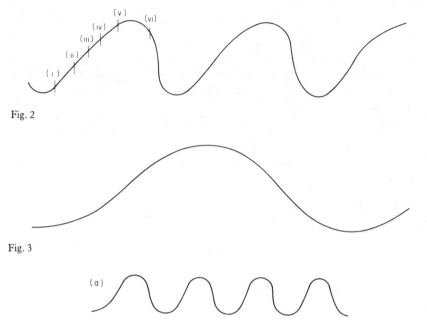

Fig. 2

Fig. 3

Fig. 4

III. EFFECTING CHANGE

A. Change in Short Sequence

A change in such a pattern would require that the sequence goes beyond its usual level of intensity of interaction. For example if in a family a sequence commonly ends with a mother rushing out of the house, saying "I am leaving for good", and returning an hour later, that event will not mean that mother is leaving to anyone in the system, but rather that that is the end of the sequence. If on the other hand, against this background the mother stays out for a week, and does not telephone, the event changes its context and meaning, and will probably have to be resolved in a new way. It is a central goal of Structural Family Therapy that a pattern of events is pushed beyond the usual limiting factor, so that new limiting factors have to be found, and thus new sequences. There is often a two-fold goal:

(a) to change immediate sequences by the therapist directly intervening in these sequences.

(b) through the medium of changing sequences to differentiate relevant sub-systems, particularly executive subsystems (Minuchin, 1974; Camp, 1973).

In the service of these two goals the therapist will try to maintain and enhance the intensity of the interactions in the family's common sequences, and as a result put the members of the family through an experience of stress. The therapist will try to enact a sequence in the course of the therapy session, or even to enact the same sequence several times and in various ways try to influence its outcome.

A classical example of this approach is demonstrated when Minuchin "pushes the parents of an anorectic girl to make her eat". That is, he provides a backcloth and frame—"she must eat or she will die" . . . "you must make her eat"—and the shape of the communicational pattern then unfolds in front of him. For example, commonly the parents will each use gentle coaxing, pleading, cajoling, blaming and denouncement in rhythmic rotation, and each will disqualify the attempts of the other as the interactions approach a certain pitch of intensity (ironically just that pitch at which the pattern could be broken). In a variety of ways, one of which is to repeat at intervals his instruction to the parents, Minuchin will intensify this pattern beyond the usual level of tolerance allowed by the family. In one well-known case he stops the interaction just as the father is trying to force a sausage down his daughter's throat. He tells the daughter that she has humiliated her parents in front of him, because this is so far the only way she can fight them. She will need to learn more competent ways of fighting them, but in the meantime she must eat. The fact that she then eats is accompanied by two other changes:

(1) She allows her development to continue, achieves some greater autonomy, and increases the emotional distance from her parents.

(2) Her parents can no longer avoid conflict by their "helplessness" in relation to her "illness", partly because they have been shamed into finding some new solution and partly because her continuing develop-ment makes her less available to be engaged in their relationship. They thus have to organize themselves into an executive, parental pair.

The rationale for trying to separate out a more defined executive pair or sub-system in a family can be seen from two points of view. First, in terms of general systems theory, this has the effect of increasing the state of order or "negentropy" (the ordering of randomness) in the system. This is a necessary precursor to developmental change, because the individual's development requires a transformation in the shape of the family: a reorganization of the pattern of alliances and coalitions. Any system requires a degree of order in its internal state before it can effectively and safely (without a threat to its survival) undergo such a transition.

Secondly, the definition of an executive subsystem in a family can have a powerful impact on the communicational patterns. One thesis of communications theory is that when a child presents as symptomatic, the parents may make digital statements geared towards control. However analogic communications from either or both parents will frequently invalidate these messages, so that the symptomatic child can either oscillate between responding to one or the other message, or is unable to respond to either. This is close in analogy to an electromagnetic sine wave. If an alternating current is to be "rectified" for direct current use, half of the sine wave has to be "cut off", otherwise the two waves cancel each other out. A strategy analogous to this "rectification" has been used by therapists from the Strategic school of family therapy (Haley, 1977) an example of which has recently been described by Madanes (1980). She advocates that the therapist should respond to only one of these apparently conflicting communications. By enhancing and supporting one of the communications (in this case the one which supports the hierarchical nature of the parents' authority) the other communication becomes relatively less powerful, the control of the reverberating sequence is lost, and a new sequence has to develop.

B. Change in Short vs Long Sequences

Using a Structural approach to family therapy, it is possible to enact a relevant sequence within a session. However if one is considering sequences whose "wavelengths" might be over many years, then clearly this is not possible. Also, increasing the time-span of the sequence beyond a certain limit not only means a quantitative difference, but also the nature of the sequences becomes qualitatively different. Using again the analogy of electromagnetic wave forms, infra-red light is a very different phenomenon from ultra-violet light, which has a much shorter wave-length and ultra-violet light is a quite different phenomenon from radio waves or X-rays or gamma rays. They all have quite different transmission properties, and the effects of their impact on matter and particularly on biological tissue differ entirely.

One example of a short sequence in a family has been given. In another let us say that the mother complains of tiredness and asks her husband to help prepare a meal. He asks Susan to "do more for your mother". Susan complains that Johnny is "let off". Johnny offers to help the mother. The father stands up for Susan. Susan calls Johnny a sneak "you wouldn't do it if I weren't in trouble". The father then provokes Johnny to do something for which he can punish him. This sequence ends slightly differently from the earlier one but the formal relationships are almost the same; that is, the interrelationship of the parts is similar. For example, in relation to Johnny and Mother, Susan and Father are in alliance; in relation to Susan or Father, Johnny and Mother are in alliance.

Within particular families the content may change but the form may remain remarkably constant.

However the *longer* the sequence is, the more difficult it is to describe accurately, or even to identify clearly. If one does examine a family history and sees that for example every second generation for three generations there is a "favourite child" who is in some way done down by a "black sheep" sibling, then one may be observing the manifestations at least of a long sequence. This may only be the visible manifestations on which hang a whole series of complex relationship patterns. In one family it could be clearly seen that there was a pattern through three generations of a "brother not speaking to a sister" for long periods. Other relationships between their parents and respective spouses could be seen to be organized around the periodic nature of these disaffections, and the latter could be seen to occur in relation to patterns in the former. Other such sequences of varying lengths are illustrated in the examples described later.

Structural family therapy, using interventions designed to influence relatively short sequences, nevertheless assumes that these relatively short focussed sequences of behaviour will represent some part of the whole functioning of the family system. This coincides nicely with the holograph analogy: each segment contains an image of the whole. Thus a structural family therapist may take one segment of the whole picture, usually that which contains the presenting symptom brought by the parents, and he will assume that this represents a restricted view of the whole system, not in terms of content, but in terms of its formal relationships. For example he will assume that if Johnny has a problem about bedtime which interferes with the parents' sleep, and perhaps their sex life, that a change in this sequence will potentially represent changes in the whole pattern of relationships between the boy and his mother, the boy and his father, the parents with each other, and perhaps all of them with siblings. Such an approach is fully congruent with much general systems and cybernetic thinking. For example the idea that each element in a system or in each subsystem will contain patterns which are analogous to those in the larger system, is implicit in the concept of isomorphism (Ashby, 1956). Recently this concept has gained neurophysiological validation in the description of "enfoldment" or the "implicate order" of the sensory/motor cortex (Pribram, 1971). It has been shown that while on the one hand, different cells in the cortex respond to different frequencies in the environment, a pattern of the whole is recorded and stored by each cell.

It is after all implicit in the concept of a system rather than a "heap" (to use the systems jargon), that a change in one segment will reverberate throughout the whole system. This phenomenon is illustrated by Ashby's Homeostat* (1956). The use of this model also demonstrates how events with a different "time space" manifest different properties. For example the time that this machine takes to go through all its gyrations and eventually achieve a "steady state", can vary depending on the kind of change initiated in any element of the machine

---

*A mechanical model whose parts are interconnected in such a way that a change in one leads ultimately to a change in all the others until a new equilibrium is established.

and on the relative position of this element within the machine. It could take anything from a few milliseconds to several hours for the machine to re-establish equilibrium. The change which takes fractions of a second leads to a change of state which is of different order to that which takes hours. In the former case the machine is "stable" much of the time. In the latter case, the machine is in a state of *establishing* stability for much of the time.

C.   The "Event Shape in Time Space"

I have so far drawn heavily on analogies from other events in working towards a framework for the shape of events in human systems. My purpose in this liberal use of analogy has been to try and disengage temporarily from our innate subject-iveness in order to isolate some generalizations. Before moving to the more vexed question of "How does it all happen? — "What controls it all?", I shall summarize the points I am making and some of the analogies used.

(1)   Patterns all have a shape, and patterns of human interaction all are events in time, and thus have a shape in time.

(2)   Such patterns have a tendency to reproduce themselves. Thus each event will tend to repeat itself at regular intervals, if other variables remain constant. I have drawn on sound and electromagnetic wave analogies to illustrate this point.

(3)   Each part of an event, while being a mini-whole event itself, also contains the pattern of the main whole event. As well as illustrating the practical application of this point in structural family therapy, I have also used analogies from the holograph and from the connections to the sensory/motor cortex.

(4)   The properties of an event are principally governed by the time space within which it occurs, as well as by the event shape.

(5)   Thus the interventions required to change the shape of an event in a short time space will differ from those in a long time space.

In the case of short sequences, occupying a relatively short time space of a few minutes, hours or days, these principles could form the basis of guidelines for interventions of the kind used in structural family therapy. The answer to the question "What keeps the pattern going?" can be assumed to be "the pattern itself". On the other hand, there is a relationship between sequences of different lengths. Short sequences can be components of medium sequences, which in turn can be components of longer sequences (see Fig. 5). Theoretically, a change in the pattern of short sequences could ultimately lead to a change in the pattern of long sequences. The husband/wife pair who successfully break a family tradition of a pattern of "alcoholic husband/long-suffering wife" characterized by sequences of drinking—violence—recriminations—and contrite guilt, could possibly have influenced a long-term family pattern for the future. This assumes that there is not some specific governor or control process, which remains relatively unaffected by such short-term changes, and which will tend to maintain the traditional pattern. Carter and McGoldrick (1980) have used the term *vertical stressors* to describe relatively stable family patterns or myths which seem to have a life of their own. If this happens, and I believe there is evidence that it does, then it is necessary to try and identify the nature of this governor or control process. I prefer the term "control process" to "governor" because I think there is evidence that it is itself an event rather than a fixed entity, such as a "thing" or a particular person. The Ps of systems terminology denotes a point in the interactional process; "the nodal point", rather than a particular element or person.

Fig. 5

D. The Nature of Control Processes

Both object relations theory, and attachment theory (Fairbairn, 1952; Cooklin, 1979; Bowlby, 1969) have provided models for control processes over longer-term sequences. Object relations theory suggests that the individual carries an internal model of an unresolved relationship which he continues to try and resolve in new relationships which are out of context. They are out of context because he is trying to solve the original relationship rather than the new one. Attachment theory suggests that in dysfunctional relationships, the individual is "anxiously attached" to a familiar albeit unsatisfactory relationship. More satisfying opportunities raise anxiety about giving up the known relationship on which one's own internal model is based. One aim of structural family therapy is that an individual will experience a new set of relationships, and thus members will participate in a new set of sequences. However sometimes the internal working models are so powerful in families that they act as a kind of "giro" or to use an electronic analogy as "reverberating circuits" which provide their own overwhelming positive feedback. It is in these situations that some different order of intervention is required.

From a different standpoint, Madanes (1980) makes a similar point about the individual adolescent:

> It may be that the disruptive behaviour *had* a protective function, but when the incongruous hierarchy stabilises and the system of interaction becomes chronic, the disturbed behaviour persists as a function of the system and independently of what set it off. It may be that at a certain point in time, there is no longer a hierarchical incongruity but simply a hierarchical reversal with the youth in a

superior position of power over the parents and with few or no situations in which the reverse is true.

This sees the "giro" as throughout the system, but the youth may be continuing to behave in a manner which has its own momentum although the behaviour may have lost any protective function. I believe for a similar reason Rosenberg and Lindblad (1978) from the Philadelphia Child Guidance Clinic recommend the use of behaviour therapy (specifically counter-conditioning) in addition to family therapy for the treatment of elective mutism.

> The individual work with the child is crucial since it affords the child an opportunity to work at changing in a context different from the one that allowed for the development of the symptom. Together these approaches offer a complimentarity that both speeds the change in the child and allows for this change to hold after a "return" to the family.

At this point however, a truly "systems" view of the control processes has not been satisfactorily described here. In fact the traditional psychiatric view of the "illness" or "condition" causing behaviour would almost fulfil the criteria that I have so far used for a control process. It could be argued that in Rosenberg and Lindblad's model, the child is seen as "embodying" the control process, but this would be an over-simplified anthropomorphic attempt to understand a complex phenomenon. Ferreira (1963) and Byng-Hall (1973) have explored the place of family myths as the "governors" controlling the course of long-term sequences. Watzlawick and others (1969) used the function of myths in regulating short and medium-term sequences. I have previously described the role of the Family Group Preoccupation (1974, 1979) around which potentially conflictual relationships are bound, as a governor of long-term sequences in certain families. The Family Group preoccupation is closely allied to the role of ghosts in family life: both those that are "as if" as well as those that are "believed in".

But all these ideas beg the question "What really is the control process?" Myths, the Family Group Preoccupation, and ghosts are after all only visual, representative, projections of patterns. Ghosts maintain an image which is often embodied in an event; a person's death in a particular way for example. Myths are patterns of relationships; the parts which the members play. It follows therefore that the control processors are themselves patterns, or at least patterns of patterns, rather as the patterns of amino acids in a protein are reproduced by the patterns of DNA in the chromosomes. It is really the configuration itself which is in charge of the sequences.

An intervention in a family can allow an apparently "impossible" father, mother, or child to leave that role. So what was impossible? It must have been the pattern itself. It is true that a pattern may be continued by an individual in a country far from his family of origin. The object relations model does provide a framework for the transmission of a pattern through such an individual. On the other hand, it is relatively rare for an individual to be totally cut off from his or her family with absolutely no communication, and if that state is approximated, the cultural context will play an even greater part in what pattern is continued. In addition, the strategic and paradoxical interventions of Haley, Madanes,

Pallazolli and others could not be effective if one followed through the logical conclusion of object relations theory as originally described. This is because all the object relations models of change rely heavily on the concept of "working through". Although made up of many repeated events in the therapeutic relationship, "working through" appears as a relatively smooth continuous process. Changes following strategic and paradoxical interventions, on the other hand, are often sudden. The shape of the event of change is more that of a step function (Hoffman, 1980) and occurs in jumps. The pattern of such change has been most clearly illustrated by Zeeman (1978) from the point of view of catastrophe theory. Because these interventions frequently do not involve the therapist in active persuasive "change encouraging" moves, in contrast with structural family therapy, they must act at the level of the patterns which control the patterns (Gorell Barnes, 1981). They achieve this by making the control processes irrelevant and therefore powerless. They do not make the actual relationship irrelevant or meaningless, a point often mistaken by therapists "trying out" paradoxical techniques. They may in fact lead to the same relationships being experienced with increased authenticity. I believe this is close to what Watzlawick *et al.* (1974) have described as second-order change. I believe this can be represented by returning to the wave form analogy (Fig. 5).

Fig. 6

This is of course a gross oversimplification, and the patterns could be represented by changes in different dimensions (Fig. 6). Second order change would have to be accompanied by some change in reality, and therefore one would expect by some change in the medium and long-term sequences.

E. Change in Short-Term Sequences Effecting Medium-Term Sequences

It has been stressed that in some situations patterns can apparently reproduce themselves. It has also been argued that when this is the predominant process, a relatively minor change in a short-term sequence could ultimately lead to change in longer-term sequences, rather as a small change in a river's banks can divert the whole course of that river. Thus small changes enacted during a family session might ultimately lead not only to change in those sequences enacted, but also to change in the family's structure and patterns of interaction. An example follows from the Anton family.

Paul was aged 13, and came with his sister Angie aged 10 and their grandmother,

Ann. The problem presented was that Paul suffered from regular, recurrent and severe vomiting, what would usually be described as Periodic Syndrome. The vomiting was said by his grandmother to occur in bouts at approximately weekly intervals, and about once a month it reached sufficient severity for him to require admission to hospital and treatment for dehydration. These events severely interfered with his life, and with those of this current family. The precipitant to the family's referral was a failed holiday in the Channel Islands. Paul had soon been admitted to hospital and the holiday was ruined. He was said to have suffered from this disorder since about the age of three, and he had been seen by at least two previous psychiatrists. In the folklore of the family, it had been talked of as having "developed from jealousy after the birth of his younger sister". The family had moved to the United States, and four years before I saw them the children's two parents had been killed in a car crash. Within the family there had been some relatively public heart searchings about whether the parents had been drinking at a party that evening, or whether any family row could have contributed to the event. At the time, the children's maternal grandmother had been on a short visit to the family. Two years before the accident, she had been divorced by her own husband just after her sixtieth birthday. Having now lost her only child as well, the opportunity to take over the children seemed to offer her a welcome new purpose to her life. In fact before the accident, Paul's symptoms had abated somewhat, at least in frequency, but within a year of the formation of this new family of three back in England, the symptoms had reappeared with all their previous ferocity. Paul also had been assessed by a local psychiatrist for learning difficulties, and had been placed in a special school. His sister Angie rarely missed an opportunity to rub in his relative incompetence with reading, by parading her own eloquence, results of tests etc.

When the three (grandmother and children) came for a family session, it was also clear that Angie was in as much of a battle with her grandmother for domination as she was with Paul. Paul presented himself as rather passive, and all his behaviour seemed directed to the goal of "keeping things calm". The family were seen for eight sessions in all. Within three sessions Paul's symptoms had subsided, and after another two, they had disappeared, apart from one relapse during Christmas which he was able to handle himself without recourse to hospital. The grandmother became less involved and preoccupied with Paul's symptoms, more able to control Angie and with less "sisterly" battles. She was also more able to enjoy activities of her own in a way which seemed in keeping with her own time of life.

Now let us consider this case in terms of stable short-term sequences, without seeking relevant long-term sequences. Paul's symptoms had disappeared relatively quickly. Although the therapist had spent some effort in encouraging and pushing the grandmother and children to re-experience more fully the mourning of the loss of the parents, at first sight this did not appear to be crucial. Recounting the details of the loss did not seem to be followed by any major change, particularly in Paul's symptom, and this symptom had been present almost continuously long before his parents' death.

The relationship Paul had with Angie and the grandmother appeared to have similarities to certain patterns in his relationship to his parents (Fig. 7). For example it appeared that by Paul staying closely involved with his mother, he had in some way acted as a safety valve in what was at times a stormy relationship between his parents. A similar kind of stormy relationship now existed between

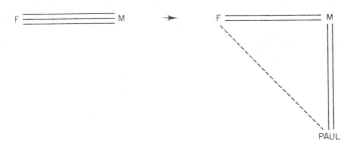

Fig. 7

Angie and his grandmother. The grandmother was often unable to control Angie, would threaten to have her "put away", while Angie would usually "win and get her own way". As the tension rose, Paul would begin to vomit. Paul's mother had responded to mounting tension in the marriage by threatening to return to her mother. Paul's father seemed unable to back down, so that an escalating series of threats would be exchanged until Paul began to vomit. Thus the relationship pattern between Paul and his grandmother and Angie, was isomorphic to that which had previously existed between him and his parents. Although the content was quite different, the pattern was the same (Fig. 8).

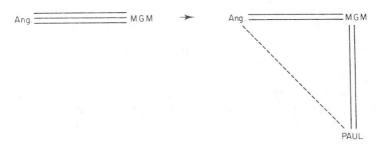

Fig. 8

The therapist directed his attention towards trying to establish a controlled hierarchy between the grandmother and children. He aimed to intensify the grandmother's attempts to control Angie, so that Paul could eventually be allowed a place as an elder brother to Angie. The effect of this was to place Angie and Paul on a similar level together, and relatively speaking more distant from the grandmother (Fig. 9). Angie, as a result, fought her grandmother less and Paul was less involved in their struggle.

It would appear that the historical significance of these encounters was less relevant to the changes in the short-term sequences. Nevertheless it could also be argued that the shared experience of mourning effected the outcome of medium-term sequences in the family. An example of such a sequence would be the pattern of over-engagement, oscillating with threats of abandonment, which

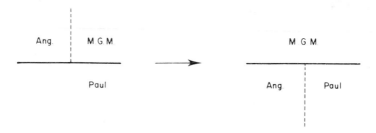

Fig. 9

occurred between Angie and grandmother, and which in turn was regulated by Paul's symptoms. If such a sequence changed, then the shifts in the more short-term sequences could be accommodated. The mourning process in which they were engaged during therapy could have led to a differentiation of the present pattern of interactions from the previous set which it emulated. The present pattern could therefore be governed more by the immediate needs of the family and less by a requirement to continue an old pattern. However, one could not predict at all how these medium-term changes might effect the longer-term pattern of relationships in Paul's or Angie's families of procreation.

F. Change in Short Sequences Leading to Interventions in the Control Process of Long Sequences

John and Sue Losey were a young couple with a 2-year-old son. John was a moderately successful businessman, and Sue had been competent in her own work as well as being a capable housewife. They had been referred by a paediatrician because their child George was described as "hyperactive". He would not sleep at night, got up early in the morning, often damaged things around the house, had tantrums if he could not get his own way, and was always on the move. Apart from slightly retarded speech, he was an otherwise normal and healthily developed boy. At different times the paediatrician had previously prescribed both tranquillisers and amphetamine-related stimulants, without effect.

John was smiling and affable, Sue worried looking, tense and rather bitter. George oscillated between them in an excitable manner until I engaged the two parents on the question of how they could co-operate in his management. As, with my encouragement, the two parents began to negotiate with each other about their approach to George, George seemed to forget them and eventually went to sleep, remaining so for the following hour. As this was some 15 minutes into a session and was dramatically different from anything which the parents had seen happen before, I was somewhat thrown from my goal of intensifying current sequences and trying to achieve shifts in their outcome. I could have encouraged them to waken George, but something about the unusual experience of peace with him asleep triggered the two of them to reminisce about how they had come to form this family. Sue's father had committed suicide shortly before George's birth. She had experienced this as extremely traumatic, feeling that she was responsible as she ''should have known that things were not right'', and experiencing the loss intensely as she had viewed her father as her only close support. His death had intensified what had been a previous pattern in her relationships. She would respond to potentially close relationships by hardening and distancing herself. With John this had been easy because his ''happy-go-lucky'' approach to life made little intrusion on her privacy. However, George's robust demands led her to retreat even further into herself, to which George naturally responded by making increasingly excited demands. Sue had been pregnant by John before the marriage but had insisted on having this aborted ''because I didn't want to have to get married for that reason and then be told by my mother 'I told you so' ''. John claimed to have been very distressed about this abortion, and thought that it had coloured his protective attitude to George. In the same breath he talked about a younger sibling in his own family who died as a ''cot death''. John had made efforts to make up to his own parents for their loss, and had developed a very protective and ''soft'' attitude to little children. This had been intensified by his hurt about Sue's abortion. Therefore in response to George he would be ''kind and explain things'', rather than assert relevant controls. This of course undermined Sue, and intensified her ''hardness''.

This family was seen for only three sessions, during which time the parents gained control of George, who had calmed down considerably, and Sue had ceased to distance herself so much from John, thus allowing John to be more assertive and direct with her. In this case, one could argue that Susan was able to change the way in which she distanced her husband once she was able to allow him to help her with the suffering and self-blame with which she continued to burden herself about her father's suicide. Similarly, John's need to ''nurture and protect little children'' could be seen both in the context of this immediate family, and as part of a longer-term sequence relating to his role in the family of origin. Although it was in fact the use of ''Structural Moves'' to enact and intensify the interactions related to the problems the family brought which was followed by this dramatic change of mood, it was the change in the control processes which allowed the new sequences to continue. In this case, the control processes were at the first level the nature of the triad between John, Sue and George, but at the second level, the processes were related to the roles which John and Sue were both asking each other to fulfil. The reason that these roles fulfilled the function of control processes was because they were non-explicit. Thus each had to fit more or less comfortably into the other's demands in order to remain within the system. Making these roles both explicit, and providing a context for their development was I believe an important part of the recalibration of the control processes in this case.

G.　Integrating Change in Short and Long Sequences

So far it has been stressed that change in short-term sequences can be affected by the techniques of structural family therapy: enactment, intensification, boundary-making, unbalancing. When used in conjunction with techniques for changing realities, and "changing epistemology", such changes will sometimes lead to a shift in the balance of interactions throughout the system in such a way that the control processes themselves will be recalibrated. In this case, a change in the pattern of the longer-term sequences may also result. However when the control processes and the longer-term sequences which they control carry a powerful momentum, then efforts to intervene with these directly will be complementary to changes effected in short-term sequences. The control processes may be effected by a number of strategic techniques (Gorell Barnes, 1982a, b) or by exploring their original context which has now become potentially irrelevant. I say potentially because, in fact, the context has not become irrelevant if the processes are continuing in the present. The typing or coding of events as belonging to the past is only useful if it relegates these events to the past. This can be achieved by changing their current context so that they no longer have a place in the present. This last point is illustrated by the following example:

The Arkwright family consisted of the mother June who was a pottery teacher, the father Stan who was a landscape gardener, and their two children, Shelley aged 10 and Neil aged 8. Shelley was in trouble at school, her work was deteriorating, and teachers had complained about her. She was involved in escalating battles with her mother, ostensibly about homework, and her mother was alarmed by the degree of violence in which the two of them were engaging. Viewing the family from the point of view of its formal relationships, Shelley and her mother were over-engaged with each other, and Stan was relatively distant. There was no hierarchical differentiation between Shelley's and her mother's roles, and Stan treated his wife in a patronizing way, as though she and Shelley were sisters. At the same time, if Stan began to address either Shelley or her mother directly, he was usually interrupted. Neil behaved "as good as gold", which engaged him actively with Shelley by irritating her, and relatively distancing himself from his parents (Fig. 10).

Fig. 10

In the first two sessions, I asked June to show me what happened when she tried to talk to Shelley the "way she wanted to". She asked Shelley "what is it about me that annoys you?" At first Shelley would not answer. Eventually Shelley responded "Why do I annoy you?" The analogic components of this question conveyed that she was asking her mother if that was what the mother's question meant. At another level, it also conveyed her confusion manifested from the lack of hierarchical clarity. In intensifying the sequence I had moved the father's chair so that he could not directly intervene with Shelley, but could only see his wife. I had asked Neil not to interrupt but to listen "for the time being". I had asked Stan to find out from his wife what she wanted to do when Shelley kept leaving her chair. After several attempts to ask June in which he made such statements as "What you want to do is . . ." or "I mean you want to make her sit down, don't you . . ." or "shall I make her sit down . . . ", he finally asked his wife "what do you want Shelley to do?" June responded that she wanted Shelley to sit down. He was then helped to support his wife in achieving this. As Shelley continued to have tantrums in the room, the therapist was able to intensify the interaction between the parents in the task of successfully managing these tantrums (Fig. 11). By the third session, the mother had established control over

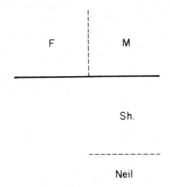

Fig. 11

Shelley, and Shelley was scowling less and looking more relaxed. However in relation to her father, she was even more mocking and dismissive (Fig. 12).

Fig. 12

The father was asked to enact what the mother had been able to achieve, and the mother was asked to sit out and watch. After several episodes, when the mother could not restrain herself from "rescuing" her husband each time as she saw it he "did it wrong", the father was in fact able to have a quite reasonable and age-appropriate conversation with his daughter. Meanwhile Neil had said to his sister "Shelley do hurry up otherwise Dr Cooklin will only be talking about you and I will never get dealt with".

I asked the mother how she thought her husband was managing to which she replied rather reluctantly and a little sourly "I think he is doing rather well". I then left the room and went behind the one-way screen having asked the father to "continue". A sequence similar to the ones I have described developed again. At a certain point, the mother leant forward to "help" her husband by talking to Shelley. This was the point of "repeat" which I had been waiting for. I entered the room and said to the mother "really, I don't understand why you must keep rescuing him. Why is it? Why must you keep rescuing him? He is really doing very well". At first she smiled nodding, and then burst into tears apparently communicating a degree of distress which seemed quite out of keeping with this setting. I had asked her "why must you keep rescuing him?"

I stopped this part of the session and asked about the origins of the family. The mother showed the same distress as she began to tell me about the death of her father when she was aged 15. She and her younger sister (at that time aged 10, the same age as Shelley now was) had been playing with an old gramophone trying to make it work. Her younger sister Sarah had been nagging her father to make the gramophone work. "Make it work Daddy, make it work for me". The father had checked the connections on the electric motor and plugged it in. He was electrocuted and killed instantly. June had told her sister that her father was not really dead, just unconscious. There was nobody else around and she had had to get help, but none of the adults would believe her story. She and her sister had never discussed the event.

What I had responded to analogically was that she was treating her husband in an inappropriately fragile way. Following this session, Shelley's relationship with her mother changed markedly, and she became increasingly engaged in school. June met her sister and discussed the incident for the first time, both acknowledging how afraid they had been about facing each other. June and Stan were seen for a number of marital sessions before June was able to treat Stan as potent enough to be of use to her. The complimentary side of this shift was that he had to acknowledge his wife as a potential adversary rather than the "best child he had got". Once the couple had separated themselves out as a marital pair, Shelley and Neil began to be more actively competitive. The therapy had lasted for 12 sessions in all, but two months later the parents returned on their own to ask for advice about Neil. I did little other than to ask them to enact discussing it together. They went home and found an easy solution to a minor control problem with the little boy (Fig. 13).

There are other frameworks within which these events could be considered. Shelley's behaviour certainly played an important part in distance regulation between the parents (Byng-Hall, 1980). They maintained some engagement through her, but did not become so intently engaged with each other that the confusions of hierarchy in their marriage would be confronted, thus avoiding the dangers of violence or abandonment between them.

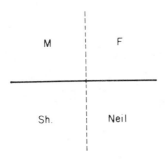

Fig. 13

There was a shift in balance between the different parts of the system through the initial work of intensification, boundary-making, and unbalancing. However, there was an overall pattern of interactions of the husband/wife pair which seemed to override these short-term changes. The intensely emotional event of the wife seeing the link between the way she treated her husband (which only could have been seen in the context of her as *mother* in the presence of *her children and* her husband), recalibrated the control process. Without this second-order change, the scene could have been set for the propagation of a longer-term sequence from generation to generation or in alternate generations. However the pattern was not carried alone by June (or of course her husband's component by him) but by the configuration, which involved her mother, her sister, and others.

H.   Medium Sequence Change

In the final example three wavelengths of sequences can be distinguished; short repetitive cycles occurring regularly throughout a session, medium sequences repeated over a cycle of a few months or years, and longer-term sequences spanning a generation or more.

The family consisted of Annie, Jack her husband, and Sheila their daughter of 24. The problem presented was that Annie was "having a nervous breakdown". The timing of this coincided with Sheila's latest bid to leave home, and to separate from the intense triangular relationship between the three of them. The short-term sequence refers to the regular pattern of interaction between the family members. This is characterized by the following moves: as Jack withdraws from Annie, so Annie becomes increasingly extreme in her demands. Jack then withdraws further. As the pitch of interaction rises, Sheila makes moves to leave the triangle. The pitch of interaction between Jack and Annie then further increases in intensity until Sheila becomes engaged in taking one side or the other. This is an example of the short-term sequence, which could occur several times in a session. The pattern will show a remarkable constancy of form although, as can be seen from the example below, the roles assigned may be swopped from time to time. The starting point of the sequence I have used is quite arbitrary as the pattern is both cyclical and continuous. The medium-term sequence is similar in form but different in its time space or wave length. The peaks of intensity are when Sheila prepares to leave home, and are ultimately followed by Annie "having a nervous breakdown", or at least Jack's complaint that she is. The wavelength varies between a few months and a year or more.

The long-term sequence refers to the pattern of relatively stable triangles giving way to relatively unstable dyadic relationships, which would in turn be replaced by stable, and therefore "clung to", triangular relationships throughout the family's available history.

Annie had come from a family where triangular relationships, those in which three people were "reliably" involved, were the stable unit. She had remained closely involved with her parents while her elder and younger siblings had responded to the freedom which this arrangement afforded them by "leaving us to it". Her own separation from her parents had not occurred until her mother died. Without her mother, the relationship with her father was unstable, and she soon began to try to distance herself. She married Jack in 1937. They had met "in service" (they were both servants in a country house), but he was soon drafted into the Army. By the time of his return from the war, she was living with another man. After an initial refusal she returned to Jack and almost immediately became pregnant. She gave birth to a boy with spina bifida who died ten days later.

Jack was the middle child in his family. His father was engrossed in his elder brother and his mother heavily involved with his young sister. The latter two were still living together. Although he often felt lonely and depressed, he was most comfortable when being relatively ignored. He had to "force" his attentions on Annie who for a time had responded to him and then withdrawn again, after the death of their child. Jack's attempts to woo Annie were infrequent, and he would usually seem relieved when he settled back into a more or less comfortable isolation. It appeared that this cycle of events lasted about ten years. They had married in 1937, the first child was conceived ten years later, and Sheila was conceived after another ten years in 1957. Annie, however, had remained closely involved with the child that died. This ghost seemed to maintain the stability of her relationship with Jack, as it completed the triangle. This "child" required Jack to stay in the marriage for the myth to maintain its authenticity. It kept Jack at a distance so that the question of whether or not the child was really alive would not be confronted. For Jack's part, the child myth had not only kept the marriage safe, not too intimate but to be preserved at all costs, for fear the myth be exploded; it also became reminiscent of the elder brother he could not displace. In fact he felt most comfortable and "knew his place" in such a context. This arrangement continued to operate throughout a cycle of about ten years. Annie maintained that the child had not really died. Jack responded to this contention as a reason why he must treat her carefully, and the myth was never truly challenged; not, that is, until the birth of Sheila.

Thus Jack had moved from being the relative outsider in a series of triangular relationships in his family of origin, to being the relative outsider in this new triangle. Annie had moved from being closely involved with her mother in such a way that her father was kept "in the picture" but comfortably at bay from both of them, to being closely involved with the dead child in such a way that Jack was kept involved but kept at a distance comfortable for both (Fig. 14).

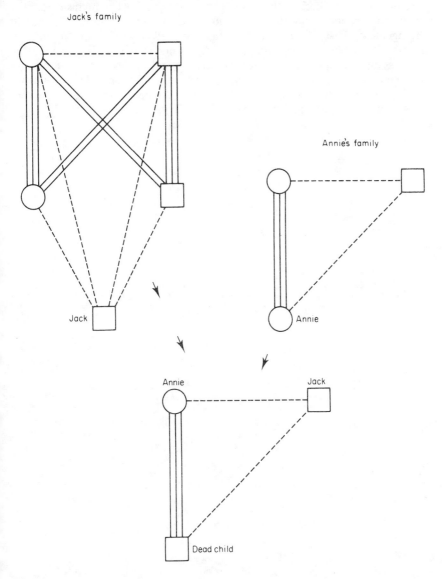

Fig. 14

This whole system was therefore initially destabilized by Sheila's birth. For her to be accepted, the myth had to be exploded, and the raison d'être of the marriage brought into question. Neither partner could contemplate this. Jack became Sheila's "protector" from Annie. Annie's position became more untenable, and she is said to have tried to smother or strangle Sheila. This then became a new myth: "Annie had tried to get rid of Sheila". As the system restabilized, Sheila became the pivot of the new triangle. The myths of Annie's attack on her, and of the son "who had not died" served only to cement this arrangement. That is the "guilt" of "having tried to kill" Sheila meant that Annie kept closely involved with her, and Jack ministered over the relationship but was outside it. The dead baby was therefore replaced by Sheila, but hovered in the background threatening to return if Sheila should leave. The implication of the return of the dead child myth was that Annie would have a "nervous breakdown", and the system would destabilize (Fig. 15).

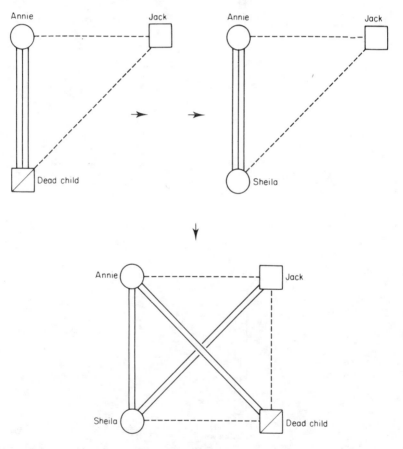

Fig. 15

Thus both myths prevented a challenge to Annie's role: "she was disturbed, could not be challenged, and needed Jack and Sheila", and her role protected the relationship between Jack and Sheila, as supportive but distant. Only the developmental process in the form of independent strivings from Sheila could really challenge this arrangement. Until recently, Sheila had shown little evidence of any such strivings. She had often stayed home from school to look after Annie, and Annie had often kept her off school to "protect her daughter". Annie would have "paranoid breakdowns", and Jack remained "long-suffering" and continued to minister to Annie and Sheila.

The family had been the subject of many therapeutic endeavours, including hospitalization and medication for Annie, medication and later psychotherapy for Sheila, "investigations" for weight loss in Jack, and recently "supportive psychotherapy" for Annie combined with family therapy for all three. When I first saw them, a medium-term sequence was in the process of being repeated. After many years of school refusal, Sheila had had similar difficulties with work, but was now settled in a reasonable clerical job. However she was isolated, without friends and did everything with her parents. The previous year she had made enquiries about training as a nurse, about thirty miles from home. She applied and was accepted. Her father began to reassure her that she'd be all right. Her mother began to complain about "spiritualists plotting against me", and Sheila wrote turning down the place on the course. However, although she stayed at home and isolated, she began fighting her mother about what she called "you trying to control me" and her father about his handling of her mother. A few months before I saw them, Sheila had again stated her intention to leave home and train as a nurse. Jack then admitted to Annie that he'd been having an affair with another woman. The nature of this affair was very unclear, and it appeared anyway that it had been going on for some years. Thus it seemed clear that it was less important whether or not this affair had happened than that it was presented as a challenge to the system. That is a different kind of triangle, in which Jack *was* involved with a third person, suddenly appeared like an omen to warn of the possible consequences of Sheila leaving, and breaking the stable pattern. The system produced an effective error-correcting negative feedback loop.

The initial response to this apparent piece of new information was an escalation in the standard pattern of medium-term sequences. Annie insisted the spiritualists were controlling her thoughts and once or twice "let out her feelings" on some members of a bus queue. Jack was demanding in-patient treatment for Annie. An increasing number of professionals became involved with the family in various ways.

The longer-term consequences were the way the families of both partners had transmitted a requirement for stable relationships, and the patterns which surrounded these. The medium-term sequences were those which maintained this pattern; the way Jack and Annie came together, separated and came together, in the company of another man, another woman, a dead child, and Sheila. Part of these medium-term sequences was enacted by the way Jack and Annie responded to Sheila's attempts to separate, each responding to Sheila and each other in a way which disqualified Sheila's bid for independence. Sheila also showed evidence of patent relief as these sequences completed their cycle and leaving became irrelevant. The interactions which I'll summarize occurred over the course of some ten sessions:

(1) "Paying off" the other therapists (no reflection on their skill but rather on their place in these sequences), and were in three phases.
(2) Dislodging Annie's role as the "one who is crazy and must be treated with kid gloves".
(3) Marshalling Annie and Jack to "parent" Sheila.
(4) Using a paradoxical challenge to Sheila to divert her from "completing the sequence" and returning home.

In the first session, Jack was insisting that Annie was "having a nervous breakdown". I asked Jack to explain what he meant in detail.

Jack: Well, you know she's imagining things.

Dr C: Please be more specific, exactly what do you mean?

Jack: If you've been a psychiatrist all these years you should know what a nervous breakdown is like.

Dr C: Not this one . . . look, let me help . . . get Annie to show me the behaviour you're worried about—try and make her show me.

Jack: [to Annie] Well you tell the Doctor what you told me—about these things you're imagining.

Annie: I'm not mad.

Jack: I never said you was.

Annie: I just said I was being victimized—the people in the office they were spiritualists and they were going to victimize me out of my job and they were right.

Jack: [to Dr C] There you are, you see . . .

Annie: [shouting] I was being victimized out of my job I tell you . . . [now screaming and standing over Jack threatening him with her fist]. You bastard . . . you won't believe me . . . why won't you listen?

Jack: [to Dr C] Now you see why I don't like coming up here . . .

Dr C: Go on—continue . . .

Jack: No, I'm not going on because this is . . .

Dr C: You know Jack I am amazed at the amount of extremism you tolerate in your wife . . . why do you allow it?

[Jack appears somewhat taken aback]

Dr C. continuing: I mean it can't allow for any pleasure, peace, *or* tranquillity . . . why do you allow it? . . . I wouldn't allow it with my wife . . . why do you?

Jack: Because . . . someone's got to keep on an even keel . . .

Annie: [taunting] Why don't you leave me?

Jack: . . . because if I didn't . . . I can see I could land up like these wife bashers.

Annie: But it's good to let go of your feelings . . . a row is good . . . why are you so passive?

Dr C: So is it, Annie, that the more passive and calm Jack gets, the more emotional and emphatic you become, the more passive and unsure Jack becomes, which makes you more determined?

Annie: Yes, he won't fight me.

Jack: Well I will sometimes . . . at least I'll argue . . .

This short sequence had occurred many times between this couple. The intervention pushed it beyond its normal limits, reframed it as a relationship pattern, and at the same time reframed Annie's behaviour in "behavioural" rather than "illness" terms. Later in the same session, much of the above history was also related by the couple. Some interventions were also made around the question of the myth of the dead baby. For example Annie claimed Jack had never shown her the death certificate, but added that she wouldn't have believed it anyway. It was therefore agreed that Jack would obtain a copy of the death certificate but keep it hidden from Annie. They might visit the grave together, but not observe the name on the headstone. Such interventions which by *reductio ad absurdum* gradually dislodged the "live-dead baby myth", also intensified the triangular relationship between Annie, Jack and Sheila. Thus within 2-3 sessions, the first phase of therapy had been completed, but with Sheila now *more* engaged in her parents' relationship. Although attention had been paid to the long-term sequences as manifested in the "live-dead baby myth", I do not believe these were effective in influencing the course of these sequences. They were, however, relevant to the short-term goal of dislodging Annie from the role of "mad woman".

I have acknowledged that the first phase left Sheila more rather than less engaged with her parents. In fact by the fourth session, Sheila had moved back into her mother's bed, while her father moved into the living room. It was reported that this was because Sheila was said to have been hearing noises in her room "like a cat scratching". I had initially responded to this information as though it were a perfectly common place state of affairs, and asked the father to join me at the blackboard to help me construct a detailed diagram of the house and where it connected with the neighbours so that we could "ascertain the nature of this sound". Eventually this was interrupted by Annie in a triumphant voice "well it was the vase coming off the mantle piece that really frightened her . . . she thought it was a ghost . . . *so* she's coming in with *me*".

Dr C: Ah, because you've got the edge on these supernatural things?

Annie: [a bit deflated]: Oh well I don't know about that.

Sheila: Yes, well I did think it might be a poltergeist.

Dr C: Now wait a minute, do you mean a poltergeist or do you mean a ghost? Let's be clear.

Sheila: Well I'm not sure . . . I think a poltergeist . . .

Annie: She thought it might be a ghost, that's why she's coming . . .

Dr C: Wait Annie, I want to hear from Sheila . . . was it a poltergeist or a ghost?

Sheila: I'm not sure . . . may be it was a ghost but . . .

Annie: It must have been a ghost because . . .

Dr C: Now wait Annie, was it you or Sheila who had this experience . . .

Annie: I expect it wasn't anything at all really.

Dr C: Sheila, what was it? A ghost or a poltergeist?

Sheila: Well . . . I think . . . yes, I'm sure it was a poltergeist.
Dr C: Good . . .

This was an example of a common short-term sequence which ended with Sheila defining her own reality. Although one might feel the content was crazy or at least bizarre, the formal relationships were isomorphic with other sequences in which the content was quite different. In future similar sessions, similar in form but not in content, Sheila gradually increased her distance from her parents to the point where she insisted she would "do the training whatever happens to them". She had moved out from her mother's bed. The parents were keeping their own conflict in check by engaging in supporting Sheila's bids for greater independence. So far, therapeutic interventions had only shifted the short-term sequence. There was no evidence that the medium-term sequence would not be completed as before, as she began to move out, so that she would not leave. A variety of strategic moves, aimed at interfering with the control process of this medium-term sequence, were used. For example Sheila was told that she certainly would not do the training, but it was a good myth to keep up as it would prevent her parents from feeling demoralized or worried that they had kept her too close. Later she was told that although she would not be able to leave, it was good training for when the time was ripe. Against this background of "training for maturity", the parents were asked to have a violent row in the next room to Sheila and see for how long she could keep the door closed and "stay out".

Sheila took up the challenge, left home five months before the training was due to start and spent this time on a kibbutz in Israel. She is now doing well in the nurse training, has had a boyfriend and has developed some other social relationships. It would appear that the medium-term sequence has been altered. It is impossible to say what will happen to the longer-term sequence, transmitted through Sheila. Annie and Jack have settled down. From time to time, Jack complains of various physical symptoms. Annie worries about him and then complains of being "victimized", but their modus vivendi is fairly stable.

IV. CONCLUSIONS

The following points have already been made (p.88):

(1) Patterns all have a shape, and patterns of human interaction are all events in time, and thus have a shape in time.

(2) Such patterns have a tendency to reproduce themselves. Thus each event will tend to repeat itself at regular intervals, if other variables remain constant.

(3) Each part of an event, while being a mini-whole event itself, also contains the pattern of the main whole event.

(4) The properties of an event are principally governed by the time space within which it occurs, as well as by the event shape.

(5) The interventions required to change the shape of an event in a short time space will differ from those in a long time space.

The following additional points have been made:

(6)   The notions of "here-and-now" change in systems as opposed to "systems over time" are artifacts. "Here-and-now" change occurs in the spatial and temporal form of short-term sequences. Interventions in systems over time can only happen "now" and *may* then influence the shape of future sequences.

(7)   The approach of structural family therapy is most powerful when the short-term patterns repeat themselves, when the parts of an event or pattern have a similar formal shape, or are isomorphic with, the larger pattern of which they are a part. When the latter is the case, the structural approach is most likely to be effective in sequences which are longer than the therapy itself.

(8)   Long-term sequences may imply a governor or control process which although itself a pattern of events, is a pattern of a different order from day to day interactions. Although this pattern will sometimes be influenced by changes in short-term sequences, sometimes it will not. In the latter case a different form of intervention is required.

(9)   While I have previously described an approach to these control processes based on object relations theory, in this chapter I have stressed the relevance of strategic and paradoxical interventions. These interventions change the pattern by removing the control process "from office", as it were, and thus making them inoperative by placing them in an untenable context. On the other hand, in my second and third examples (the Losey and Arkwright families), I contend that the control processes were manifested by the couples maintaining roles which were inappropriate to their present context. By establishing the context in which these roles *had* been appropriate in their families of origin, they were divested of their potency as control processes in the present context.

Thus when the control process is vested in crucial relationship patterns hinged to powerfully emotive events, it may be necessary to name these events in the process of shifting the locus of control. In the work of the Milan group, one can see both principles operating.

This leaves the question of "what to do when?" The nature of control processes can only be implied. Any attempt to search for the "real truth" carries with it dangers. One of these is of entering a "linear pursuit" for the "true culprit" or cause. Another is of entering into a cognitive search for this "truth" with the family, which keeps the intensity of interactions below a level at which change can occur. It follows that a structural approach to short-term sequences is a rational starting point, not only because it attends to the bread and butter of what the family has brought, but also because one cannot at the outset know where a small change will end.

REFERENCES

Ashby, W. R. (1956). "Introduction to cybernetics", John Wiley & Sons, New York and London.
Bateson, G. (1979). Mind and Nature, Wildwood House, London.

Beels, C. C. and Ferber, A. (1969). Family Therapy: a view. *Family Process*, **8**, 280-332.

Bentovim, A. (1979). Theories of Family Interaction and Techniques of Intervention. *Journal of Family Therapy* **1**, 321-345.

Bowen, M. (1975). Family Therapy After 20 Years. *In* "American Handbook of Psychiatry V", Basic Books, New York.

Bowen, M. (1976). Theory in the Practice of Psychotherapy. *In* "Family Therapy" (P. J. Guerin, ed.), Gardener Press, New York.

Bowlby, J. (1969). "Attachment and Loss, Vol. I, Attachment", Hogarth Press, London.

Box, S. J. (1979). The Elucidation of a Family Myth. *Journal of Family Therapy* **1**, 75-86.

Byng-Hall, J. (1973). Family Myths Used as a Defence in Conjoint Family Therapy. *British Journal of Medical Psychology*, **131**, 433-447.

Byng-Hall, J. (1979). Re-Editing Family Mythology During Family Therapy. *Journal of Family Therapy* **1**, 103-116.

Byng-Hall, J. (1980). Symptom Bearer as Marital Distance Regulator: Clinical Implications. *Family Process* **19**, 355-365.

Calcraft, L. (1980). *In* "Einstein: The First Hundred Years", (M. Goldsmith, A. Mackay and J. Woudhuysen, eds), Pergamon, London.

Camp, H. (1973). Structural Family Therapy: An Outsider's Perspective. *Family Process* **12**, 269-277.

Carter, E. and McGoldrick, M. (1980). The Family Life Cycle: An Overview. *In* "The Family Life Cycle", (E. Carter and M. McGoldrick, eds), Gardner, New York.

Cooklin, A. (1974). Family Preoccupation and Role in Conjoint Therapy. Paper to Royal College of Psychiatrists, June 1974.

Cooklin, A. (1978). Cultural reflections in British Family Therapy, *Group Analysis XI*. **3**, 212-222.

Cooklin, A. (1979). A Psychoanalytic Framework for a Systemic Approach to Family Therapy. *Journal of Family Therapy* **1**, 153-165.

Dowling, E. (1979). Cotherapy: A Clinical Researcher's View. *In* "Family and Marital Psychotherapy: A Critical Approach", (Walrond-Skinner, ed.), Routledge & Kegan Paul, London.

Fairbairn, W. R. D. (1952). "Psychoanalytic Studies of the Personality", Tavistock Publications, London.

Ferreira, A. J. (1963). Family Myths and Homeostasis. *Archives of General Psychiatry* **9**, 457-463.

Friedman, E. (1981). Systems and Ceremonies: A Family View of Rites of Passage. *In* "The Family Life Cycle", (E. Carter and M. McGoldrick, eds), Gardner, New York.

Gorell Barnes, G. (1982a). A difference that makes a difference. I. *Journal of Family Therapy* (in press).

Gorell Barnes, G., Jones, E., de Carteret, J. (1982b). A difference that makes a difference. II. *Journal of Family Therapy* (in press).

Hardy, T. (1891). "Tess of the D'Urbervilles", MacMillan, London.

Haley, J. (1977). "Problem Solving Therapy", Jossey-Bass, California.

Hoffman, L. (1980). The Family Life Cycle and Discontinuous Change. *In* "The Family Life Cycle" (E. Carter and M. McGoldrick, eds), Gardner, New York.

Kinston, W., Loader, P. and Stratford, J. (1979). Clinical Assessment of Family Interaction: a reliability study. *Journal of Family Therapy* **1**, 291-312.

Kinston, W. and Bentovim, A. (1981). Creating a Focus for Brief Marital or Family Therapy. *In* "Forms of Brief Therapy", (S. Budman, ed.), Guildford Press, New York.

Lieberman, S. (1979). Transgenerational Analysis: The Geneogram as a Technique in Family Therapy. *Journal of Family Therapy* **1**, 51-64.

Madanes, C. and Haley, J. (1977). Dimensions of Family Therapy. *Journal of Nervous and Mental Disease,* **165,** 88-98.

Madanes, C. (1980). The Prevention of Rehospitalization of Adolescents and Young Adults. *Family Process,* **19,** 179-191.

Miller, E. J. and Rice, A. K. (1967). "Systems of Organisation", Tavistock Publications, London.

Minuchin, S. (1972). Structural Family Therapy. *In* "American Handbook of Psychiatry Vol 3" (G. Caplan, ed.), Basic Books, New York.

Minuchin, S. (1974). "Families and Family Therapy", Tavistock Publications, London.

Northrop, F. (1958). Causation Determinism, and the 'Good'. *In* "Determinism and Freedom", (Hook, ed.), New York University Press, New York.

Palazzoli, M. S., Boscolo, L., Cecchin, G. and Prata, G. (1980). Hypothesising — Circularity — Neutrality: Three Guidelines for the Conductor of the Session. *Family Process* **19,** 3-11.

Paul, N. L. (1967). The Role of Mourning and Empathy in Conjoint Marital Therapy. *In* "Family Therapy and Disturbed Families". (G. Zuk and I. Boszormenyi-Nagy, eds), Science and Behaviour Books, Palo Alto, California.

Pribram (1971). "Languages of the Brain: Experimental Paradoxes and Principles in Neuropsychology", Prentice-Hall Inc., Englewood Cliffs, New Jersey.

Rosenberg, J. and Lindblad, M. (1978). Behaviour Therapy in a Family Context: Elective Mutism. *Family Process* **17,** 77-82.

Ryle, G. (1949). "The Concept of Mind", Hutchinson, London.

Santa-Barbara, J., Woodward, C. A., Levin, S., Goodman, J., Streiner, D. and Epstein, N. B. (1977). The McMaster Family Therapy Outcome Study: I. An Overview of Methods and Results (unpublished manuscript).

Sluzki, C. (1978). Marital Therapy from a Systems Theory Perspective. *In* "Marriage and Marital Therapy" (I. Paolino and S. McReady, eds), Brunner/Mazel, New York.

Street, E. and Treacher, A. (1980). Microtraining and Family Therapy Skills — Towards a Possible Synthesis. *Journal of Family Therapy* **2,** 243-257.

Treacher, A. and Street, E. (1980). Some Further Reflections on Family Therapists as Scapegoats — A Reply to Robin Skynner. *Journal of Family Therapy* **2,** 1-22.

Watzlawick, P., Bevin, J. H. and Jackson, D. D. (1969). "Pragmatics of Human Communication", Norton, New York.

Watzlawick, P., Weakland, J. and Fish, R. (1974). "Change", Norton, New York.

Wrate, R. (1980). The Development of Family Therapy in the U.K.: A Minority View? Newsletter for The Association of Family Therapy. Autumn: 14-18.

Zeeman, E. C. (1978). A Catastrophe Theory of Anorexia Nervosa in Hunger Models (Booth, ed.), Academic Press, London and New York.

Zinner, J. and Shapiro, R. (1972). Projective Indentification as a Mode of Perception and Behaviour in Families of Adolescents. *International Review of Psychoanalysis,* **43,** 523-530.

Zinner, J. and Shapiro, R. (1974). The Family Group as a Single Psychic Entity: Implications for Acting Out in Adolescence. *International Review of Psychoanalysis* **1,** 179-186.

Chapter 3

Dysfunction of Feeling: Experiential Life of the Family

J. Byng-Hall

I. INTRODUCTION

Emotion provides the thread and the colour in the tapestry of family life. The full range of every experience is felt most profoundly within family relationships: bliss, contentment, sexual ecstasy, loyalty, remorse, loneliness, frustration, boredom, fear, murderous rage and so on. Feelings provide the impetus for staying together and for leaving. They energize relationships. The experiential life of the family is generated by the interplay between feelings and interaction. This interplay is creative when each facilitates the other. A husband feeling affectionate reaches out to touch his wife on the arm. She feels warm and smiles back; seeing this exchange, the children settle to play together.

When an experience is, or has been intolerable, the family may defend itself by avoiding the situations in which either the affect or the action may arise. This may be called family defence. The parents in the family might have experienced intolerable rejections. The husband feeling affectionate but not sure how to express it, may tentatively put his hand out to touch his wife; she withdraws, perceiving the hesitancy in his approach as showing insincerity. The children, sensing the parents' vulnerability, start a fight which draws attention away from this marital interaction. The danger is past. The risk of putting intimacy to the test has been avoided. Every family needs some defence. However, dysfunction may follow when there is a serious disconnection between the feeling and the appropriate action; either the disconnected feelings such as depression, or the out of kilter action such as vandalism may then be experienced as the problem.

Experiential techniques in family therapy are aimed at helping family members experience feelings in their appropriate interpersonal context. Experiential family therapy can be described as a method or school of family therapy (Kemplar, 1973; Duhl et al., 1973), or it can be one set of techniques within a much wider repertoire, which is the author's practice. Madanes and Haley (1977) stated that a major characteristic of experiential techniques is the introduction of new experiences within the session. In order to choose an appropriate therapeutic strategy, it becomes imperative to understand the family system: to know what is dysfunctional and what is not. For this reason, the author will describe various experiential techniques in relation to his formulation of family conflict; he will not list techniques 'à la carte'. Readers who espouse a different conceptual framework must also undertake a similar linking exercise. Without

Family Therapy
ISBN: 0-12-089355-X

this discipline a mish-mash can occur; indeed the therapist can find himself merely reinforcing the family defences by following their cues to avoid particular actions or feelings.

II. THE ROLE OF AFFECT IN HOMEOSTASIS

Homeostasis, the way the family system maintains itself and prevents any major changes, provides limits to excesses of experience by curbing certain interactions and feelings in the family. Hence it may be used in the service of defence.

A. Establishing Experiential Limits: Marking Boundaries

The limits are set down in the family script which each member of the family is taught. The homeostatic boundary is tested, often by adolescents and the consequences remembered and handed on by being recounted in family stories and legends (Byng-Hall, 1979). If a member of the family approaches the limit, warning will be given, if this does not check him sufficiently, threats of what will happen follow. Sometimes these threats are carried out. In this way, the imagination or phantasy life of the family and its memories play important roles in boundary-setting. The emotions of guilt, fear, anxiety and loyalty are all evoked.

A family drama may be enacted etching the family script on the family memory. In one particularly tragic example, the 14-year-old girl drowned following a rough and tumble with some boys on the jetty of a harbour. The parents labelled this as murder and their two sons were warned that the murderers were outside waiting for them as well. Needless to say the family became totally housebound; their boundary became the front door.

The drama can represent a replay of a scene from the family script. It emerged that the mother of the drowned girl had nearly been drowned herself by some boys when she was six. She warned her daughter never to go swimming, indeed she prevented her from learning to swim, and even identified the fatal jetty in her warnings. The drowned girl had acted a role in her mother's script. In the family sessions following this tragedy, it became clear that the murderousness within the family, especially between the father and mother was very intense. These dangerous impulses had been displaced and they were now united against the outside world. Murderers were now seen to lurk everywhere. In this instance, the replay of the script led to a fearful narrowing of the external boundary as the price for reinforcing limits within the family itself.

III. AFFECTIVE BALANCING

Most families, however, are able to adjust and extend their boundaries in the light of experience. One reason for a failure to adjust may be that an excessive preoccupation with one boundary is used to distract from or balance another diametrically opposite boundary. For instance, a fear of intimacy may be hidden by a preoccupation with loss. It is easy to imagine that someone who cannot bear to be left alone is automatically at ease in intimate situations. This is often not so. Conversely, someone who cannot tolerate being held down by anyone may appear to be free of anxiety about being alone. Again this is often not so. If a couple with these two styles get together, they may establish an interaction in which one is overtly clinging and the other overtly pulling away. The clinging spouse can then deny her fear of intimacy, and the independent spouse can deny his fear of loss. This results in what is known as a too close/too far system (Byng-Hall, 1980) in which the relationship is simultaneously too close for comfort and too distant to feel secure. This, however, is a potentially unstable bond. The more she clings, the more he tries to escape. This can escalate in what in cybernetics is known as mutual positive feedback. That is, each person's action produces a reaction which in turn encourages an increase in that action. The resulting escalation can break up the relationship.

The parents of the drowned girl had separated for a while, father demanding that his wife should stop holding him down. Byng-Hall (1980) goes on to describe how a third party, often a child who is ambivalent about the marriage may be given the role of distance-regulator or stabilizer to the marriage, holding them together if they become too far separated, and keeping them apart if too close. Parents, relieved that they do not have to take responsibility themselves for their tensions, unwittingly exploit their "go-between" child's role. The child's natural ambivalence, wanting to get each parent to herself, but also wanting them to stay together, becomes increasingly intolerable and he or she becomes a patient.

Before she drowned, the girl had been depressed. This brought father home again to help mother look after her. She was also sleeping with her father, with the collusion of her mother who on her part had one of the adolescent boys sleeping in her room. Thus the girl kept her father at home but also kept her mother out of his bed.

The drowning provided a classic, although tragic, example of how the symptom is frequently a compromise between opposing themes. She went dangerously far away from home, but in her physical contact with the boys on the jetty became too close, dramatically proving the danger of this contact through the final enactment. On examining the evidence, it was clear that she provoked the boys to throw her in. Her incestuous guilt was finally punished. Following the drowning her parents became united, in order to hunt down her killers. In her death she became an even more effective distance regulator.

This family is of course a highly dramatic and unusual one. They were used by the author because they vividly illustrate several aspects of his thesis. Byng-Hall and Whiffen (1981) describe how mood swings can be countered in the family. Depression in one member may for instance be balanced by elation in another. If the mood reaches certain thresholds, family anxiety may trigger a swing into the opposite mood. This anxiety might for instance be about suicide in depression or loss of control in manic episodes. It can be seen then that either excessive affect or extreme action provokes homeostatic controls.

IV.   EXPERIENTIAL TECHNIQUES IN FAMILY THERAPY

A.   Changing Boundaries: The Therapist as Boundary Marker

Who monitors boundaries? Often it appears to be one person concerned with limits. However, on careful examination the whole family is involved, and if the boundary keeper is away someone else takes over. Even the person who most frequently transgresses can take over this role, much to everyone's surprise. This can be vividly demonstrated when the therapist asks family members to change roles. One delinquent boy was asked to reverse roles with his father. He ticked his father off with such intense feeling that neither could doubt that his disapproval of delinquency was his own, not merely belonging to his father. The ultimate power to control the homeostasis, however, lies with the person who can change or reset the boundary: the boundary marker. If that person is in the family, then the potential for change and growth is present. If the boundary marker is in the extended family, or in the form of an internal unmourned dead family member, or disputed in the family, change can be more difficult.

The therapist can become a temporary boundary marker (Byng-Hall and Campbell, 1981). He can become an attachment figure (Bowlby, 1969) who can provide a safe base from which to explore. Winnicott (1971) discusses the role of *play* in which symbols are used to explore new dimensions to feelings and relationships. If exploring new forms of interaction in the presence of the family therapist shows them to be safe, these can then be added to the permitted family repertoire.

Winnicott (1971) contrasts play with playing *games* where rules are firmly established and then experienced within the intense action of the game. The authority of the therapist can be further enhanced by setting new rules for family interaction and then ensuring that the accompanying interaction occurs. He can then give blessing to new boundaries. This approach is found in structural family therapy described by Minuchin (1974), and discussed by Cooklin (Chapter 4). In this technique, family members are taken during the session beyond their normal homeostatic limits. The therapist has established a boundary beyond the family norm. The intensity required to break through the barrier may be provided either by the severity of the symptom, as in anorexia nervosa, or by the therapist's very active pushing of the family homeostasis. In both situations, the therapist's skill lies in keeping the family to the task and preventing them from defusing the tension or from using homeostatic mechanisms. Finally, sometimes quite suddenly, they are forced into quite a new way of relating.

In one family, the daughter had reached 6 stone, and her weight was dropping steadily. In an outpatient session, it emerged that father covertly undermined his wife's attempt to force their daughter to go to hospital if this was needed. The therapist discussed with the family the weight at which she might die. The tension rose. The girl shrieked at her mother that she would rather kill herself than go into hospital, adding that she would eat enough anyway. Mother countered this by pointing out that that was what she had said every time but nothing had changed. The therapist noticed father sitting back. He sided heavily with mother while making them decide when she should come into hospital. Both parents shouted at each other. Mother screamed "murderer" at father who suddenly switched into making a decision about how his daughter should come into hospital the next day both to stop her "suicide" and her self-starvation. The tension dropped, the daughter started to eat, and hospitalization was not needed. Here the rule forbidding any hostility between parents was changed, allowing them to set effective limits.

B.   Extending the Therapist's Own Emotional Thresholds

This work engages the therapist in emotional experiences which are often way beyond his own family norms. Empathy is the key to experiential change. The therapist cannot carry his clients beyond where he himself can journey, which through empathic process is only as far as his own emotional defensive cut-off point. When he retreats, they have to as well. To be helpful to a wide range of clients, the therapist's experiential journey has to be beyond not only his family but also the social norm. In analogy a surgeon who does not get over his normal revulsion to cutting flesh, will be of no help to his patients. The other side of the coin is that he has to be sensitive to his patients' pain, or he may indulge in surgical practices which increase rather than decrease suffering. Similarly, the therapist also needs to acknowledge and even value his own limits, but he should ponder their significance.

Family therapy training must provide the setting for trainee therapists to extend their emotional limits. This may be done through live supervision (Whiffen and Byng-Hall, 1981), in which the supervisor watches the therapist working and keeps him to the task, thus preventing him from using too many homeostatic manoeuvres of his own. Another approach is to work with the trainees' own families, either as it is represented internally, or by helping him (Bowen, 1972) to go beyond his normal lifelong routines within his family. McGoldrick (1981) describes very vividly how all three methods can be used together to reset trainee and family boundaries simultaneously. She selects what she calls trigger families, that is, those families which have similar difficulties to the trainee therapist (e.g. failure to mourn), and then works on that issue as it manifests in trainee and family. This can lead to a break through for both family and therapist. In these techniques, the trainer becomes the attachment figure, or potential boundary marker for the trainee therapist.

Personal therapy: either family, marital, group or individual can provide settings where experience is allowed to extend and blossom. Support groups consisting of colleagues can help to share the task of going beyond the norm. Sometimes personal reflection provides the means for change.

I was able to work with the grieving and despair in the drowned girl's family. I could stand the pain of standing by the dead girl's bed with the whole family weeping and wailing. I could even ask, "Where is she now?" to be told, "There sitting next to you on the bench"! When, however, the murderous rage started to emerge in full force, I and my co-worker became seen by the family as potential murderers. I was unable to tolerate the anxiety despite my co-worker's willingness to soldier on. I stopped the therapy. Instead I alerted the network to the danger; for instance, the housing department was warned that to carry out an eviction order might be very dangerous. There was plenty of evidence to support this thesis. For example, father threatened to use an axe on us if we came again, and he told us that he and his sons were going out to discover and hunt down the murderers.

I ponder whether my anxiety provided a link to reality and appropriate limit setting, or whether through my limits, this family missed a crucial opportunity to resolve their fundamental problem. My co-worker experienced the threats as having a histrionic quality. Probably she was right. My inability to contain the murderous fury that we were being asked to hold for the family was nevertheless making further work impossible, whatever the reality. I need to learn to defuse hostility before it reaches this level in the future. As I write this, I become aware of the need to examine whether my own fury coloured my view of the family. One hour later I have. It was helpful but uncomfortable. Reflection is one important method for re-experiencing and *preparing* to reset the point at which one has to cut out of experience: to "not know" or "not do". My boundary will not actually be changed until after the next encounter with an experience which resonates in type or intensity with the previous one. Reflection and action must complement each other; one must not be used to avoid the other.

Most experiential exercises can, and should if possible be entered into by the therapist himself beforehand. This usually involves working with a group of colleagues who will simulate or enact a family in therapy while the therapist tries out the technique. This gives the therapist the experience of doing it and also the participants an inside view of what it feels like. These groups are best led by an experienced teacher, or by someone who has used experiential techniques. Watching an experienced therapist treating a family with experiential techniques either on video-tape, through a one-way screen, or by sitting in the same room is also invaluable. If these opportunities are absolutely unavailable, it is possible to start afresh. I started using some techniques in this way.

Therapists and agencies have a duty to structure enough time for reflection and training. It is far easier to labour greatly, rushing from one task to another without experiencing the pain of growth. The cost of this defensive manoeuvre is diminishing efficiency, absenteeism, and a failure to confront society with the realities of employees' appropriate emotional boundaries. This perpetuates the syndrome of an overworked inefficient demoralized system, which is often merely a reflection of the client population. On the other hand, endless navel gazing can of course be equally task avoiding.

V. SPECIFIC EXPERIENTIAL TECHNIQUES

Some guidelines can now be given. But unlike a game with strict rules, the most alive experience for the therapist and the family is play, where their combined creativity will give a fresh and refreshing twist to each and every situation. Once a technique has become stereotyped and boring to the therapist, it is no longer experiential. The family only moves in an experiential event if the therapist is also on the move. Luckily like all play, there are an infinite number of possibilities allowing for something new to emerge each time. It is, however, probably best to weave the variations around some basic strategies. This provides more security for play. Occasionally a completely new approach can be tried, but devising some totally new game each time will be too confusing.

VI. SPACE

A. Altering the Balance Between Verbal and Non-Verbal Communication

The family system is often expressed in seating arrangements at home, or in the arrangement of the house. These become routine, and are frequently reflected in the way the family sits in the therapist's office. A therapist who wants to provoke minimal change in spatial experience (a quite legitimate strategy), will go to the family home and sit in the visitor's seat. There are a myriad ways of providing new spatial experiences.

The power of changing the usual spatial arrangement was discovered by Freud. He put his clients lying down with the therapist out of sight. Not surprisingly, he discovered that among other things, this evoked experiences related to childhood and to sleep: namely, dreams. It also removed much of the non-verbal interaction and placed what remains out of sight, thus freeing the patient's phantasy to roam. The family therapist, who wants to promote phantasy can ask family members to close their eyes, while he is asking them to imagine something. An example would be in asking for metaphorical images to represent each family member. Animal imagery can for instance reveal that a son perceives his father like a huge grizzly bear and himself as a mouse, something not easy to appreciate when visually that son is a hefty 27-year-old and the father an arthritic 60-year-old. Visual cues can also be removed by the therapist putting two members back to back and asking them to discuss something, thus forcing them to communicate accurately with words; a valuable communication exercise especially for families who are typically non-verbal.

The aim of the therapist may in contrast be to increase the use of all the modes of communication. In one family, whenever conflict emerged all members of the family would look away from each other, even shutting their eyes. When the next topic of disagreement emerged, he asked the parents to sort out the disagreement together, not to address everything to him. After several promptings they talked to each other, but looked at the therapist. He moved the patients' chairs to face each other, and looked away himself if they tried to catch his eye. Only then were they able to engage in discussion and to reach an agreement.

B. Triangles: How to Discover a Dyad

In one family, everyone continuously monitored everyone else with their eyes. Whenever the therapist wanted the parents to work something out together, one of the children, often cued in by a parent, created a lively distraction. He put the children together to play on one side and placed his own chair so that it blocked the view between parents and children. This gave the whole family the experience of parents being able to resolve conflict without the children intervening. The alternative of seeing parents on their own does not provide this experience.

The one-way screen can also be used for this purpose. In one very enmeshed family, the 19-year-old girl monitored and dominated her parents' every action. They were "separated" but still living at home while father was awaiting new housing. The girl was sent to sit next door to watch the therapist and her parents through the screen. They discussed how to find father a flat. After a while, the therapist joined the daughter who was agitated about what would happen to each parent. He discussed her fears of her parents' possible suicides. The discrepancy between this nightmare vision and the middle aged couple sitting next door calmly discussing arrangements enabled the therapist to confront the daughter with what she was projecting onto them. After a while, the parents got bored, mother took out a book, curled up on the couch and started to read. The therapist and girl burst out laughing. On returning to the room, the parents exclaimed how much easier it had been without their daughter's "help". The issue of suicide was then discussed openly and realistically.

C. Symbolic Use of Space

One couple asked to discuss their marriage. They talked endlessly about "mother-in-law" instead. After some time, the therapist said that he was going to play mother-in-law. He stood in between them, and insisted that they continue their discussion. He moved repeatedly to block their views. Getting exasperated, each in turn asked him to sit down but he merely responded by swivelling round to look at the other. When they consulted with each other and asked together he finally sat down. They laughed. They no longer brought the topic of mother-in-law up as a diversion, or if they did, the therapist merely made a move to get up and they stopped with a laugh. This family is described in detail in Byng-Hall (1980).

One couple, Sarah and George, presented with serious fights and wife-battering. They described an incident in which a row had escalated into violence after shouting at each other through a closed door. This had followed an earlier row in which George had threatened to leave, and then locked himself into the sitting room. When the door was finally opened, George punched Sarah, breaking her nose. The therapist tried to get the couple to discuss the episode. They were too agitated. The therapist decided to role play the door. He stood between them, told them that he would represent the door, and asked each to say exactly what was shouted.

Sarah (S): Let me in!

Therapist (T): [to George (G)] What did that make you feel?

G: I just wanted space to think.

T: What happened next?

S: I said, "Don't leave like this when you're upset".

T: How was it, George?

G: I felt hemmed in.

> [The therapist asked where the door was. It was the only exit from the sitting room and *en route* to the front door.]

T: You were hemmed in. Sarah, could you say it a different way?

S: I—er—I could have said, "Are you going to go away again?".

G: Yes, then I would have just explained.

T: You see, Sarah, "Are you going?" feels different to "Don't go", when you feel hemmed in.

T: [turns to G] How did you respond?

G: I said, "Leave me alone!"

T: But Sarah was afraid of being left, I expect she heard the "leaving" bit.

G: I could have given more detail.

T: Such as?

G: Leave me for a while.

T: Sarah, how would you have reacted?

S: It would have reassured me a bit.

T: But not enough?

G: Perhaps, "I need time to think".

S: It would have left me in doubt, I just needed reassurance that he wasn't leaving.

T: George, could you have given that promise at that time? Let's be realistic.

G: I just needed five minutes to think. I didn't know what to do, I locked the door because I knew she would be at me.

T: Does that give us a lead?

G: How do you mean?

For several minutes the therapist struggles to get George to think about what he might have said. Finally:

T: You remember the five minutes?

G: When? Oh yes, I suppose I could have said, "Just give me five minutes, I don't know what to do".

Sarah: [relaxing visibly] "I would have stopped pestering you then.

The therapist, still standing between them, says, "The problem is that you, George need space. But Sarah, you want to be close because you're afraid of desertion. Unfortunately the messages you each got through the door was (T advancing towards George, arms out in enclosing gesture) "I've trapped you"! So you respond by replying to Sarah, "Go away"! Therapist turns round and gives sudden dramatic pushing away gesture to Sarah. "The trouble is that makes you cling even tighter—and you George end up punching her to get her away—and so on." All three then sat down and discussed ways in which they could make simple clear factual statements to each other when a similar situation next occurred. They could then choose to de-escalate rather than escalate.

This example illustrates the problem of experiential work. It was unique to the situation, and will never be repeated in precisely the same form. It followed a failure to get the couple to confront each other. The therapist wanted to maintain the intensity of the situation. His involvement and proximity ensured this, but it also provided the safety each needed. The therapist took on the distance-regulation role in a very concrete way. One technique, that of asking the couple to re-enact what happened, suitable to some situations, was too frightening here. The way in which the exercise developed reflected his theoretical view of the too close/too far system found in this family (Byng-Hall, 1980) in which Sarah was too close for George and George too far away for Sarah. The therapist wanted to provide a way in which each could back off the impending escalation always incipient within that system.

It cannot be emphasized enough that experiential exercises are only as good as their aim. If the therapist has a hypothesis about what is wrong and what needs changing, he can improvise on the technique. The flourish in which the therapist enacted the reciprocal phantasy of envelopment/rejection only occurred to the therapist as the intervention unfolded; it was not foreseen. Indeed it would be dishonest to say that what he was going to do was planned. He only started with a rough idea. Another approach might have been to interpret George locking himself up as representing his wish to stay and to be controlled, and Sarah's combination of provocation and then staying to be punched after the door was unlocked as representing her wish to be punished. This would have clashed with the therapist's aim at that moment to interrupt the mutual positive feedback which was acting to escalate each other's behaviour. Later when the fighting had stopped, there were plenty of opportunities to make those interpretations.

VII.   FAMILY SCULPTING, VIDEO-REPLAY AND MIME

A.   Family Sculpting: Methods

Family sculpting in which family members are placed in spatial relationships symbolic of their relationships, has a specific methodology and can be learned and used in a more planned manner. The technique was developed at the Boston Family Institute (Duhl et al., 1973) and described by Simon (1972) and Walrond-Skinner (1976). Those interested should read further, and preferably explore the technique using colleagues before trying with a client family.

Dolls can be arranged in relationship to each other by a client to show his picture of his family. In family sculpting, the dolls are dispensed with and the actual family members used instead. Needless to say this provides a powerful and vivid picture of the family as well as a profound experience for each family member. For instance, one father who saw himself in the very bosom of his family, was profoundly shocked when placed by his son outside the door. He had to acknowledge how little time he spent at home and what this meant to his family.

Each member of the family is asked by the therapist to place family members, including himself in positions which represent the family as he sees them now. This is done with as little talking as possible, thus forcing the person to act in non-verbal mode. He should be asked to position limbs, body and head to represent each person's typical attitude, and to do this without thinking too much. It is not, however, a non-verbal technique. After the whole family tableau has been set up, each family member is then asked to share his or her experience of being placed in this position. This provides material for therapeutic work either at the time or later. After this procedure is finished, each person is asked to put the family in the positions that they would prefer, which is usually closer and more loving. This second stage provides some goals for therapy. It also provides an experience of how things could be improved, and of how good that might feel.

B.   Sculpting: Facilitating the Process

This represents the bare bones of the technique, which like any art has to be practised. Some brief hints may be useful. First, how do you start? Standing up, the therapist may say,

> As a way of helping me to get to know your family, can you show me how you see yourselves? First can you stand up please? Joan (he walks over to her and holds her by the arm), can you put your family as you see them? Who is close to whom, put them in a position which shows their personality, what they are like [pause] each of you will have a turn to give me your picture of the family. Now Joan, whom do you want to start with?

Each therapist and each family has a different style. Many require further explanation, but the use of too many words at this point can block the exercise. The therapist has to model what he wants the family to do. Note how he stands up first and then goes to Joan to hold her arm just as she is going to be asked to mould or sculpt her family. The family usually looks perplexed and the therapist may say, "O.K. you've chosen Mum—now how do you see her, head up? angry? [miming this for the family] or down trodden? or sad?" [therapist drops his head in despair]. Humour obviously facilitates this process, and the family usually gets the point quickly, especially when the therapist is himself at ease with the process.

C.   Sculpting: Indications for Use

When do you use it? Some therapists use sculpting routinely at some point to expose and explore relationships in the family. It can even be done within a few minutes of the beginning of the first session. The author prefers to use sculpting for specific reasons. When a family is very verbal, with many intellectual insights, a sculpt can cut right across this and reach the raw emotions underneath.

It may be done when the therapy has reached a standstill, or lost direction. In other families, where words are woefully inadequate, they can tell the therapist, and each other much more in a sculpt. It should be remembered that the technique is symbolic and aimed at generating understanding. This might interrupt problem-solving techniques. It should then be avoided or postponed if the therapist is struggling painfully to help the family solve a particular real-life problem. To sculpt at that time might be a defensive manoeuvre. Space should in that case be used to provide a better setting for resolving that problem, in which case structural family therapy techniques such as changing seating arrangements may be more appropriate.

D. Sculpting: Case Example

In George and Sarah's family, a sculpt was used in the second session. George was being ultra-intellectual about his view of Sarah's problem. The therapist asked him to sculpt how he saw the family. He placed himself "out in front" leading the family with Sarah and their two children, Derek aged five and Florence aged three, five strides behind. He held his arm out sideways in front of Sarah. When asked how he would like it, he said that he wanted her more equal. The therapist explored how this change could happen. He could fall back. No!, he did not want that. For her to step forward meant that she had to drag the children with her or leave them behind. The therapist asked the family to rearrange itself. Two interesting things happened. Sarah struggled forward, the five-year-old son, Derek, tripped up and hurt himself as he was dragged forward, and simultaneously she banged her face into George's outstretched arm. She already had a black eye from a fight with George, and so the therapist worked on the idea that George's shield was also his punching arm which kept her down. George was able to share his fear that she might walk right past him and do better than him. As he was out of work, this fear was more vivid. Sarah was asked how she would like the family. She wanted to be level. How was this to be symbolized? She let go of Derek's hand, stepped forward and held George's shielding hand, thus lowering it. Derek lay on the floor crying. The therapist asked how they could manage this. Sarah let go three-year-old Florence's hand and picked up Derek. Now Florence was adrift. Eventually after much struggling with what to do, George picked Florence up and held her. In this exercise the rivalrous tensions between the parental subsystem, and mother/child subsystem were revealed. Sarah's need for George's help in parenting emerged as the problem and not Sarah's depression which George had initially been complaining about.

The difficulties in the dimension of closeness/distance can be revealed in sculpting. In one very tense family, the 8-year-old Timothy placed his mother in the middle of the room with his 5-year-old brother Jack hidden behind her and his father in front of her. When asked what he felt about this, father said that this was probably to put his wife in between himself and Jack to stop him beating Jack.

This led to a discussion about how mother interfered with her husband's discipline. Jack's behaviour had for long been out of control and the therapist pointed out to mother how she needed the help of her husband's authority. In the meantime, Jack lay on the floor kicking and screaming. His mother tried to stop him, failed, and then picked him up and exasperated, carried him over to her husband. Jack continued playing up. The tension rose considerably and the therapist felt a very powerful pressure to intervene but managed to restrain himself. Finally father, who was furious, smacked Jack on the arm. Jack glanced at his mother who showed that she supported what his father had done, and he stopped misbehaving. For the next ten minutes Jack leaned up against his father in a relaxed manner. His disobedience started to decrease after this session.

This episode illustrates how the therapist should be able to allow the tension to rise until resolution occurs. If he had intervened, he would merely have become another part of the family homeostasis, proving that father was dangerous to Jack and reinforcing the need for mother to go on policing father's smacking, which incidentally also provided a distancing mechanism between the parents: they fought over his discipline.

E. Sculpting: Adding Video Play-Back

This theme required further work. Single therapeutic interventions rarely completely change a system, as so often implied in the literature. In a later session, Jack was disobedient again, rushing over to Timothy to grab his drawing. His parents failed to discipline him. The therapist stopped the action and suggested a replay or rerun of this episode. They returned to their original places, Jack again with gusto making to grab Timothy's drawings. Father held his arms. Jack continued to struggle. Mother looked on. Jack watched her to see her reactions. After his mother said, "Stop it," he quite suddenly relaxed and stopped misbehaviour. The therapist wanted them to have an experience of success and to see for themselves how they had achieved it. He replayed a videotape of this segment of the session four times to the family. Finally they were able to see for themselves how they had succeeded when acting as a team, which was when mother supported her husband. Video playback provides a particularly powerful experience. Members observe themselves in context. They see themselves contributing to something instead of merely responding to things being done to them.

F. Sculpting—Adding Intensity

Intensity can and should be an ingredient of experiential exercises. Sometimes, as with Jack, a child or another member of the family adds fuel to the situation. On occasions, however, it is the therapist who has to ensure this. In one family described in detail by Byng-Hall and Whiffen (1981), in a typical ending to the family sculpt, Zoe aged 9, the identified patient, when asked to put the family as she wanted them, placed them in a small entwined hugging circle. Everyone agreed that this was lovely and close. The therapists let this go on until the tension rose intolerably. Zoe then said, "We can't stay like this. Dad won't be able to go away to work and Mum—she couldn't go shopping". This led to laughter and disentangling of the group. The conflict between clinging and autonomy was experienced. Byng-Hall (1981) discusses other methods of adding intensity to sculpting.

G.   Sculpting with Miming Added

Mime can be added to sculpting. Instead of keeping their positions still, the participants can be asked to mime some daily event without words. This could for instance be father coming home from work and his family's response (or lack of it). The family can then be asked to repeat this many times until they are thoroughly fed up with it. The intensity and energy is now available for change. If they are asked to do it in a new way the next step can be taken. In the family discussed earlier in which the therapist role-played the mother-in-law (Byng-Hall, 1980), the couple was able to mime a symbolic interaction between themselves.

> Margaret stood still facing her husband. He came toward her, opened his arms when he got closer as if to hug her. Margaret then put her hands up to keep him at a slight distance. David dropped his hands to his side in a resigned way and walked away towards the door as if to leave, however, before reaching the door he turned back and walked towards Margaret once more. The whole cycle would then be repeated. After this cycle had been repeated about ten times, with an increasing sense of frustration, Dr B. asked the couple whether they would like to try the cycle in a way in which they would both prefer. After a series of tentative efforts, they finally managed to embrace each other. Dr B. stood by silently and allowed the tension to rise. Finally they had to pull away again from each other. The therapist asked what it was that they were afraid of in their intimate contact. They said that they did not know but that they would like some help with their sexual relationships which were unsatisfactory.

The last two families illustrate how important it is to allow tension to build up in the close apparently loving positions. In too close/too far families, intimacy is as problematical as loss. The family may recognize the need for work on it after this exercise.

VIII.   TIME: PAST AND FUTURE IN THE PRESENT

A.   Exploring Time Past

Changing the experience of time can alter current behaviour. Usually the therapist takes the family, or an individual in a family session, back in time to re-experience in the present what was avoided in the past. Time can be taken forward as well. In the Right family, each member presented with great vehemence, conviction and in detail how he or she had been badly done by by the rest. The therapist listened patiently to each story. He then said, with equal conviction because he felt it was true,

> You, Angela, are *absolutely* right — completely correct — you, Ben, are equally right . . . etc.

Saying this to each member of the family in turn.

> Isn't it marvellous! You have all worked out a beautiful system in which you can be so perfectly right — *every* one of you! It would be a shame to change that. Clearly in your family being right is more important than sorting out differences. I suggest you continue this for a number of years. In my experience with such a beautifully balanced dance, you could carry on without changing it except for minor interesting variations for the next ten, fifteen years — perhaps shorter — usually a great deal longer. Let's see, Gill, you would be thirty-one after 15 years at home proving that you are entirely RIGHT! Marvellous! You, Alex, would be 29, etc.

Techniques for looking backward in time have a number of aims:
(1) To mourn unmourned figures from the past, who because their image is kept alive usually haunt a current member of the family;
(2) To give an appropriate historical context for the current family problem. This can save the scapegoat from feeling that he has caused all the problems *de novo;*
(3) To join in a therapeutic alliance with the family;
(4) Cementing alliances between family members by increasing empathy;
(5) To understand the origin of their current predicament;
(6) To alter or re-edit family legends from the past, and in this way change the family rules which are carried from generation to generation through its mythology (Byng-Hall, 1979).

The central technique involved is to evoke memories of past experiences, but the mode of change is through altering the relationships in the session. In families the past is the present; the memories or stories are there now, in the session.

Family sculpting can be used for this purpose, members of the family, and/or the therapist can be asked to represent figures from the past. Parents can be represented as they were envisaged before children were born, and then each child in turn placed in relationship to the couple. This is a powerful way of evoking the experience of the change in the couple that children bring. Usually the couple are together, the first child placed between them or in front of mother. Father then has less attention. When more children arrive, there is often no space for them. The experience of the new child struggling for a place is balanced by the feeling of the first child being displaced. Deaths can be portrayed by asking the dead person to lie down, or to stand on a chair like a haunting ghost. The feelings evoked can be very strong.

This method of exploration of family history is often done with groups of professional colleagues, where one colleague with help of a consultant sculpts his own family of origin or a client family. As many as sixty or more people can be involved in sculpting the extended family. This technique is such an effective way of demonstrating family systems evolving over time that it is often used in teaching events, and it may be what is best remembered by the participant. Indeed some novice therapists then imagine sculpting to *be* family therapy.

The technique can be used with client families. One dead, unmourned child was represented by a cushion. In another family, an empty chair represented a dead grandfather. The therapists can be used to represent grandparents, which is like sculpting the family transference.

B.   Family Trees: Geneograms

The use of family trees or geneograms are described by Lieberman (1979). Some therapists do most of their family therapy around the family tree, in much the same way as the analyst uses the couch. Byng-Hall (1979) discusses when an exploration of history is necessary as opposed to when it is a tool that both therapist and family can choose to use because it suits them. Those families which misuse their history need help. Two misuses are common. First, those families that see the present merely replicating the past without any choice, and secondly those families that deny that the past has any relevance whatever. These misperceptions of the historical process appear to be opposites but are really similar. The families which deny the past usually unwittingly re-enact the past faithfully in the next generation, as do the families that know their family script and faithfully replicate it.

An appropriate historical context is one in which each family member has a sense that his background provides a tradition and impetus for what happens but that he is in charge of the form that his life takes. It is important for therapists to experience this sense of being supported by tradition while simultaneously holding one's own destiny in one's own hands. The best way of achieving this is for the trainee therapists to explore his own past family. This can be done unguided, although it is preferable to do this with the help of a supervisor, or of a colleague in which a co-counselling relationship can be established.

There are a number of ways in which the memory of past figures can be intensified in family therapy. When asking about figures in the family tree, it is valuable to ask for family legends or stories about them. These can then be written on the family tree. Sometimes children will draw faces in the squares or circles. These can be very informative. The therapist can ask for family photographs so that a visual image can be added. Getting out the old photos can also start the family reminiscing even before coming to the session.

C.   Differentiating Images of the Past from Present Reality

Paul and Paul (1975 and personal communication) asks for a photograph of a client's parent of the same sex. He then enlarges it and videotapes the photograph. This makes the dead person seem alive. Furthermore he can, with his videotape mixer superimpose the living picture of the son on the photo of the father. This gives a quite extraordinary haunted look. The live picture can then be faded or the two images separated to either side of the screen. In this way he merges and then separates the two people in an attempt to disentangle the introject of the parent from the client's current self-image.

The equipment of course is not available to many therapists. Paul however uses audio cassettes of each session which the clients take home and play later. He also instructs them to play cassettes at the time of important anniversaries, to enable them not to unconsciously re-enact some unresolved drama. For instance, he may make a tape of a mourning experience that occurred in

October 1963 in October 1977. He will instruct the family or couple to listen to this tape every October, but especially October 1983.

There are many techniques for intensifying, and reliving a bereavement. Paul (1967) calls this operational mourning. The client, in the presence of the family, is asked to recount all the details of the death, of his or her reactions, of what happened and how were they told of the death. The therapist empathizes with the pain of the experience. In this way, the memory and the appropriate affect are both brought together, and re-experienced in a way in which proper mourning can be completed. The client can be asked to visit the grave. Williamson (1978) describes how he instructs the person to say the things which he would like to have said at the grave, in short to talk with the dead person. This can be recorded on a cassette recorder and brought back to the therapy session. This can provide a very powerful experience for the patient and therapist. Paul describes this when done by a man who visited Dachau where both his parents died. This tape provides an unforgettable experience for anyone who has heard it. Paul also uses material related to other families' mourning processes to play to new clients. This may be cassettes, videotapes or letters. They are chosen because they resonate with the client's problem. This stimulates the affect which has often been buried.

Past ceremonies which had disastrous effects can be rerun with a different outcome. In one family, the parents could be sexual together in private, but had to be stiff and formal in front of anyone else including their children. The children's developing sexual identity was threatened by this denial of adult sexuality. It emerged on exploration that neither parent had been properly given away at the wedding. Indeed both families had disapproved. The therapist asked whom on each side disapproved most: it was mother's father and father's grandfather. The therapist then conducted a marriage ritual in which he at first played the mother's father, in which he gave the bride away, and then as father's grandfather blessing the groom instead of disapproving. Following this the couple could be more demonstrative.

IX. SHARING THE THERAPIST'S EXPERIENCE WITH THE FAMILY

In all these techniques, the therapists obviously share the overall experience. This however can be taken further. Therapists can openly share their own pain, confusion or sense of madness with their clients. This can provide a profound linking experience. It is especially useful in rescuing the scapegoat. A girl was referred because she was crazy. Half way through the first session in which each parent bombarded the other, the client and the therapist with questions, demands and contradictory statements, the therapist felt he was going mad. He burst out: "If this goes on a moment longer I think I will go crazy, I feel smashed into a thousand pieces, if I can feel like this in half an hour I wonder what it is like at home twenty-four hours a day, seven days a week". For a while the family treated him as crazy, but his co-therapist rescued him and slowly over time, the focus shifted to what happened between people, not how crazy they were.

A direct interpretation of how the parents were driving their daughter crazy would have alienated the parents who would then have had to prove once and for all that she was crazy in her own right. Whitaker (1978) is a grand master in use of his own craziness and phantasy in entering the family system and then changing it. His approach is, "Hey! don't leave me out of this amazing world of yours, I want to enjoy it as well". He often uses a co-therapist to rescue him. The artistry with which he tunes into the family imagery is truly amazing. He uses the vitality of daily conflict but defuses the terrifying phantasies.

X. CONCLUSION

There are many more ways in which the therapists can introduce new experiences into the sessions, family drawings, tasks in the session such as "Arrange the furniture here to make a home," or "Draw your house as it is, then how you would like it," communication exercises, encounter techniques, Gestalt techniques etc. etc. Space in this chapter only allows a brief sketch of the techniques familiar to the author. The guiding principle is, *"Know what you are trying to achieve",* then experiential techniques can add to the effectiveness of therapy. Doing exercises for their own sake confuses and defuses. The author uses experiential techniques at some time in most families varying from 5% to 15% of the treatment time, rarely more or less. Because they are fun to describe, they probably rate a higher percentage of his writing.

REFERENCES

Bowen, M. (1972). Towards the Differentiation of a Self in One's Own Family. *In* "Family Interaction", (J. L. Framo, ed.), Springer, New York.

Bowlby, J. (1969). "Attachment and Loss, Vol. I: Attachment", Hogarth, London.

Byng-Hall, J. (1979). Re-editing Family Mythology During Family Therapy. *Journal of Family Therapy* **1**, 103-116.

Byng-Hall, J. (1980). Symptom Bearer as Marital Distance Regulator: Clinical Implications. *Family Process* **19**, 355-365.

Byng-Hall, J. (1981). Therapeutic Confusion Produced by Too Close/Too Far Family Systems. *In* "Questions and Answers in the Practice of Family Therapy", (A. S. Gurman, ed.) Bruner/Mazel, New York.

Byng-Hall, J. and Campbell, D. (1981). Resolving Conflicts Arising Out Of Family Distance Regulation. *Journal of Family and Marital Therapy.*

Byng-Hall, J. and Whiffen, R. (1981). Family and Marital Therapy in Affective Disorders. *In* "Handbook of Affective Disorder", (E. S. Paykel, ed.), Churchill Livingston, Edinburgh.

Duhl, F., Kantor, D. and Duhl, B. (1973). Learning Space and Action in Family Therapy: A Primer of Sculpture. *in* "Techniques of Family Therapy: A Primer", (D. A. Bloch, ed.), Grune & Stratton, New York.

Kemplar, W. (1973). *Principles of Gestalt Family Therapy.* A. S. J. Nordahls Trykkeri, Oslo.

Lieberman, S. (1979). Transgenerational Analysis: The Geneogram as a Technique in Family Therapy. *Journal of Family Therapy,* **1**, 51-64.

Madanes, C. and Haley, J. Dimensions of Family Therapy. *Journal of Nervous and Mental Disease,* **165, 2,** 88-98, 1977.

McGoldrick, M. (1981). Through the Looking Glass: Supervision of a Trainees Trigger Family. *In* "Supervision in Family Therapy: Recent Advances", (R. Whiffen and J. Byng-Hall, eds), Academic Press, London and New York.

Minuchin, S. (1974). "Families and Family Therapy", Tavistock, London.

Paul, N. (1967). The Role of Mourning and Empathy in Conjoint Marital Therapy. *In* "Family Therapy and Disturbed Families". (G. Zuk and I. Boszormenyi-Nagy, eds), Science and Behaviour Books, Palo Alto, Calif.

Paul, N. L. and Paul, B. B. (1975). "A Marital Puzzle: Transgenerational Analysis in Marriage", Norton, New York.

Simon, R. M. (1972). Sculpting the Family. "Family Process", **11,** 49-58.

Walrond-Skinner, S. (1976). "Family Therapy: The Treatment of Natural Systems", Routledge & Kegan Paul, London and Boston.

Whiffen, R. and Byng-Hall, J. (1981). "Supervision of Family Therapy: Recent Advances", Academic Press, London and New York.

Whitaker, C. A. and Napier, A. Y. (1978). "The Family Crucible", Harper & Row, New York and London.

Williamson, D. S. (1978). New Life at the Graveyard: A Method of Therapy for Individuation from a Dead Former Parent. *Journal of Marriage and Family Counselling,* **1,** 93-101.

Winnicott, D. W. (1971). "Playing and Reality", Tavistock, London.

Chapter 4

Pattern and Intervention
Research Findings and the Development of Family Therapy Theory

G. Gorell Barnes

I. RESEARCH AND CLINICAL WORK

A. Introduction

Researchers and clinicians in the field of human development and psychotherapy often find it hard to bridge the gap between their different kinds of enquiry. Researchers are concerned with the measurement of categories of things in a valid, reliable and replicable way while clinicians face each event as it comes to their clinical attention, responding to the unique qualities of the particular constellation that make up the person, family or problem before them. The two do not have to be mutually exclusive, but it is often difficult as a clinician to know where there are links with scientific thinking. How do the frameworks that people who class themselves as family therapists use, relate to other frameworks where change is studied. It seems important to me that the way in which people who work and teach in the family therapy field are seen to think, should not be characterized only by their difference from other more traditional psychotherapies, but by their areas of convergence with the approaches of different disciplines studying learning and change, and the research that has taken place within them.

According to the Oxford English Dictionary, a science consists of systematic and formulated knowledge. Hinde (1979) declares that,

> The study of interpersonal relationships and the treatment of these lacks as yet an overall and comprehensive measure for systematizing knowledge. Only when we can describe relationships, categorize their properties and classify them, can we transform our limited knowledge and experimental findings into generalizations with specific ranges of validity.

He covers many of the ways in which attempts are made to measure relationship, and charts some of the complexities of this process as it has been attempted within different disciplines.

Family Therapy
ISBN: 0-12-089355-X

B.   Relationship and Pattern

Following his approach, the variables involved are considered briefly here. Inter-personal relationships represent a coming together of individually specific constitutions and histories. There may be a shared social network and culture to provide common elements of history, or these also may be different and specific to each person involved. Many variables therefore affect the course of each relationship, and these are hard to differentiate within any given interaction. From the interactions developing between any two people over time, new and specific properties emerge, some of which can be observed, and others which are invisible and intangible. These can be classified as the behavioural and the emotional properties of relationship. While any pattern of interaction possesses subtle qualities that may be beyond the early reach of observational analysis, it is likely that most of the behavioural properties are accessible. What has preceded the interaction, as well as expectations of what will follow in the future, will inevitably influence its course.

C.   Measurement of Family Pattern

Measurement of such patterning is difficult.

> Given the possibilities for unidirectional, bidirectional, direct and indirect effects of individuals and for dyads, triads and quadrads, it is an understatement to say that a four element system is complex (Lewis and Feiring, 1978).

This is seen as a major obstacle to the transfer of scientific attention to units larger than the dyad and to the measurement of the notion of a system, a problem to which developmental psychologists have recently drawn attention.

In videotape recording of families, we have been greatly helped as clinicians in our observations of family pattern within sessions. For example, the child may produce a stomach pain or an obsessional symptom such as the need to wash his hands when tension in the room mounts. To measure this scientifically is possible but complex. Hartup (1978) has referred to "The tyranny of data"! In measuring family interaction, 30 minutes of observation yields 360 discrete, 5-second inter-vals on each participant in a dyadic situation. Scores may be generated on any number of different variables in each of these intervals. The reduction of such amounts of data is a task of staggering magnitude. Campbell (1981) recently de-scribed the Tavistock Clinic, Department for Children and Parents, Family Therapy Programme research team's 5-year struggle to do this, and the complexity of the task. Other British studies of family interaction related to measuring intervention in-clude most notably the many studies from Great Ormond Street (Kinston *et al.*, 1979, Bentovim and Kinston, 1978 and Kinston *et al.*, 1981) in their developing work on Brief Focal intervention, have devised techniques for relating past and pres-ent patterns in a relatively economic way. In attempting to describe families more efficiently, they are looking at the reliability of clinical description and judgement of family atmosphere, based on the observation of behaviours and the inferred relationship of these to the underlying pattern of historical events.

D. Variations in Traditional Family Pattern

Further variables would include the many family forms with which clinicians now meet. A "normal" model of family may still be a two-parent family with their own children, but it is equally likely to be two-parent families where one parent is not the original parent of the child, single parent families, multiparent families where divorce and remarriage has led to at least two sets of parents for the children, adoptive and foster families, and homosexual couples with children, who are seeking an outside viewpoint. It would not be possible to cover adequately in one model the variables these different family clusters add to the already rich complexity of a family life based on continuous development from birth.

E. Intervention in Family Pattern

For clinicians, the relationship between interactions, relationships and the properties of these relationships; the overall family pattern and the symptoms of any one member may be said now to be the basis of family therapy. The debate about procedure in therapy, how to intervene in the organization of pattern over time, the family system, is related chiefly to whether intervention should be at the level of the interactions themselves as they occur in the room; or at the level of the pattern of their emergent properties, what the therapist understands about the meaning of the interactions he observes. Does he go for the more concrete or the less overtly definable aspects of relationship? Concern over what constitutes an effective therapeutic intervention and the proper role of the therapist, can be seen as centring here.

II. FAMILY PATTERN AND INDIVIDUAL DEVELOPMENT

Pattern exists in the eye and mind of the observer, and the way he chooses to punctuate it will depend on his own context and vantage point. Nonetheless, to punctuate pattern at the boundary of the family can be said to be legitimate from the contextual viewpoint of professionals other than family therapists. While the boundary that focusses on the family, at the expense of school, of community or at a supra level, of region or cultural group, is an arbitrary boundary; research has shown that it can be an appropriate one for clinical rather than political attention. The family is a unit where leverage for change can be effectively applied both on behalf of individuals within the family, and in order to develop the family's capacity to act effectively on their environment. If the family can develop belief in their capacity for problem solving, they and the individuals they nurture, can develop the capacity for autonomous action, and can apply what has been learnt outside the family as well. Haley (1976) has pointed out that whatever radical position the therapist takes as citizen, his obligation as professional is to define the social unit that needs to change to solve the presenting problem of the client, and to act effectively on that.

The influence of family patterns on individuals has been shown in diverse ways, three of which are particularly relevant to professionals who work with and hope to influence families: pattern as it affects social change, pattern as it affects mental illness and antisocial behaviour; and pattern as it affects stress.

A. Family Pattern and Social Change

Although the way in which the family mediates between its members and the world outside is so diverse that it cannot properly be noted here, the findings of Rutter and Madge (1976) in Cycles of Disadvantage are worth noting. They have shown that while familial continuities do exist especially with respect to intelligence, educational attainment, occupational status, psychiatric disorder and multi-problem families, there are also striking discontinuities. At least half of the children born into disadvantaged homes do not repeat the pattern in the next generation. Over half of all forms of disadvantage arise anew in each generation. Even where continuity is strongest, many individuals break out of the cycle. There is also a marked reduction in continuity over three generations. While the impact of professional intervention is not part of their study, it provides evidence that it is not misplaced to attempt intervention in family pattern.

B. Family Pattern and Mental Illness

We know that family pattern has an effect on forms of illness and social behaviour. Four recent quite different research studies may serve as examples to demonstrate the effect of family interaction upon one of its members. The replication by Brown et al. (1972) of an earlier study predicting the relapse of discharged schizophrenic patients, found that the measure of "expressed emotion" and in particular the number of critical comments made by a key relative about a patient, was the most important predictor of relapse and a suitable target for intervention. Other components of expressed emotion were emotional "overinvolvement" and "hostility". Above 35 hours a week of face to face contact with a highly emotional relative greatly increased the chances of relapse. This was equally true whether the relative was a parent or a spouse. Falloon and his colleagues (Falloon et al., 1981) have recently reported some success using this as a target for sustained professional intervention. Kreitman (1970), studying 60 male patients receiving outpatient treatment for neurosis or personality disorder, found that while the patients' wives did not differ from the control group in terms of mental health early in marriage (i.e. it was not a question of assortative mating), at time of study they had higher ratings both of impaired health and of psychiatric illness. It was found that (as in Brown's study) more time was spent in face to face interaction with each other with no one else present than in the control group. It was hypothesized that in such a case of modelling process takes place in which the husband was the dominant model. In a third study, this time of behaviour problems among children in their own families, Patterson (1975) assessed the frequency with which hostile behaviour from a child was followed by a response from another family member likely to induce another hostile response, and found that such sequences were five times more common than in the control group.

A fourth interesting and relevant study by Bugental (1971) analysed video-taped parent/child communication in families containing a disturbed child of 8–12 years, referred by the school for chronic behaviour problems, and found messages nearly six times as likely to contain conflict between the verbal, vocal and visual channels than in the control group, (for example, a critical or disapproving statement spoke in a positive or cooing voice). Conflict was found between verbal content and facial expression and between verbal content and tone of voice, but not between face and voice. Such behaviour is similar to that described by Bateson and his colleagues (1956) and hypothesized as the basis of the Double-bind theory of schizophrenia. While much of this theory is now taken as an elegant model of transactional confusion and the basis for other kinds of analysis of discrepancy in family message giving, rather than as relating specifically to schizophrenic illness, the existence of such conflicting messages in families with disturbed members is common knowledge among those who work with them.

C. Family Pattern as it Affects Stress

It is clear that aspects of family patterns are also important under special circum-stances of stress. In Brown and Harris's study of depression among women in south London (1978) the presence of young children in women with a stressor increased the risk of depression from 17% to 93%. On the positive side, the presence of a good relationship with one parent does a lot to ameliorate the effects of parental discord for the children (Rutter, 1971, 1979). Of the children in discordant homes with a good relationship, only a quarter showed a conduct disorder, compared with three quarters of those lacking such a relationship. A similar finding is discussed by Lewis (1976) whose study of seriously disturbed, midrange and optimal families will be referred to again. It is also discussed by Skynner (Chapter 1, p.32).

III. MUTUAL INFLUENCE IN FAMILIES

In turning to the effects of pattern in families we can find much more open acknowledgement of mutual influence than would have been the case 10 years ago. Most interaction studies before that time were concerned with mothers and infants. Studies have now demonstrated the impact which each member can have on another. Fathers as well as mothers respond to their newborn infants, infants respond to their fathers by 7 months at least (Lamb, 1976) and interactions with elder siblings, cousins and other kin or network also play a crucial role in social development and may be seen to compensate for parental deficiencies or parental absence. Babies and children affect parents, both structurally and emotionally. It is not a one way process (Lewis and Rosenblum, 1974). As Dunn (1977) states:

We can only understand the growth of a child's relationship with his parents if we see them as interacting pairs from the earliest days, and we can only understand the origin of later individual differences between children if we take real account of differences from birth.

A. Healthy Family Patterns and Stress

The development of the structure of the healthy family itself contains stresses. Dunn's work has also shown how ordinary family events like the arrival of new babies create stress in family patterns. She and her colleagues found that more than half of the forty 2- to 3-year-old children in their sample became more tearful after the birth of a sibling, nearly one half showed new toiletting problems, and a quarter developed sleeping difficulties. Mothers tended to play less with the first child and spent more time in prohibiting, confronting, and in negative verbal interactions (Dunn, 1980).

Intact families will vary in their response to life stresses such as illness, hospitalization or bereavement. Such stresses can impinge powerfully on the pattern of relationships. On discussing how stress affects later development, Rutter (1981) pointed out that stressful early events may operate on later action by altering sensitivity to stress or in modifying styles of coping which then protect from or predispose towards disorder in later life only in the presence of later stress events. All children are likely to encounter stress events as they grow up, and it is very unlikely that the long-term outcome will be determined by the number of such stresses. It is more probable that it will be determined by how the stress is dealt with at the time; and perhaps particularly on whether the result was successful adaptation or humiliating failure. We might cautiously say that helping families solve problems successfully in the present is also preventive against future stress, since if we help them achieve adaptive and flexible solutions to stress that simultaneously help diminish sense of failure and humiliation, they will have a larger repertoire of problem-solving behaviour to draw on (Aponte, 1978) and they will keep open a flexible, curious and hopeful attitude to the outside world and the dilemmas it imposes which Lewis et al. (1976) have shown is one of the characteristics of healthy and functional families.

B. Stress, Intervention and Future Development

While one could argue that helping a family cope better with current life events is a worthwhile aim in itself, those who observe families without the intention of intervening, suggest caution in attempting to alter interaction as a preventive measure (Dunn, 1976; Kagan, 1978; Stern, 1979). The predictions between particular influences in early childhood at any one time and the child's subsequent behaviour are not clear.

As Kagan puts it,

Maturational forces direct the basic growth functions for many psychological systems that emerge during the first two years — reaction to discrepancy, amplification of memory, object permanence and stranger and separation fears. Experience determines the age at which these competencies appear or disappear and during the period of their emergence the intensity and frequency of display.

Dunn and Bateson (1976) argue for the idea of equifinality as an important notion in development to which we should all attend. As children arrive at similar end-states by very different developmental routes, we should intervene in what may appear to be "abnormal" with caution. They remain scientifically cautious, however, about which aspects and parameters of relationship can be safely ignored. "We do not know which aspects of a relationship are essential, which can be transferred and which are harmful." Hard data on what family interactions are optimal is rare. Some of the epidemiological work in this country (Richman, 1978) would suggest fixed qualities in family relationship which correlate with persistent disturbance in young children, and the many studies from Professor Rutter and his colleagues give further guidelines on behaviours in families that correlate with psychiatric disturbance in older children (Rutter, 1975, 1978).

While on the one hand, behaviour relationships (and therefore patterns) in families are observed as changing over time, Dunn also comments that although behaviours themselves change, the core characteristics of a set towards behaviour is often maintained (Dunn, 1981, personal communication). This is a helpful and relevant observation for family therapists who have learnt to consider "classes" of behaviour with different discrete performances by family members at different times. It is relevant to the discussion on levels of change within systems which ends this chapter in which change is considered not only as it relates to particular interactions but to the class of interactions of which that behaviour is a member. The way in which change may be pushed through whole family systems in a change in subsystemic sequences, or alternatively the way in which a change in a class of behaviours will affect a series of interactions, links to this independent observation of family behaviours from a different source.

Dunn and Bateson (1976) also discuss the existence of stabilizing tendencies (homeostasis) both in given interactions and within the developing organism, pointing out that while not every aspect of mother/infant interaction matters, the absence or exaggerated presence of aspects of relationship may lead to divergence or disruption. Where stabilizing mechanisms do operate successfully, they will do so only as long as the divergence lies within certain limits. For example, small divergences such as a temporary loss of temper or withdrawal of attention may be unnoticed, moderate ones like brief or regulated absence adequately compensated, while larger ones such as severe physical abuse or sustained marital tension are disruptive. The consequences of any given degree of disruption will always depend on the impact of other variables in the system. The Tizard's work on children in different contexts both in institutions and in families, highlights this crucial variable of context (Tizard, 1975, 1977). Hinde states:

> We cannot yet tell without empirical data what aspects of a relationship are essential to its nature. Indeed the answer to that is liable to depend on circumstances.

In intervention with families, we would normally have to use clinical judgement about whether our job was to promote stabilizing tendencies within the family as in times of family crisis, or to increase divergent tendencies within a family who appeared to be stuck within a frame too narrow to enable them to cope with the problems confronting them, which might be necessary prior to better and healthier stabilization being achieved. This is unfortunately an area where clinicians must work with their own judgement in the absence of clear knowledge about what constitutes crucial aspects of relationship and therefore satisfactory resolution of crisis. As clinicians then we are still very much in the dark about what behaviours and what patterns exemplify the Winnicottean notion of "good enough parenting". Recent work (Rutter, 1978, 1979) has recently outlined further research evidence in this area.

C.   The Circular Nature of Developmental Interaction

Within developmental psychology, the circular nature of developmental interaction has recently been emphasized by Lerner and Spanier (1978) whose dynamic interactional model proposes the view that individual development may only be adequately understood in the context of the constant reciprocal interaction between a changing person and his or her changing environment, and suggest that such continuous circularity implies a need for new statistical models and new conceptualizations of the variables analysed within these models.

> If development is conceptualized in a circular manner, then the utility of linear statistical models seems limited. In time the variables involved in this circularity may not be appropriately seen as antecedent to or consequences of one another. The components of development — the components of this circle, constantly change; as such, since each component is a source of every other, as each constantly changes, so do all others. Accordingly rather than the social universe being seen as constant and permanent and change being the to be explained phenomenon — this model assumes that change is the rule.

Such views chime closely with current thinking in family therapy where we are being urged to lose the constraints of Aristotelian logic and linear thinking (Dell, 1982). It seems important to remember at the same time a distinction between mutual influence and an awareness of the imbalance of power inherent in family relationships in the different developmental capacity to choose how action is taken upon the impact of that influence. The properties of a relationship involving a child are in a part a consequence of the child's immaturity, and whatever influences the child brings to bear in his interactions with parents, he does not have the same developmental capacity to choose how he acts (Stern, 1979, Brazelton and Main, 1974) in response to the influence of the other. To recognize the circularity of mutual influence is not to accord equality of power of thought, choice and action in terms of maturation, and it may be important to keep this in mind when the relationship between professional intervention and family distress is considered.

IV. MUTUAL INFLUENCE, PATTERN AND SYSTEM

In moving from interaction, relationship and pattern to considering how the relationship pattern is organized in time, we move into the concept of system. It is important to remember that a system is a model, an abstract representation of how a series of repeated events within a limited frame or boundary are construed. As an operational model for thinking about family functioning, it is worth asking in what ways thinking of families as systems have been useful. Systemic models of aspects of family functioning have been used in different ways in the theory building of family systems, and this difference is confusing, since the relationship properties described are not necessarily of the same category.

A. Physiological Systems Model

For example, in thinking about physiological response, a systems model has been used in describing the origins of reciprocity by Brazelton (1974); introducing the physiological component linking relationship pattern to individual organisms

> Just as there is an oscillating regulatory mechanism that maintains homeostasis in physiological parameters such as temperature control, cardiovascular mechanisms, the curve of activation, discharge and recovery seems to be necessary for attention in an ongoing interaction. The autonomic system is dominated by this kind of homeostatic mechanism. This homeostatic model which underlies all the physiological reactions of the enonate might also represent the immature organism's capacity to attend to messages in a communication system.

The relationship of system pattern to physiological response in the individual organism has been excellently documented in this country by Lask (1981) in relation to psychosomatic illness; chapter 23. It has been perhaps most strikingly demonstrated by Minuchin and his colleagues (1978) in a series of trials in which they measured the increase in free fatty acid response in diabetic children witnessing parental conflict from behind a one-way screen. This provided physiological evidence that psychosomatic diabetic children were not only more seriously affected by the family conflict than the control group of diabetic children, but that they took much longer to recover following termination of the witnessed parental row.

B. Systems Theory and Attachment Theory

Following John Bowlby's original work on attachment in systems theory in terms of set goals, goal correction and function leading to the maintenance of caregiver/infant proximity, Bischof (1975) modified Bowlby's systemic approach to include the move to maintenance of distance from the familiar and towards exploration of the stranger. Sroufe and Waters (1977) described attachment as an organizational construct which links individual difference to the requirements of development in different environmental situations.

"A behavioural system operating in terms of set goals mediated by feeling and in interaction with other behavioural systems." They make a distinction important to family therapy thinking, about behaviours and classes of behaviour; in response to criticism that specific behaviours as instances of attachment behaviour did not show stability over time. Sroufe and Waters argue:

> Since multiple behaviours can have similar meanings — prediction becomes not that behaviour A will be correlated with behaviour across situations of time but rather that behaviour A as members of class X will predict the occurrence of behaviours in class X in that same context.

(This is similar to Dunn's comment that while particular types of mother/child interactions show little consistency over time, patterns of interactions assessed as wholes do show consistency.)

This distinction between a single behaviour as an instance of a predictable class of behaviour is important as it relates to patterning in families, to the learning that is made possible or that is constrained by such patterns that I shall refer to later and to the class and level of interactional behaviours that are selected by the therapist for intervention.

Ainsworth (1977) emphasizes a distinction between attachment and the behavioural terms that mediate it; and views attachment as

> An inner organization of behavioural systems which not only controls the 'stable propensity' to seek proximity to an attachment figure but also is responsible for the distinctive quality of the organization of the specific attachment behaviours through which a given individual promotes proximity with a specific attachment figure.

Heard (1978) further extends the model to clinical work with the family system and suggests how it may be used both for assessment and as a design for therapeutic intervention (a) to evoke exploratory behaviour, and (b) to promote reappraisal of internal images of self and others in such a way that inner needs for attachment are assuaged by subsequent interactions.

C. A Systems Base for Family Intervention

Systems thinking derives principally from the concept of organization and reflects the proposition that events can usefully be represented in terms of their participation within a network of interrelated events. A system is usually defined as an organized arrangement of elements which comprise a network of inter-dependent and co-ordinated parts which function together as a unit. Open systems require energy and information from outside to accomplish their operations and to perform their functions. What the system can and cannot do at any particular place and time relates to its organization, the input it is receiving, and its environment. Systems can be categorized on a continuum from chaos (entropy) through rigidity toward greater flexibility with further evolution of coherent structure (negentropy). Families can be placed along this continuum in terms of their capacity to develop adaptive and flexible structures in response to feedback from the environment or from its members (Lewis et al., 1976).

"Feedback" is characterized as either negative or deviation countering which maintains homeostasis, or as positive deviation amplifying operations, through which growth or creativity may occur within a system. Therapeutic intervention with families who are stuck rather than in dangerous crisis would be characterized by deviation amplification, i.e. the introduction of complexity to the system. In order to survive; complex, adaptive systems must be capable of positive feedback (i.e. move away from homeostasis) which leads to change in structure, organization and values as family or development requires it.

(1)   Health and Dysfunction in Family Patterns
Speer (1970) characterized a maximally viable social system (such as a healthy family) in the following way:
(a) Complex structural relationships in communication and interactions.
(b) A highly flexible organization capable of change from within the system.
(c) Highly autonomous components with a minimum of constraints in inter-component relationships.
(d) Considerable intrasystem determinism and causality of system and component behaviour.
(e) The ability to tolerate basic change in the system.
(f) The necessity of a constant flow of a wide range of information experience and input into the system.

The notion of health on families has been further discussed in the Timberlawn research comparing healthy and disturbed families (Lewis *et al.*, 1976) and is discussed at greater length by Skynner (in chapter 1). Two studies influencing their work are worth mention. The first by Westley and Epstein (1969) looked at a normal population of 96 college students, their health ratings by psychological testing, psychiatric interview and parental interview. Family variables distinguishing healthy from "sick" students included problem-solving capacity and style of communication, and the balance of autonomy and independence as important groups of variables. The factor critical to emotional health in children was the nature of the relationship between the parents. The second study by Mishler and Waxler reported a long-range interactional study comparing three groups of families, two with a schizophrenic child, with good and poor premorbid adjustment, and a control group with no child having a history of psychiatric hospitalization. These families were studied in a session involving the parents and a well sibling. Areas of differences among the groups were (1) expressiveness, (2) and (3) power: the strategy of attention and personal control, (4) disruptions in communications, (5) responsiveness. In the control families, there was more expressiveness, more positive affect and more flexibility. There were clear generation boundaries with a complexity of power although this was not exercised in a rigid or authoritarian manner. The parental coalition was strong, communications were more responsive and more disruptive than in families containing schizophrenics.

For the purposes of discussion in this chapter the Timberlawn findings about rigidity in dysfunctional family systems and flexibility in optimal family systems are worth noting. Speer (1970) in reviewing several interaction studies postulates a healthy family system as flexible with an absence of rigid constraints in system structure and a high capacity for tolerating autonomous behaviour.

The Timberlawn research interviewed 56 intact families with the oldest child in mid-adolescence in all, 31 of whom maintained 6-month records of family events, health and professional care. All families had no member in psychological or legal difficulty for the previous year. Each family was videotaped for initial data gathering, life history, medical history and interactional pattern. Four psychiatrists independently rated their health at a global rating and subsequently six families at either end of the health spectrum were interviewed for three hours. The findings bore out Speer's earlier work in confirming that physically healthy families with no evidence of psychiatric disorder and effective functioning were more open systems, tolerating a much greater receptivity and responsiveness to new ideas and capable of sustaining contradictory feelings and viewpoints without distress. There was greater respect for difference both within and outside the system boundary and greater individual autonomy. Severely dysfunctional families in contrast were run on a basis of "mutual intimidation"; responses had to be within narrow limits and little attention was paid to individual perception and feeling, or to any view that did not fit the family's "group think". Such families were reluctant to accept loss or change, and were held together by incongruous myths maintained by denial of reality and careful family teaching.

(2)   The Maintenance of Equilibrium

In family problem-solving, we are always confronted by some fear of change and a corresponding wish for "homeostasis" or the maintenance of things as they are. At one end of a continuum, this shows the wish for a healthy and necessary stability, as Hinde, Dunn and others have indicated; representing the family's capacity to survive over time and make healthy developmental adaptations as a social group with some cognitive congruence (common sets of meanings, values and expectations). At the other end of a continuum, however, it can become the stagnation of structure and the denial of individuation and growth, as the Timberlawn research demonstrates. What is important for the therapist is to be able to identify where the wish for homeostasis will actively prevent the intake of new information which might lead to new solutions because the family fear change more than they experience discomfort. If he does not take this fear into account, he will fail to understand why all that he does is useless. The family "tends to maintain itself" around some ideal (or idealized) point of equilibrium which has been established as the system evolves. As a system containing young children is a growth system and therefore on the move and not static, there is a continuous process of new input into it and thus a tendency for it to be pushed away from equilibrium. Over time, the family may develop certain repetitive enduring techniques or patterns of interaction for maintaining its equilibrium when confronted by stress and this pattern may be activated appropriately and inappropriately whether stress is internal or external, acute or chronic, trivial or gross. It is always essential to keep in mind the positive function of these homeostatic mechanisms for maintaining the "togetherness" of a family as they see it.

(3) How Does Systems Theory Help Family Problem Solving?

Haley, one of the original contributors to systems thinking in families, attacked systems theory recently (1978) as unhelpful to therapy.

> The merit of systems theory is that it makes things predictable — the demerit is that it focuses on how a family remains the same — it is not a theory of change but a theory of stability. In that it is not functional for a therapy based on restructuring and reorganizing the family hierarchy and in that it takes away individual responsibility from participants it is not a theory of how to proceed in therapy.

In the long-term debate on family systems theory which Haley is referring to, there was much emphasis from groups studying families with schizophrenic members and a cybernetic model based on closed-system feedback prevailed. The focus was on how the family homeostasis which involved the regular rehospitalization of the patient, was maintained. Many psychotherapists reacted against the way in which individuals in the debate appeared to be considered only as if they were components of a system. Focus was on input-output aspects of the system as reflected in family transactional processes which were assumed to be governed by rules based on maintaining homeostatic principles which both constrain and regulate intrasystemic behaviour. Discussion was largely based on clinical observations and studies of disturbed behaviour, and arose in reaction to clinical despair at the ineffectiveness of individual psychoanalytic psychotherapy for this patient group. Don Jackson said:

> It is significant in the development of family theory that it was the observation of homeostatic mechanisms in the families of psychiatric patients that led to hypothesis of family as homeostatic and eventually specifically as a rule governed system.

Dell (1981) has recently attacked the model as limited and inaccurate, and Hoffman (1981), in reviewing the development of systems thinking in the USA, confirms that this debate largely ignored biological systems with their innate capacity for adaptation and change. This may have been because much of the initial theory was based on work with young adults who were not seen to be developing further; and interest was drawn rather to communication patterns within the family. While a more cautious attitude to the cybernetic model has always prevailed in this country largely because of the development of family therapy within a health service and social service framework with a strong commitment to families with young children, the awareness the cybernetic model has offered of the transmission of rules in families at both verbal and non-verbal levels, and the potential for disturbance, held by conflict in the class of response required by a message, has been invaluable. It has inexorably led to the question of how the therapist himself should class his own messages and give information to a family, who themselves always communicate at conflicting levels. It has therefore led to the development of strategy and paradox in the interventions of the therapist (Watzlawick et al., 1967, 1976, 1978; Cade, 1979; Papp, 1980; Madanes, 1981).

In family work with dependent and developing beings, we always need to keep the push for growth and development in mind as a force for creating change and not take too much upon ourselves. Alongside Winnicott, it may be useful to ask, "How little need we do?" As Dunn *et al.* (1976) have indicated, there is evidence that despite difficulties along the way, the same end-point may be reached by many different routes. Our job is often to provide the information that is missing to help the biological family system find its own solution to the dilemma in hand rather than offer a premature or forced solution ourselves. Bateson has defined information as "a difference that makes a difference", and it is exactly this that the professional, an outsider to the system, can provide if he can develop a clear hypothesis and understanding of what "information" is required. Clearly what will make a difference is the million dollar question; and it is around this question of what will make an effective difference to the family's capacity to find solutions to their problems that the wide variety of techniques incorporated into family therapy can be seen to be arrayed.

V.   LEARNING AND PATTERN

A.   Learning, Storage and Habit

Before some aspects of work with "rules to change the rules within a system" are examined, some interrelated issues such as learning (coding and classification), habit, i.e. what happens to previous learning and past experience, and how it is stored; will be touched on briefly. How experience is stored must be the source of most controversies in therapeutic attempts to help people retrieve; re-work undo and find new solutions. What follows is an arbitrary *aide memoire* to thinking afresh about changing pattern, not an academic review of different therapeutic positions.

Foss (1973) in talking about human learning, reminds us of the mechanisms brought into play by interaction between the main thinking and the object thought about, coding, classification and the learning of patterns.

> When an object is categorized this normally carries with it a process of coding; one remembers seeing 'an angry boy-bad girl', there is much less load on memory as compared with having to remember the total original percept . . . but this advantage is gained at the expense of discarding much of the original information.

The object is remembered not for its unique qualities but as more like a "typical instance" of the category in which it has been placed. Accuracy of learning and remembering, will therefore depend on the number of categories and sub-categories available to the learner which will vary from person to person. The remembering of pattern will depend on two main processes: (1) autonomous processes including possible tendencies to simplicity, symmetry and fading, (2) categorizing, in which the pattern will be recalled as a typical instance of the category in which it has been put.

Bateson (1967), relating to this learning of pattern as it is reprojected in art, discusses habit formation also; as the sinking of knowledge down to less conscious and more archaic levels. The unconscious contains not only the painful matters which consciousness prefers not to inspect; but also many matters which are so familiar that we do not need to inspect them. Habit therefore is a major economy of conscious thought. (p.114)

Both Foss and Bateson from very different positions point to the price paid in the problem of information storage. The "sinking" process, though economical, may lead to over simplification in how we think.

B. Habit and New Learning

This may affect our capacity to think afresh since new learning depends on prior learning. Everything that we learn depends on constraints and predispositions resulting from what we are, and what we learn must include the rules that we learn and most of the rules determining what we learn (Seligman and Hager, 1972; Hinde and Stevenson Hinde, 1973). How learning takes place and how it is constrained remains a matter of differing opinion, but the debate is highly relevant to professionals intervening in a pattern since it relates to what can be undone, reworked and thought about in a new way.

What a person experiences depends both on physiological arousal and on how he labels the situation (Singer and Schachter, 1962). In interpersonal relations, emotions will therefore be affected by how an individual has learnt to label his feelings in the light of the circumstances he knows to have produced them. What he believes about what has happened, the meaning he ascribes to events, will determine the map he makes of his own experience and the way he subsequently describes them. Experience is stored as symbols which can be manipulated. In spite of selectivity and distortion there will be for him a relationship between what happened and what he describes about past interactions with others. His behaviour and emotions will also be influenced by his anticipations about the future. As Hinde (1979) points out, in spite of debate about precisely how it happens, A's perceptions of people, situations and behaviour, his feelings about them, his thoughts about his feeling, and his thoughts about the behaviour and feelings of others are coded, and stored in symbolic form (Hebb, 1969; Ash, 1959) which results in dynamically organized and interrelated schemata of cognitive representations of individuals and events (Neisser, 1976).

C. Pattern and Anticipation

Neisser (1976) argues for models of learning based on anticipatory schemata which operate at ranging levels of generality. Perceptions and cognition are transactions with the world that do not merely inform but transform the perceiver, in turn modifying the anticipatory schemata. This affects the capacity to receive certain information where there is no prior anticipatory set "information can be picked up only if there is a developing format ready to accept it" (p.55) and has implications for what the therapist does in problem solving. How he prepares the ground for his own intervention and uses the material of the session as governing information for his input into the system will be crucial for its effectiveness.

D. Variety in Learning

Bindra (1978) has proposed a model of learning which is particularly relevant to the relationship between the influence of pattern and the choice of action. The essence of his proposal on how individuals learn relates to the variety in the conditions of learning and the resulting train of appropriate responses that any individual therefore has at his command in response to subsequent eliciting stimuli (a view widely held by ethologists). Where there has been a narrow learning pattern in the first place ("a limited range of environmental spatio-temporal patterning"), subsequent eliciting stimuli will therefore call forth limited rather than various and flexible chains of "overlapping" or "nesting" of association. By stimuli he includes a full range of human experience sights, sounds, smells, temperatures, crying children, sexual attraction and fear of attack.

Bindra says that the mechanism by which these "pexgos" (presently excited genetic organizations with spatially and temporally ordered activation) are translated into a particular act is not known; and that the problem of a meaningful relation between perception and action is a fundamental one for psychology. He suggests however that since a response is a fresh construction in the brain every time it occurs, we must look to the lack of variation in relationship between space and time in learning pattern to account for stereotypes of response. Where these are altered, flexibility in response can occur within the same context (what Bateson has called Learning II). He proposes therefore that the analysis of behaviour should rest not on relating specified responses to specified stimuli but on the study of the total range of actions that occur in relation to the larger patterning of areas of behaviour in space and time. He suggests that the alternation of uniformity and stability in the patterning within which individuals happened to be confined may well relieve them of possible continuing stereotypy and persistence in their own responses. The implications of this for therapy and intervention in pattern will be apparent. Similar ideas arising from different sources will be found in this book in chapters by Cooklin and Byng-Hall. From a different perspective again P. P. G. Bateson and Hinde have both emphasized the importance of diversity in learning. P. P. G. Bateson's experimental chicks developed flexibility in attaining the goals they were seeking in response to the introduction of slight novelty to the usual pattern of experiment, learning rules to change their own rules. Although the problem of identifying where the starting rules are stored "which may be largely cellular and beyond analysis at the level of the whole", remains; Bateson and Hinde both argue that presented with diversity of interactions in learning, young animals can be equipped with "rules for changing the rules" and thus develop greater functional reciprocity with their environment (Bateson and Hinde, 1976). This complements Fentress (1976) who states that in the early stages of activation of learning, a wide variety of behaviours may be facilitated, but as the organization increases, the dynamic structure becomes more tightly constrained, requires less information (i.e. becomes habitual), is less easily interrupted by external factors, produces more linked sequences and blocks behaviour patterns associated with other systems.

E.   Links to Learning in Families

Thus from different fields, we see strands of argument and thinking developing which are similar and relevant to systemic thinking within the field of family therapy. Pattern constrains the capacity of the individual interactions, affects their process and also affects the capacity to receive new information. Information will only be effective if attention is paid to context and to the pressure of time and space that if uninterrupted will constrain an increase in flexibility of responses whether in thought, feeling or action.

F.   Therapy as Punctuation of Pattern

All therapy may be seen as offering a new punctuation, arbitrarily imposed by the therapeutic persuasion of the professional, to the experience of the patient. The provision of a different experience to that to which the patient is habituated, and which is causing pain is the beginning of providing a basis for new learning.

A note from Piaget links the role of active participation in learning to the kind of punctuation family therapists tend to offer to the experience of the family. He distinguishes objective knowledge, i.e. something someone else knows about; knowledge that is integrated, calling these states *vs* transformations. He describes how children learn better when they act on the thing to be learned, rather than when they simply watch and remember the relations between mental images and operations.

> The image is useful to the operation, to the extent that it symbolizes an exact knowledge of states, but it is by no means sufficient to furnish an understanding of transformations. To understand those it is necessary to act on the object and to co-ordinate the modifications into a coherent whole. (Piaget, 1977)

Piaget emphasizes that the process of learning is a process of dialectic. Something is learnt through the process of application to the issue in hand in which the properties of the object are freed from the subjective illusions of the person who is learning. Piaget has called this process "decentration". It links to the question of how a problem for a family can be distanced enough for them to do some work on it. Minuchin (1967) made this an important feature of his early work with families talking about the movement from interpersonal blame within the family to a joint focus on the third thing "the thing to be learned" which the family could work at together. The Milan group provide a similar experience using the different method of neutrality and circularity in the way they ask questions, punctuating the experience of the family in new objective ways (Palazzoli *et al.*, 1980).

VI.   PROBLEM-SOLVING APPROACH TO WORK WITH FAMILIES

A.   What Stops Them Doing the Work Themselves

Problem-solving therapy as a whole may be seen as focussed on the issue of what stops a family from learning or from decentring themselves enough from the problems they have in hand to do the work necessary to finding solutions to them. A number of reasons have been discussed, including the lack of prior information and experience on which to draw, a difficulty in assigning appropriate common meanings to the nature of the problem, and an inability to hold onto and store problem-solving solutions, so that they can be experienced and used again.

Another potential set of situations which the various examples of how we may be said to learn point to, is where the nature of the problem activates unpleasant stimuli or "anticipatory schemata" or associative chains that are maladaptive to problem solving because prior experience has led to learning of the wrong kind. Incorrect or oversimplified classification may be the least difficult area to remedy since other classifications may involve physiological responses of a complex order. There may be conflict between one set of responses which might be appropriate and another set at a different level which prohibit the employment of the first. McFarland (1973) has described one of the constraints on learning as "ambivalence in the environment". A family may not solve a problem when the solution may be seen as creating another problem at another possibly more threatening level. Inability to solve problems in family life is both very common and sometimes very complex since it may involve pattern development over generations as well as over time within one generation. Because families live together and interact in close physical proximity, they arouse one another very deeply often in the course of minor events. What appears to an outsider to be a small problem such as a baby crying, a child refusing to eat his potatoes, or a child's wish to go out with friends rather than joining a family outing, can become the ingredients of major problem development within families; invested with dramatic feeling which relates to the context in which these events were originally experienced, coded, categorized and stored (Gorell Barnes, 1978).

Families may also try to solve problems from their store of available ideas, not seeing how their persistent attempts to solve the problem have become the problem. The system they have arrived at for attempting solutions has itself become the problem. For example, we observed the family of a child with a hysterical dislocation of the shoulder which could be performed at will (but not backwards apparently) and which had involved eight years of attendance at different hospitals. The family was observed to be in disagreement and concerned over a number of other issues. The function of the symptom appeared to be to unite the family in concern over her as a distraction from their quarrelling and anxiety. It also brought the secondary gain of personal concern and attention. However, the problem solution, to attend hospitals, as a way of uniting the family in common concern, had become the problem, since the maintenance of the problem-solving pattern in one area of family life or at one level depended on the symptom continuing in another.

In thinking about families so far we have considered interactions, relationships, and the properties and pattern of relationship, defining a family system as being the organization of this pattern over time. Over time, pattern itself influences the properties of a relationship and therefore interaction and individual perception. Many social psychology experiments have shown the effect of group influence on individual perception (Asch, 1952).

In families, permission to perceive in a certain way, the coding and categorizing of information, are framed by relationship properties expressed through interactions, and by the pattern that governs these.

B. How Family Therapists Work with Rules

Rules constrain the system and control the way information is allowed in and processed; therapists struggle with these rules in their work with families and the different ways in which they address rules is the subject matter of this book. Here I would like to highlight briefly three styles of intervention as they relate to rule change in family systems.

Therapists aim to change rules so that new perception and action are permitted at different levels within the dysfunctional system the family show. However, there are different levels of rule that a professional might address themselves to in problem solving: a ground-level rule or rules at higher levels. The choice for the therapist will be which of these he will choose for his point of intervention in trying to change a pattern that has become habitual and simplified, distorted or rigid in ways that are causing distress.

Strategies for change in family systems, defined loosely here as structural, strategic and systemic work, can be seen as linked to Bateson's definition of the levels of learning of which organisms or systems are capable (Bateson, 1972). Ground rule problem-solving work, which includes structural work and some strategic work, is linked to a second level of learning, "Learning II"; in which through therapy, members of a family are moved beyond the stimulus response patterns of the first level of learning "Learning I", and learn to act on, not simply respond to their environment, in a variety of ways (generalized learning). The therapy aims to repunctuate their sequences of experience and have them enact a variety of new responses within the same context. The members of the family learn to learn, and learn also how to transfer their learning to new situations.

The structural model developed by Minuchin (1967, 1974) and Haley (1976) has taken on a more strategic layout in the more recently published work of Papp (1980) and Madanes (1981) which include the use of different kinds of strategy. It continues to address itself to change through the minutiae of interaction in subsystem sequences. These sequences which are in operation from the moment a child is born into a family generate certain characteristics of the individual self which are in turn fed back into the system. Bateson calls these "the cybernetic circularities of the self and the external world" and Stern (1979), watching mother–infant play sequences, Minuchin talking about therapy with families call these "the dance". While the family context remains unchanged, certain behaviours, whether verbal or non-verbal will be read within the family as cues (or markers) for sets of perceptions and expectations to be brought into play, which stimulate further predictable patterns of behaviour. Such expectations as have been discussed are normally determined without conscious thought, having sunk to the level of habit, and the original reasons for categorizing them in a particular way being forgotten. They are not therefore available for discussion and repetition. The way that the truth as the family see it, is punctuated, can neither be true nor false in any absolute sense since there is no such thing as objective truth, but it represents the powerful view of reality within which the dysfunctional behaviour or "problem" is embedded (Bateson, 1964).

The therapist using a problem-solving approach working at ground rules, would aim to repunctuate sequences between family members so that experience in these sequences takes on different meanings. Ground rules carry the detail of family structure. Many transactions obeying the same meta rule will therefore be equivalent to one another (isomorphic) so that challenging one transaction is not an isolated event. Such work requires energy, focus, precision and intensity, through repeated repunctuation of sequences that have rigidified thereby decreasing options for problem solving. By encouraging family members to enact new ways of talking and behaviour with one another, the repeated challenge of isomorphic ground-rule transactions will amount to a challenge to a meta rule. Minuchin (1981) recently summarized this elegantly: "Intervention can focus on therapeutically relevant transactions and bring seemingly disconnected events into a single organic meaning increasing family members' experience of the single constraining rule".

Strategic work also requires the therapist to work with the behaviours of the family, at ground-rule level to achieve change, but always aimed more specifically at reframing the meaning of the behaviours. Watzlawick defines reframing as "an alteration in the conceptual or emotional setting or viewpoint in relation to which a situation is experienced" and the placing of the experience in "another frame which fits the facts of the same concrete situation equally well or even better thereby changing its entire meaning". Systemic work (Palazzoli *et al.*, 1980; Campbell, this book chapter 17) does not require the therapist to act upon the behaviours of the family to achieve a change in the system, but thinks more specifically about a change in the context of *meaning* ("reframing") within which the behaviours take place, a change at the meta level or second order rule level (or higher), "the highest possible rule". Notions of step by step learning through action are not part of the session, which is used for circular questioning to gather information about the way the family view the problem and the way they view each other's perceptions. The therapist addresses himself to change in the system as a whole, usually in relation to a wider system that frames the meaning of what he sees before him with a message or a task at the end of the session. The mechanism of change resides with the therapist's positive connotation of all the behaviours in the family. The family is thrown into a bind by being asked to accept the positive qualities of the symptom they ambivalently ask to be rid of. This is one way of distinguishing different styles of strategic work since the system is always seen in the context of the family system unlike the work of Watzlawick and his colleagues (1967, 1976) where the unit of behaviour treated may be taken right outside the context of family. This way of working, the systemic approach in which the whole system is addressed through the highest rule that the therapist can understand (Campbell, 1981) can be related to Bateson's "Learning III". In this third level of learning, a system may theoretically be freed from the bondage created through adherence to its own processes of second-level learning by perceiving the issue of choice in a new way. The paradoxical rules that have developed as a result of the conflicting attribution of meaning over time that govern current perceptions and therefore learning, are transformed by the introduction of new meaning and experience that affects each member of the family simultaneously. An overall change in pattern is aimed at, not just a change in part of the pattern.

C. A Hierarchy in Rule Change?

Haley, originally a pioneer in the use of strategic therapy (1963) suggests more recently a simpler way of viewing an approach to rule change or problem solving in families. He suggests

> A way to view the approach is to give directives doing directly to the goals, such as getting the child to school. For those families in which a direct approach is not effective, the therapist falls back on an alternative plan that will motivate the family toward the goal. If that alternative is not effective, fall back on yet another alternative plan.

The more clear the problem and the goal of the therapy, the easier it is to design directives.

Papp (1980) distinguishes a hierarchy in approach to rule change in systems between interventions that are compliance based or direct, referring to the therapist's expectation that the family will comply with them, and those that take the resistance of the family to change into account. Compliance-based interventions: advice, explanations, and suggestions; include promoting open communication, coaching parents on how to control children, redistributing jobs and privileges among family members, establishing disciplinary rules, regulating privacy, and providing information that the family members lack. *Defiance-based or paradoxical directives* are those that depend for success on the family's defying the therapist's instructions or following them to the point of absurdity and recoiling. They rely on (1) defining the symptom as benignly motivated to preserve family stability; (2) prescribing the symptom-producing cycle of interaction; and (3) *restraining* the family whenever they show signs of changing. Another way of thinking about her work would be to suggest that its success lies not only in the wish of the family to defy the therapist, but in the way the tasks prescribed show them the logical absurdities within their own rule system.

Within family therapy and within this book, the issue of how to address the rules relating to the problem behaviour with the system, is obviously a key one. It has resulted in many innovations in therapeutic technique devised to invite or organize the family into reframing their dilemma in such a way that therapeutic work is done on a number of levels. The size of the system that is seen by the therapist and the time scale required for the change in the system to be worked through, are among elements contributing to diversity of approach and technique used. The flexibility or rigidity of the family system relating to their degree of dysfunction is likely to be another. The development of different ways of addressing changes in family rule structure will be the subject of further discussion (Gorell Barnes, 1981; Gorell Barnes *et al.*, submitted, 1981).

This chapter, reviewing some aspects of work in related disciplines that are of relevance to family therapists, places their ideas in a different context. It has been shown that family therapy has potential and exciting links with other areas of system thought about pattern and change. The links with ethology and with the constraints on learning imposed by context, seems particularly exciting and relevant; relating as they do to different ideas about rule change, the possibilities of flexibility and rigidity in learning within a system, and the introduction of new information into dysfunctional family systems. It is important that we continue to jump context and consider the relevance to our work of what colleagues in other fields are thinking and doing, so that as a group of clinical practitioners, we continue to be an informed open and flexible system ourselves.

REFERENCES

Aponte, H. (1978). The anatomy of a therapist. "Full Length Case Studies", (P. Papp, ed.), Gardner Press, London and New York.

Asch, S. E. (1952). "Social Psychology", Prentice Hall, New York.

Asch, S. E. (1959). A perspective on social psychology. *In* "Psychology, a Study of Science", (S. Koch, ed.), Vol. 3, McGraw Hill, New York.

Bateson, G. (1964). The logical level of learning and communication. *Reprinted in* "Steps to an Ecology of Mind", (1973). pp. 250-279, Paladin, St. Albans.

Bateson, G., Jackson, D., Haley, J. and Weakland, J. (1956). Towards a theory of schizo-phrenia/Behavioural Science. *Reprinted in* "Steps to an Ecology of Mind", (1973). pp. 173-198, Paladin, St. Albans.

Bateson, P. P. G. and Hinde, R. (eds) (1976). "Growing Points in Ethology", Cambridge University Press, Cambridge.

Bateson, P. P. G. and Klopper, P. H. (1978). "Perspectives in Ethology 3: Social Behaviour", Plenum, New York.

Bentovim, A. and Kinston, W. (1978). Brief focal therapy when the child is the referred patient. *Journal of Child Psychology and Psychiatry*, **19**, 1-12.

Bindra, D. (1978). How adaptive behaviour is produced: a perceptual-motivational alternative to response — reinforcement. *The Behavioural and Brain Sciences*, **1**, 41-91.

Bischof, M. (1975). A systems approach towards the functional connections of attachment and fear. *Child Development*, **46**, 801-817.

Bowlby, J. (1973). "Attachment and Loss. Vol. I. Attachment", Hogarth Press, London.

Brazelton, T., Koslowski, B. and Main, M. (1974). The origins of reciprocity. "The Effect of the Infant on its Caregiver", (M. Lewis and L. Rosenblum, eds), Wiley, New York.

Brown, G. W., Birley, J. L. T. and Wing, J. K. (1972). Influence of family life on the course of schizophrenic disorders: A replication. *British Journal of Psychiatry*, **121**, 241-258.

Brown, G. W., Bhrolcrain, M. and Harris, T. (1975). Social class and psychiatric disturbance among women in an urban population. *Sociology*, **9**, 225-254.

Bugental, L., Love, L. E., Kaswan, J. W. and April, L. (1971). Verbal and non-verbal conflict in parental messages to normal and disturbed children. *Journal of Abnormal Psychology*, **77**, 6-10.

Cade, B. (1979). The use of paradox in therapy. *In* "Family and Marital Psychology: A Critical Approach", (S. Walrond-Skinner, ed.), Routledge & Kegan Paul, London.

Dell, P. (1982). Beyond homeostasis: Towards a concept of coherence. *Family Process*, **21**, 21-41.

Dunn, J. (1976). How far do early differences in mother–child relations affect later development. "Growing Points in Ethology", (P. P. G. Bateson and R. Hinde, eds), Cambridge University Press, Cambridge.

Dunn, J. (1977). Patterns of early interactions: Continuities and consequences. "Studies in Mother Infant Interaction", (H. R. Schaffer, ed.), Academic Press, London and New York.

Dunn, J. F. and Kendrick, C. (1980). The arrival of a sibling: changes in patterns of interaction between mother and first born child. *Journal of Child Psychology and Psychiatry*, **22**, 1-19.

Falloon, I., Liberman, R., Lillie, F. and Vaughn, C. (1981). Family therapy of schizophrenics with high rate of relapse. *Family Process*, **20**, 2, 211-222.

Fentress, J. (1976). Dynamic Boundaries of Patterned Behaviour. *In* "Reaction and self organization" *In* "Growing Points in Ethology", (P. P. G. Bateson and R. A. Hinde, eds), Cambridge University Press.

Foss, B. M. (1973). Human and Animal Learning: A Caution. *In* "Constraints on Learning", (R. Hinde and J. Hinde-Stevenson, eds), Academic Press, London and New York.

Gorell Barnes, G. (1978). Infant needs and angry responses. A look at violence in the family. "Family and Marital Psychotherapy: A Critical Approach", (S. Walrond-Skinner, ed.), Routledge & Kegan Paul, London.

Gorell Barnes, G. (1981). Family bits and pieces: Framing a workable reality. "Developments in Family Therapy", (S. Walrond-Skinner, ed.), Routledge & Kegan Paul, London.

Gorell Barnes, G. (1981). A Difference that makes a difference (1). *Journal of Family Therapy* (in press).

Gorell Barnes, G., Jones, E. and de Carteret, J. (1981). A Difference that makes a difference (2). *Journal of Family Therapy* (in press).

Haley, J. (1973). "Strategies of Psychotherapy", Grune & Stratton, New York.

Haley, J. (1976). *Problem Solving Therapy.* Harper Colophon Books.

Hartup, W. W. (1978). Perspectives on child and family interaction. "Child Influences on Family and Marital Interaction. A Life Span Perspective", (R. Lerner and G. Spainer, eds), Academic Press, London and New York.

Heard, D. H. (1978). From object relations to attachment theory. A basis for family therapy. *British Journal of Medical Psychology*, **51**, 67-76.

Hinde, R. and Stevenson-Hinde, J. (eds). (1973). "Constraints on Learning", Academic Press, London and New York.

Hinde, R. (1978). *Towards Understanding Relationships.* Academic Press, London and New York.

Hinde, R. (1981). Family influences. "Scientific Foundations of Developmental Psychiatry", (M. Rutter, ed.), Heinemann, London.

Hoffman, L. (1981). "Foundations of Family Therapy", Basic Books, New York.

Kagan, J. (1978). Continuity and stage in human development. "Perspectives in Ethology, Vol. 3", (P. P. G. Bateson and P. H. Klopter, eds), Plenum Press, New York.

Kinston, W., Loader, P. and Stratford, J. (1979). Clinical assessment and family interaction: a reliability study. *Journal of Family Therapy*, **1**, 291-312.

Kreitman, M., Collins, M. J., Nelson, B. and Troop, J. (1970). Neurosis and marital interaction, I. Personality and symptoms, II. Time-sharing and social activity. *British Journal of Psychiatry*, **117**, 33-46.

Lamb, M. (ed.). (1976). "The Role of the Father in Child Development", John Wiley & Sons, New York.

Lewis, J. M., Beaven, R., Gossett, J. T. and Phillips, V. A. (1976). "No Single Thread: Psychological Health in Family Systems", Brunner/Mazel, New York.

Lewis, M. and Feiring, C. (1978). The child's social world. "Child Influences of Marital and Family Interaction: A Life Span", (R. Lesner and G. Spanier, eds), Academic Press, London and New York.

Loader, P., Kinston, W. and Stratford, J. (1980). Is there a psychosomatogenic family. *Journal of Family Therapy*, **2**, 311-326.

McAuley, R. and McAuley, P. (1977). *Child Behaviour Problems: An Empirical Approach to Management.* Macmillan, London.

McFarland, B. J. (1973). Stimulus relevance and homeostasis. *In* "Constraints on Learning", (R. A. Hinde and J. Stevenson-Hinde, eds), Academic Press, London and New York.

Madanes, C. (1981). "Strategic Family Therapy", Jossey Bass, San Francisco.

Minuchin, S. (1976). *Families and Family Therapy.* Tavistock, London.

Minuchin, S. and Fishman, C. (1981). *Family Therapy Techniques.* Harvard University Press, Cambridge, Mass.

Minuchin, S., Rosman, B. and Baker, L. (1978). "Psychosomatic Families", Harvard University Press, Cambridge, Mass.

Mishler, E. and Waxler, M. (1968). "Interaction in Families", Wiley, London.

Neisser, U. (1976). "Cognition and Reality: Principles and Implications of Cognitive Psychology", Freeman, San Francisco.

Palazzoli, M. S., Boscolo, L., Cecchin, G. and Prata, G. (1978). Paradox and Counter Paradox: A New Model in the Therapy of the Family in Schizophrenic Transaction. Jason Aronson, London and New York.

Palazzoli, M. S., Boscolo, L., Cecchin, G. and Prata, G. (1980). Hypothesizing-circularity-neutrality: Three guidelines for the Conduction of the Session. *Family Process*, **19**, 1.

Papp, P. (1980). The Greek chorus and other techniques of family therapy. *Family Process*, **19**, 1, 45-58.

Patterson, G. R. (1975). A three stage functional analysis for children's coercive behaviour. "New Developments in Behavioural Research Theory, Methods and Applications", (B. C. Etzel, J. M. Le Blanc and D. M. Baer, eds), Elbaum & Hilldale, New Jersey.

Piaget, J. (1977). The role of action in the development of thinking. "Knowledge & Development Vol. 1. Advances in Research and Theory", (W. F. Overton and J. M. Gallagher, eds), Plenum Press, New York.

Rutter, M. (1978). Early sources of security and competence. *Human Growth and Development*, (J. S. Brunner and A. Gorton, eds), Oxford University Press, London.

Rutter, M. (1979). Protective factors in children's responses to stress and disadvantage. *Primary Prevention of Psychopathology, Vol. 3. Social Competence in Children.* (M. W. Kent and J. E. Rolf, eds), University Press of New England, Hanover, N.H.

Rutter, M. (1981). Stress, Coping and Development: Some Issues and Some Questions. Emmanuel Miller Lecture. Association of Child Psychology and Psychiatry. To be published in the Journal of Child Psychology and Psychiatry.

Rutter, M. and Madge, M. (1976). *Cycles of Disadvantage: A Review of Research.* Heinemann, London.

Schachter, S. and Singer, J. E. (1962). Cognitive, social and physiological determinants of emotional state. *Psychological Review*, **69**, 379-399.

Speer, D. C. (1970). Family systems: Morphostasis and morphogenesis or is homeostasis enough. "Family Process", **9**, 259-278.

Sroufe, L. A. and Waters, E. (1977). Attachment as an organizational construct. *Child Development*, **48**, 1184-1199.

Tizard, B. (1977). "The adoption of children from institutions after infancy", Association of British Adoption and Fostering Agencies, London.

Tizard, B. (1977). "Adoption: a Second Chance", Open Books, New York.

Tizard, J. (1975). "Varieties of Residential Experience", Routledge & Kegan Paul, London.

Urban, H. (1978). Development from a systems perspective. "Life Span Development and Behaviour, Vol. 1", (P. Baltes, ed.), Academic Press, London and New York.

Watzlawick, P. (1978). "The Language of Change: Elements of Therapeutic Communication", Basic Books, New York.

Watzlawick, P., Bevin, J. and Jackson, D. (1967). "Pragmatics of Human Communication: A Study of Interactional Patterns, Pathologies & Paradoxes", W. W. Norton & Co., New York.

Watzlawick, P., Weakland, J. and Fisch, R. (1974). "Change: Principles of Problem Formation and Problem Resolution", W. W. Norton & Co., New York.

Part II

Practical Issues in the Therapy of the Family

Chapter 5

Preparation of the Referral Network The Professional and the Family

W. Roberts

I. INTRODUCTION

Whether or not a family attends an initial therapeutic session will depend, to a large extent, upon the preparation of all concerned: that is, the family, the therapist, the referring agent and any other relevant professional workers. "Good enough" preparation should aim at ensuring that the expectations of all those involved in the process are understood and clarified, for although family therapy is a treatment method increasingly available in a variety of settings, it is still common practice for one member of the family to be selected as the nominated patient at the time that the referral is made. It is therefore essential that the therapist is alert to the many factors which are present during the referral process, and is able to take appropriate steps to ensure that progress is as smooth as possible.

II. ROUTES TO THE FAMILY THERAPIST

A. Varieties of Agencies

The avenues through which a family finds its way to an agency are numerous, and although some families are sufficiently motivated to refer themselves, it is still true to say that the majority come into therapy because one or more of its members is showing signs of stress, the symptoms being as varied as the agencies or settings in which they may be presented. The majority of helping agencies, whether voluntary or part of the Welfare State, tend to focus on a particular age group, symptom or disability, and although many are increasingly aware of the implications of a stress signal being transmitted by a family member, may still make the referral for family therapy in such a way that the family themselves are unaware that they are expected to be involved in the assessment of diagnostic procedure.

With the growth of understanding that individual disturbance may represent family dysfunction, it is not only "helping agencies" who make referrals to family therapists. Schools are often alert to the difficulties of the children they are teaching: disruptive behaviour, academic underfunctioning and inability to make relationships are, among others, commonplace foci for referral. In some

Family Therapy
ISBN: 0-12-089355-X

areas, the Police Juvenile Bureau have been known to make appropriate referrals, and in one instance, at least, the leader of a holiday play group, concerned about an aggressive boy, sought the help of a family therapy practitioner.

B. Historical Factors

If one considers not only the variations among helping agencies, but also the orientation and training of their workers, it is hardly surprising that difficulties occur, and it is relevant to look back in history if we are to understand this. During the era of the Welfare State, services have developed piecemeal, and were generally planned as a response to individual needs as they were recognized. Thus, Infant and Child Welfare Clinics were set up to cater for the under-fives age group, while on the other hand, services for the physically and mentally handicapped, span all age groups but tend to have symptom-orientated boundaries. Education Welfare Officers deal with problems affecting school children and their families, with the availability of the school psychologist, should need arise. The blind, the deaf, the spastics and others had voluntary organizations available to them to meet those needs not met by the State services, and because of the multiplicity and overlap of services, choice often depended upon the attitude of the sufferer or of the referrer. Despite the fact that in recent years, steps have been taken to change and improve this situation, (Seebohm, 1968) many families continue to be attached to more than one agency, and are seldom recognized as a "whole".

C. Multiple Agency Allegiances

Examples of this are numerous, and the following situation is not as uncommon as one would hope it might be:

The M family consisted of Father, Mother and two daughters, Betty and Mary. At the time that they came to the notice of a family therapist, Father was the nominated patient and was referred by his general practitioner for depression, leading to outbursts of violence. When the family were seen together, it came to light that Mother and daughters had another general practitioner who had referred Betty to a hospital child psychiatric department because of her mother's complaints about her difficult behaviour. This was the first time that Father learned of this situation, and he was understandably angry at being kept in the dark. Before the family were seen for the second session, it was learned that Betty had also been seen by the school psychologist to whom the teacher had turned for help when she became so disruptive as to be threatened with suspension. The school psychologist had spoken to Mother, but she said nothing about the steps she herself had taken and agreed to be referred to the educational authorities child guidance clinic, although when she failed two offered appointments there, the referral was not pursued. This clinic overlooked communicating with the General Practitioner. Meanwhile, the child psychiatric department had seen Mother and Betty and offered individual treatment to both. Soon afterwards, the Education Welfare Officer called to investigate Betty's prolonged absence from school, having been asked to do so by her colleague who was attached to the School. (The reason for two E.W.O.'s being involved was because, at that time, the Department was organized in such a way that officers worked on a "patch" system, and in some instances the family home and the school were not in the same "patch".)

Later it was learned that Mary, who was 3 years of age, was known to a health visitor who was keeping closely in touch because of her concern about Mary's slow development. This concern had recently led her to alert the Social Services Department for she suspected ill-treatment, and wondered whether Mary should be entered on the "non-accidental injury" register. A social worker from that department had just begun to visit the home. This is not an unusual situation, horrific though it may appear when actually faced in this way. We need to ask ourselves what it is that makes it difficult to change or avoid such situations; for once they have occurred, changed they must be if family work is to be successfully undertaken, and what needs to change is the failure of agencies to effectively communicate with each other.

III. BLOCKS IN REFERRAL TO AGENCIES PROVIDING FAMILY THERAPY

Let us instead try and understand what it is that creates such situations in order that, as family therapists, we may be sensitive to the roles of other workers, the policy and structure of their agencies, and so aim at improving collaboration between us.

A. Problems within the Referral Agency

Agency workers, and in this context I include school teachers, G.P.'s, health visitors and all who are likely to make referrals to a family therapist, have generally received a training which befits them for the kind of work they are expected to undertake within the confines of the orientation of their profession, and although many such workers are increasingly aware of the dynamics of family relationships, they may be restricted both by training and agency boundaries to working with an individual family member. Referral to a family therapist, even where this is relevant, depends upon a number of factors: (Menzies, 1970; Hornby, 1979).

(1) The level of trust which has developed between their agency and others,

(2) The degree of responsibility they feel they carry (an example of this being the local authority social worker who has statutory responsibility for a family member)

(3) The desire to practise family therapy themselves, even although this is not considered to be a function of the agency

(4) The fear of having undermined or undervalued the work they have so far done and

(5) The often unrecognized fear of losing a patient or client.

There are no doubt many more, not so easily recognizable but equally important factors. Perhaps we all need, from time to time, to stop and remind ourselves of the motivation which led us to choose our particular area of work and to realize that this, and our investment in training, may lead to serious ambivalence in referring on to others those with whom we have become involved.

B. Problems within the Family Therapy Agency

At the other end of the spectrum, family therapists may need to guard against inappropriate referrals which come their way because of the despair (or anger) of a worker. In this respect, unless the situation is appropriately handled and the reasons for refusal to accept such a referral fully understood, the resultant unexpressed feelings of frustration between referrer and family therapist may lead to a failure of future referrals being made. I cannot emphasize too often, the importance of "good enough" communication between family therapists and referrers if treatment is to be effectively carried out. Ambivalence between workers is not limited to inter-agency relationships. In some instances the agency offering family therapy as only one method of treatment, may have failed to resolve differences of opinion between its own workers about when it is appropriate to see and assess the whole family. In this case, they run the risk of the ambivalence and/or disagreement being conveyed to referrers in such a way that the referrers are confused about what is being offered and failure results (Skynner, 1976).

C. Recognizing Mixed Messages

The manner in which referrers convey ambivalence is varied. In one clinic in which I worked for many years, we became familiar with the referrer who informed us that although he was convinced that the problem was linked with relationships in the family, he was equally convinced that either one or other of the parents would not attend, or that the parents would not agree to any of the children other than the nominated patient being present. Experience taught us to enquire whether the referrer had actually *seen* both parents together to discuss the question of attendance, or to clarify the relevance of the siblings being included. It was not unusual to learn that this had not happened, and that information given by one parent about another had been accepted as valid: "my husband leaves all the matters about the children to me", being a commonplace statement. We were remiss in not recognizing that we had failed to ensure the referrer understood the relevance of the presence of both parents and all the children at a therapeutic session.

Many family therapists will no doubt recall their own past misgivings in this respect, for I well remember the long and difficult discussions that took place in the clinic where I first practised family therapy; the doubts and fears that we aired then are still being expressed by those to whom the treatment of a whole family is a new and unknown procedure.

D.   Who Gets Referred and Why

I think it is appropriate to state that currently, the majority of families who find
their way to a family therapist do so because one or other of their children is seen
as the nominated patient; although it is also true to say that other agencies such
as Marriage Guidance Counsellors, Probation Officers and others, are increasingly
recognizing that difficulties presented by adult family members may be symptomatic of family disequilibrium.

Where a child is the presenting problem, it is frequently because of the
concern of somebody outside of the family. It therefore becomes essential for that
person (school teacher, playgroup leader, or whoever it is who is feeling concern)
to inform the parents. In so doing, it is not unusual for tentative ideas to be
floated as to the possible cause of the difficulties; the general public are being
increasingly alerted to the symptoms of psychological stress by the media, and in
addition, the training of all of those in the helping professions includes some
aspects of this.

Unfortunately the ideas floated may not only be inaccurate, but may tend to
apportion blame: "it's because his father is always out", "his mother makes a
favourite of his sister", and so on. Alternatively, the cause may be attributed to a
particular event: "he's been like it ever since we came to live in this neighbourhood". Such discussion between informer and parent, or between professionals
as a result of a conversation with a parent, provides the opportunity for thoughts
and ideas to be aired in such a way that the focus is on one family member who is
seen as the patient or client; as the "victim" to be helped or rescued, or as the
family member with a vulnerable personality unable to deal with stress. These
perceptions, and there are innumerable variations, must affect the attitude and
expectations of all concerned.

IV.   PRINCIPLES TO ENSURE SUCCESSFUL REFERRAL

From the foregoing, it is evident that if family work is to be successfully undertaken, as much care and attention must be given to those who, although outside
the family, are part of its system (the supra-system), as to the family itself when it
is eventually seen. I hope it is also evident that "good enough" preparation needs
to allow time and opportunity for misunderstandings and differences of opinion
to be aired, and if possible, resolved.

A.   Have the Whole Family been Prepared for Invitation?

With the foregoing in mind, what steps can a family therapist take to ensure that
a referral is more likely to achieve a successful outcome? In the first instance,
unless the referrer is well known (or the referral document makes clear), it will be
necessary to enquire whether or not the whole family have been prepared for an
invitation. It is not sufficient to be told that one parent was seen alone and
promised to *try* and get the other to attend. I discovered how risky this can be

when a head teacher volunteered this information and I later learned that a wife's message to her husband had been: "The Head says you will have to go to the clinic because she thinks you are too soft with Tom"! On other occasions there was no message to father. Referrers sometimes need convincing (preferably by personal contact, but at least by a telephone conversation) of the importance of the need for them to speak directly with important family members. Their reluctance to do so can not only be attributed to the demands on their time, for in discussing this topic with numerous referrers, they have aired their anxieties about meeting with parents who are known to disagree, their fear being that they will not be able to handle the disagreement.

In such a situation, it may be helpful to arrange to join in the discussion about a referral, thus not only providing a model of how such a meeting may be conducted, but also allowing the opportunity for the parents, or whichever family members are attending, to meet an agency member and have answered some of their questions. Some agencies provide a form which referrers are asked to complete and which requests relevant information. A referral form with which I am familiar asks the following questions in addition to name, address, occupation or school, name and profession of referrer:

(1) Other agencies involved (e.g. Social Services, school psychologist, health visitor, voluntary bodies) etc.
(2) Are these agencies aware of this referral?
(3) Reason for referral (the problems and their duration) as seen by the referrer.
(4) *The problems and their duration.*
     (a) As seen by the patient(s), adult or child
     (b) As seen by the family
(5) What is the attitude to referral of the patient(s) or the family?

The form then requests specific details of all family members, i.e. name, age, occupation or school, etc. plus details of other important family members or friends (if known). An additional paragraph states: "Before completing this form (which is provided as a framework for your comments), please discuss the reasons for referral with the patient(s) or family concerned to ensure their agreement".

Do not ignore uncompleted parts of the form however much you are tempted to do so. Their incompleteness is probably very relevant. For example, a referrer may be aware of the involvement of other agencies but not considered them relevant; like the G.P. who had seen both parents of a child in trouble and from them learned about a problem with a neighbour and of their request for rehousing made to a Social Services Department. The General Practitioner presumed that the Social Worker concerned was dealing with the housing situation, whereas the request had been seen as symptomatic of other difficulties and exploratory home visiting was arranged. Failure to inform about this very relevant agency led to confusion for this particular family.

B. Sharing Understanding with Agencies

What other steps may be taken to encourage "good enough" communication between professionals in order that the preparation of a family for therapy is adequately carried out? In some areas, regular meetings are arranged which provide an opportunity for workers to get together. Such meetings can be task-orientated, i.e. to discuss particular problems, but they nevertheless offer the chance for sharing ideas; for discovering what one has in common and what is the particular speciality of each; for learning about the problems and difficulties inherent in the work of each agency; for sharing understanding about the various methods of working and for developing trust. Care is needed in the arrangement of such meetings: place, timing and purpose need to be discussed and agreed. Changes of workers may necessitate a recurring series of meetings at agreed intervals. In the initial planning stages, ambivalence is almost inevitable and will be expressed in numerous ways: late arrival at meetings, misunderstandings about date, time and place, and so on. But if this can be recognized and tolerated so that negative feelings about frustrations, disappointments and unmet expectations are aired, there is a good chance of the group working well together. The knowledge that families are often expert in playing off one agency worker against another may be an incentive for attendance!

A commonplace criticism of family therapists is that they are fortunate in only working with families who are motivated. While there may be some truth in this, the demands made upon referrers in the preparation process make it clear that the degree of motivation depends, to some extent, upon their own contribution. Nevertheless, the complaint may be linked with the awareness that referrers are left with many difficult problems, particularly those instances where a family is resistant to treatment. Staff in schools and childrens' homes are examples of this and often feel that they are not helped with some of the more problematic situations which are daily occurrences. Some family therapists have found ways of helping by meeting regularly with interested staff to discuss ways in which they may work more effectively. This has also offered the opportunity for supporting workers who are often left feeling helpless and despairing. Better and more appropriate referrals can result from such meetings, particularly when the improved understanding between agency workers is reflected in discussions with families. The following model which was successfully established is offered as a guide to those who are interested in improving communication with prospective referrers:

Three team members, representing three disciplines in a Child Guidance Clinic arranged, after initial exploratory meetings with senior staff, to meet fort-nightly with a group of Educational Welfare Officers. The place for meeting alternated between the working premises of each group, and the agreed plan was for the Educational Welfare Officers to present a situation with which they were experiencing difficulty. It was expected that the presenting problem would be discussed in depth so that sufficient understanding could be reached for practical suggestions to be made about how the situation could be handled more effectively, an important part of these meetings, for endless discussion without decisions can be an abortive experience!

The clinic workers, in turn, discussed families known to the Educational Welfare Officer, demonstrating in discussion their understanding of family dynamics and thus the relevance of the need for the whole family to be seen and assessed. As trust developed, the Educational Welfare Officer expressed fears that family therapy could be "dangerous" and lead to violence between family members; that getting everyone together was like "building a bonfire" to which the therapist would "set alight" with the additional risk of them being sent away leaving others (i.e. the Educational Welfare Officer) to "quell the flames". The Educational Welfare Officer who made these comments was not alone in expressing such anxieties; indeed, I recently learned of a teacher who had said to a parent:

> You should ask your doctor to send J to "X" Child Guidance Clinic where they'll see her by herself. If I ask our psychologist, he'll refer you to "Y" department where they insist on seeing all the family together, and *in my opinion*, that's not necessary as J's the problem, and needs the help.

It is evident that we should not be complacent about the presence of such anxieties and their effects on the preparation of a family when a referral is being made.

C.   Sorting out Territorial Rights

Before initiating any meetings it is important to ensure that the appropriate agency staff have been approached and are in agreement. In schools for example, you may need to meet with those who have "professional territorial rights": the educational psychologist, the educational welfare officer and of course, the Head teacher. If you are interested in meeting with the staff of a residential institution, you will need to communicate with the appropriate hierarchy of the Social Services Department. Unless care is taken to work through the correct channels, your offers of help may prove abortive. Care must also be taken to ensure that your offer is not misunderstood, for a "them and us" situation is not unknown in some areas, the "us" being seen as the experts who have all the skills, and the "them" those who have none.

There are of course, other ways of dealing with resistances in professional workers once one is aware of their existence and of the need to try and overcome this in the interest of effective therapeutic work with a family. Case conferences to which all known workers are invited can be arranged, care being taken in considering the advantages and disadvantages for meeting before or after one has met with the family. Some therapists are resistant to having more than the minimum information about a family prior to their being seen, while on the other hand, where it is known that a family is likely to be resistant, it may be more helpful to gain the support of all known agencies before attempting to contact the family itself.

It is no doubt clear by now that I consider the preparation of referrers to be of the utmost importance if the majority of families requiring therapeutic help are to find their way to an appropriate agency. "Good enough" preparation not only deals with resistances, but gives support and encouragement to the family; prevents conflicting and confusing communications; and avoids the possibility of the family being pushed and pulled between rival agencies.

V. INVITING THE FAMILY

A therapist who feels confident that this groundwork has been successfully undertaken can now address himself to the preparatory work that is still required to be done by him. The referral having been received and accepted, the next step is to invite the family for the initial session, the invitation making clear who is being asked to attend. This may appear to be stating the obvious but in my experience, letters of invitation are sometimes so vague that it is hardly surprising when either the nominated patient only (in the case of an adult) or a parent and child alone respond to the letter.

A. Letters of Invitation

The letter needs to state very clearly that all of the family are expected to attend . . . "If I am to be of help to you, it will be important for all of the family to attend at least for the first session".

It may be helpful, in view of prior information you have received, to suggest other relevant persons be included . . . "you may feel it could be useful to include others in your household in addition to members of the immediate family".

In this case, the letter is worded in such a way that the therapist is indicating a knowledge of other persons who could appropriately be included, but leaves the final decision about their inclusion to the family members.

It can also be helpful to recognize that some adults in a family may be required to take time off from work . . . "should you require a letter for your employer in order to be allowed to take time from work, I will be pleased to provide this".

Since attendance of a whole family may mean that some members are likely to be inconvenienced and a compromise about availability reached, the therapist can be helpful in indicating that alternative appointment times are possible . . . "can you please confirm that you are able to accept this appointment. If, on the other hand, the day and time are not convenient for you all and you would like me to arrange an alternative, I will be pleased to do so". Such a statement can also prevent the waste of therapeutic time since most families seem able to respond to a request for confirmation.

It may be helpful to send a copy of the initial letter to the referrer, particularly when resistance has been met and worked with, for this enables the referrer to continue to be encouraging. Or, where authority issues are at stake, as may be the case with a school truant, or a Court report, the referrer can take whatever steps they may feel appropriate to ensure that the appointment is kept.

B.   Inviting Family Members not "Living Together"

Where a referrer indicates that:

(i)   parents of a family are either separated or divorced,

(ii) there is a co-habitee currently involved,

(iii) a grandparent, or other relative is either living in the household or sufficiently close as to be considered an important member to include,

then a decision must be made about whether and how they should be invited. Parents who are apart may yet continue to share parenting functions in such a way that unless they are both included, therapy will create conflict and confusion even where this may not be already in evidence (Skynner, 1971).

One family known to me were considerably helped through the steps taken by the therapist to ensure that a reluctant father (separated but maintaining contact with some of his children) was present at the initial session. In order that this could be possible, the therapist first met with the father and his current co-habitee and helped them to understand why the request was being made. In this instance, the letter had to be carefully worded and the co-operation of the mother and the referrer gained.

Initial communication can also be made by telephone: to get permission to invite a separated or divorced parent and ensure that the reasons for suggesting this are fully understood; to arrange the first appointment and discuss who of importance in the family should attend; or to talk with a reluctant member where this is known about from prior information.

C.   Case Examples

This method worked well with the "J" family who were referred by an E.W.O. when their 14-year-old daughter was refusing to attend school. The E.W.O. reported that Mr J was unlikely to attend (information given by Mrs J); he believed that his daughter, Betty was the problem and should be seen. The therapist telephoned the home and spoke with Mrs J to whom he offered an appointment while at the same time explaining that he would want to see the whole family. He asked who would be coming and whether they would find it helpful to have an appointment card or letter in order to have time off from work or school. This conversation, relaxed and friendly but also enquiring, allowed the opportunity for Mrs J to talk about her husband's doubts about therapeutic help, and his unwillingness to be involved in any way. The therapist expressed his wish to speak with Mr J and enquired about a convenient time to ring him, having first gained Mrs J's agreement. When Mr J was contacted, the importance of his contribution in the understanding of his daughter's difficulties was stressed and when he continued to prevaricate, the therapist said firmly that he expected Mr J would want to take his share of the responsibility in any decisions concerning his daughter. The therapist's expectations of the importance of Mr J being present were evident throughout the telephone conversation, and days and times when he could arrange to take time from work were discussed.

With another family, some considerable work was done by the therapist on the telephone before they were seen. The G.P. for the "P" family telephoned the hospital family therapy department to request an urgent appointment for a 14-year-old patient whom he considered to be seriously disturbed and a possible suicide risk. The boy's mother had been to see him to tell of her concern and described some worrying behaviour. The therapist rang the boy's home to offer an early appointment to which all the family were asked to attend, and the mother with whom he spoke, accepted. Some hours later Mr P telephoned to cancel the appointment saying that he had spoken with his son and there was no need for further intervention. Thereafter followed several calls from each parent in turn, Mrs P asking for an appointment, and Mr P cancelling. The therapist then spoke to each parent in turn saying that they would need to talk together and agree whether or not there was a problem, and that if they agreed there was, she could arrange to see them. The G.P. was informed of the situation.

Some days later, the school asked the parents to a meeting to discuss their son's continuous truancy and difficult behaviour in school. During the course of the interview, referral to a Child Guidance Clinic was suggested, whereupon Mrs P revealed the situation concerning the hospital appointments, and the disagreement between she and her husband. This led to the school stressing the importance of Mr P's involvement, and urging both parents to telephone and speak with the therapist with whom they had already had some contact.

Some therapists have expressed doubts about using the telephone in this way, particularly before they have met with a family in person, but where there is sufficient information to indicate that a telephone conversation may be helpful, it has been found to be very effective (Coppersmith, 1980). When members of a family are required to take time from their employment, it may be helpful to give some indication of the length of time they are likely to be in a session. This can be particularly helpful when the family are attending a hospital for the expectation may well be that of having to spend a long time waiting to be seen.

D.   Practical Preparations

Next, therapists must address themselves to the practical preparations necessary for the initial assessment session. This should include a room with the appropriate number of chairs arranged in a circle so that communications can be seen and heard by all. In addition, a low table and play materials for young children should be placed in the centre of the circle of chairs to ensure that the children's play can be observed. Materials are important and should be appropriate to the ages of the children, yet not likely to be intrusive. Plasticine, crayons, coloured pencils and paper are perhaps the most popular and the least noisy! For younger children, a small box of miniature dolls, farm and zoo animals, etc. may be useful.

E.   Therapist's Personal Preparation

Finally, the therapist's own preparation will need to include an adequate space of time for thinking about the task ahead. Depending upon style of working, a preliminary hypothesis may need to be thought out, or a decision about a technical approach in relationship to a particular symptom or age of family members. If a co-therapist is to be used, time will be needed for both therapists to talk together about the family they plan to meet, and the manner in which they aim to work. It may also be necessary to make arrangements for supervision, and if a one-way screen is to be used, it will be important to ensure that therapists, supervisor, rooms and equipment are all available at the time planned for the family session. This is stating the obvious, but in the experience of myself and numerous other colleagues, the minute details of preparation are not infrequently overlooked until a late stage so that the therapist arrives at the scene of action with tensions additional to those inherent in the prospect of meeting a family for an initial session.

F. Introduction to Family Therapy Notions

With the arrival of the family, the therapist now faces the task of introducing them to the notion of family therapy (Franklin and Proesky, 1973; Haley, 1976; Stierlin *et al.*, 1981). Again this depends on the way the therapist works, whether "close" to the family or taking a more "distant" position (Minuchin, 1981).

Despite "good enough" preparation, it is possible that the family will have failed to all come together. In this case, it may be worth enquiring about this before taking the family to the room in which they will be seen and waiting for latecomers to arrive. If on the other hand, it is evident that important family members are not intending to come, the therapist will have to decide how this should be handled, and whether the initial session should be focussed on why the member has not come, and how he or she can be encouraged to attend the next session, or whether to work with the subsystem present.

Once seated in the room where the session is to take place, the next step is for the therapist to introduce him or herself. Then, if each member of the family is encouraged to introduce themself, not only may this throw light on how the family functions, but it can give the therapist the opportunity of indicating that he is beginning to understand this . . . "does your mum always like to help you by telling people your name?". Taking trouble to find out how each member wants to be known can help to relieve tension, and again indicates the therapist's wish to be attentive to everyone . . . "do you like to be called Mrs Smith, or do you have another name you'd like me to use?" if the family all wish to be known by their christian names, the therapist must decide about his or her own name. If you are quite clear about how you wish to be addressed, there is no problem, but on the other hand, you may prefer to give the family the choice. Having introduced yourself as "Bill Jones" initially, you can, after learning the family's names, ask . . . "What would you like to call me: Bill or Mr Jones? What would help you to feel most comfortable?" However you undertake this, it is important that everyone is clear about how they wish to be addressed.

The therapist may quickly discover that the family have come with the idea of presenting one of their members as the patient or problem, and skill will be needed in dealing with this. "Engaging with the family", "joining", "accommodating": these are some of the current terms used to describe this process (Minuchin, 1974, 1981).

Some therapists like to address themselves to one member (it could be the nominated patient), and to ask them to "help me to understand about your family: Who is the boss?; Do you do things together or are you all very separate?; See if you can give me a picture of the kind of family you are", and so on. Alternatively, they may ask one member to introduce the rest: "I'd like to get to know you and your family: Can you tell me who everyone is". Whatever opening comments are made are an attempt to convey the therapists' interest in the family as a whole.

Some families will rush to point out that "we've come because of Johnny", and then it can be helpful to ask Johnny whether he knows what they mean, and then to invite him to check out by asking his family directly. Generalized terms ("He's always difficult") should not be acceptable, and in such a discussion detail must be insisted upon: "Johnny, can you find out what your mum means when she says you are a problem"; or "Mrs T, how can Johnny help you to understand what he means when he says you always go on at him. See if you can get him to explain more fully". It is not unusual for family members to wrongly assume that they are talking about the same thing, and this method can lead to the opening up of an area of disagreement between family members allowing the therapist to learn something about the process of communication in the family.

However the beginning of a session is undertaken, whatever technique or approach the therapist may choose, the task is clearly that initially, the therapist must join the family, and in so doing must also introduce the notion that it is the family as a whole who are the focus of the session.

REFERENCES

Coppersmith, E. (1980). Expanding the uses of the telephone in family therapy. *Family Process*, **19**, 411-417.

Franklin, P. and Prosky, P. (1973). A standardized initial interview. *In* "Techniques of Family Psychotherapy A Primer", (D. Bloch, ed.), Grune & Stratton, New York.

Haley, J. (1976). "Problem Solving Therapy", Jossey-Bass, San Francisco.

Hornby, S. (1979). Collaboration—a report of an interagency consultation. (to be published).

Menzies, I. E. P. (1970). "The functioning of social systems as a defence against anxiety", London, Tavistock Institute of Human Relations.

Minuchin, S. (1974). "Families and Family Therapy", Harvard University Press, Cambridge, Mass.

Minuchin, S. and Fishman, H. C. (1981). "Family Therapy Techniques", Harvard University Press, Cambridge, Mass.

Seebohm Report (1968). Report of the Committee on Local Authority and Allied Personal Social Services. H.M.S.O., London.

Skynner, A. C. R. (1971). The Minimum Sufficient Network. *Social Work Today*, **2**, 9.3.

Stierlin, H., Rucker-Embden, I., Wetzel, N. and Wirsching, M. (1980). "The First Interview with the Family", Brunner/Mazel, New York.

Chapter 6

Initial Work
with the Family

G. Gorell Barnes

I. INTRODUCTION

Beginning work with a new family is always accompanied by a small surge of anxiety. On each occasion there is uncertainty about whether a claim to professional understanding and skill as vested in the therapist by his setting, and the expectations of those referring to him, will be justified. Although he may have had something to offer a family yesterday, or earlier in the same day, this new group may present themselves in ways that leave him newly helpless and wondering how to proceed. Therapists have developed many devices, and familiar routines to help them through this difficult period of joining with the family, and some of these will be recorded in this chapter; but there is a necessary uncertainty in each therapeutic encounter which is an essential aspect of exploration. Without this professional alertness, he is not fully tuned to a difference in information between this family system and others with which he is already familiar.

A. Initial Approaches

For the majority of those working with families regularly, there is now some agreement that certain sorts of beginning are more productive than others. Within the treatment setting created by therapist sitting down with family, there are processes that facilitate the family's capacity to work on their own anxiety; that help them begin to define why they think they have come or sought outside intervention (or face the reality of why it has been imposed upon them by law), and that are more likely to help them begin to do some work on this between them, with the outside agency of the therapist. There are, however, distinct divergencies between theoretical approaches to subsequent therapy with families related to the level at which the therapist chooses to intervene in the family system. Some of these differences in approach and their implications for engagement are discussed below.

B. The Problem in Context

A therapist who invites a family to see him has, for the purpose of that interview, committed himself to an approach to problem solving in which the person

Family Therapy
ISBN: 0-12-089355-X

expressing the problem is interviewed within his primary social group. The therapist is availing himself of the opportunity to observe the problem in the context of the social situation which will largely be contributing to maintaining it. He may not as yet have committed himself to continuing with the whole group, since he may feel that professional intervention to bring about change will not be best offered in this way. But recognize it or not, he is beginning on the process of acknowledging that change will involve everyone. In this country, a greater proportion of professionals see families for first interviews than continue to work with them as a group (Gorell Barnes, 1980a) since nearly all therapy takes place within contexts that believe in offering a variety of professional interventions to the families they see. These other interventions and forms of treatment are however increasingly considered within the context of the family as a whole (see Roberts, Chapter 7).

II. INITIAL WORK: THE PLACE

A. The Home Interview

A very high proportion of first interview family work takes place within the family's own home, and yet this is little discussed. Bloch (1973) discussed the clinical home visit in a detailed way that reads strangely to those English professionals accustomed to conducting much of their work in the home. Exactly because he uses visits so purposively, he highlights many of those potential aspects of making a visit to the home that can easily go unconsidered. These include a tour of all areas of the house, including those not normally on show; consideration of contrast between public and private areas of the house; the assessment of emotional exchange through the serving of food; a considered view of the style and management of family space. Lindsey (1979), Cade and Southgate (1979) and Clarke (1980) have each written about family work in the home setting in this country. Lindsey in particular has emphasized the importance of establishing a setting which makes clear to all the members of the family that the purpose of the visit is for therapeutic work to be done. She emphasizes the importance of the workers' belief in their own authority and right to be there as essential to making the family take proposed work seriously, and comments that she neither sits down, nor starts the interview until all who are expected to be there are present.

Other problems commonly found on home visits include television, acceptance of hospitality, and seating arrangements. Each worker must make their own decision about whether they will work with the TV or not; but a statement such as, "Please turn it off because I can't work when it's on", emphasizes that the interview has a purpose. Similarly, cups of tea can be deferred with a suggestion that work be done first, postponing rather than rejecting offered hospitality. It is important that the worker finds a chair from which they can see all members of the family and they may have to settle for a small hard back chair, rather than an offered corner on a low sofa between the dog and the wall.

The use of pets and toys can be important information during the interview, so it may be necessary to emphasize that everything is available for comment during the time the worker is there. Children or adolescents will therefore not be allowed to skip out unnoticed during the session. I make my personal boundary for behaviour the door of the room, since I have started interviews with mother ironing, father reading the paper, eldest daughter dressmaking, middle daughter drying her hair and youngest daughter playing in a corner with the cat. The work of the early part of the session then became the involvement of the family in listening to each other and to me (see also Byng-Hall, Chapter 19, Vol. 2).

B. The Agency Interview

An interview will start better if the therapist feels he is providing a reasonably comfortable environment for the family to be in. However, he does not want to create envy by having it too comfortable, nor curiosity by having it too personal. Problems of luxurious furnishings are unlikely to be affecting many people in the health or social services in Britain today, but too personal a style in the room should also be avoided. It is unsatisfactory for family work to be attempted in rooms that are too small for the right number of chairs to be included, in addition to containing a small table to have some toys or drawing material for younger children who will get restless without things other than "words" to relate to. Most agencies are able to provide at least one room which can be seen as a family or group room, in which adequate furniture is available for both purposes. It helps to have a large cardboard box labelled with the family name into which any drawings, or other offerings can be put, along with small toys or plasticine models which are kept safe between sessions. Children of all ages, as well as adults seem to enjoy plasticine. Felt tip pens and sheets of paper are useful.

III. INITIAL WORK: WHO COMES

A. Who is the Family?

Who comes to the first interview and who does not come is always of interest. Why does mother turn up with her own mother and not her husband? Why does a younger sister decide that her imminent exam is more important than her sister's threatened attempt at suicide, when her parents feel the case is too serious for them to delay the appointment until the following week when she could also come? Why do two parents refuse to bring their teenage children until they have "sniffed out" the "family" therapist, although they have been taking them to different hospital paediatric departments for the last seven years? Why does a mother whose son has been taken into care and whose daughter has been expelled from five schools insist that she has to carry the problem alone and that father cannot be involved because his job is too responsible? Why does a wife refer her first husband and girlfriend, her second husband and son and herself for help, and be the only one not to turn up at the arranged time? These are all questions that will involve us in understanding each different system the problem is lodged within, and the meaning of the symptom to each person in the system as well as to the system as a whole. My personal approach is to see whoever turns up, rather than insisting on whole family arrival, since if the preparatory work has been properly done, this is itself information about the way this family operate in relation to the outside world. The meaning of the absences and the absent members of the system always needs to be borne in mind during the interview, since it is in itself a communication that may be important. In this following extract, the inexperienced therapist is trying to focus on the meaning of the father's absence and is floundering in the face of the united solidarity of the three generational system of the women of the family.

B.   Case Example

Extract 1: Mother, maternal grandmother, Brenda (14, I.P.) Paul (3)

MGM: Well he's been bullying her and ignoring her because she's not conforming.

Therapist: Tell me about Bill, why isn't he here.

Mother: Well, his job is important.

Therapist: You obviously don't think that's why he's not here.

MGM: (Shakes head sadly) He's not mature enough love, look I'll tell you what, he's got thousands in the bank and he won't buy himself new clothes. They have their food and he makes sure they have their £40 every month, but we buy in between—*I* do. Doreen hasn't had new clothes—she's had that coat three years—You couldn't go to Bill for help, he needs help himself in my opinion. (3-year-old son of Bill and Doreen bashes radiator loudly during this.)

Therapist: Is that why you think he isn't here.

MGM: He's not here because you can't tell him and you can't tell him lots of things.

Mother: (simultaneously) Because he's at work.

Therapist: I know he's at work but I wrote to both of you offering to make a time when he could come. Did he read the letter?

Mother: No, well to tell you the truth I didn't show it to him.

MGM: No, nor would I. Not Bill.

Mother: He would have gone mad.

MGM: Well, we don't know if he would have gone mad.

Mother: When the headmistress told us we should take Brenda to the Clinic he said yes, he would come.

Therapist: Then why didn't you show him the letter. Does he act for Brenda as her father—I'm not clear what happened to her own father.

MGM: Oh well, Doreen divorced him, he was no good for her, she'd known him as a child and she said, "I'm going to marry him", and I said I'd never interfere with my kids and I didn't. And what he wanted was a mother—he loved me—he needed my help.

Therapist: You're telling me now your daughter has married two men who need help — (looks to Brenda who is now giggling) is that right — you've a strong nan there Brenda (patting MGM — all laugh — youngest son stops bashing radiator and joins group).

C. Comment

In this extract it is only when the therapist temporarily "joins" the system by acknowledging the strength of the grandmother that she begins to make headway. In this family it became clear that the two independently powerful systems, that of maternal grandmother, daughter and granddaughter, and that of husband-wife-children could not meet in the same room. In order to begin work with the family that took primary responsibility for the children, it was first necessary to work with and make a boundary between the family of primary responsibility and the family to which the children ran away when things got too hot: their "dear hardworking nan" and her co-habitee.

The question of who to define as the family and who to work with in the system is never fixed, and will relate to any one person's "style" of therapy and theory of change. Since I have always worked in a setting where the parents or their surrogates appointed by law are legally responsible for the welfare of dependent children, I find a minimal systems boundary definition helpful. I work with those legally responsible as well as those actually taking care of the child referred. This often means that social workers and residential workers will be present as part of the family system. Further criteria that I use, in deciding who to work with relate to the age and stage of the children, their current developmental needs, and who may need to be brought into the therapy to see that these are being attended to. I emphasize this since if the successful development of the children is the focus of the therapist's rational attention in irrational or unconventional family systems, it helps the therapist to focus on "who should be there" (Bentovim and Gilmour, 1981; Bentovim, Chapter 28). Are the parents able to treat their children in a manner that appears to recognize the age they are at and the stage they are at? Are the children being used to look after their parents' needs in ways that are grossly inappropriate, by caring for them physically; or in terms of need for emotional companionship, or sexual titillation? Are children being asked to perform tasks that are wholly unsuitable for their age and abilities? If the parents are confused, and confusing their children in this way, who is acting to give the parenting instead? (Rutter, 1974; Gorell Barnes, 1978). Outside agencies often need to be involved as part of the process of helping the family face these issues in cases of gross distortion.

IV. DEFINING THE FAMILY

A. What is a Family?

What the "family" system is will to some extent be defined, by what the functions of the agency, carrying out its meta-parental role on behalf of society through the welfare state require it to be. In general, a family is a unit of more than one generation, although sibling sub-groups have been the focus of therapeutic work. In some families, the system requiring attention will be a man, a woman and some children, but increasingly different varieties of family structure present for help. Many families will have only one parent, although an essential part of the family system will be the person or group to whom mother or father turn for support and confirmation of their own adult capabilities, as well as for sexual needs. These partners may be either male or female. We are relatively unknowledgeable as yet in this country in attending to the family structures of homosexual couples and the ensuing problems (Lowenstein, 1980) that may develop in the child. For example, in a family where the nominal parents are a white lesbian couple, the children are all West Indian boys, and there are additional issues of cross generation coupling and sexual attraction. Here, it seems particularly important to be linking intervention to the developmental needs of the children and things that any *parent*, regardless of their sex, has to be able to do on behalf of a *child* of a particular age and stage in order to help the family discover what they can do as a healthy parent-and-child unit; rather than the worker setting up unrealistic goals of achieving "normality" which fail. Hopefully whatever the nature of the sexual relationship, the single parent will be relating to other adults who confirm her sense of identity in an age-appropriate way for herself; since many of the problems arising from single parent families relate to the crossing of generation boundaries to the disadvantage of the children. Sometimes the parent herself is infantilized by her own parents who insist on keeping her in their own "parent-to-child" relationship when she needs her adult identity to be confirmed, in which case three generational work will be needed at some stage.

B.   Step Families: a Case Example

The question of who should attend is often particularly complex in step families. Many step families use the help of professionals to sort out the problems of being a "second" family. Clarifying which of those in the former families need to attend in relation to the presenting problems may be an essential part of the first interview. I have focussed on this in some detail in the extract below.

The family is composed of husband and wife and three children, two from previous different families. The children have been invited to come on behalf of Vivian, mother to two children and stepmother to the two others in the household they all lived in most of the week. She has been severely depressed for two months and has ceased to care for the house at all following an attempt to leave with Sam, her lover. The therapist is trying to establish who should be there to work on the problems the family are bringing. The eldest girl has refused to come, but the other three children, who are father's son, mother's daughter and Jo, son of this marriage, are present; one child representing each of three marriages. The therapist is discussing the absence of one member, Sue aged 18, father's daughter and the eldest child in the combined sibling group.

Extract 2

Therapist: So Sue didn't think it would "help" — what is it she didn't think it would help?

Father: The situation between Vivian and I.

Therapist: I invited all the children to come today because there were several things I thought as a family unit you might want to think about.

Father: (frames Sue's absence in terms of her moving away from the family appropriate at her age)

Vivien: (cross) That's got nothing to do with it, if she didn't want to come, she didn't want to come.

Therapist: (to father) but Sue is one of the people *you* saw as very concerned and important to the family.

Vivien: (cutting in) Yes, but I think she saw this as a very private thing.

Therapist: Well it may be that that is how all the children see it — do you know what we are talking about Jo?

Jo (7): (shakes head)

Therapist: Well I don't think we should talk about things you don't understand — why did you think you had come here today?

Jo: (squeaking): I didn't know.

Therapist: Ask one of the others to help you.

Father: Yes, you did know Jo.

David (13): I told you in the kitchen when doing washing up.

Jo: I know; I've forgotten.

Therapist: David can you help Jo out?

David: Well Vivien and Dad are coming here to try and solve their problems.

Therapist: You see it as problems between Viv and Dad as well, do you?

David: I'm not sure.

Therapist: Janet what do you think?

Janet (14): I don't know either.

Therapist: But you see things going on at home.

Janet: Arguments.

Vivien: You do know really, it's alright you *can* say.

Janet: I don't really know it's so muddling.

Therapist: I don't *really* know either, which is one reason why we are meeting together to try and sort out what it is that's not working in the family.

Jo: Well, there's a man called Sam who tries to take mummy away from daddy.

Therapist: I see — and did that make you feel unhappy?

Jo: Yes.

Therapist: I see — and now Mummy's come back.

Jo: Yes, but they are *still* arguing.

Therapist: What happens when they argue Jo?

Jo: I don't know — I go away — I go with David or Janet.

Therapist: That sounds good, so you children all go somewhere and keep out of it.

Jo: Yes, normally in the kitchen eating food.

Vivien: (tries to minimize) "not always eating".

Jo: (emphatically) Yes we were, last time we were eating CARROTS.

(Therapist finds out more about how different children respond to "rows" in the family)

Therapist: David, you've been through some upsets before you came to live with Dad.

Did you know about that Jo?

(Jo denies) (He recounts his knowledge of the process of David joining family)

First Sue came to live here and went to school with Janet and then David came.

Therapist: Why was that David?

David: I didn't like school.

Therapist: I see. I thought it was also related to something that happened at your other house.

David: Yes, I took an overdose.

Therapist: Uh huh, what does that mean exactly, do you know what an overdose is, Jo?

Jo: No.

Therapist: Could you ask David?

Jo: What's an overdose David?

David: I took too many pills.

Jo: (interested) Oh and did they take you to hospital?

David: (very brief nod)

Therapist: Did you know about that Janet?

Janet: Yes

Therapist: Do you think it's right to know something about why he did it or do you think that's his business?

Janet: His business. I'm not really involved in David's business. (David is not any blood relation to Janet being her stepfather's son by his first marriage.)

Therapist: I see are you saying you like to keep yourself separate and he also can do this.

Janet: I suppose so, but we get on very well when together.

Therapist: Of course you also lived in another family before too.

Jo: She used to live with her nanny.

Therapist: When did you join *this* family?

Janet: A long time ago — I've been here for years.

Therapist: That's one thing you all have to manage in this family — that is the three families that are part of your present family.

Jo: What's that.

David: It's not the same for you Jo 'cos you only live in one.

Therapist: Can you explain that David, because Jo is very good at understanding.

David: You actually live with your *real* Mum and your *real* Dad which Janet does not and I don't, but also we have got our real mums and real dads which is a separate family. As you know I go home to see mum every weekend, and sometimes Janet goes to see her father and her nan.

C. Comment

In this extract we can see the therapist tracking the content, getting to know the family issues, and finding out something about the complex family patterns and the way family members function under stress, both in this present family and the other families they visit regularly. In such a complex family, it is important to bear the larger system which is *four* families not *one* in mind, and to see how these other three families (the ecostructure for the presenting family) interconnect. However, the focus for the therapeutic work has to be clearly defined and maintained so that it is the family who are coming that are worked with, rather than the three that are absent, which could be an evasion from what *was presenting* in the focal parent child unit.

V. INITIAL MOVES

A. Opening the Session: Theoretical Viewpoints

For many family therapists, questions of where they will do the work and who they are going to work with in the family relates to the theory of systemic change that they believe in. My ideas about change in systems, usually defined in family therapy as structural or strategic work, are linked to Bateson's ideas about levels of learning in systems (Bateson, 1964).

(1) A structural approach to change through work with sub-systems in the family can be seen as Learning II: *"A change in how the sequence of experience is punctuated"*, whereas

(2) a whole system strategic approach can be as a change at Level III; *"A corrective change in the system of sets of alternatives from which choice is made"*, (Gorell Barnes and Campbell, 1982).

Working at either of these two levels of change would be related to different ideas about the therapist's use of himself and the setting he is in.

B. Structural and Strategic Approaches

These levels can be loosely related to styles of work known as structural and strategic. As there are many ways of defining structural and strategic work, the following brief definition must be taken as personal and arbitrary. Structural work in practice addresses itself to change in family systems through the minutiae of interactions manifested in sub-system sequences. These sequences, in operation from the moment a child is born into a family (Stern, 1977), generate certain characteristics of the self. In rigid systems, or at time of crisis when a normally more flexible system rigifies, homeostasis prevents the discovery of new pathways to problem solving. A change created within a sub-systemic loop in the system will, however, spread and if properly focussed and intensified will make an impact on the system as a whole. Working in this way the therapist gets close to the family, uses many of their words and movements, and while maintaining necessary distance works within the systemic style that presents. This kind of work fits well with home as well as professional environments.

Strategic work may equally address itself to sub-systems, since all intervention is a form of strategy and can be directed towards creating learning in a system at level II or level III, but as I am using the term here, I am considering work that is primarily aimed at creating a change in the rules that govern the system as a whole. Such work aims at a transformation of the overall contexts within which the family views their situations (that they can see the frog as a potential prince rather than as a better class of frog) (Gorell Barnes and Campbell, 1981 in press). The therapist addresses himself then to change at Bateson's level III, aiming to change the frame of the rules governing the second-level behaviours. Working in this style, the therapist maintains professional neutrality and distance from the family in a manner more akin to analytic practice and often works with colleagues behind a screen; who help him make interventions that address the system as a whole rather than the individual or sub-systems within it (Palazzoli et al., 1978). Work of this kind would be difficult to transfer to a home setting. However, there is in addition a style of strategic work that combines elements of both these approaches and that cheerfully moves levels within and between sessions. This style has developed through the Palo Alto group in California (Watzlawick, 1967, 1974; Haley, 1963; Madanes, 1980), and has been extensively developed by the Family Institute, Cardiff, in this country in both clinical and home settings (Cade, 1979; Gorell Barnes, 1982a, b).

C. Opening the Session-Practical Issues

Whichever style of addressing the system the therapist chooses, there are certain areas of family behaviour and family functioning he will want to attend to. Most family therapists prefer to dispel the anxiety to do with the setting itself in order to concentrate on the purpose for which the family have come. Preliminary courtesies are part of therapeutic work. There should be enquiry as to whether everyone knows why they are here today, personal contact with each family member to find out about their anticipations in coming to a family interview; discussion of neutral topics such as schools and work, clarification of family names and ages, and forms of address (see Roberts, chapter 7).

In the course of this process which different schools of theory give different names, the therapist has the chance to begin to learn about the relationships between family members, as well as demonstrating by his manner his respect for the family. He begins to assess their mood and pace. Is it appropriate to the occasion?: too angry, sad or hilarious? How do the parents treat the children, and how do the children respond to the requests of the parents? Do the family present a united front . . . if not, who looks at whom before speaking and who disagrees? Who sits next to whom is used as information by all therapists and commented on by some. In all his noting of the process, the therapist has to maintain an open mind about the meaning of the information.

Although he begins clocking up detail from the beginning, he is not in a position to use that valuably on behalf of the family until he has a greater overall view. He may or may not wish to use his observation for the family to change the rules of behaviour in the session: "I notice that you always look at your mother when you speak . . . in this time we are together I want you to speak for yourself . . ." This decision to change family rules, to intervene during the session, will of course depend on the style and theoretical frame of the therapist. However in general, in the first half of the session, it is of greater value to understand and observe accurately the rules of the family system than to be intent on creating new ones for the therapy. In some families, however, the problem is stated from the moment the family sit down in the room, as when a mother tells her 17-year-old son to take off his coat because the room is warm. It will be the therapist's choice about whether he makes the material the focus of his professional attention, and uses that issue as part of the joining process ("Well, Sam, I can see you have a mother who takes good care of you, does she always worry about you as well as that?") or whether he prefers to distinguish between a "hello" stage and a problem-focussed stage.

D. Slowing Down

Some families would not allow such a distinction, and the therapist has to slow them down enough to begin to keep himself and what he can offer separate from the huge network of professionals and expected solutions the family have already come to rely on.

> Well we're here today because my probation officer said you could help with Mandy's appeal; and when I told my general practitioner he said why not go and see if they can help her and it might do my depression good too. The psychologist at the school was very helpful to Mark although I didn't like the type of child at the school he recommended, and so I thought I'd ask you while I was here if you could help on that one as well, as the headmaster said well if you can get the clinic to support you it might pull some weight at County Hall.

In these moments when the therapist is about to go under, some distancing tactics are necessary. Commending mother on the speed and detail with which she has opened the session, but placing oneself in the position of the slow-witted outsider who needs more time to understand what is going on, is one way of putting on brakes; another might be to admire the teenage daughter Mandy's shoes and ask her if she bought these for herself. This could be used to repunctuate the stream of experience so that the topic could be broached from a different stance. Alternatively, the therapist could use this opening statement of mother's as the focus for further information gathering; trying to elicit difference in the family's perception of the problem by taking one aspect of the problem and asking one member of the family who between two other members is most anxious about it. However he proceeds, he will want to keep the details of his information precise and put it together piece by piece so that the family follow him as he proceeds.

VI. DEFINING THE PROBLEM

A. Sharpening the Focus

The therapist may find there is difficulty in getting to a problem. He may see the family busy chatting away in the *manner* of those presenting a problem and find himself concerned at the apparent ease with which they quarrel, complain and present material for him to work with. In these circumstances, to express bewilderment or curiosity about his own experience of the interview can be a very valuable way of learning more about the family dysfunction. For example, in a recent session where father and son were arguing vigorously about whether the boy looked after his dog and took him out for walks often enough, the therapist said, "I find I am anxious that in showing us how well you can worry about your dog, you will leave without having really shared with us your worries about each other". In another session with a different family bringing problems of uncontrolled violence in a teenage daughter, the therapist congratulated the parents on their ability to allow the young members of the family equal say on every topic but wondered if this was allowing *them* proper space in the session to express their concern as *parents* on behalf of their children.

B. A Problem-centred Approach

In the extract below, the referred child is approached in the general context of a family and an area of skill which is seen as problematic by the family. The therapist is finding a way of joining the family while retaining neutrality, in a way that leaves her sufficiently comfortable to start noticing the anxieties and reactions of the family; the point of the first few minutes is not for the family to admire the therapist's technique. The therapist begins with the youngest child who is not the referred patient, and moves on to meet other family members from there. From the beginning, the family's own commonsense and awareness in relation to different areas of the information they are bringing is emphasized and restated to them, often with a slight reframing of the context to increase the opportunities for perceiving the problem in a different way. Issues such as age and sex can be highlighted to underline children's sense of competence. To an older sibling anticipating being in the hot seat, it is reassuring to have his additional two-years' wisdom pointed out by the therapist as an asset in approaching the anxieties about school which a younger child is voicing, and to be asked his views on how these anxieties might be handled in the light of his own experience. Similarly, a same-sex sibling can be brought in on the grounds of "special understanding" of a parent or another child, or a younger child can be used to teach an older child or a parent about ways of "reaching" a parent. While the therapist will always need to be sensitive not to violate the accustomed hierarchy of the family too early, he can nonetheless make it clear that each person present has something of value to contribute about how the family operate in their daily lives, and therefore potentially about how a problem is to be solved.

In this beginning sequence, the therapist is focussing on the difficulties the children are having to the exclusion of other aspects of the family and its functioning, because the parents had presented in a crisis around the issue of reading and the violence it provoked between mother and son. Exploring more positive or resourceful aspects of the family are delayed until later in the interview. However, while impressing the parents with the fact that the problem is being taken seriously, it does not free the children to participate and the therapist has to be prepared to sit with that polarized discomfort.

C.   A Problem-focussed Beginning

Therapist: [non-specific] [to parents] I've heard a bit about the problem from Mrs Smith [E.W.O.] and I thought it would be useful to meet as a family; no one has ever met you two girls and when something like this has been going on in a family for some time everyone has usually got something to say about it.
    [to girls]—I don't know your names. [to youngest] You're . . . ?
Catherine: Catherine
Therapist: Catherine, and you're how old? Let's see now.
Catherine: Seven
Therapist: Seven, and which school do you go to?
Catherine: St Veronica's
Therapist: Is that the same school as Patrick? [Here therapist assumes naïve role of one who knows less about school system than children, so that they can tell her all about it, confirming them as experts in their own field.]
Catherine: No he's moved onto the big school now.
Therapist: So where does he go to school then? [remembering to talk directly to him rather than about him] Where do you go to school Patrick?
Patrick: St Christopher's
Therapist: What sort of school is that: girls and boys or just boys?
Patrick: Just boys.
Therapist: And was it difficult moving on from St Veronica's? [Attempt to be sympathetic too early is poor move to get child at ease.]
Patrick: [squeaky] Not much.
Therapist: Did you have to do much more work in your secondary school?
Patrick: Yes
Therapist: And is it more difficult?
Patrick: Yes much more.
Therapist: Is the reading more difficult?
Patrick: Yeah
Therapist: Uh huh: That's tough. How's the reading for you, Catherine?
Catherine: All right, sort of.
Therapist: Are you just starting to read?
Catherine: [nods and kicks her feet.]
Therapist: Can you read a little bit?
Catherine: [shakes her head.]

Therapist: Are you finding it quite difficult as well as Patrick?

Catherine: [nods vigorously.]

Therapist: Yes it *can* be difficult, words look very funny sometimes I think . . . How about you, what's your name?

Angela: Angela.

Therapist: And you're . . . how old?

Angela: Ten

Therapist: Ten—what's your name, Angela—and Patrick you're 14—and Catherine you're seven. Which school do you go to, Angela?

Angela: St Catherine's

Therapist: And how's reading for you—are you a good reader?

Angela: [nods and looks pleased.]

Therapist: Ah, you're a good reader are you—[looks at parents] is she a good reader for the family?

Father: Yes, she's the one, she's the one that can do the reading for us all.

Therapist: Uh huh, I see, you're a good reader—well that must be quite difficult for Patrick and for Catherine. That must be tough, Patrick, having a 10-year-old sister who can read so well (a mistake as he can only disagree to save his pride here).

Patrick: [squeaks] No, I just ignore it.

Therapist: [realizes mistake, laughs] Well *I* would find it tough, I bet it's difficult to ignore it sometimes.

Patrick: [relaxes six inches.]

Therapist: Well who else worries about reading in the family?

Mother: Well we do—Mum and Dad—we get very het up.

Therapist: Mum and Dad—mmm. What sort of effect does it have on you all when Mum and Dad are worrying about reading? It must have quite an effect on you all when they get so bothered about it.

D.   Family Members as Expert Witnesses

The use of family members as experts on the detail of their own problems, and eliciting of this detail, is a way of breaking down the process of the interview into manageable sequences which is particularly valuable with young children. In the following extract of a family where the 13-year-old is creating havoc in the class at school and on the point of exclusion the children have been led to discuss the process of disagreement *in the family* and the therapist is helping them track some of the detail that lies behind the presenting problem.

Therapist: I don't know much about the detail of this but I gather the school is complaining. What are they complaining about, Pearl?

Pearl (13): I don't go to maths and I don't like French. I don't do my homework.

Therapist: [repeats] You don't go to maths, you don't like French and you don't do your homework . . . uh huh, and is there anything else?

Pearl: Well I do work, but I sometimes make trouble.

Therapist: In what way do you sometimes make trouble?

Pearl: Well I sit and I don't do what the teacher tells me and I'm rude to the teachers.

Therapist: I see. Are you rude to your parents?

Pearl: Yeah

Therapist: Which one are you rudest to?

Pearl: My Dad.

Therapist: You're rudest to your Dad. Why are you rude to him?

Pearl: Because he shouts at me.

Therapist: Tell me something more about your dad; what is it that makes you want to be rude to him?

Pearl: Well when there's been trouble with my sister and mother, he always takes their side.

Therapist: He doesn't listen to *you* then?

Pearl: Well he will listen to my mum more than he'll listen to me but he listens to Babsie most of all.

VII.   MIDDLE STAGES

A.   Focussing and Clarifying

To illustrate the issues of the middle stages of the initial interview, I will continue with the same family. Later in the session, the therapist is trying to make the children sort out and agree on their reality in such a way that they can do some work on it in an age-appropriate manner.

Therapist: Well make sure that's what she's trying to say.

Pearl: I think that's what she's trying to say.

Therapist: Well make sure, ask her.

Pearl: Is that what you're trying to say?

Babsie (7): No

Therapist: Are you sure that you two understand each other—let's just get straight what really happens between you two. [focusses] Now Babsie what happens when Clive comes into your room.

Babsie: If I'm doing something he comes and you know he just says "Oh you're doing that because you want to take the cat away from me", and he puts on his silly voice and then I get so annoyed.

Clive (5): Well she started it coming into *my* room.

Babsie: I didn't, silly, I didn't. You just annoy me putting on that silly voice, calling me a cissy girl and all that.

Clive: Well she started it, hitting me and sticking out her tongue like this. [makes horrible face to show T]

Therapist: Well now let's slow this down a little.

B.   Tracking the Problem

Therapist: So then the problem is you two, is that right, you have a quarrel, a fight and you run into Pearl to sort it out?

Pearl: Yeah

Therapist: Is there anything else?

Pearl: No, that's most of it.

Therapist: How does that lead you to be rude to your Dad?

Pearl: Because he says I shouldn't smack them, but I think I'm supposed to look after them when Mum is out, then they cry and they go and tell Mum when she gets back and she says I shouldn't smack them and tells Dad and he yells — and bawls me out.

Therapist: So you would like your Mum and Dad to listen more to you and less to your sister and brother. O.K. It looks as though the responsibility . . . who's in charge . . . needs sorting out here. Who would you like to discuss this with Pearl, your Mum or your Dad—which one would you like to talk to first?*

   In this last example we are moving towards the middle stage of a first session. The question of what the therapist should have achieved by the end of the session and the links he should be making to further work, will now be in his mind. The lesson we have all learnt most powerfully in our work with families has been the importance of accepting and confirming the system the family bring, however dysfunctional it appears in the therapist's eyes, and of not letting the family go away without this sense of confirmation well established. Only if they have received this somewhere along the line are they likely to accept any initiated change, to continue working in between sessions, and want to come back. Where a family have felt that their reality has been understood, accepted and confirmed as having validity in terms of the options they had open to them, it becomes possible to challenge what is dysfunctional in the system in a variety of ways. Some of these ways are the subject matter of further chapters.

C.   Contracts

Where a family is anxious or suspicious about continuing to work in an open ended way, it can be helpful for them to agree that there is as yet no way they can know whether the process of family work is of any use and to set a contract of a limited number of sessions after which a review will take place with them to see how useful they are finding it. Such a review date should be used for joint examination of what has been achieved and for the basis for a further contract if this is thought useful on both sides.

   This limiting of sessions is especially helpful for families who cannot plan very far ahead in any aspect of their lives. The power of renegotiation is very important. Where "family therapy" has been recommended as part of a court

---

*With thanks to Harry Aponte whose patient way of working with child sub-systems in families I would like to acknowledge here.

order, it is essential to plan with the magistrate (usually in the juvenile court) that the case can be brought back for review if this approach is *not* found to be useful *on either side and other plans made*. Especially where planned as part of a possible or an actual Care Order, it is important to stick to the length of the contract made since it gives both adolescent and parents a breathing space to consider further separation in a less dramatic and crisis centred way. The fixed number of sessions act as a containment for the family during which time they know they will have a third part intermediary in sorting out habitual quarrels within a different context.

There are also families who will come for therapy with a readiness to make the clinic their home and the therapist one of their family. In such cases, the therapist may find it valuable to fix a number of sessions and then review the work in order to prevent himself making a lifelong contract. However the need for contracts to provide therapist protection are likely to diminish as the experience and confidence of the therapist grows.

For many strategic therapists, the notion of a contract of more than one additional session at a time would go against the principles on which they are working. These would include the capacity of the family to change without the further interest of the therapist or therapeutic team provided the principles on which the prescriptive intervention they had formulated for the family were systemically correct. The notion of contract might be decided session by session depending on the self report of the family and the assessment of the therapist as to whether further involvement would be therapeutically valuable in achieving systemic change.

D. Tasks

Tasks are ways of giving families concrete aspects of the therapy to take home and continue themselves. These may be given in a straightforward or in a more complicated manner. In that tasks require performance, they remind the family of the therapist and whatever containment he represents to the family that makes it safe for them to risk the improbable, which is to activate a change in their habitual system. It is thus important that tasks are set with assurance within the context of the family's confidence in the overall competence of the therapy. Two kinds of task need distinguishing.

(1) Straight Tasks
Straight tasks should be directed towards changing some piece of action either within one or more subsystems in the family. If it is overtly addressed to one subsystem only, the therapist will have to warn the family of the likely consequences for the others so that they are not taken by surprise.

> If Tom does manage to make his bed every day this week and tidy his own room you, mother, are going to find yourself with time on your hands and you, father, will have to find something else for her to worry about — or you could even find her something to enjoy.

This kind of comment which addresses itself to only one small aspect of a subsystem in a very enmeshed family can be offered both as an encouraging directive, "Let's see if you can do it", where there really appears to be some willingness to change, or perhaps as a challenge which still ascribes the best intentions to the family for resisting: "I doubt if the family will be able to allow Tom to do it on his own because they are so good at worrying for their children that they will hate to let him make his own mistakes".

(2) Strategic Tasks

Strategic tasks which address themselves to the unconscious wishes of the family as well as to their conscious and declared wishes and which aim to address themselves to the rules governing the overall patterning of the family are of a greater possible complexity than can be properly covered here. They may be directed to the system as a whole with required instructions for each person's behaviour during the coming interval; they may give reasons for the requirement or they may withhold these; they may be delivered with optimism or pessimism, with humour or with the utmost gravity.

> We believe that as a family you have a latent talent for healthy arguing which is not being properly exercised. We would like it therefore if every night you sit together round the kitchen table with an alarm clock and each take ten minutes to hold forth on the topic of your choice. The others are not to interrupt but are to wait for their turn (Gorell Barnes *et al.*, 1982b).

Alternatively, there may be no general request for action, but simply a systemic message which observes the meaning of the behaviours of each member on behalf of the system as a whole, and delegates the action to one member, often the referred patient: "It will be up to Julia to find a way to lead you to success." Letters may also be sent to ensure that the task is clearly understood by the whole family with an instruction that it be "read aloud to the family at breakfast".

The sense of humour in the average English family has provided some interesting feedback on the use of these messages. What remains fascinating is the power they have if properly construed, to bring about change even in the face of open family resistance. "We had one of your funny letters last week; we agreed about the first part but the rest of it's a load of codswallop and we've been discussing it ever since . . ."

An essential feature of paradoxical work is the therapist's proper appreciation of the function of disturbed behaviours for the family system as a whole. He is therefore *unwilling* to prescribe change, respecting the family's grasp of their own safety margins. He may indeed prescribe no change: "It is very important that you two do not get any closer at the moment because the family just aren't ready to handle that; stay just that distance apart." Alternatively, he might thank the presenting patient for "keeping the family just the way they are" and ask the family to help the patient maintain their symptom, while putitng it more consciously under the patient's control for the following week: "It is important that you practice your temper for at least 15 minutes every day and you, mother, must make sure she is really taking it seriously. Tom and Father are to remind you when it's time to practise" (Gorell Barnes, 1982, a, b).

VIII. ENDING THE INITIAL WORK

It is important to end the first session with everyone agreed about when the next one is taking place. Whether this is in a week's time or a month's time, the family need to know how long they have got to digest whatever has taken place in the session. The length of time between sessions will largely depend on therapist style, choice of theoretical model, and time he has available rather than any known index of family need. A guideline is to consider how long the family can hold onto the "representation" of the therapy, or the change resulting from the session, and at what point these representations will be lost, and the system readjust to its former state, perhaps requiring another input. As yet we know little about this.

In the engagement phase of therapy, it is usually important for the gap to be small while family and therapist achieve a working alliance, but those who work primarily with paradox feel that the time span is lengthier and that at least a fortnight is needed between sessions. The therapist working with whole-system prescriptive strategy who is aiming at transformation of the overall rules of the game, would argue that if the family's view of reality has indeed been transformed, i.e. become a new entity with formal characteristics different from its predecessor, a much longer time must be allowed for the implications of this radical change in view to be carried through to the behaviours of the family members. Links with any previous view or with the person of the therapist, would be irrelevant so that a number of weeks or months might be left between appointments. The length of time, however, would be determined and stated before the prescriptive message was given, so that a date was firmly fixed in the family's mind.

Successful therapy, as we all know, is not achieved by sticking to a rule book; but each therapist has to learn the basic rules of the theories of change he is following. He can then develop his clinical judgement about appropriate procedures between him and each new family with a greater degree of confidence.

REFERENCES

Bentovim, A. and Gilmour, L. (1981). A family therapy interactional approach to decision making in child care, access and custody cases. *Family Therapy*, **3**, 65-78.

Bloch, D. (1973). The clinical home visit. *In* "Techniques of Family Psychotherapy", (D. Bloch, ed.), Grune & Stratton, New York.

Cade, B. and Southgate, P. (1979). Honesty is the best policy. *Journal of Family Therapy*, **1**, 23-32.

Cade, B. (1979). The use of Paradox in Therapy. *In* "Family and Marital Psychotherapy: A Critical Approach", (S. Walrond-Skinner, ed.), Routledge & Kegan Paul, London.

Clarke, A. (1980). (Unpublished paper), Kettering Family Centre, Northants.

Gorell Barnes, G. (1978). *In* "Good Enough Parenting", C.C.E.R.S.W. Study 1. Report of a group on work with children and young people and the implications for social work education.

Gorell Barnes, G. (1980). Family therapy in social work settings: a survey by questionnaire 1976-1978. *Journal of Family Therapy*, **2**, 357-378.

Gorell Barnes, G. (1982a). A difference that makes a difference. I. *Journal of Family Therapy*, (in press).

Gorell Barnes, G. (1982b). (With Jones, E. and de Carteret, J.) A difference that makes a difference. II. *Journal of Family Therapy*, (in press).

Gorell Barnes, G. and Campbell, D. (1982). From frog to prince: the impact of structural and strategic approaches on the supervisory process. *In Family Therapy Supervision: Recent Developments in Practice* (R. Whiffen and J. Byng-Hall, eds), Academic Press, London and New York.

Haley, J. (1963). *Strategies of Psychotherapy*. Grune & Stratton, New York.

Lindsey, C. (1979). Working with rage and anger — the establishment of a therapeutic setting in the homes of multi-problem families. *Journal of Family Therapy*, **1**, 117-124.

Lowenstein, S. (1980). Understanding lesbian women. *Social Casework: The Journal of Contemporary Social Work*.

Madanes, C. (1980). Play, paradox and pretending. *Family Process*, **19**, 73-85.

Palazzoli, M. S., Boscolo, L., Cecchini, G. and Prata, G. (1978). Paradox and Counterparadox, Aronson, New York.

Rutter, M. (1974). *Helping Troubled Children*. Penguin, Harmondsworth.

Stern, M. (1977). *The First Relationship: Infant and Mother*. Fontana Open Books, New York.

Watzlawick, P., Beavin, J. H. and Jackson, D. D. (1967). "Pragmatics of human communication", Norton, New York.

Watzlawick, P., Weakland, J. H. and Fish, R. (1974). "Change: Principles of Problem Formation and Problem Solution", Norton, New York.

Chapter 7

Maintaining Family Motivation During Treatment

A. Elton

I. INTRODUCTION

Maintaining a family in treatment presents one of the greatest therapeutic challenges. This may apply equally to a planned short-term contract as to an open-ended long-term treatment. Perhaps it would be truer to say that keeping the family involved in and working actively to change is the problem, since there are many families as well as individuals who may come compliantly to sessions, but may, once there, appear to use them to maintain the family status quo; indeed there may be families who oppose finishing treatment out of just such a need to keep things the same.

A. Some Basic Factors Motivating Families

Families who attend do have some wish to change, and many put considerable energy and much hard work into the process. Their enthusiasm and capacity to do so relates to the presence of various conditions. First, they *hope for relief* from their presenting symptom, whether that be identified by them as behaviour of an individual or as relationship problems. Many families may experience some relief of such symptoms from the outset of treatment, or even if there is no early symptoms change, they may be very reassured by having their worries and complaints listened to and taken seriously. Continued experience of relief, even if periodic, occurring through treatment keeps the family hope of change alive. Secondly, families may *be interested, even excited, in discovering new facets about their behaviour;* in doing this, possibilities of expansion in their family life may become evident. Finally, *they may actually enjoy treatment* despite the hard work they put into it (sometimes indeed because of the hard work and their own and the therapist's acknowledgement of this). Naturally such enjoyment has to be transferable and transferred to other situations if the family is to be able to stop treatment without undue anxiety.

The therapist has to bear these three needs in mind throughout treatment and meet at least one of them for much of the time. Indeed, if he cannot meet any of these needs for a prolonged period, his own motivation with that family is likely to weaken and he, too, may become hopeless. This can obviously be fatal to the treatment since its continuance and success depends on the therapist's interest and enthusiasm as much as on the family's.

Family Therapy
ISBN: 0-12-089355-X

B. Resistances

In previous chapters, a variety of therapeutic approaches have been described, all of which may be employed to help bring relief of painful symptoms, to widen the family experience, and to deepen their understanding and appreciation of each other. However, it is not enough for therapists to be skilled in techniques of change and sensitive to understanding very indirect messages about a hope for change. All therapists come up against the strong need of the family not to change: the positive resistance to any real alteration in the current situation, however painful it is. It is this resistance which makes the task of maintaining the therapeutic alliance so difficult. All families, however great and true their wish to change the painful situation which brought them into treatment, have a simultaneous and powerful wish not to experience certain changes; the very changes which may be essential to the achievement of their motivating goal.

II. RESISTANCE AND PREVENTION OF CHANGE

A. Psychodynamic Theories

(1) Individual
Resistance to change has been observed since the early development of psycho-analysis. Freud described it as a "vigorous and tenacious resistance" maintained throughout the whole course of treatment. He went on to discuss the very varied and subtle forms such resistance can take, and understood the phenomenon to arise from the same powerful forces which produced the symptomatology, namely from repression. He postulated that certain impulses are felt to be too dangerous to allow into an individual's consciousness and so are repressed: A defence system is necessarily erected to keep these impulses unconscious, but in doing this, the defences become an integral part of the personality. Indeed, they are the part of the personality which has to be changed in order to allow expression and understanding of the original repressed impulse and so relief of the symptoms. Naturally, defences are very strong, necessarily to do their work of repression, and so of course they are also very competent to resist any attempt to modify them themselves.

(2) Group
While in 1916 Freud expected his audiences to regard this phenomenon and the strength of it as improbable, his influence, and that of other analysts since has led to its existence being generally accepted, and to analytic and psychodynamic treatments focussing on many aspects of the resistance. Working with groups in the 1950s, Ezriel developed the theory of required and avoided solutions, which mirrored the idea of repression and the defence system, but described it in group terms (Ezriel, 1956). The required solution, including the symptomatology, is manifest and is produced in order to avoid some more painful situation. This

situation, if not avoided, it is feared would lead to some catastrophic occurrence. More recently, Malan (1976) has restated this concept further, and describes the *required* solution as the defence system, the *avoided* solution as the impulse or wish, and the *catastrophe* as the painful feelings which would be experienced if the avoided solution was allowed to occur.

(3) Family

The understanding that symptoms arise as a result of the attempt to avoid painful conflicts does, of course, make the existence of resistance to change understandable, indeed logical. Who would court the very disaster they have spent their lives, individual or group, trying to avoid? The Ezrelian concepts of required and avoided solutions can as well be applied to family dynamic life as to group process. Family therapists who work with family myths such as Byng-Hall (1973), Stierlin (1977) and Ferreira (1963) emphasize the way in which family myths have a homeostatic function since they act as strong defences, often stronger because they are passed on from one generation to another and so cannot easily be challenged. Equally, it may be very difficult to challenge what Stierlin describes as "loose myths", vaguely formulated assumptions held by family members. Such assumptions are powerful defences against examining the truth of family relationships since they obscure the real quality and variations in such involvements. Being over-determined, myths inevitably lead to labelling either of individuals or of relationships, and so distort reality. As with repression in individuals, myths serve both a defensive and a protective function; defensive against forces from within (the individual or family) and protective against forces from without (the therapist). Thus they constitute a strong resistant mechanism.

B. Systems Theories

(1) Steady State Maintenance .

Systems theorists also postulate a force analogous to resistance to change as central to the maintenance of the system. They see systems as requiring a state of equilibrium or "steady state" in order to continue functioning successfully; this is produced by feedback mechanisms which convey information to the system allowing it to correct either for its own malfunctioning or for any environmental change. In this way a steady state or homeostasis is maintained. As Katz and Kahn (1966) stress, in open systems the most important principle is "the preservation of the character of the system" rather than a rigidly precise homeostasis. Thus, if one part of the system changes, another part will alter in a compensatory direction; this capacity of systems to adjust allows them to continue functioning in different situations. This principle provides the basic axiom of systems theory as applied tc family therapy. If one part of the system (individual) changes, then other parts have to change too in order to preserve the system as a functioning whole. The simplest type of change is an adjustment made to compensate for the initial change; this means that the steady state of the system is maintained. However, the aim of family therapy is to alter the system, and the ready activity of natural feedback mechanisms provide the resistant force.

(2)   The family's Special Ability to Resist

The fact of a family's being a group does not make it less resistant to change than an individual, but more so. A family will have a greater variety of possible manoeuvres to employ by way of indicating pseudo-change than an individual has. If an individual learns to accept unacceptable feelings or practice new behaviours, they may become a meaningful part of himself and so lead to a real change. But if family member A in the family context does this, he may not be indicating real system change, but merely expressing something hitherto manifested by another family member, B, and so in a sense borrowed from him, so that B has now lost it.

The essential circularity of systems which arises from their need to maintain a steady state can ensure this. For example, it is not unusual to meet families where one person acts as spokesman for all; their words may be listened to with eagerness, fear, impatience, or boredom by other members. During treatment, this phenomenon may be noted and commented on; other members will be encouraged to speak, and may do so. An apparent improvement may occur, but the therapist may then become aware that A's overwhelming monologue has just been replaced by B's intrusive chattering. The system has not changed; that would require every member to speak for him or herself with a frequency appropriate to their age, and to be able to listen attentively to others. It is precisely this change which is so difficult to achieve. As Wynne (1965) has put it, "families have a staggering capacity to remain the same". Framo (1965) has described the massive resistance presented by families in treatment, a description which echoes Freud. Ferreira (1963), as discussed above, has pointed to the power family myths have in maintaining homeostasis and keeping the required solution alive. The strength of the barriers to change raised within a family is greatly increased just because each individual may not only be resisting change within himself, but is also resisting change in other family members either protectively or in self-defence.

(3)   Case Example: The K Family

A striking example of such openly manifest resistance was shown in the K family. the Ks were a family consisting of parents and three teenage children, girls of 17 and 13, and a boy of 15. There were frequent violent arguments in this family, and members tended to take up very entrenched positions, with a great deal of mutual labelling. The mother talked in a particularly battering and intrusive manner in a loud and high voice, often in the plural and at great length. She herself became aware of how aggressive her style of talking was, and of how easily it could spiral off one of the frequent rows. Her distress at recognizing this was quite real, and she made determined and sincere attempts to alter her way of speech. Although her son supported her, and as a result she and he greatly decreased their arguments, the daughters vigorously and openly opposed her quieter approach, even mocking it. Her husband more subtly opposed it by failing to notice the change. After a short time, the mother (and son) gave up the attempt to change. The pressure of the family as a whole was such that it could not adapt to this change without some other member having to make a totally unpalatable change; for example, the two girls to have more open disagreements with each other. Still less could the family bear to consider at this point what pain the system of continuous rows over trivia avoided.

In such ways there can be active, albeit at times secret, coalitions between family members to maintain people in their assigned and familiar rôles. Fortunately, the converse is also true, and is what contributes to the effectiveness of treatment; that is, co-operation to achieve change. The therapist has to work to keep this active co-operation alive throughout the treatment process. This means treading a difficult balance between pushing the more optimistic members to changes which the others might resist, and letting the whole family fall into despair at the lack of change if they go at the pace of the slowest. It means keeping alive hope for the family at the times when they are struggling to change and failing to see results. It means being sensitive to the family's fears and defences even if they are not openly acknowledged and recognizing when it is helpful to change therapeutic emphasis from process to content and vice versa. All this is done in the context of recognizing the immense struggle between the wish to change and the fear of doing so.

III. TECHNIQUES AIMED AT MAINTAINING MOTIVATION IN THE FAMILY

In order to maintain the therapeutic alliance, it is obviously essential to have the family's co-operation. In the previous chapter, the work of engaging the family, formulating the problems and agreeing on a work contract have been described in detail. I will only refer to some of these tasks insofar as the therapist may need to refer back to them himself in helping the family deal with its resistance and carry on with the work.

A. Establishment of the Therapist's Authority

As Skynner (1976) has pointed out, "issues of authority, hierarchy and control occupy a central place in the concepts and techniques of almost all family therapists". The therapist establishes his control at the beginning by deciding which members he will agree to see together, when he will do it, and how he works. The aims of work are agreed upon. Having done this, the therapist is then much more likely to be able to deal successfully with drop-outs, absences and other such manoeuvres designed to undermine the treatment at a later stage. Although the therapist's control is generally speaking confined to the actual sessions, he is much more likely to succeed in getting the family to carry out tasks between sessions if the family acknowledges his direction, and of course perceives the task as relevant.

Once the therapist has succeeded in getting the appropriate members present at an agreed time, he then has to show that he expects the family to do quite a lot of the work themselves. He neither can, nor will, provide the answers, nor will he take over care and control of family members during sessions, although he may help. These functions belong properly to the family. Parental failure to comfort, control or attend to children can only be assessed and worked on if it is clear to all that the therapist does not intend to take over these functions. Parents have to be asked to carry them out. In this way, it is possible to see how success-fully they can care and control, and how well the children respond. Similarly, most questions raised within family sessions are implicitly, if not explicitly, directed at another family member; families really wish to hear their own relations' views on important issues and not just the therapist's. The therapist has to be able to redirect questions from himself to an appropriate family member. Minuchin (1974, 1981) has described the need to avoid getting too strongly put into the "helper" rôle; if this does occur, it can prevent the family discovering its own independent strengths and capacities. It also means that the family when struggling with its own resistance to change, is much more likely to be able to recognize that this resistance arises from within itself, and not attribute it to a mean withholding spirit in the therapist.

B.   Creating a Focus and Changing it

An essential part of the engagement process is the agreeing of a focus of work. The therapist may wish to concentrate on the presenting symptom, or he can make his initial formulation to the family in terms of broader issues in the system. For example, if a child is presented as having temper tantrums, the focus may be simply helping the family manage the tantrums, or it may be stated as including a parental difficulty in expressing anger. Whichever is the case, the family and therapist have to agree on the difficulties they wish to change at the outset. A working alliance can only be maintained until those initial aims are achieved. A common experience in family, as in individual, work is that as the work proceeds, more problems may be highlighted. A change of aim or focus may then be indicated. If that is the case, a new agreed target must be negotiated. This shared target is important in maintaining the working alliance, since it provides necessary boundaries to the work in hand which could otherwise be felt to be endless. It also allows the family space to think about what they really want. A common expression of resistance is a belittling of their own needs. Families say things like "there must be people worse off than us, aren't we just wasting your time?" and "perhaps things are not really so bad". Such moves commonly occur near the beginning of treatment, although they may also be heard around significant anniversaries or holidays. If the basic problems are still manifest, the family is usually helped by being able to re-identify them.

It seems to me very helpful to be able to formulate the focus in such a way that the family cannot only accept it, which is essential, but also make sense of it, enlarge on it, and broaden the area of work themselves. This means that they do much of the work of overcoming their own resistance to moving into new thera-peutic areas. If we consider the situation suggested above of a family referred because of a child with tantrums, an agreed formulation which refers to the parents' difficulty in expressing anger can allow that couple to move into looking at their own relationship or their relationships with extended family should that seem appropriate.

C. On-going Therapeutic Approaches and Techniques

I feel that there are two major elements to the work done with families in treatment. One is directed at the *"here and now"* process, the current feeling atmosphere and style of interaction between family members, and between family and therapist. The second is concentration on the *"content and meaning"*, discussion and understanding of the topics raised which can be seen as reflecting the thoughts and preoccupations of the family. Work on family myths comes into this category. My own personal view is that in order to maintain a satisfactory and helpful alliance, the therapist has to take due account of both elements. This does not necessarily mean that he has to work directly with both, nor that he has to select the one the family is overtly presenting. Therapists are well aware that families may produce content issues as a defence against working on control difficulties and structural problems as a defence against intolerable fears.

Those struggling to learn the theory and techniques of family therapy may often feel that there is a basic dichotomy between these two elements. This feeling may be exacerbated by reading such papers as Beels and Ferber (1969) on types of therapy and therapist, distinguishing *"active conductor"* and *"passive reactor."* In addition, the fact that family therapists have come from a wide range of theoretical backgrounds means that they have introduced techniques from such different orientations as psychoanalysis and behavioural theory. It also means that some workers are definitely inclined to be more symptom-orientated, others less so. Behavioural approaches tend to be labelled as active and directive (which may be true), and as taking no account of complicated feelings and past experience (which is not so). In distinction to this, the psychoanalytic method is seen not just as undirective (which it is), but also as passive and purely concentrating on past experiences (which it is not). Indeed, the whole concept of transference brings a technique of working with here-and-now processes, albeit in the context of content about past as well as present.

Family therapists may incline much more strongly either to a model concentrating on current behaviour (including relationship) change or to one struggling to understand the roots of the problems and thus achieving change. However, I feel that in order to maintain the family's motivation and so help bring about change, it may be most appropriate to be flexible: to be able to concentrate on here-and-now processes at certain times, and at other times be content to let past experience be the focus. Above all, it seems to me important to be able to distinguish when one must work with one element in order to be free to work with the other.

IV. "HERE AND NOW" INTERVENTIONS
TO MAINTAIN MOTIVATION

"Here and Now" interventions comprise those techniques aimed at working directly with the structure of the family: techniques such as work on communications, work on control and boundary issues, on family alliances and task setting; and those aimed at working on the family/therapist relationship, such as transference interpretations (transference in the traditional analytic sense). Use of paradox, which is a direct and immediate challenge to the resistance, is also a here-and-now move.

A. Communications and Boundaries

I am linking communication and boundary issues, since dysfunction in one almost inevitably is associated with dysfunction in the other. In clinical practice, we frequently see families with striking problems of confused communication pattern and boundary keeping. Some families continually interrupt each other, or more than one person speaks at once. Others avoid talking directly in the first person, or else the individual addressed does not respond, but rather another does for him. In a similar way, if one family member is requested to do something, another may take over and act for him. While all families obviously do most of these things some of the time, families presenting for help may manifest such patterns to a very high intensity. Clearly if A or B speak for C, as often as he does for himself, there is likely to be little real sense of boundaries between individuals. If a family's pattern is for all to talk at once, or indeed never to talk freely at all, there may be a very impoverished awareness of each other's thoughts and feelings. There is also likely to be a general feeling of lack of control; that is, a lack of caring and an absence of parental authority. Naturally the parents share in this feeling, as they share in not being heard, and consequently their actual capacity to exert control when appropriate is likely to be diminished.

Such families can confuse and overwhelm the therapist with the amount and speed of information given and feeling projected, as well as by the actual noise level. It is often worthwhile for the therapist to make a statement about his own confusion or his inability to hear anything clearly. If the family responds to that spontaneously, it indicates that their pressure of talk arises from anxiety in the new therapeutic situation and that they themselves can modify it. However as is more often the case, such a comment has no effect, the therapist may have to work directly on the communication pattern shown before he and the family can do any other work.

B. Case Example: Robert's Family

(1) Introduction
Robert was an 8-year-old boy who was referred because of fairly severe behaviour problems both at home and in school; he had tempers, was distractable and

disobedient and had had to be contained in a special small class. He was a boy who was excessively short for his age, being considerably smaller than his two younger sisters, Ann aged 7, and Susan aged 6. Mother was the only remaining parent, the father having deserted when the youngest child was only months old. It was immediately clear to the therapist that Robert was never treated as the oldest child in the family, Ann being given that rôle. It was also evident on meeting the family that Susan was at least as disruptive as Robert and that all three children talked and interrupted continuously. Mother rarely spoke except to give weak or ineffectual negative injunctions. As well as talking for each other the children haphazardly used each other's toys and drawings in such a continuous way that the victim of such an abuse often did not notice its occurrence until later.

(2) Initial Therapeutic Moves
The therapy initially concentrated on three issues. First, mother was asked to treat Robert as the oldest child giving him some obvious privileges such as a later bedtime. Secondly, the therapist made a rule that there was to be no interruption, and the children were asked to put up their hands when they wanted to speak. Thirdly, mother was asked to monitor this and attend when a child wanted to speak and had been waiting. During sessions the family were encouraged to talk to each other. Although the first task was fairly readily carried out, the family had more difficulty with the others. The children responded easily to the notion of raising their hands, after all such behaviour is often expected at school, but they continued to speak for each other. The therapist then teasingly asked who they were: if Ann answered for Robert, she was called Robert, and so on. This amused the children, but also was effective in helping them identify themselves and each other. They began to use each other's names much more often and more appropriately. Interestingly, some time later on in the treatment when the chidlren wanted to show off their prowess in writing to the therapist, what Robert and Ann chose to write was: "We are learning to listen", and this indeed had been the explicit message of much of the treatment. Other techniques were also used. The family played a game in which members took it in turns to build up a story; this necessitated listening carefully. They were also shown video playback of parts of their sessions, Robert and mother particularly being shown bits where they had switched off and stopped listening and then introduced a red herring topic.

It was most difficult to help mother take over an appropriately active rôle and also a listening one. In playing a structured game early on, she had demonstrated that she could teach the children how to do this and hold their attention success-fully. In that kind of unemotive situation, she could be both active and responsive. It needed more work, not only on the here and now, but on the feared content of what she *might* hear if she listened attentively to the children in more spontaneous interaction, for her to be able to begin to respond more positively to the children's general needs.

(3)   General Implications

Robert's family was a complicated one with many problems. Nonetheless it was obvious that the children appreciated being listened to and given space as individuals from the outset and that mother eventually did so too. Many families with confused and interruptive communications may respond more quickly to having their interruptiveness pointed out. They may be relieved to be allowed to stop such undermining behaviour, and will readily continue to check interruptions themselves. Some families will follow such changes by admitting to shared feelings of low self-esteem (a feeling which was confirmed by knowing that no one ever really heard). This in itself may be enough change; the family may be able to start to enjoy each other's company in a much more positive way. If the family can recognize the painfulness of the pattern and yet not be able to stop it with help from the therapist, then it may be necessary to consider with them what it is that is too frightening or painful to hear.

Very enmeshed families often show more severely disturbed communication patterns which are more resistant to change and may be more difficult to identify in the first place. The use of "we" instead of "I", the silent looking to another family member for approval or permission to speak, coalitions to silence certain members, all occur. Such systems show an insidious encroachment on to one another's psychological territory; often it is not clear who is encroaching and who is the victim. The moves may not be as equal and balanced as in Robert's family. This causes deeper enmeshment and confusion. Nonetheless, although much work on understanding feelings and history may need to be done in gaining understanding of why, here and now work must be done in identifying the pattern and pointing out actual occurrences.

(4)   Therapist's Rôle

The therapist's rôle in this is an active one insofar as he must be able to observe the communication patterns accurately and then help the family see them. The family then has to take over the task of monitoring those. Games and rules may help as may video playback if it is available. Indeed, some families derive enormous help from the impact of seeing themselves as they are, and can use this to increase their own motivation to change.

C.   Changing Alliances

All families have numbers of natural alliances within them; that between parents, between certain siblings, between parent and child. Such closenesses occur inevitably and only lead to dysfunction if any given alliance prevents one or both members of it being as close as they might be to other family members. Obviously negative alliances or coalitions exist with the implicit purpose of preventing closeness between members (Haley, 1967) and such coalitions are always pathological.

(1)   De-triangulating Children

They probably always indicate that there are significant problems in the marital relationship and the therapist's first task must be to detriangulate the child caught in the coalition and then work with the parents together, either with the rest of the family there or not depending on the case and on the therapist's preference. My own is for working with the couple alone in such situations. However, in order to reach that point, it is necessary to have overcome their resistance to having the problem labelled primarily as a marital one. If a couple are able to acknowledge some difficulties they are more likely to see that they are drawing a child, or children, in unhealthily and so may well accept the reformulation. However in some situations, the couple are determined not to look at their own relationship, and in such situations, it may be impossible to let the child out of the treatment. Such families are again likely to be highly enmeshed and may need a long time before changing at all, and perhaps the highest drop-out rate is among such families. If they are not so resistant, they are likely to highlight the marital conflict fairly early on, often over management of the children, and from then on may agree to work on it; indeed, are often relieved to do so.

(2) Strengthening Sibling Alliances

There are, however, many other ways of helping families change and shift the balance of alliances. Siblings may be helped to learn to enjoy activities together (as in Robert's family). Another common shift is in helping an adolescent or near-adolescent child make a closer alliance with the parent of the same sex. Often a young adolescent may be presented as having a problem such as not working in school, general negativism or mild unhappiness. Sometimes when the family is seen, what is revealed is a considerable distance between the adolescent and parent of the same sex. While this may co-exist with an apparently over-close relationship with the parent of the opposite sex, this may occur not because of significant distance between the parental couple or overprotectiveness from the close parent, but more from unfamiliarity in how to approach each other. Helping the child and parent find ways of getting together can alter such distance and so change the existing alliances. The two may do this over talking together or having an activity together.

(3) John's Family: Case Example

John, a 15-year-old with a sister of 20, was presented as being completely disinterested in any activity: home, school or leisure-based. He and his mother appeared to be very over-involved with each other. Father was asked to talk with John and share with him his own experiences of growing up especially at this age. Following this John became much more lively and active, and it also became clear to the therapist that the parents still had a great deal actively in common and did pursue their joint interests together, despite mother's apparent closeness with John.

(4) Lindsay's Family: Case Example

Lindsay was an attractive 13-year-old whose parents complained of her temper tantrums and generally negative behaviour. She was also failing in school and had a long-standing speech defect. During the treatment the difficulty she and her mother had in achieving any positive closeness was highlighted; it was clear that both felt they were in some ways failing the other's expectations and so were continually unable to make friendly approaches. Both parents were rather concerned about some of Lindsay's normal adolescent interests in dress and appearance etc.; father definitely more so. The therapist picked up on mother's sneaking sympathy with her daughter and with mother's own rigid upbringing, and got them to talk together ("girl talk") without father and younger brother in the room. Mother was able to open up to Lindsay about some of her own adolescent "goings on", and to help her daughter express some wishes about make-up and so on. The two then were set the task of going shopping for make-up together, and also of playing around with it at home together on occasions. In this way they began to feel closer to each other, and consequently less dissatisfied; father was able to take a back seat on this issue and allow his wife to deal with it alone.

D. Control

Problems in control clearly relate to boundary dysfunction. Many families with children present with difficulties in this area. Sometimes they themselves are complaining of their children's disobedient behaviour; at other times they are not aware of a control problem, and are afraid that the child is very unhappy, anxious and so on. Of course a child who is allowed to have inappropriate control over his own and his family's life is likely to be unhappy, but that may often be secondary to the problem. Tantrums, behaviour problems and school phobia are common examples of dysfunction in control.

(1) General Principles
With many symptoms parents can be encouraged to find ways of establishing appropriate control both within the sessions and at home. Setting tasks and then supporting the parents in carrying them out can help. If parents succeed in stopping their infants' temper tantrum or in getting their children to listen attentively in a session, they gain an experience of success which often provides a basis on which to build at home. Families presenting with a school-phobic child may respond immediately to a new or heightened awareness that this symptom is, in part at least, expression of a control problem, and the child can then return to school at once. Such symptom improvement is of course unlikely to be maintained unless some further work is done on the family system, and part of the initial aim must be to identify such needs.

(2) Martin's Family: Case Example
Martin, aged 13, was brought by his parents having been out of school for 6 weeks. The boy had increasing anxieties about his performance, and felt that he could not cope with the work. Significantly, his much older sister had had a change of schools at about 13 because her school "was not right for her". During the interview, Martin was able to say quite clearly that he felt burdened by his mother's anxiety, worse since a recent illness. The mother's anxiety and ambivalence about her son's growing up were obvious, the father's equally

strong although not manifest until later. Father, who was nearing retirement, was confused and rather ineffective, torn between supporting his wife and his son. All three could agree, however, that they would like the mother to be less anxious and protective. With the hope of this being achieved, the parents were able to reassert their authority and help Martin return to school the following day. (As often seems to happen, this was done after father made a telephone call to the therapist during his struggle to get Martin out of the house, asking for confirmation that it was alright to be firm.)

Having achieved this success, the family was then well motivated to continue in treatment for a number of sessions during which they could continue to work on the separation problems underlying the original symptom. As in many families, task-setting as well as discussion of anxieties around independence could be helpful. Ideally, tasks should either involve all family members in the therapeutic group together (such as a shared activity) or else should give each member separately some task, which individually they might wish to achieve, but also which involves all members dealing with the same feeling difficulty. In Martin's family, he was asked to go out to a football match with a friend (he had only been with father before), and the parents were asked to have an outing together. This allowed each member to have some chosen pleasure but at the cost of having to separate from the other generation.

E. Transference Interpretations

A very different "here and now" technique, that of transference interpretation, is much more rarely used in family therapy, although certain groups of workers such as Boszormenyi-Nagy and his colleagues (1965), Zinner and Shapiro (1972), Box *et al.* (1981) and Stierlin (1977) have worked on intra-familial transferences. However, interpretation of family/therapist transference may be helpful in response to resistance at certain points, especially in long-term treatments. Distress and acting out around holidays may be one such time, or therapist behaviour may quite accidentally seem to mirror actual experiences in the family, and so arouse similar feelings of anger or sadness.

An example of this occurred in Robert's family (see above). On one occasion, one of the co-therapists had to miss a session to deal with an emergency. The children began talking about the mother's co-habitee, who had recently left the family, in such a way as to indicate direct fears about the therapist's capacity to wish to continue "caring." A transference comment about this produced open acknowledgement of such anxiety, and the children were then able to continue to discuss their feelings about the co-habitee much more freely.

Transference interpretations may be made in relation to the whole family, as in the above situation, or may be directed at one member only, usually the one who is most vigorously expressing the resistance. In some ways, this latter approach is one form of the familiar technique of allying strongly with a particular family member.

F. Paradoxical Injunction

During the last decade, various family therapists have developed techniques of utilizing the resistance and the very symptom itself. Watzlawick *et al.* (1974), Haley (1977) and others (who in any case eschew attempts to help clients gain understanding of their problems), instead focus on changing behaviour, and counter resistance to change by paradoxically agreeing that the patient has found a better way of life than others can help him achieve. Palazzoli and her colleagues (Palazzoli *et al.*, 1978) who do work to understand relationships, will in very resistant situations provide carefully worked out prescriptions which appear paradoxical in that they reframe the pathological behaviour or system positively. In fact, they are providing a counter-paradox to the conflicted and bound situation in which the clients find themselves. In connoting this painful situation positively, they give the family a new feeling of self-esteem which may then help them find a new solution and to continue in the therapeutic alliance. This is a different approach from that of Haley and others, who may facilitate change by altering the focus of the resistance. Instead of the family struggling to prevent change, they may now fight to stop *not* changing, so that any change must be labelled as "too fast" or potentially dangerous, and to be resisted.

Many families seem to be helped sufficiently by interventions in the "here and now." They make improvements which can be maintained without any underlying pathology being revealed. Such dysfunctional patterns may arise as a result of severe stress such as illness or bereavement. The family might have coped well had it not been for great accidental problems. Or it may have coped well with such problems on the feeling level, but been unaware that in doing so, the children had had to "grow up too fast" in one way, and so took over control inappropriately in other ways. Dysfunction may also arise because the parents have a particular difficulty in taking responsibility for setting limits. If a family can enjoy its new freer opener communication and happily take responsibility for control appropriately, the work may be confined to this sphere. The "avoided solution", acceptance of boundaries, proves to be a paper tiger, not a real toothed beast.

V. INTERVENTIONS IN CONTENT, MEANING AND HISTORY TO MAINTAIN MOTIVATION

A. Introduction

Some families present without striking problems in control or communication, but express feelings of not understanding each other. Equally there are many families who do not respond much to interventions in the here and now, or who, having been helped achieve a more open and shared communication, find that they are unhappy with it. In such cases, one suspects that the manifest inter-actional difficulties have arisen as a defence against underlying fears. Indeed, sometimes this is obvious right from the outset, but it may also be clear that the taboo about open discussion of such fears is very strong and time is needed for the family to develop trust enough to do it. These families may be defending against a feared and all too likely catastrophe; illness and breakdown in one or more members, loss, either by death or total separation. Such events may actually have occurred already in the family's life or may have occurred in the past. The parents may themselves have been brought up in deprived or very disturbed situations. It is also possible that such fears were present in past generations and so have been transmitted as a part of family history or myth.

Therapists like Pincus and Dare (1978) and Byng-Hall (1973) give numerous examples of families who presented with problems which had their roots in a fear of repeating past history and so reexperiencing the miseries of painful relationships. As Stierlin (1977) and Boszormenyi-Nagy and Spark (1973) have pointed out so forcefully, family loyalty is immensely powerful and people feel unable to break the pattern of dysfunction, however painful, set by their parents. Herein lies another resistance to change; even when the family may have gained some understanding of itself and its relationships, the parental loyalty to their own families of origin can make it very hard for them to change and do "better" than their parents.

Even if families are responding well to treatment, concentrating predominantly on current interaction, many may be interested in how they came to operate in their dysfunctional way. Often some exploration of history is helpful, both in revealing ways and in maintaining a therapeutic alliance, since the family curiosity deserves to have some satisfaction having been aroused (Martin, 1977). The therapist, too, may be able to use such information to appreciate and convey understanding of the family pain and fears without necessarily dwelling on it at length. This may happen very naturally if labelling people with rôles and personality types is marked in the family.

B. Myth and Labelling

Exploration of family history and myth can free families to concentrate on working on their current relationships and may be a necessary first step when history is continually brought to the forefront.

(1) The "G" Family: Case Example

The G's were a couple who requested marital help following an earlier period of family work. The husband, a rather depressed and anxious man, described himself as coming from a "bad" rather harsh and uncaring family, whereas the ebullient wife came from a very warm, close-knit family and saw the husband as the ill partner. The husband tended to share this view, and moreover felt guilty that all the problems in their family must stem from his rather deprived past. The couple were asked to bring their family trees and describe their extended families. In doing this, they threw a completely different light on the matter; the husband's family emerged as fairly ordinary and likeable, albeit with certain personality difficulties. The wife's family, on the contrary, came out as depressed and enmeshed; the wife had had a real period of painful separation and two siblings were severely disturbed. The normality and likeableness of the husband's "bad" family was conveyed by both partners, who agreed in their descriptions but did not realize that they were describing "nice" as opposed to "dreadful" people. When the therapist commented on this, it came as a revelation to both of them and relieved the husband of an enormous burden of guilt about his "hard" family. Indeed, it allowed him to establish warmer relationships with his family of origin. In the marital treatment, it brought the wife in equally as a patient, and the couple then allowed work to concentrate on their current relationship.

C.   Content of History and Work with the Past

(1) Introduction

Exploration of family history is not only very rewarding therapeutically at times, but has the added advantage of bringing in past (and absent) generations and so putting the growth of problems into a multigenerational context (see chapters 10 and 12). This can help relieve the family in therapy from feeling inappropriate guilt for all their problems. In doing this, it cannot only help maintain the therapeutic alliance which might otherwise feel too persecuting, but it can gradually help the family feel appropriate guilt and responsibility and so motivate them to change. Often such change will extend to the grandparental generation and so go to improving relationships there. As Boszormenyi-Nagy and Spark (1973) and Stierlin (1977) have described, such work may be of considerable importance for families with severely disturbed and deprived relationships, not only in the present but also in the past. In such families, the avoided solution is always likely to contain such strong and persisting fears that they cannot be adequately relieved by work concentrating on present interactions. For families with less disturbed backgrounds, there is still often a bonus of gaining increased appreciation of the grandparental struggle and of then being able to forge closer bonds. Often these moves may come when the adults in treatment are able to identify themselves as clearly separate from their parents, even at the cost of some argument, and can then enjoy warmer, less tied relationships with the older generation.

(2) The "Y" Family: Case Example

The Y's were a family with seriously disturbed backgrounds. They were referred with an obsessional difficult 13-year-old girl. Initially they presented as a confused and enmeshed mass; the two children, especially the younger girl (a 10-year-old), were positively invited to tell the tragic and disturbed family history which was then discounted by the parents. During the first contracted period of work, issues of boundary and control were quite successfully worked on; each member did overtly want some more privacy and some increased parental control. The "history" was deliberately ignored by the therapists. A better balance between parents and children was achieved, the children feeling some relief. The improvements, however, highlighted the marital dissatisfactions and their shared depression. At the end of the first contract, the couple were able to accept continuing help for the marriage. Although it was obvious that the difficulties related to deep-seated shared experiences of loss and deprivation, the wife was still unable to dare acknowledge her fears openly. These were made easier to hide as the husband's background was more dramatically disturbed and he became seriously depressed.

This resistance to looking at the past meant that the early part of the marital work still focussed on helping the couple work on their own communication problems, their shared distance from each other. Facing the past was avoided because of a feared catastrophe of total loss and madness, the loss which had been experienced in the husband's family and the madness in the wife's. Instead of facing the past, the couple turned every minor current event into a potential disaster. Very gradually this was understood and improved and along with this the couple were helped to dare look at their fears about themselves, their deep disappointments and their anger. Again, the husband led in this, the wife maintaining a front of denial about her depressed and frightened feelings for about a year. The husband, who could not bear to meet any of his wife's extended family, knew that this was because his parents-in-law were looking after two orphaned grandchildren. He himself had been partially brought up by grandparents after being deserted, and on marrying had hoped to be parented by his in-laws. His jealous rage at the intruding grandchildren had led him to quarrel bitterly with his mother-in-law and to fear his own violent feelings to the children.

Later, the wife was able to reveal something of the roots of her obsessional behaviour, understanding it as a retreat and defence against the loneliness and fears of living in a family which was supporting at least one overtly psychotic member. Once the couple were able to look more openly at their own experiences, they were able to understand why they had made such demands on each other and failed to meet them; they were now able to give each other more mutual caring and to accept less violently some of each other's failures. They also began to re-establish some of the broken relationships with their extended families, taking a more realistic view of the likely disappointments but also writing, telephoning and talking to their families in less hostile and provocative ways.

While the therapists had been aware of some of the history and of the weight of incipient depression from the beginning, the work had to be taken very slowly and to vary its overt focus in order to maintain an alliance and avoid a resistance which frequently threatened to take the couple out of treatment. The open focus of feared depression and the work on the history took about a year to reach and a further six months to work on.

VI.   DROP-OUT FROM TREATMENT AND ITS PREVENTION

A.   Therapist Alliances with "Doubtful" Motivation

In family, as in individual treatment, resistance can be acted upon by certain members of the family dropping out before they have achieved their stated aims.

Often this wish to stop is voiced openly or hinted at in a session. In such situations, it is likely to be helpful if the therapist can ally strongly and empathically with the resistant member. In the Y family described above the wife came to the final session of the initial contract determined to stop; the female therapist allied strongly with her, empathizing with her feelings of doubt, and to the husband's amazement she changed her mind and agreed to continue with the proposed marital therapy. During the initial period of marital work while the couple were still see-sawing with doubts about continuing, the therapists deliberately allied rather more strongly with the partner of the same sex, aware that both had particularly deprived relationships with the parent of the same sex. Once the couple were well settled into treatment, such specific sex-linked alliance was not necessary.

B. Dealing with Collusive Exclusion

In other families, it might be more helpful to make such alliances on a hetero-sexual basis because of client need. If the therapist has some knowledge of the family history, he is perhaps more likely to be sensitive to such need. Often too, one is working as a single therapist and so the possibility of choice does not arise. The family therapist, therefore, has to be able to ally with any member positively; he also has to be able to do so with what Stierlin (1977) describes as "involved impartiality" which conveys to the family trust in his basic fairness. If this trust is established, it can help avoid the major problem caused by drop-out of a family member.

One important technique designed to demonstrate this is the therapist's refusal to continue the "work" when anyone is out of the room. Should a child or adolescent actually fail to attend, the therapist can encourage the parents to use their authority to bring him back, thus confirming that control is in their hands. If an adult drops out, the situation is rather more complicated, but nonetheless the responsibility often lies with other family members who collusively wish for that person to absent himself. Situations of this kind often arise when one parent and child, or children, are in open or covert alliance against the other parent and so wish to exclude them. They may do this because they want to complain about them: "he is always drinking", "she is ill and can't stand the hassle", "he isn't really interested in the family anyhow." If the criticisms are open, the therapist can point out that people cannot usefully be discussed in their absence, since such discussion is not only unlikely to help the absent person but might well add fuel to the fire of existing disagreements. In this way, a manoeuvre to label the absent member as the difficult one can be foiled. The attending group may well decide that in that case, they would prefer everyone to come so that they can at least voice the complaints. The family then accepts the responsibility for negotiating with itself. If the alliance against the absentee is covert, the situation is more difficult since the family may present a front of concern for him. Under-standing of the kind of perverse coalition described by Haley (1967) can help the therapist intervene in ways which drive a wedge into the coalition either by unmasking it or by continuing an open empathy with the absentee.

C. Dealing with Drop-Outs

If a member drops out, the therapist can sometimes help him back by a letter or a telephone call. If the family resistance is all being carried by that person the more positive co-operation in the work is being carried by the others, and that coupled with their own warm feelings towards the absentee may help him return.

In my experience, it is more common for the whole family to stop attending than for one member to drop out. The fear of change, the exposing of myth or revealing of secrets, is likely to affect all together. A family may be unable to give up its symptom or scapegoat, and in resisting any improvement will of course feel that the treatment is useless, as it is in such cases. More commonly a family may get some gains from alleviation of the presenting problem only to discover a new discomfort which threatens their security more. A common example is the uncovering of marital unhappiness. Sometimes an offer to see part of the system may help overcome such resistance and help the family decide to return all together, or the therapist may decide to work only with a subsystem. The capacity of the therapist to be flexible enough to work when he considers it appropriate with part of the whole system may be as important a therapeutic technique as being able to use a variety of approaches.

REFERENCES

Beels, C. C. and Ferber, A. (1969). Family Therapy: A View. *Family Process,* **8**, 280-318.

Boszormenyi-Nagy, I. and Framo, J. L. (1965). "Intensive Family Therapy", Harper & Row, New York.

Boszormenyi-Nagy, I. and Spark, G. M. (1973). "Invisible Loyalties", Harper & Row, New York.

Box, S. *et al.* (1981).

Byng-Hall, J. (1973). Family Myths used as Defence in Conjoint Family Therapy. *Brit. J. Med. Psychol.,* **46**, 239-250.

Ezriel, H. (1956). Experimentation within the psychoanalytic session. *Brit. J. Philos. Sci.,* **7**, 25-41.

Ferreira, A. J. (1963). Family Myth and Homeostasis. *Arch. Gen. Psych.,* **9**, 457-463.

Framo, J. L. (1965). Rationale and Techniques of Intensive Family Therapy. *In* "Intensive Family Therapy", (I. Boszormenyi-Nagy and J. L. Framo, eds), Harper & Row, New York.

Haley, J. (1967). Towards a Theory of Pathological Systems. *In* "Family Therapy and Disturbed Families", (G. Zuk and I. Boszormenyi-Nagy, eds), Science and Behaviour Books, Palo Alto.

Haley, J. (1977). "Problem Solving Therapy", Jossey-Bass California.

Katz, D. and Kahn, R. (1969). Common Characteristics of Open Systems. *In* "Systems Thinking", (F. Emery, ed.), Penguin, London.

Malan, D. H. (1976). "The Frontier of Brief Psychotherapy", Plenum Press, New York.

Martin, F. (1977). Some implications from the theory and practice of family therapy and individual therapy. *Brit. J. Med. Psychol.,* **50**, 53-64.

Minuchin, S. (1974). "Families and Family Therapy", Harvard Univ. Press, Cambridge, Mass.

Minuchin, S. and Fishman, H. C. (1981). "Family Therapy Techniques", Harvard Univ. Press, Cambridge, Mass.

Palazzoli, M. S., Boscolo, L., Cecchin, G. F. and Prata, G. (1978). "Paradox and Counter-Paradox", Jason Aronson, New York.

Pincus, L. and Dare, C. (1978). "Secrets in the family", Faber & Faber, London.

Skynner, A. C. R. (1976). "One Flesh: Separate Persons", Constable, London.

Stierlin, H. (1977). "Psychoanalysis and Family Therapy", Aaronson, New York.

Watzlawick, P., Weakland, J. and Fish, R. (1974). 'Change: Principles of Problem Formation and Problem Resolution", Norton, New York.

Wynne, L. C. (1965). Some Indications and Contra-Indications for Exploratory Family Therapy. In "Intensive Family Therapy", (I. Boszormenyi-Nagy and J. L. Framo, eds), Harper & Row, New York.

Zinner, J. and Shapiro, R. (1972). Projective identification as a mode of perception and behaviour in families of adolescents. *Int. J. Psycho-analysis*, **43**, 523-530.

Chapter 8

Family Legends
Their Significance
for the Family Therapist

J. Byng-Hall

I. INTRODUCTION

Family mythology (Byng-Hall, 1979) consists of a complex set of self-perceptions and stories which give the family its sense of identity. Mythology is an interesting blend of reality and fantasy. Only outsiders see the distortion involved and hence would call it mythology. To the family it is their reality. Among the stories of mythology are legends. These are coloured and often colourful stories which are told and retold down through the generations. All families allow many fascinating episodes to fade into the past unless someone takes the trouble to go and ask the ageing members of the family before it is too late. Why in contrast is great care taken to make sure that certain stories are told to the next generation? The main thesis of this chapter is that these stories are often moral tales which convey the rules and obligations of family life. Legends are moulded by the narrator and are "here and now" not "past" phenomena. Each telling produces a version which is edited to fit current distortions in family myths (Ferreira, 1963; Byng-Hall, 1973) and family rules. Thus while the family system remains unchanged, so too do the family stories, and legends can help to prevent change because they have a homeostatic function. Neither teller nor listener is usually aware, however, of when re-editing takes place in line with a shift in family structure. Each imagines that the past, as now depicted, led up to the present family predicaments: a far cry from the idea that the past has just been altered by the present. Thus legends can also consolidate and maintain change, reinforcing the new "reality".

Because legends are involved in changing and maintaining family rules, family therapists should be aware of them, both as phenomena and as potential tools for change. As most families have some legends, there are opportunities for family therapists to explore this dimension within their own families. This chapter includes a description of the author's exploration of one of his own legends. The use of legends in family therapy and in training will also be discussed.

Family Therapy
ISBN: 0-12-089355-X

II. THE INFLUENCE OF FAMILY LEGEND:
A CLINICAL EXAMPLE

Both family myths and cultural myths are descriptive and prescriptive, but family myth differs from cultural mythology in one important respect: ownership has to be acknowledged. As implied in the old adage "blood will out", stories about ancestors are more compelling for each family member than are more general stories. The moralizing in family legend usually leaves it clear that the "black sheep" is the odd one out in the family; but of course every member then has to struggle hard to avoid being the one to follow suit. It is after all "lurking in the blood". Scanning the present family cast in order to spot the next villain becomes a powerful mechanism in self-fulfilling prophecy.

A.   Clinical Example: The "X" Family

In the X family, as will become clear, violence was considered to be the problem. Mrs X, a pretty petite physiotherapist, referred the family over the telephone because of her two teenage sons fighting, but added that she was worried about telling her epileptic husband about making the appointment. He would, she said, be absolutely furious.

In the first session, it became clear that one of the functions of the boys fighting was to reroute potentially disastrous marital or father/son violence. Mr X would rush in to stop their fighting, his wife would then storm up to stop him damaging her sons. They would then disagree with each other on how to stop the fighting. The fighting acted as a distance regulator (Byng-Hall, 1980). It brought the parents together, but not too close. In that context, there was no danger of the intimate marital contact of which they were both so scared.

Father, who was a Scottish architect, described how in his family of origin:

> My father threw his father out when he was only ten. My alcoholic grandfather was drunk one day when he came home and started beating up my grandmother who was blind. My father got hold of a piece of wood, hit him, and threw him out of the house.

The therapist asked whether the rest of the family knew this story. They all contributed additional snippets of information showing that this was a well-worn legend. "He never came back, leaving his blind wife to look after him and his five blind brothers and sisters!" (there was a form of congenital blindness in the family). "The only one who could see properly was grandpa who was the youngest." The imagery of legend is often vivid. In this case it was epic in quality. There was a hero, a heroine, a villain and victims. The villain not only assaulted a blind wife but deserted his pathetic almost totally blind family.

B.   Legends as Condensed History

Legends are condensed history. What takes a minute or two to tell often depicts something which unfolds over several years. The legend encapsulates a scenario, and stands as a graphic analogy for the whole process. In the X family, it was of course not one but many episodes which led to grandfather's departure. The implied blame was the family's own current interpretation of what must have been a breakdown in the family and marital systems of the previous generation.

III. RE-EDITING FAMILY MYTHOLOGY

A. The Illusion of Alternatives

It seems that one of the reasons that certain legends are told and retold is that there is an unresolved theme in the family involving an illusion of alternatives (Watzlawick, 1978), implying that one of two particular choices has to be taken, e.g. either you fight your father and get rid of him, or you let your father beat up your mother. Either way the son is wrong. The theme also remains unresolved, because the way the problem is framed implies that it is only the son(s) who can provide the answer. The chooser *has* to choose one of the alternatives. This is the illusion. He can of course choose not to get involved in parental battles at all, leaving them to resolve their own difficulties. The real alternative is to be, or not be, involved. By posing the question as, "In what way are you going to be involved?" the real choice is obscured. Watzlawick (1978) illustrates the illusion of alternatives with the Nazi slogan "National Socialism or Bolshevik chaos?" The real choice is of course between dictatorship or democracy.

The story illustrating the illusion of alternatives is then told to maintain the family structure, e.g. keeping sons triangled in, reminiscent of the binding dimension of double bind. The function is to avoid an even more feared solution, e.g. one or other parent may be damaged, or they might separate. When this pseudo dilemma is resolved by discovering other options (e.g. marital rows can be survived and sons can leave home), the stories pertaining to it may die out, unless that is, they are so entertaining that they survive for "after dinner" purposes.

B. Editing the Past to Fit the Present

Editing the past to fit the present is of course a well-known phenomenon. Linnemann (1966) describes the editing of Christ's sayings by the gospel writers so that the parables carried significance for the young church at that time. He describes a parable as a "language event". At each telling the context is different. Christ preaching in his lifetime to his uninitiated followers was done in a very different context from that of the gospel writers who believed him to be the Messiah. Preaching is, in Linnemann's words, "Updating or providing new exposition to each generation". The moral to be drawn in each context, as with family legends, is somewhat different. In a secular context, history has also often changed to fit the present. Stalin and Hitler changed the official histories of their countries and then changed the course of history.

IV. "BYNG MYTHOLOGY": IN SEARCH OF ALTERNATIVES TO ILLUSIONS

After writing the article on family mythology (1979), I realized that if I was going to take my own ideas seriously, I would have to examine my own family mythology.

A. The Choice of Legends

I sat down and set myself a number of rules. I would select one of my family legends and proceed chronologically throughout my life tabulating all events which linked with the theme of the legend. I would also try to read the moral of the story. The first legend which came to my mind seemed safe enough. It was 222 years old.

I tried to remember the legend as it was first told to me.

> Admiral Byng was an uncle of yours. He was only an admiral because his father, your great-great etc. grandfather was a famous Admiral of the Fleet. He was sent to relieve Minorca which was being attacked by the French. He was sent under-equipped, and when he got there, the French fleet was much larger and so he did the most sensible thing which was to keep out of range, exchange a few shots and sail home again. Unfortunately he was then found guilty of cowardice and shot on his own quarterdeck.

The illusion of alternatives was you either attack or run away, either way you die.

B. First Association

At first glance, this seemed to have very little personal relevance. I was brought up in Africa a full 300 miles from the sea. I then recalled that despite the remoteness of the sea, I had as a boy wanted to join the Navy. The ownership issue was however quite clear. I was to identify with the Great Admiral of the Fleet, of whom I was a direct descendant, as opposed to this uncle of whom we were all somewhat ashamed. I could not remember being told the date of the battle, 1756. Anyway to a child, the story would have been timeless and vivid.

What other connection did I have with ships? When I was eighteen months old, in 1939, my family was sailing through the Mediterranean when war was declared. My parents told me that much of the time was spent looking over the side for submarines and torpedoes. I have no recollections of this, but the impression made on a toddler must have been powerful.

By the time I was 12-years-old, my wish to join the Navy was very strong and was taken seriously by my parents, so when an old family friend who was captian of a British Naval Cruiser wrote to say that his ship was visiting Momoasa, my parents arranged for me to spend some time aboard to see if I enjoyed it. The whole experience was frightening. Naval discipline was totally mystifying to someone brought up on a huge farm. The most vivid memory for me was standing to attention, upright and rigid, on the quarterdeck, looking very intently at the second in command, terrified lest he saw that I was scared stiff. This episode had puzzled me until I saw it in the context of the legend. Now it made startlingly good sense. I recalled that Admiral Byng was said to have been shot by his own men on his own quarterdeck: presumably at the order of his second in command.

C.   Cowardice as a Theme

The theme of cowardice evoked powerful themes for me. I spent all my childhood frightened. I lived through some dangerous times. Kenya was dangerous both in its wild life and during the African Mau Mau rebellion against us white colonials, during which we lived in an isolated farmhouse in the forest. The family was fully armed against a Mau Mau attack which was a constant possibility. Indeed it was discovered later than a main Mau Mau trail ran a few hundred yards from our house. By the time I was conscripted to the Army the fighting had died down, and much to my relief, I never needed to shoot at anyone. Some of my best friends were Kikuyu.

I was much preoccupied with the question of whether I was a coward or not. Was fear evidence of that shameful (and dangerous) condition? Faced with a charging lion or an attack would I prove cowardly and run? My problem then was that never having "engaged" the enemy, I had not dispelled the fear of being a coward.

The next contact with boats had until then also puzzled me. After leaving the Army, I spent a holiday on the East African coast. In a fishing boat with some friends and an African fisherman, I noticed a shoal of six or seven sharks, not very large ones, but about 20 yards from the boat. I found myself diving in and swimming towards them. My friends told me to get back aboard but I watched the fisherman. As soon as he looked anxious and beckoned to me, I came back and climbed aboard. The Byng legend helped me to understand how I sought out a "real" seaman to help me know when I had got close enough to "real" danger to dispel the haunting label of cowardice.

Soon after this I sailed to Britain to go to University. I slept on board deck through the Red Sea and developed acute pain in the back and paralysis of the legs. This was polio. One fleeting fantasy was, however, that I had been shot in the back. Where are you shot if you are a coward and run away? The illusion of alternatives seemed to hold its spell. The option of leaving the danger zone (an alternative to fight or flight) seemed to have the same catastrophic result as flight.

D.   The Double-ended Catastrophe

Before re-editing this legend, something I clearly needed to do, I tried to experience the power of the legend's moral injunction. My theory at that time (Byng-Hall, 1979) proposed that legends acted as a guide to which choice to make when there was a dilemma. The way this legend was remembered implied that attack when outpowered by an opponent was potentially disastrous, but retreat was just as catastrophic, constituting a double-ended catastrophe (Byng-Hall, 1980). Put into relationship terms, either separating or becoming over close could in phantasy and/or fact lead to catastrophic results, and thus articulation of the dilemma acted as a bimodal homeostat, preventing relationships becoming too close or too distant. Features of too far/too close family systems are discussed further by Byng-Hall (1980, 1981).

In this legend, the scenario was set in a wider social context. If you get too close you may be wiped out, but moving too far leads to execution. As Watzlawick (1978) points out, the act of presenting an illusion of alternatives represents an exercise of power. The listener thinks he has to choose one or the other, thus obscuring the fact that there may be many other options. The only apparent solution to this dilemma which did not invite disaster was to hover between the two alternatives, ultimately to stand absolutely still. Anyone who knows wild life knows the wisdom of that rule; either running off or attacking invites an attack. It might also be said to be a wise stance if one is outnumbered 150 to 1 in a civil war. What is obscured is the option to refuse to get into or remain in the danger zone. British pride disallowed that. Another family legend which reinforced this whole stance went as follows: my grandfather, who at the time was Governor of Northern Nigeria, was warned of an imminent attack at dawn for which he was totally unprepared because of a late night party. He placed his chair outside the house, which was on a hill, and sat in it, quite still. He was wearing a white dinner jacket. At dawn, the attackers fled when confronted by this ghostly still figure.

The Admiral Byng legend, as it was told, implied that attack plus posthumous glory was on balance better than public shame and execution. The British Empire in the 1950s could not lose face by conceding that Mau Mau had a good cause to want Africa for the Africans. They could only do this after first defeating them (or appearing to have done so). Similarly two centuries earlier, the English could not accept that the French might reasonably be expected to have more influence in Minorca than the British. To concede that would have meant harbouring the idea that the whole British Empire was an outrageous anomaly.

E. Family and Cultural Overlap of Legends

In legends, family and cultural values often overlap. The twin set of rules: don't either go too far off or get too entangled clearly had a family function especially in a very isolated situation. British society as a whole is also rather preoccupied with maintaining the correct distance between people. The Byng legend proved to be particularly valuable to study because it is both an international and family legend, hence it is well documented from many perspectives, English, French and from within the Byng family. Because it is old, it is also possible to trace some of the editing, re-editing processes.

As I had experienced the power of this legend, I felt I needed to find out whether I had imposed it on the rest of my family. I asked my three sons separately the question, "Who was Admiral Byng and what did he do?" Our 13-year-old replied: "Well a message was sent and Admiral Byng was sensible and did not get into a battle he knew he would lose; but he was shot for cowardice". He had picked up the gist of the legend. As an afterthought he said, "When I was younger I thought he was shot aged 12". This came from the title of a book about Admiral Byng entitled *At 12 Mr Byng was Shot* (Pope, 1962). Our 12-year-old said: "He was the bloke who was shot at midnight by his own men, he gave the order himself". He did not know why. He got this idea from the cover of the same book about Admiral Byng. In the picture on the cover, Byng is shown dropping his handkerchief to order his own execution. (Note that the second in command did not order the execution.) The sky was painted dark blue, and it could have been midnight, not midday. Our 8-year-old son promptly replied: "He was Admiral of the Fleet, like Nelson". This was entirely correct, we had recently been to the Maritime Museum where a painting of Admiral Sir George Byng (the admirable admiral who was father of the Byng of the legend). When asked about the nephew, he did not know anything except, "Didn't something happen to him, wasn't his throat slit?"

I was intrigued by what each of my sons had focussed upon. Editing occurs at the hearing stage as well as through the telling. Each version seemed to me to reflect something of their personalities as well as age. Perhaps bravery or cowardice in face of the enemy and naval battles were now less powerful themes in our family and culture. Other themes were more relevant, e.g. danger at night.

I felt that because of the lack of consistency in their accounts, I had probably not talked much about the episode, nevertheless they had all picked up something ominous. Much of the information seemed to come from cultural sources, not from family story telling. If I had not chosen to take an interest in the legend, would it have died out in the next generation?

I asked the same question of my 18-year-old nephew whose second given name was Byng. He knew the legend in much the same form as my original legend (page 216). Despite all evidence to the contrary, it emerged that he was preoccupied by the idea that he was a coward. Family legends can of course be kept alive in some branches of the family and die in others.

V. RE-EDITING THE BYNG LEGEND

A. Exonerating Byng

I thought it was important to give my sons a more accurate picture. I told them about what I had learned from the book (Pope, 1962) which I had read 15 years before. The book had aimed to exonerate Byng and show that he had been scapegoated. This is what I told them.

> Newcastle, who was Prime Minister at the time, was politically insecure. He had been warned many times that the French were planning an invasion of Minorca but he did nothing. Minorca was attacked and he had to act. He sent Byng at short notice which meant that his ships were ill equipped and his crews untrained. The

battle itself was inconclusive, but the French and English Admirals in time honoured manner, each sent home news of their own great victory. Unfortunately for Byng, the British Secret Service was most efficient and intercepted the French message of a French victory long before Byng could sail home with an account of his victory. Newcastle was panic-stricken because he knew that he would be held responsible for the loss of Minorca through his tardy action. He launched a political campaign to blacken Byng's name before he arrived home. This included hiring professional writers to write damning lyrics about Byng, which were sung by bands of singers roaming the streets of Westminster. Byng was arrested on arrival at Portsmouth and the trial was rigged to find him guilty.

How much this account was also an edit of the book can be assessed by those who want to read the book which is incidentally fascinating reading. While I was giving this account, my 8-year-old wrote this poem:

Newcastle was a silly old thing,
    He sent Admiral Byng to fight over Minorca without a thing.
Finally Byng was shot,
    Do I like Newcastle? Not a lot!

One re-editing had been completed.

B. Exploring the Context Removes the Illusion of Alternatives

I decided that I wanted to know more about Byng as a person and the context in which all this happened. I told the story to Professor Howard Feinstein who is a psychohistorian and psychiatrist. He became intrigued, and we went to the British Museum to find the documents about the Battle. Some of those old documents had clearly not been touched for 223 years; others had been handled only once or twice. This was an incredible experience. The smell and texture of the paper itself was mesmerizing. As paper after paper revealed more and more unexpected information, the pull of history was almost tangible. Beware therapists! You can be lured here for a lifetime.

The pictures were most exciting. Here was visual proof that Byng engaged the enemy. There was a picture and commentary for each half hour of the battle, which could be followed in detail. In one picture both fleets were shown closely engaged with each other. There was a written description of Byng coolly discussing tactics with his captain. No sense of cowardice here. At one moment he had to veer away from the enemy to avoid ramming the dismasted ship in front of him. This could be seen in one of the pictures, and was later used as evidence that he withdrew from the enemy. Perhaps the most moving account was that given by an English sailor who described a rising tide of cheers from the English crews and marines as the French sailed away. Clearly they considered that they had won.

Evidence about Byng's dignity was plentiful. He wrote a long speech to be delivered before his execution. This speech was angry; indignantly proclaiming his innocence, but also forgiving. It conveyed a presence of mind which was in conflict with the picture I had built up of him which was of a haughty pompous, rather stupid man who did indeed have a streak of cowardice in him. It took, however, a long time before I allowed myself to be convinced by my new findings. Howard kept on remarking how I took every piece of evidence and twisted it to fit my preconceptions. Sometimes I did not even see some evidence in front of my eyes, at others I reversed the evidence. For instance, Byng never read this speech. I took this as evidence of fear (which may be true) rather than consider that he was not given the opportunity to make the speech, especially as it placed his executioners in such a poor light. This confirms my clinical impression that family mythology is extraordinarily difficult to shift.

Much of the search was interesting in itself. There were of course no daily newspapers. Instead political pamphlets were distributed. These were often written by well-known writers. Dr Samuel Johnson wrote pamphlets which were pro-Byng and carried some marvellous political invective. He wrote two, each in a different style: one in similar vein to the popular press for the less sophisticated, with simple arguments; and the other in which he used highly complex reasoning, more like the *Times*. Unfortunately he overdid it, and his highly convoluted arguments lost credibility.

To a family therapist, scapegoating is a highly understandable process. But why execution? Countless commanders had made far worse muddles. Was there something in the context to explain this extreme form of scapegoating, or did he like some victims invite persecution?

I discovered that Tunstall (1928), a naval historian who was keen to place the blame on the politicians as opposed to the Navy, has painted a most intriguing picture. All the leading politicians were involved: Newcastle, Fox and Pitt, each apparently either trying to save face or exploit the situation. The court martial failed to find him guilty of cowardice, indeed all the evidence given suggested that he was courageous. To emphasize this, he insisted on ordering his own execution by dropping his handkerchief. The Court only found him guilty of an error of judgement, not itself an offence at all. Quite erroneously from a legal point of view, this was then equated with negligence, for which the death penalty was mandatory. Probably the court martial assumed that the King (George II) would be bound to grant a pardon, and hence they did not have to face the full consequences of the decision. Byng himself did not want a pardon. He wanted the verdict reversed. He preferred to die rather than accept a pardon and hence admit his guilt.

The king was outraged by the request for clemency. George's own position in England was insecure. He was seen as more German than English, and he needed the support of the City who sponsored his expensive operations in Hanover. The City merchants were most annoyed by Byng's failure to regain Minorca from the French. It was an important Mediterranean base for British trade. The King felt that the politicians had whipped up public fury against Byng about the loss of Minorca. If he were to pardon him, where would their fury then be directed? Here I felt were sufficient ingredients for killing a scapegoat; money, power and the throne at stake. Later the nation itself felt the need to purge itself of this legacy to Byng. There was a vast list of publications which depicted him as a political victim.

C.   Further Exploration of the Context

This may have sufficed to salve the national conscience about Byng, but family scapegoating is different. Did he invite it? Also how did our family react? This sent me on another quest. To decide for myself, I needed further sense of the battle itself. Here was where I dug deepest. Was he really a coward? I had to forget what the world made of it afterwards; that is always falsified anyway. Systems theory told me that he must have colluded in some way. First of all, what were the odds he faced? I already knew that his fleet was ill-equipped, ill-manned and far from home, and that he was facing a well-prepared fleet, roughly equal in numbers, fresh out of harbour. For someone brought up in the spirit of the British Empire, however, victory would be expected in those circumstances!

A complete shift in my view occurred when I read that 15 000 of the best French troops commanded by Marshall Duc de Richelieu were already on the island besieging the English garrison at Fort Mahon, which was commanded by Lieutenant-General William Blakeney aged 84, suffering from gout, and in bed most of the time! Byng had only 13 ships, and had been refused extra marines by the commander at Gibraltar, despite orders from Whitehall that he should be given them. It was as if a myth had been exploded for me. At last the incredible British self-deception was fully exposed. It seemed that it had been easier to focus on the deeds of one man than to ask the whole nation to open its eyes to its own stupidity. I think this resonated strongly with my Kenyan childhood experience, where the illusion of everlasting superiority was maintained despite being outnumbered 150 to 1. Bluff carried the British far, but this included self-deception as well, often based on the idea of intrinsically superior British qualities and inferior foreigners.

In the forest, my family had to maintain the same myth. I knew the truth. One of my closest friends was a Kikuyu teenager of my own age. We hunted together. I knew that not only were we outnumbered, but that the Africans could, quite naturally, run rings round us in their own environment. (This situation is not to be confused with South Africa where racial ratios are very different.) I had now been able to re-edit my view of my childhood experience after re-editing the Byng legend. I could now ask the question, who were the cowards? Those who refused to see real dangers, or those who dared to look and risk being appropriately scared? I was now able to ask my parents and my sister about their experience during the Mau Mau period. We had, it appeared, all been frightened but each carried the idea that the others were not. We imagined that sharing our fears would have undermined the other's courage.

D.   Byng's Collusion

I then pursued the question of how Byng might have colluded. Horace Walpole described Byng as haughty and arrogant. He seemed by most accounts to have been more concerned with doing the correct thing than with the pragmatics of the situation. At every decision point he called a council of war, a sort of committee meeting, in which the majority made the decision. This hardly made for dynamic leadership. For instance, he did not insist on being given the marine reinforcement by the Gibraltar garrison despite orders from Whitehall; he allowed a Council of war to override this order. He also fought the battle exactly according to instructions devised 50 years before. It seems he found it difficult to take an initiative, allowing the rules to decide the action rather than risk opting for one of the alternatives. He could have engaged the French for a second time and presumably risked victory or defeat. He could also have refused to engage the enemy in formal battle. Tunstall (1928) argues (with modern tactical hindsight available to him) that a better tactic would have been to ensure that no French ships landed on Minorca; a much easier objective, and one which could have led to a successful siege of the besiegers, because the island could not support 15 000 troops, whereas Fort Mahon had ample supplies. Yet Byng had other options. He could have fought in an unexpected way, instead of predictably following the rules. It is interesting that the slavish following of battle procedures used very successfully by his father possibly served him ill. Perhaps that was his real error of judgement. It would have been interesting to know what legends he was told about his father's famous victories. It seems that he was chosen to command this expedition partly because he was expected to somehow emulate his father's domination of the Mediterranean.

By exploring Byng's context, I had shattered the power of the illusion of alternatives. Catastrophe did not automatically follow either alternative. The illusion of alternatives itself now also dissolved as I sensed that there were instead multiple options open to him. I could sense, however, the power of his historical context to encourage him to behave in certain ways.

VI.   PASSAGE OF THE LEGEND OVER TIME

A.   The Enemy's Views

Scapegoating can always be seen more clearly from outside. The French saw it immediately. The Duc de Richelieu was indignant about what was happening to Byng. He wrote a letter to Voltaire which included

> Whatever I have seen or heard of him does him honour . . . all Admiral Byng's manoeuvres were excellent . . . had the English persisted in the engagement they would have lost their entire fleet [possibly a French myth?]. There has never been such an act of injustice as that now directed against Admiral Byng, and every officer and man of honour ought to take note of it.

Voltaire sent this letter straight to Byng for him to use in his defence. It was discounted as having been solicited by Byng. In *Candide*, which was published shortly afterwards, Voltaire describes how, to paraphrase the passage, Candide while in Portsmouth sees an admiral being shot and asks why. He is told that he was not close enough to the French admiral, to which Candide asks a good systems question: was the French admiral also not close enough to him?!

"Cela est incontestable", lui repliqua-t-on; "mais dans ce pays-ci il est bon de tuer en temps en temps un admiral pour encourager les autres".

This particular famous quotation has done more than anything else to ensure that Admiral Byng is remembered. It assured the story legendary status. This piece of history is, however, now taught less and less frequently in British schools. As the British Empire has gone, perhaps this is less interesting or relevant.

B. Some Conclusions

To explore details of the changes in the legend over time, requires further articles. Suffice it to say that there are quotes by historians which, interestingly enough, support my original version of the legend. For instance Macaulay, writing in 1834: "But he did not think fit to engage the French squadron and sailed". Guedalla, in 1913, wrote: "Was militarily wise as it was politically foolish". The message that it is more praiseworthy to lose one's life bravely than to survive with shame is important to convey especially when, as is so frequently the case, the battle at the front is so clearly a complete, horrifying, bungled mess. The knowledge that retreat might lead to being publicly shamed and punished is a universal phenomenon of war. The Byng execution provided a vivid scenario not only for his, but for all ages. Legends have to resonate with universal themes, otherwise why would they pass from tongue to tongue.

The family was apparently solidly and unreservedly behind Admiral Byng in his direst hour; in one case surprisingly so. The fifth Viscount Torrington was his nephew and had been looked after by Byng after his own father died when he was 8 years old. He wrote extensive diaries which were later published as the Torrington Diaries (1934). He had clearly hated his uncle. In one poem he wrote:

> But I, soon sent abroad, to range at large,
>> By death divested of a parent's charge.
> That parent so beloved so truly dear;
>> An uncle lived, like Hamlet's uncle he
> Meet that I set it down, such this to me!

(It sounds as if there is a good family secret to pursue!) Despite his hatred, when the time came, he sent a petition on behalf of his uncle. Byng's younger brother Edward hurried to Portsmouth to meet him despite extreme ill health; indeed he was so ill that he died the day after arrival. The most vigorous of his supporters was his youngest sister Sarah, married to Admiral Osborne. She petitioned and pleaded at each level and opportunity. Members of the family were depicted crying in handkerchiefs in one picture of the execution. I visited the family mausoleum. His plaque was just underneath his father's, Sir George Byng's; a place of honour. On it were the following words:

> To the Perpetual Disgrace
>> of Public Justice.

The Honourable John Byng, Esq.,
    Admiral of the Blue,
Fell a Martyr to Political Persecution,
    March 14th, in the year MDCCLVII;
When Bravery and Loyalty
    Were Insufficient Securities
For the Life and Honour
    Of a Naval Officer.

On the front page of Tunstall's (1928) book given to my father by one of his aunts who was the matriarch of the family, I found written:

> An ancestor of ours who became the scapegoat for the blunders of the Government of his day to "their everlasting shame".

In public anyway, the family refused to join in the scapegoating. By the time the legend reached me, however, he had clearly been disowned.

On reviewing my original legend, very little remained as "true", not even the detail of being shot on his own quarter deck. The Monaque was not his flag ship. Did that edit relate more to my childhood experience of danger on our "own" farm? The Byng legend is clearly unusual in its age and documentation. More recent legends can, however, be explored along similar lines except that information about the event has to be collected from people rather than books. This, of course, gives the exploration a greater significance as a family event.

VII.   IMPLICATIONS FOR FAMILY THERAPY

A.   Family Legends in Other Families

Is my family unique in the power of its legends? To investigate this, I have been exploring legends with client families, colleagues and trainees. I have used the following experiential exercise in family therapy workshops. I ask the participants to close their eyes and

> imagine some current unresolved issue: we all have them; it might be trivial such as whether to buy a new washing machine, or perhaps involves some more important issue. Try to build up a picture of yourself and other people grappling with this decision.

This is to elicit the unresolved theme for which the legend might provide rules.

> Now think of the first family story that comes into your mind which was told to you about a period before you can remember. Again it does not matter if it is trivial. Stick to the first story. Try to get a vivid picture of the person telling you and how it felt.

I give about 2 minutes for them to do this and then say, "Now turn to your neighbour and share this experience with each other". This part takes about 12-15 minutes. Then

> Explore whether there was any connection between the unresolved dilemma and the story. There may or may not be. If there is a link, are there any clues from the story about how you should resolve your dilemma?

Not surprisingly, there is usually a significant connection reported; occasionally none. This proves nothing of course, but the reporting back is usually fascinating. Often a story pops into the participant's mind immediately without much internal scanning, and its relevance only emerges in discussion. Indeed some participants drop the story as irrelevant, hence the importance of the instructions to keep to the first story however apparently trivial. Legends have much in common with dreams. The connection between conflict and legend is frequently clearer to the listener than the narrator. If the workshop meets over a period of time, the way in which the story changes can be explored. Many participants have told me how important the story turned out to be, and that they have explored it further. The richness of the stories shows that they come in many forms. Those including an illusion of alternatives account for a number.

In some families story telling is less important, or the family is totally cut off from its past. In these families, exploring the stories "made up" or phantasies about past figures can be fascinating.

B.   Legends in Family Therapy

In family therapy, change may precede or follow re-editing of legends. In my practice (Byng-Hall and Campbell, 1981), at the beginning of therapy I usually work structurally to help change the current relationships, and work with history at a later stage. I work mostly with family interaction, and with history only for a small proportion of the time. Drawing a genogram reduces the intensity and speed of work produced by structural techniques. For this reason I have techniques for eliciting the relevant rules from the past as quickly as possible.

I may ask the family to think of the first story that came into their heads. This usually provides a rich source of material related to the current therapeutic theme. In the family with the epileptic father mentioned earlier, immediately following an exploration of their profound fears about epilepsy, I asked for their stories. Father's story was

> It is curious but this keeps popping into my mind . . . My father telling me about how he used to stand on the bank of a river and dive right under the barges and come up again on the other side.

The family produced a rich network of interlocking stories about danger at sea, near drownings, and saving others who were drowning. It was then possible to link these with the many aspects of the epilepsy experience. Like all fantasy material, it is so rich that the therapist has to focus and select the relevant stories. Like metaphor, the story which resonates best with the therapist provides the communication. It becomes important for the therapist to be aware of the colour he adds to the mix. The Byng legend resonated with this.

In longer-term therapy, the genogram (Leibermann, 1979) provides a useful format for exploring legends. The main modification of the technique is not to ask what an ancestor was like, but to ask for a story about him, or better a story to show how "those two" got along. The story is then written down (the paper needs to be large enough) and any subsequent editing can be noted. The other advantage of constructing a genogram this way is that the stories are interactional which is congruent with working with the family system.

Re-editing my legend had involved exploring the context of the legend, exploding some of its myths and seeing that other options were open.

C.   Clinical Example: The "X" Family Legend

In the X family, as the family system stabilized, the legend of the drunken great-grandfather thrown out by his 10-year-old son was revisited several times. They decided that he could have chosen to come home, or perhaps his wife did not want him. It emerged that the blindness was of late onset and so only the great-grandmother would have been affected, not brothers and sisters. Mr X came to one session complaining bitterly about his son's rudeness to him. I asked the family to recall the legend. I suggested that perhaps it was ringing bells for them now which could be frightening. I asked them to put themselves in imagination into that legend, as if it were now. They could hardly bear to think about it, but keeping them to the task, they eventually accepted the roles while acknowledging them to be fantasy. Mr X discussed with Brian whether he felt he had to intervene to stop him beating up his wife. The reality of the present family interaction was compared and contrasted with the legend. I point out how they had corrected the legend so that father emerged as the strong one who could beat up his sons if necessary. The fighting which was valued was largely restricted to that between the brothers, a much more appropriate place. I also suggested that they had to exaggerate this correction perhaps unnecessarily, because they were haunted by the legend. Father's epilepsy made potential violence feel more real than it might have been otherwise. Fact and fantasy, past and present, were disentangled.

VII.   EPILOGUE

One more important personal change came from quite an unexpected source. I was telling the Byng story at a party when someone, who possibly had the influence to put it into effect, suggested that Parliament should ask the Queen for a public pardon for Byng. A curious sense of release followed, perhaps because justice could finally be acknowledged, where it needed to be: with the monarch. Despite the fact that this was 224 years later the legacy had still weighed on me. Boszormenyi-Nagy and Spark (1973) discuss the concept of a family legacy. Although the nation had not repaid its debt to the family, in some symbolic way, it was now showing its willingness to do so. I could now feel free of the obligation to collect that debt, although it could be argued that I am doing so through this chapter.

REFERENCES

Boszormenyi-Nagy, I. and Spark, G. M. (1973). "Invisible Loyalties", Harper & Row, London.

Byng, J. (1934). Extract from a poem on his youth. *In* "The Torrington Diaries", (C. Andrew, ed.), Vol. 1. p. 345, Methuen, London.

Byng-Hall, J. (1973). Family myths used as defence in conjoint family therapy. *British Journal of Medical Psychology,* **46,** 239-249.

Byng-Hall, J. (1979). Re-editing family mythology during family therapy. *Journal of Family Therapy,* **1,** 103-116.

Byng-Hall, J. (1980). Symptom bearer as marital distance regulator: Clinical implications. *Family Process,* **19,** 355-367.

Byng-Hall, J. (1981). Therapeutic confusion produced by too close/too far family systems. *In* "Questions and Answers in the Practice of Family Therapy", (A. S. Gurman, ed.), 143-146, Brunner/Mazel, New York.

Byng-Hall, J. and Campbell, D. (1981). Resolving conflicts arising out of distance regulation. *Journal of Marital and Family Therapy,* **7,** 321-330.

Ferreira, A. J. (1963). Family Myths: The covert rules of the relationship. *Archives of General Psychiatry,* **9,** 457-463.

Lieberman, S. (1979). Transgenerational analysis: the geneogram as a technique in family therapy. *Journal of Family Therapy,* **1,** 51-64.

Linnemann, E. (1966). "Parables of Jesus: Introduction and Exposition", S.P.C.K., London.

Pope, D. (1962). "At 12 Mr. Byng was Shot", Weidenfeld & Nicholson, London.

Tunstall, B. (1928). "Admiral Byng and the Loss of Minorca", Philip Allan, London.

Watzlawick, P. (1978). "The Language of Change: Elements of Therapeutic Communication", Basic Books, New York.

— Chapter 9 —

The Strengths and Weaknesses in Co-therapy

— W. Roberts —

I. INTRODUCTION

It would be true to say that when family therapy was first practised in England, it was commonplace for practitioners to work in pairs, and although initially it often appeared to take place because of the level of anxiety about the ability of one person to manage to work alone with the complexities of family interaction, it was also recognized that working as a therapeutic pair offered a number of additional advantages.

Currently the situation appears to be changing, and an increasing number of family therapists are choosing to work alone, or, if they have co-workers, to use them in a more supervisory role; whether or not this can be considered co-therapy is debatable (Hannum, 1980). How has this change come about? In part it can be attributed to the interchange of ideas and cross-cultural learning which arose from the visits of various American practitioners during the 1970s when new and relatively unfamiliar methods of working with families were introduced (methods which required more activity on the part of the therapist), reinforced by the contributions made by some of our own family therapists when they in turn visited the United States. It may also be due in part to the disenchantment experienced by therapists who had difficulties in establishing a satisfactory co-therapy relationship. My own view was personally influenced by the combination of these factors, and led to me choosing to see families alone rather than with a co-worker.

II. EARLY CO-THERAPY EXPERIENCES

A. Basis in Multi-disciplinary Clinic Settings

If we re-trace the development of the family therapy movement in this country, we find that initially it was most commonly practised in child-centred settings, i.e. Child Guidance Clinics or hospital departments of Child Psychiatry. This may be one of the reasons why co-therapy was so immediately popular, for these settings were generally staffed by inter-disciplinary teams accustomed to working together in other ways. The majority of these settings were psychoanalytically orientated, and the techniques used were based on a psychodynamic model using

Family Therapy
ISBN: 0-12-089355-X

interpretation and taking account of transference and counter-transference phenomena.

The co-therapy relationship was considered to be very important for a number of reasons: it provided a relationship model not only for the marital couple, but for the family itself; it introduced an additional relationship dimension, since the interaction between the workers became part of the process and was available for use in the interest of the treatment process. Skynner (1976) suggests, for example, that in providing a role model for the family, "mutual trust and the combination of personal spontaneity with attentiveness and responsiveness to the partner . . . mirror closely the relationship necessary for the most satisfying sexual intercourse". It allowed the opportunity for carrying out planned strategies aimed at bringing about change as, for example, when one worker agreed to "take sides" with one or more members of a family in an attempt to restructure a pattern of behaviour; or when the therapists adopted a pre-determined role such as one remaining passive leaving the other to be more dominant. In addition, it not only allowed "hand-holding" for workers who were keen to learn to practice, but also increased the learning opportunity when workers could share their differing perspectives of the family and become aware through their own interactions of relationship aspects projected onto themselves.

B. Some Disadvantages of Co-therapy: Personal Experiences

Aware of the value of co-therapy and the essentials needed to reach a satisfactory level of working together, many practitioners attempted to set up co-therapy relationships, some of which were highly successful and others of which continued over a prolonged period of time. This was largely my own experience when working in a Child Guidance Clinic with a fairly large staff, most of whom remained in post long enough to allow satisfactory co-relationships to evolve. Despite the apparent advantages of such a situation, the kind of difficulties common to agencies less well-endowed were still experienced. As members of an interdisciplinary team, we were encouraged to form an alliance with more than one member of the team, and although there was apparent freedom in the way in which partners selected a co-worker, nevertheless there were occasions when the unmet demands of a particular worker led to pressure from team members for demands to be met. It was this situation which led to an unfortunate early experience for me.

In the clinic to which I am referring, it was at that time customary for new referrals to be discussed at a staff meeting, and it was at such a meeting that a recently appointed colleague accepted responsibility for the "S" family. She immediately invited me to be her co-worker after the two male staff confirmed that they had no vacancies. My prevarication led to my colleagues' firm request that I should consider helping "J" who as a new member of staff, was eager to learn to practice family therapy. My hesitation was due to a number of factors: I was reluctant to expose myself to somebody I felt I had not yet come to know very well; I was aware that she saw me as "experienced" while I considered myself still to be a beginner; I was in the stages of developing a co-worker relationship with two other members of staff, and did not feel that I was ready to attempt a third. My doubts were overruled and I gave in to the pressure! At this stage, we were not yet sufficiently aware of the importance of preparation, and so my colleague and I met for a very short preliminary discussion before we saw the family, but together we wrote the letter of invitation to them.

(1) The Family Interview

The family comprised Father: a small, passive man who was frequently out of work because of recurring bouts of sickness for which no physical cause could be found; Mother: a part-time domestic worker who had difficulty in travelling on any form of public transport; and Billy, 14, the youngest of three children. His brother and sister were married and living away from home and had apparently given the parents no cause for concern. Billy on the other hand, was said to be finding it difficult to get to school, the parents describing the scenes in which he lay on the floor "writhing in agony".

My colleague had asked me to "take the lead" with this family, saying that although she had read quite a considerable amount, she had had no opportunity to practise. I was a dilatory reader and felt rather threatened by her theoretical knowledge! However, I liked her enthusiasm and had been impressed by her contribution at a recent case conference. I failed to say anything to her about either of these factors. While we waited for the family to arrive, we talked over the information given by the referrer and speculated about the symptom and its relevance to the family, and as the clinic was using a psychodynamic model of working, we focussed on the emotional tie between Mother and Billy, and were curious about his early history. During the early part of the session my colleague, whom I will refer to as AB, remained very quiet and passive and left the running to me as we had agreed. The session moved slowly with Mother insisting on giving a graphic description of Billy's symptomatic behaviour while I attempted to explore what might have precipitated the symptom; Father shared Mother's extreme anxiety that Billy was "*really* ill". After about half an hour, my silent colleague sprang to life and began to be quite active in making suggestions about how Billy should be got back to school, directing Father to carry these out and insisting that his florid behaviour should be ignored. Mother's anxious reactions were ignored; and so was I! The session ended in this flurry of activity between my colleague and Father, while Mother shed a few tears looking appealingly in my direction. I could only look back helplessly. There was no time immediately available to discuss what had happened, only time for AB to comment "that was interesting", and for me to acknowledge, with a multiplicity of feelings, that indeed it was.

An hour later the mother telephoned, asked for me, and complained about the task her husband had agreed to do. She tried to make me her ally reminding me that I had indicated that I was aware of her anxiety and I was too close to the experience to be able to think rationally. I found myself torn between supporting my colleague's strategy and empathizing with the mother's distress. Later, despite the efforts we made to discuss what had happened and to try and agree a way of working in which both of us would feel comfortable, the tension we brought to the next session transmitted itself to the family in such a way that they failed further appointments and asked to be transferred to another agency. I was later to discover that this experience was more commonplace than I had known it to be, and that others, like AB and myself, were sometimes able to use it constructively. In our case we sought the help of a colleague, and made time to talk about the experience in some depth, airing and sharing the positive and negative aspects of the contribution we had each made in such a way that we felt the relationship was enriched, and were able to continue to do some rewarding work together.

C. Agency Disadvantages of Co-therapy

When difficulties could be resolved satisfactorily, co-therapy was an obviously advantageous method of working. Circumstances sometimes meant, however, that this was not so easy to achieve. Discussion at a depth that often becomes necessary if two people are to reach a degree of compatibility for successful co-therapy to take place, not only needs time and space, but also requires that the workers are likely to be able to continue to develop their skills together by remaining in the same agency over a long enough period of time. Too often, particularly in Departments of Social Service, where there appeared to be a more frequent turnover of staff, co-therapy relationships tended to end with the termination of a worker's term of employment before the full potential of the therapeutic pair had been realized, leaving one frustrated worker feeling ambivalent about starting again to develop another co-worker relationship.   '

In speaking with social workers, I learned that it was often because of this kind of experience that they had decided against practising family therapy until they could either find work in an agency where they believed there would be less likelihood of staff mobility, or until they had successfully negotiated a co-therapy relationship with a colleague who was aware of what was needed and prepared to commit themselves to an agreed period of working together. Others took steps to approach workers in another agency in an attempt to find a solution, one example of this being the work undertaken when both the Probation Department and the Social Services Department had responsibility for one or more members of a family. This method of working made extra demands on the workers since each was accountable to their own service, and additional meetings which included senior management were often necessary.

In the clinic where I was practising, we began to invite the agency worker who had referred the family, to become the co-therapist with the member of the clinic staff who had accepted the responsibility for the referral: a method also used by many other clinics. This brought other problems:

(1) The workers were not always clear about management responsibility.

(2) The "hidden agendas" of the referrer: "please take this difficult family off my hands", and of the clinic worker: "I'll only take this family if I can work with them", were not recognized or acknowledged!

Again the varying levels of expertise between the workers, or the unrealistic expectations of one about the other was not discovered until they attempted to practice together. This latter situation was often intensified by the fact that the two workers may have been of different disciplines, each having unaired fantasies about the role of the other. In addition, practical considerations such as finding time together when both could be free to meet, and where to do so in order that travelling time was not too onerous, often led to a reluctance to continue.

Despite these difficulties, however, the motivation of many practitioners to learn family therapy techniques played a large part in the efforts made to overcome them, with benefit not only to the workers, but also to the agencies whom they represented, for the need to improve inter-agency collaboration became evident.

As skills developed, so it seemed did the level of expectations rise. Some of the difficulties which might have been ignored or tolerated in the early stages seemed to assume greater importance, and when they could not be overcome, they led to the breakdown of the co-therapy relationship. Similarly, if one of the pair developed at a faster pace than the other, frustration again led to an end of the partnership leading one or both therapists to seek alternative workers with whom to pair. It was out of this shifting and changing that some of the more lasting co-therapy relationships emerged and grew from strength to strength.

Dowling (1980) has carried out a detailed study in which she explores clinical issues regarding co-therapy as a method of therapeutic intervention. She found that

the therapists were consistent in their personal style of intervention . . . behaved in a similar manner with different therapists and different families — expressed that they would want similar characteristics in a co-therapist regardless of the type of family.

Reference is also made to the need for empirical study into the value of co-therapy as compared to single therapist intervention.

III. ASPECTS OF THE CO-THERAPY RELATIONSHIP

A. Personal Qualities Necessary

The fact that co-therapy is still widely practised is an acknowledgement that it has value despite the continuation of some of the problems experienced in the early stages. Many of those who have written about family therapy have commented about the co-therapy relationship; Boszormenyi-Nagy and Spark (1973) are of the opinion that

an unusual amount of flexibility and creativity are required on the part of both co-workers who should have empathy, compassion and trust, and in addition a capacity for complementarity.

They also suggest that ideally the couple should be heterosexual. This poses problems for agencies where the majority of the staff are female: a not unusual situation in this country, although my impression is that there has been a change in recent years. On the other hand when working with the psycho-dynamic model, the co-therapists may be experienced as heterosexual by family members, investing them with feminine and masculine characteristics. In making reference to this, Dowling (1980) points out the importance of the therapist's awareness of this phenomenon.

Walrond Skinner (1976) lists the most important criteria of choice of partner as

> one with whom one will feel comfortable in sharing and exchanging ideas, feelings and problems as these are experienced both within the treatment situation with the family, and within the co-therapy relationship itself.

By committing themselves to working together over a prolonged period of time, some therapists have achieved a complementarity which has enabled them to work with the most seriously disturbed families. Complementarity can be seen as a counter-balancing of therapeutic input, and may be achieved by, for example, one worker being supportive while the other is more confronting. In an article describing a method for working with schizophrenic families, Mueller, McGoldrick and Orfanides (1976) speak about the need for co-therapy being prompted by the power of such families in keeping their boundaries rigidly closed to outsiders. The co-therapists adopt structured roles: the male supporting the males and setting limits for the females and vice versa, and this is said to greatly facilitate the task of keeping the family engaged whilst working for change. Furthermore, it is claimed that it is extremely difficult for a lone therapist to maintain the required balance between support and confrontation in families who are disorganized yet rigid.

B.   Co-therapy with Disadvantaged Families

One of my own experiences is of working with a high percentage of families with a history of severe deprivation (physical, material and emotional) and I found that the heavy demands made by such families became more tolerable when there was a co-therapist to share the task. One particular male colleague and I, able to work together over a long period of time, developed a method whereby we would take it in turns to manage a particularly noisy and disruptive situation, such as that of a family expressing very angry feelings and making demands for action. The "J" family are an example of this as can be seen from the following short excerpt:

Husband: (in loud voice and gesticulating wildly) You get into my guts, stop telling such lies — you're a downright liar — take no notice of her, Miss, she wants you to believe her . . .

Wife: (at the same time and in equally loud voice and sobbing) Stop him, Miss, he's telling lies — how can you sit there and say such things — don't believe him, Miss . . .

My co-therapist and I learned that if one of us stayed "out of the fray", as it were, by remaining less engaged while the other was more active in making comments, clarifying what was being said or demonstrating by non-verbal behaviour that he or she was intent on listening and prepared to speak, then the inactive partner could wait for the moment when the intensity had begun to diminish and then "move in" to focus on one particular aspect he or she considered would be amenable to more coherent discussion. Minuchin *et al.* (1966) give a very good description of this approach:

> Whenever one therapist is involved in interaction with a family, the co-therapist's field of observation includes the therapist, not just the family alone. He learns to watch specifically for the ways in which the family organises his partner into behaving along lines which do not permit family change . . .

In the incident referred to above, I had been making such comments as "I can see you are both very angry with each other", or "it must be difficult to hear each other when you believe that what you are hearing is all lies", and "I hear you both saying that you are worried about whether we will be taking sides . . .", to little or no effect. My almost silent colleague eventually spoke quietly yet with a firm voice addressing himself to me:

> Win, I don't think we will be able to begin to help Mr and Mrs J until they can stop talking together and begin to listen to each other. Could you tell us, Mr J, more about the incident you've just been describing so that we can understand it from your point of view, and then we can hear how Mrs J felt about it.

When, at times, we had not used this technique but had both chosen to be active, we had found it difficult to see "the wood for the trees", and shared the family's exhaustion at the end of the episode.

An additional factor which had to be managed when working with families were the children, often equally deprived, who themselves made constant demands on the therapists. In such circumstances, our strategy was sometimes to decide that one would give attention to the children and attempt to get them to settle down, while the other focussed solely on the parents. It then became possible to bring adults and children together in a discussion when the therapists took the side of either the parents or the children. Nowadays one would ask the parents to settle the children.

C. Making Co-therapy Work

It is evident that the requirements necessary for a co-therapy relationship to reach this level makes heavy demands on the workers; time for talking together before and after each session with a family in order to be open to each other's difficulties, to respect each other's limitations, to recognize and value each other's strengths, and to develop a degree of mutual trust that will safeguard against a family's attempts to split or scapegoat. Frequent and regular communication of this kind can lead to growth for the therapists, both personally and professionally.

It is difficult to know at what stage my colleagues and I began to consider the possibility of practising without a co-worker. In our frequent discussions about this we shared similar doubts and anxieties. Concern centred around such areas as the difficulty for a lone worker in dealing with feelings of extreme helplessness and despair being projected by more than one member of a family; what would be lost by not having a partner who could be used as a "sounding board", and who, having been present, provided the opportunity for detailed discussion of the family and its problems. It was apparent that many of the needs inherent in the concern being expressed were in the nature of having available a kind of "hand-holder", and although there was in addition the recognition of many of the positive aspects of pairing already referred to, when the prospect of working without a co-therapist was being aired, the argument against change was more generally linked with doubts about being able to manage.

Another factor which was frequently referred to as justification for co-therapy was the suggestion that the risk of being "sucked in" to the family pathology was such that a co-worker was essential to "pull one out" before one went "completely under", and although this seemed to imply that family therapy was fraught with potential dangers, there was often more than a grain of truth in the possibility of this taking place, particularly in families where individual boundaries were very diffuse. Having recognized this phenomenon, some co-therapists adopted a way of working in which one of the workers deliberately allowed himself/herself to become involved to a point where it became apparent that he or she was displaying signs of having got caught into the emotional level of family interaction, at which stage the partner would intervene to extricate him. This is a particular feature of Whitaker's work (Napier and Whitaker, 1978).

(1) The "G" Family: Case Example

The following example of work carried out by myself and a male colleague demonstrates some of the points I have been making. My colleague and I had paired on many occasions, and were very comfortable in the way we worked together. Our co-therapy relationship was the result of spending time together before and after each family meeting when we would explore in some depth our separate experiences of the session and discuss areas of disagreement looking critically at each other's contribution. From prior information we were aware of the fact that the "G" family were likely to be somewhat chaotic, the parents having recently re-married following a divorce some years previously. The referrer also told us that during the period of the divorce, when Mr G lived with an unmarried brother, he had returned to his wife and children for most weekends. Mrs G had taken care of many of his material needs, washing his clothes and cooking some of his meals. They had had an annual holiday together as a family, and were sometimes joined in this by Mr G's brother. The children had remained with their mother, but had also spent time with their father. They were referred because Peter, the oldest son aged 13, was not only having difficult in getting to school, but also in mixing with children of his own age. Both he and John, aged 11, were unaccustomed to leaving the house to play with other children because the parents considered their neighbours were "too rough". Any social event had to involve the whole family, so for example, the parents had located a pub with a beer garden so that Peter and John could always accompany them when they went out for a drink together. Likewise, visits to the cinema were always made *en famille*.

My colleague, "C", and I agreed that we would want to try and establish some boundaries between adults and children in the first session, but speculated that this might not be easy. So we planned that we would attempt to find some areas of disagreement between parents and children and then "take sides" in so far as he would join with the children while I would ally myself with the adults. We also agreed that alternatively if disagreement became difficult to locate, he would join fully in family discussion moving freely between all family members while I would maintain a distance and be ready to extricate him when I thought he was becoming too enmeshed.

"C" began the session engaging the family in talking about the problem with which they had come, and then he was active in getting them to describe their family life and relationships and the "togetherness" indicated in the referral became apparent. I remained passive while this was taking place, observing how "C" was joining with the family by showing keen interest in their description of their life together, commenting upon their closeness in such a way that they elaborated upon the detail and I became increasingly aware of the feelings of suffocation being engendered. At this point I commented quite brusquely, for I was beginning to fear that C might not heed me,

> C, I can't agree with you that this family are as close and loving as you seem to think they are, because I find myself wondering whether Mr G might sometimes like to take his wife out alone for a couple of hours without the children. I thought he gave some indication of this when he spoke of looking forward to the day when he could take Mrs G out for a meal. [He had commented that he wasn't able to afford to take all the family out to eat together.]

Mrs G immediately began to deny this, but the look her husband gave me confirmed that I had struck a chord to which he could respond although he needed some support from "C", who now joined me in exploring this possibility before he felt able to do so.

Before the end of the session, we had also been able to establish some boundary between parents and children. This became possible when the boys talked of playing football at school, whereupon C engaged them in "football talk" while I explored interests that the parents had enjoyed together before the birth of Peter. I learned that they had been keen cyclists, but had discontinued this activity when Mrs G became pregnant and were waiting for the boys to be "a little older" before they started cycling together as a family. During this part of the session we changed the seating, C placing himself between the boys and the parents, while I sat opposite to him with the parents on my right; thus we created a physical boundary between parents and children. These moves were established with comparative ease which was, I believe, entirely due to the way in which C had initially allowed himself to be drawn into the family.

IV. DEVELOPMENTS IN CO-THERAPY

A.   Co-therapy with a Difference

Reference is made at the beginning of this chapter to the changes that took place during the 1970s when many family therapists, accustomed to working from an analytic understanding, became interested in systems theory, and in particular in the structural approach which demanded new skills and techniques. These changes appeared to give an impetus to the move away from co-therapy in which the two workers stayed together with the family group and towards the situation of having one's partner and sometimes partners, behind a one-way screen. It is possible that the increased activity demanded by the new techniques led to difficulties in working with a colleague in the same room largely because of the uncertainty of being able to ascertain that the colleague was sharing the reasons for the moves being made. Working with the feeling content of the family inter-action allowed space for co-workers to become aware of the direction in which the process was moving, as for example, when two therapists were attempting to explore how a family *felt* about a particular piece of behaviour, each could move in and out of the discussion and so on: sometimes active, sometimes passive, but generally staying with the feeling level being explored.

If, on the other hand, these same workers were focussing on the *process* of the communication rather than the *content*, and aiming at effecting some change in this within the session, confusion might well arise unless both were clear about the direction of the change; in addition the authority required to elicit change could become diminished. One example of this was when a therapist, aware that a wife was disqualifying her husband, attempted not only to recognize this, but also to get the couple to interact in a different way in the "here and now"; the intervention needed to be made quickly and firmly, and allowed no time for the workers to discover whether they were in agreement. In other words, it seems that working to effect change in the "here and now" gives no opportunity for co-therapists to communicate about possible strategies without losing the necessary authority unless they can discuss the situation away from the family.

B.   The Advantages of "Distance"

The distance created by the one-way screen is particularly helpful in allowing the therapist working with the family to remain "in charge" as it were, while at the same time having available the comments, understanding, suggestions and criticisms of his co-workers, who, at this distance are often able to see more clearly how the family are interacting with the safeguard of not becoming involved in the emotional aspects of the situation. I consider that when a co-worker behind the screen makes live interventions by, for example, entering the room, he or she can correctly be called co-therapist, and many of the strengths and weaknesses already discussed can be equally appropriate. For example, when a therapist is working alone, the question of "where does the authority lie?" may be problematic unless the co-worker, in making interventions, is careful to avoid undermining or disqualifying the therapist. When co-workers remain together throughout the session, areas of disagreement can be talked about in the presence of the family, giving the opportunity for "modelling" a way of dealing with differences of opinion. Although this may also happen when the co-worker intervenes from behind the screen, unless handled skilfully, the impact runs the risk of removing the authority from the therapist.

This way of working does not mean that the workers have to be constantly in agreement; on the contrary, they may choose to employ a strategy of disagreement although the family is not made aware that this is an agreed decision. Papp (1978) gives a detailed account of a family who were helped by this method, and has developed the notion of the "group" behind the screen: a sort of Greek chorus commenting on the action.

V. CONCLUSION

Co-therapy is considered as a part of the developmental process of Family Therapy practice. It is suggested that it was widely used in the early stages as a method by which therapists could support and help each other while learning to work with families. It was seen to have particular advantages in psychodynamic work in so far as modelling, complementarity and mirroring were concerned, although success was to a great extent dependent on the quality of the relationship between the co-therapists.

The introduction of Systems Theory and consequent development of new skills and techniques appears to have led to therapists choosing to work alone more frequently, although the co-worker(s) may continue to be part of the process behind a one-way screen. The need for ongoing research with particular reference to the value of co-therapy as compared to lone therapy intervention is recognized.

REFERENCES

Boszormenyi-Nagy, I. and Spark, G. M. (1973). "Invisible Loyalties", Harper & Row, New York.

Dowling, E. (1980). Co-therapy: A clinical researcher's view. In "Family and Marital Psychotherapy", (S. Walrond-Skinner, ed.), Routledge & Kegan Paul, London.

Hannum, J. W. (1980). Some co-therapy techniques with families. Family Process, 19, 161-168.

Minuchin, S., Montalvo, B., Cuerney, B., Rosman, B. and Schumer, F. (1966). "Families of the Slums", Basic Books, New York.

Mueller, P., McGoldrick, M. and Orfanides, M. (1976). A Method of Co-therapy for Schizophrenic Families. Family Process, 15, 179-191.

Napier, A. Y. and Whitaker, C. (1978). "The Family Crucible", Harper & Row, New York.

Papp, P. (1978). The family that had all the answers. *In* "Family Therapy: Full Length Case Studies", (P. Papp, ed.), Gardner, New York.

Skynner, A. C. R. (1976). "One Flesh, Separate Persons", Constable, London.

Walrond-Skinner, S. (1976). "Family Therapy", Routledge & Kegan Paul, London.

Chapter 10

Going Back
to Your Own Family

S. Lieberman

I. INTRODUCTION

In this chapter I shall present reasoned arguments to persuade you to use your family of origin as a personal resource in your work. Your experiences in your own family of origin should already have taught you a great deal about the structure, transgenerational influences and resistances which are universally found. Further work with your family can provide added knowledge, skill and personal growth.

Going back to your own family of origin to study it and change your relationships within it is a novel and controversial act. Its novelty stems from its rarity as a prescribed part of training. English family therapists have yet to adopt this procedure within their training programme. It is a rarely described, taught or written technique. Going back to your own family is controversial in that it raises the spectre of confidentiality, personal insight and growth, and involvement of "innocent" bystanders (the therapist's family members) on the road to becoming a family therapist.

A search of the literature reveals a paucity of material which discusses the issue of going back to one's own family of origin. The seminal article was published anonymously (1972) at first, and later published by Bowen (1974). But the original airing of the issue, "Differentiation of a Self in One's Own Family", was presented in 1967 to a family therapy research conference following the breakthrough in Bowen's efforts to work with his own family. Bowen believed that

> the family therapist usually has the same problems in his own family that are present in families he sees professionally and that he has a responsibility to define himself in his own family if he is to function adequately in his professional work.

His attempt to differentiate himself from his parental and extended family was guided by his theoretical postulates of family functioning (Bowen, 1976). Differentiation for him meant being able to "maintain emotional objectivity while in the midst of an emotional system in turmoil, yet at the same time actively relate to key people in the system". I have summarized all of his theoretical concepts elsewhere (Lieberman, 1980), but it is necessary to understand his techniques for working with families in order to grasp why he did what he did with his own family.

Family Therapy
ISBN: 0-12-089355-X

II. APPLICATION OF BOWEN'S TECHNIQUES

The three main techniques are detriangling, reversal of emotional cut-off, and increasing the differentiation of self.

A. Detriangling

In detriangling, the therapist investigates a particular family triad. He excludes the most vulnerable individual, whether child or parent from further sessions, and arranges to meet with the remaining family members. The therapist then sits back and awaits triangling moves. When they come, they are resisted and explored by the therapist. The end result is an alteration in the needs of the family members to emotionally bring in (triangle) vulnerable family members which will generalize to the family environment.

B. The Reversal of Emotional Cut-off

This requires only one family member in therapeutic sessions. Bowen coaches individual family members, not necessarily the identified patient, to re-establish relationships with relatives who were emotionally cut off so as to reverse the process. Once in contact, he coaches them to establish a new type of relationship based on "solid selves" rather than "pseudo-selves".*

C. Increasing the Differentiation of a Self

This describes the method by which Bowen attempts to raise the level of differentiation for his patients. He asks individual patients to work with their family of origin so as to continually detriangle themselves from the family. The result of this manoeuvre is meant to be an increased level of

---

* *Editor's note:* Although this term is in common usage by the Bowen Group, it is both distinct from, and overlaps with other writings about "true" and "false" self from a psychoanalytic perspective (see Balint, 1968; Guntrip, 1968; Rycroft, 1968; Winnicott, 1971; Lomas, 1973). There are at least three distinct uses both of *Ego* and of *Self* in the Psychoanalytic and Family Therapy literature. Bowen appears to derive the terms from the American psychoanalytic writings at a time when Hartman (1965) and others were defining the Ego as an adaptive mechanism, very similar to the error-control cybernetic model. "Self", on the other hand has usually been defined experientially in "who I am" terms. The "false self" is the character played by an individual in life-events while the "true self" refers to the individual's authentic experience of him- or herself if and when it can be realized. In contrast, Bowen's "solid self" refers to the level of differentiation, viz. it defines a level of ability to perform certain behavioural and interpersonal tasks which is fixed at a certain point in development, and is relatively uninfluenced by context. "Pseudo-self" on the other hand, is a definition of performance which varies according to the anxiety and relationship context. For further development of these concepts, see Bowen (1966) and Kerr (1981).

self-differentiation.[†] This technique is especially useful when faced with adults emotionally arrested in their adolescent stage of development. While differentiating a self, the individual establishes a new responsibility for himself as he is coached to make his own therapeutic manoeuvres. Bowen, after beginning therapy with adults individually or in marital or family therapy, sends his adult patients home to visit their family of origin, supervising them in their differentiating struggles.

All of the above techniques are used in Bowen's work with his own family. After an account of his family background and history, he details preliminary work which consisted of person-to-person communications over a period of 12 years. These attempts were supposed to enable him to develop independent personal relationships with members of his extended family (reversing emotional cut-off). He hoped he would then be able to break the existing family triangles and prevent himself from fusing into his family's emotional system. This strategy alone proved unsuccessful. "Action is required when words fail to detriangle in emotional systems." Bowen set up a situation in which he precipitated a confrontation between himself, his brother and his mother. His mother would often relate stories about his younger brother to him, while his brother avoided him entirely. Bowen wrote down many of these stories in a letter sent to his brother and primed many of his relatives in various ways for his next visit to the family home. A 2-hour personal discussion with his brother and his brother's wife resulted which was full of fire and thunder while his wife, his mother and his father hovered in the background. During this trying period, Bowen reports that he was able to stay completely outside of his family's emotional system (differentiating a self).

His success and its resultant effect upon him led Bowen to begin coaching his trainee family therapists to achieve a similar goal in their families of origin. He claims that

> Those who had been most successful with their families developed unusual skill and flexibility as family psychotherapists. They were adept at avoiding intense emotional entanglements with families in their practice and they could work comfortably with upset and distraught families.

III. FURTHER DEVELOPMENTS

Although Bowen's presentation predates all other existing written material on this subject, in 1968 there appeared the first published article (Framo, 1968) by a

---

† *Editor's note:* The concept of self-differentiation has been elsewhere clarified by the author (Lieberman, 1981, p.340):

> The concept of differentiation is defined rather tortuously by Bowen. Those individuals with high levels of differentiation of self are emotionally and intellectually integrated with intellectual control maintained. Individuals with low levels of differentiation of self are said to have emotional and intellectual fusion. Here, the control of the self is muddled so that the individual's reactions are liable to be determined by the relationship (family) system and develop a pseudo-self, a concept similar to Winnicott's false self (Winnicott, 1965).

family therapist devoted entirely to the impact of one's family of origin on families in therapy and vice versa. Framo starts from the premise that treating families "revives the specters of one's own past family life" as well as the "subtle suffusing effects on the therapist's current personal family relationships". The remainder of the article he describes as "a kind of self-indulgent labour of love and pain", in which he anecdotally catalogues and compares statements from various family therapy sessions followed by his own personal reflections or vicarious participations. It is a curiously moving paper which Framo later described as his favourite (Framo, 1976). He maintains that a "critical but unnoticed ingredient in all family and marital therapies is the presence of the ghosts of the therapist's own family".

In 1970, there appeared the first of many articles later to be published using Bowen's techniques and theory to describe work with the therapist's own family (Friedman, 1970). Friedman indicates that his goal was to obtain change in his extended family, and that his most potent tools were verbal and behavioural reversal. Specifically, he used himself as an antitherapist in his family "by *not* helping precisely where because of my professional expertise I could have been most helpful". He closely follows the Bowen model of re-establishing individual relationships with each family member and altering those relationships systematically.

In 1972, a systematic attempt to describe both the work on one's own family and the task of the supervisor of such work was published (Guerin and Fogarty, 1972). Guerin first gives a detailed description of a three-generation geneogram which is a starting point for a trainee's work on his own family. This blueprint or map of family relatedness plays a central role in the planning of work with the family. Existing frequency of contact and physical location of each family member are determined, and then the existing family triangles are explored. He reports that 25% of his trainees actually take on the project of working with their own families, all of whom found it personally and professionally helpful. The goal of the project is described as the differentiation of the self from others in the family.

Ideally, the planning and accomplishment of such work is guided by a trained supervisor (who has undergone a similar experience). But Fogarty describes such supervision as a battle for the mind of trainee therapists, as if it were a seduction of the trainee into a new way of thinking. Wooing trainees away from psychoanalytic viewpoints has less relevance in England* and detracts from the real work of supervision as it can occur with a willing and motivated therapist-trainee. Fogarty traces the reluctant path of a trainee from supervision of a case to supervision of the trainee's work with his family; a path which ends in failure

---

* *Editor's note:* The statement is relevant in terms of the different development of both Psychoanalytic and Family Therapy thinking in England, from that in the USA and parts of Europe. The object relations views of an individual (see Winnicott, 1971; Balint, 1968; Guntrip, 1968) have been more readily applied to a family context than the classical psychoanalytic approaches more prevalent in the USA. At the same time, the process of the development of Family Therapy in Britain took a different course, which at least initially meant that theoretical polemics were less relevant (see Cooklin, 1978).

to convert his young disciple. He concludes that family systems cannot be truly understood without personal application of the theory. Ferber's critique of this article is discussed in the section on a family training analysis.

Three further articles detail the intimacies of family therapists using Bowen's approach to working with their families of origin (Colon, 1973; Anon, 1973; Anon, 1974). Finally, two papers which deal with the importance of the family of origin as a resource in therapy (Framo, 1976; Carter and Orfanides, 1976) also touch on the importance of the family of origin of the therapist. It is noted that all of the above work is American in origin. The first presentation of work using a similar approach in England was the presentation of work with my own family to the Family and Marital Course of the Institute of Group Analysis on 21 January, 1975.

IV. A FAMILY THERAPIST'S TRAINING ANALYSIS

In another work (Lieberman, 1980) I have attempted to explore a model for a family training analysis. The necessary and sufficient components of such an analysis would include:

(a) Providing opportunities for insight and self-understanding,

(b) Increasing the empathic skills of the therapist,

(c) Providing an apprenticeship experience,

(d) Teaching a model for working with families,

(e) Providing experiential input through work with the therapist's own family members,

(f) Providing a therapeutic experience where necessary for the trainee and his family.

Insight and self-understanding have been traditional goals of training analyses for psychoanalysts and group analysts for many years. Insight is valued for its ability to warn therapists of their own compulsive and destructive helping behaviour. Insight into one's own family dynamics and relationships would result in similar protection for our client families. Although such insight may be obtained serendipitously, through a do-it-yourself process (such as Freud's self-analysis) or other haphazard means, the family training analysis would be an organized and supervised experience within a training programme for family therapists.

Accurate empathy is an established and important primary therapeutic quality (Truax and Carkhuff, 1967). Research has shown that training programmes can and should aim to increase the abilities of a therapist in this dimension. Empathy refers to the ability to detect another person's emotional state without interfering in it. It has been enhanced by specifically teaching individual therapists to detect feeling states in patients, peers, and standardized audiotapes. Accurate empathy is one of the qualities in therapists which behavioural therapists value (Marks, 1976) as well as family therapists (Minuchin, 1978; Bowen, 1974; Lieberman, 1980). Understanding of one's own family members would provide valuable empathic training in the following way. Family members who are most likely to arouse sympathy, hostility or other emotional reactions provide an ideal testing ground for the development of accurate empathy as defined above. For example, a family therapy trainee was unable to work effectively with a client-family due to the hostility of the father. Work with his own father enabled him to gain the necessary empathy to side with the client father in subsequent sessions. Previously his hostility towards his own father prevented him from being able to feel accurately what the position of his client father was.

An apprenticeship training provides the opportunity for a trainee to work closely with a skilled therapist. The advantages of such an arrangement include exposure to the expertise, and guidance through the literature and the various techniques of family therapy. Family therapy skills are partially intangible and defy concise definition. The art of family therapy is best learned through observation and tuition by experienced practitioners. A family therapy training analysis which links a skilled therapist with a trainee who is investigating his own family of origin can provide a close working relationship which is otherwise unavailable. Given adequate safeguards in the choice of competent trainers, an experienced therapist should be able to provide satisfactory personal tuition in the art of family therapy.

The training analysis will also provide a model for working with families. The trainee, by going back to his family would be learning a model of intervention of use to his clients. Not only would he learn the finer details of the process, he would be intimately aware of the problems involved, having experienced them himself. This experiential input should prove emotionally useful for the trainee when involved in client family sessions.

The model has been described in much greater detail elsewhere (Lieberman, 1980). Briefly, the supervisor-trainee dyad mirrors the therapist-client family relationship. Both involve the exploration of history through use of the geneogram. Both require analysis of the resulting family information. Both provide a rationale for setting tasks which real family members would then complete outside the sessions. The model can be used conjointly or singly with the individual family members.

One final useful outcome of the family training analysis is deeply personal. Individual and group training analyses have often been therapeutic in their effect on trainees, and this effectiveness has enhanced the use of the particular form of therapy by the therapist. The family training analysis might also become a therapeutic experience for the trainee and his family of origin as well as his current nuclear family. This experience might provide certain trainees with confidence in family therapy's effectiveness while rescuing the trainee and his family from their own pain and suffering.

V. FAMILY ANALYSIS: A PERSONAL ACCOUNT

My own search for identity as a family member and as a family therapist has been published (Lieberman, 1980). Since doing that work and speaking and writing about it, I have attempted to internalize the work which I did with my own family and to integrate it with theories of family intervention. The following account presents my work with my own family members tabulated with my retrospective comments in three different theoretical frameworks (see Table I).

Presentation of my own work with my family has raised the important issue of confidentiality and the involvement of innocent family bystanders in what is actually an attempt to change them by changing oneself. That is, although they have of course participated in the maintenance of the family patterns, they may not have asked for any change or played any part in the contract between trainee and supervisor/therapist. Bowen's defence of his work is that no one is an innocent bystander in a family, and that the change attempted is that of the therapist only. This "naïve" position ignores the primary system theory postulate that change in any part of a system affects the whole. The intent of a person may be to change himself, but his alteration is never encapsulated. This is true of individual and group therapy as well as family therapy.

VI. THE PLACE OF WORKING WITH THE THERAPIST'S OWN FAMILY

Perhaps a more honest statement would be an admission that working with your own family of origin changes relationships and may be helpful to some member but harmful to others. Bowen cautions that resistance will be created in family members if you tell them what you are up to. This secrecy of motivation may be viewed by some as dishonesty, trickery and manipulation. There are no independent accounts from family members on the receiving end of this type of approach, nor have negative results been published. Caution with any new and powerful technique is wise since its limitations are often determined after its successes have been reported.

Ferber (1972) presents a reasoned critique of working on one's own family. This critical evaluation is worth reading before any family therapist embarks on a journey through his family. Ferber begins by comparing the family training analysis to a ritual indoctrination so that the trainee may become the special sort of man in his culture that his role as a family therapist requires of him.

> Working with one's family is a ritual journey that one must undertake if one is to return with the grail of extraordinary competence as a family therapist.

His tongue-in-cheek critique continues with a description of the process of work between the supervisor (the master) and the trainee (apprentice) as set out below.

    (a) The master establishes a relationship with someone who may benefit from working on their own family.
    (b) The master tells the apprentice anecdotes about the master's family.
    (c) The master produces postulate I: "Self-control is the only sure posture".
    (d) The master produces a parable of his work with his own family.

Table I

Family Systems	(Bowen) Theory[1]	Structural Theory[2]	Transgenerational Theory[3]
Construction and analysis of your own family system	1. Discover relevant triangles. 2. Uncover evidence of fusion. 3. Determine levels of differentiation. 4. Determine presence of emotional cut-off.	1. How enmeshed is your family? 2. What are your family boundaries? 3. How overprotective is your family? 4. How rigid (resistant to change)? 5. What evidence of conflict avoidance?	1. What evidence of family collision? 2. What bonds exist based on family constellations and sibling position? 3. What are the timings of losses and gains in the family system? 4. What secrets exist between family members? 5. What replacements have occurred in the family system?
Set goals and work for change in your family system	1. Reverse emotional cut-offs. 2. Detriangle yourself. 3. Differentiate yourself by taking the "I" position. 4. Resist fusion.	1. Challenge the status quo. 2. Seek constructive conflict. 3. Stop overprotection. 4. Avoid enmeshment.	1. Uncover secrets. 2. Cross generational boundaries. 3. Share unmourned losses. 4. Absorb and reconcile family cultural differences.
Successful Conclusion	"To be with family members without fusing with them"	"To be able to work in high affective moments create and maintain, and be comfortable with moments of high intensity without being drawn in to 'help'."	"To provide a personal growth experience and insight while providing also a personal experience of working within changing a family system".

In 1970, during my first three months of training in Psychiatry, I used geneograms on my patients. Their usefulness led me to an awareness of my uneasiness about my position within my family of origin. I constructed a geneogram of my family and found there were gaps in my own knowledge which I felt impelled to fill. During the following year, I searched for the missing data. I wished to develop character sketches of relatives who had not previously seemed important, either due to distance or death. I was interested in discovering family secrets. Lastly, I sought information about the effects of significant life events upon my relatives. I thought of it as a search for my roots. When my parents decided to visit my home in Boston, I prepared myself for their visit by organizing a list of questions in my mind. On their arrival I	Recognition of my fusion with mother, emotional cut-off from father, eldest brother and extended family. Taking the "I" position in the presence of older family members was unsuccessful. Many triangles but especially the oedipal one.	I recognized my use of conflict avoidance with all family members. Father's rigidity and mother's overprotectiveness were noted. I was part of an enmeshed family system.	I involved myself in a search for my own identity and roots. I wondered what transgenerational influences moulded me into the person I had become. I used my family geneogram as a blueprint.
	First goal was to reverse emotional cut-offs.	I decided to challenge the status quo by avoiding enmeshment and seeking information which might lead to constructive conflict.	I sought data about death and illnesses in my extended family. Secrets and the boundaries they created, reactions to lost sibling positions, bonds and family cultural differences were to be sought.
	Detriangling moves	Here I challenge the status quo	I sought to cross generational boundaries by uncovering secrets
			I probed, clarified and questioned,

[1] See Bowen, 1976.
[2] See Minuchin, 1978.
[3] See Lieberman, 1980.

Family Systems	(Bowen) Theory	Structural Approach	Transgenerational Approach
approached each of them separately. I asked specific questions about their life history and mine which were a mystery to me. For example, I asked my father to share his feelings and thoughts about our move from Chicago (1951) when he first separated from his family of origin.		by speaking separately to my parents.	signalling to my parents that I had crossed the boundary between childhood and adulthood. Family secrets reserved for the elder generation could be shared. The collision of their family backgrounds was broached.
I asked my mother about her own mother's illness and death. Much of my probing produced embarrassed silence or hesitant vague replies. Many of their answers awakened my dormant memories. My parents sidestepped some questions leaving me puzzled about many details, but as I left my parents at the airport, I was seized by a pang of mixed grief and joy which brought tears to my eyes. My mother felt similarly on the plane. Weeks passed in which a feeling of freedom and sadness mingled, preventing full concentration.	Challenging fusion	A small measure of constructive confrontation as I avoid enmeshment and reject attempts to protect me.	
	Response to small permanent increase in level of differentiation.	The feeling of release from a trap with less rigidity and overprotectiveness.	A change in family bonding occurred.
I wrote letters and telephoned my geographically scattered relatives. Separate letters to my	Further reversal of cut-off through letters etc.	Exploration of family boundaries.	I sought to alter my family bonding by sharing new feelings and ideas.

parents requested detailed histories of their lives.		
My mother responded swiftly with a 9-page letter. She began with a list of her medical illnesses during my childhood which had required that I board with uncles and aunts. She wrote of her siblings' lives and characters, adding facts about two deceased siblings of whom I was unaware. She included secrets about her father's disreputable behaviour. (He was a powerful family figure.)		Transgenerational influences were revealed. Sharing of secrets and knowledge that showed me the origin of family collisions and pattern.
The deprivation and hardship she described during her first year of life reduced me to tears. It contrasted starkly with the relative luxury of my life and increased my compassion for her. Some of my anger and resentment abated. Buried feelings of loss surfaced when I read of my dead maternal grandmother's life in Russia and France.	Solidifying the gains made in my level of differentiation.	
I next contacted my mother's eldest brother asking for his memories of life in Europe and Chicago before my mother's birth.	A detriangling move with my mother which also reversed emotional cut-off with my uncle. I challenged the status quo by establishing my right to contact my uncle without going through my parents. Inviting conflict.	Recognition of an unrelinquished bond. This move let me create another generational boundary. My mother's family's secrecy revealed.
His reply came after he wrote	Her overprotective stance was greatly altered.	

Family Systems	(Bowen) Theory	Structural Approach	Transgenerational Approach
my mother. He wanted to know what she had written before he answered my letter.			
I sent a copy of my mother's letter to him and again asked for his help. Finally I spoke to him on the phone. He disagreed with some of my mother's letter and told me a great deal which he was unwilling to commit to paper.	Further detriangulation, also aiding differentiation.	A constructive conflict developed which also led to avoidance of enmeshment.	More secrets were revealed. Another boundary crossed. I altered my place in mother's family of origin.
I next sent copies of all letters to my brothers. I asked them for their memories and their reactions to me. My letter to my younger brother also contained my usual advice about his career. He replied bluntly with confrontative honesty which was new. I had felt protective towards him while his reply showed emotional maturity beyond mine.	Further detriangulation and reversal of emotional cut-off from my siblings. Recognition by my brother of my new level of differentiation allowed him to take the "I" position with me.	Writing about feelings challenged my siblings. No conflict avoidance here anymore!	Sharing secrets. Altering bonds. Changing family patterns.
My father failed to reply to my letters. I resolved to visit him and continue my work. In March, 1972 I stayed with him for 2 weeks. I brought the family album out and my father spoke freely about his family.	Emotional cut-off remained. Limited reversal of cut-off noted.	Enmeshed and rigid I had to force a conflict.	More gentle work of exploration. We spoke and shared more. Losses and cultural differences were revealed.
I visited my maternal grandmother's grave and spoke to my	Reversal of cut-off and		

grandfather about his turbulent life. I felt free and easy with my parents.	detriangling move between him, my mother and myself.	Enmeshment was minimal.	The letter signals a change in our relationship.
On my return to Boston a letter arrived from my father. Two stories explain influences which moulded him. One illustrates the value of being a good neighbour. The other tells of my father hitting a neighbour's son. He fled in fear when the boy fell to the ground. This story was an explanation of my father's repressed temper.	Further reversal of cut-off. Some differentiation.	Status quo change some conflict resolved.	Much greater understanding of transgenerational influences and family patterns.
I obtained other information from my father's sister when she visited Boston. I learned that my father was the second born in his family. My father carried the name of the eldest who had died in his first year. Also, his family moved from Poland to America after the death of a brother during the war.	Detriangling move with my aunt. Reversal of cut-off.	I was becoming known as a family member who faced conflict and needed no protection.	Information from my aunt which was later shared with my father. Uncovering secrets and crossing generational boundaries.
Two years after starting work with my family, the wedding of a cousin became an opportunity to visit my extended family. My intention was to experience the impact of a large extended family while revisiting the city of my childhood. I hoped to test my new position	A test of my new level of differentiation by being fully engulfed by my extended family.		The large extended family group would test my new position in the family. Family cultural differences and patterns would be evident.

Family Systems	(Bowen) Theory	Structural Approach	Trangenerational Approach
within the extended family. I set as a major goal the viewing of family cine films which dated from 1948-56. Deaths in the family had prevented them from being shown. I found there was great resistance. Each relative said they wouldn't be upset but refused out of concern for someone else. Finally, after asking all of them and receiving their individual approval, I negotiated an occasion for the films to be shown. I also visited old neighbours, taped conversations with many relatives and filmed many of my extended family. I considered my work completed to my satisfaction.	Extensive detriangulation allowed me to work in contact with my family members without fusing with them. able to negotiate a new event	I created a new family structure. Unhealthy overprotectiveness was challenged. In the moments of high affective intensity I was able to negotiate a new event without being drawn in as a compulsive helper.	My success led to a feeling of elation and satisfaction. I maintained my new position within the generational hierarchy of my extended family. My work gave me confidence in dealing with my nuclear family, provided me with resources and understanding which have proved valuable in my clinical work and provided awareness of the fears and problems involved attempting to alter human relationships.

(e) The apprentice learns how to do similar work:
   (1) Identify problem areas in your family.
   (2) Go back and develop relationships with every family member.
   (3) Don't change their behaviour; change yours.
   (4) Open up closed topics.
   (5) Become close to those who are distant and vice-versa.
(f) Deal with problems in step 5 by backing off, rethinkng and re-entering when control is established.

The resulting therapist is described by Ferber as a "lone wolf", training people in the tradition of self-sufficiency and self-control in relationships.

That this end-point is not universally sought is a clear indication that the supervised family training analysis must have proper feedback between the therapist, supervisor and family members as a responsible approach to working with one's own family.

Ferber (1972) has described other ways to work on or with one's own family. These include the presentation of one's family at group seminars either through discussion, audiotape or videotape presentations of structured or unstructured interviews, personal appearances of family members or role-playing of family members. He has himself role-played his family network, shown videotapes and home movies of his relatives, brought his family in for an interview together behind a one-way screen and gone back to various of his family members a la Bowen.*

Throughout the discussions of the use of one's family of origin as a resource, the prime emphasis must be "who is this person; where is he going as a family therapist; and how if at all might he change his position in his family system to further his development as both a person and a family therapist".

REFERENCES

Anonymous (1972). Towards the Differentiation of a Self in One's own Family. *In* "Family Interaction: A Dialogue Between Family Researchers and Family Therapists", (J. L. Framo, ed.), Springer, New York.

Anonymous (1973). A Family Therapist's Own Family. *The Family,* **1,** 26-32.

Anonymous (1974). Taking a Giant Step: First Moves Back into My Family. *In* Georgetown Family Symposium Papers II (1977), (J. E. Lovia and L. McClenathan, eds), George University Press, Georgetown, Virginia.

Bowen, M. (1974). Towards the Differentiation of a Self in One's Own Family of Origin. *In* "Georgetown Family Symposium Papers I", (F. Andrew and J. Lorio, eds), Georgetown University Press.

---

*Editor's note:
   How this development of the therapist as a person will in fact influence his competence as a therapist will depend also on the model of therapy he or she is using, and his or her level of experience in that model. However, the reader of this volume will be able to take the relevant issues raised in other chapters and consider the development of their own competence in the light of this chapter (see also particularly by Byng-Hall in this volume).

Bowen, M. (1976). Theory in the Practice of Psychotherapy. *In* "Family Therapy: Theory and Practice", (P. Guerim, ed.), Gardner Press, New York.

Colon, F. (1973). In Search of One's Past: An Identity Trip. *Family Process*, **12**, 429-38.

Ferber, A. (1972). Follow the Paths with Heart. *International Journal of Psychiatry*, **10**, 23-33.

Framo, J. L. (1968). My Families, My Family. *Voices*, **4**, 18-27.

Framo, J. L. (1976). Family of Origin as a Therapeutic Resource for Adults in Marital and Family Therapy: You can and should go home again. *Family Process*, **15**.

Friedman, E. H. (1971). The Birthday Party: An Experiment in Obtaining Change in One's Own Extended Family. *Family Process*, **10**, 345-359.

Guerin, P. and Fogarty, T. F. (1972). The Family Therapist's Own Family. *International Journal of Psychiatry*, **10**, 6-50.

Lieberman, S. (1980). "Transgenerational Family Therapy", Croom Helm, London.

Marks, I. (1976). Behavioural Psychotherapy. *British Journal of Hospital Medicine*, p.253.

Minuchin, S., Rosman, B. and Baker, L. (1978). "Psychosomatic Families", Harvard University Press, London.

Truax, C. B. and Carkhuff, R. R. (1957). "Toward Effective Counselling and Psychotherapy", Aldine, Chicago.

EDITOR'S REFERENCES

Balint, M. (1968). "The Basic Fault", Tavistock, London.

Bowen, M. (1966). The Use of Family Theory in Clinical Practice. *Comprehensive Psychiatry*, **7**, 345-374.

Cooklin, A. (1978). Family Therapy in the British Concept. *Family Process*, **17**, 99-105.

Guntrip, H. (1968). "Schizoid Phenomena Object Relations and the Self", Hogarth Press, London.

Hartmann, H. (1964). "Essays on Ego Psychology", International Universities Press, New York.

Kerr, M. (1981). Family Systems Theory and Therapy. *In* "Handbook of Family Therapy", (A. S. Gurman and D. Kniskern, eds), Brunner/Mazel, New York.

Lieberman, S. (1981). The Extended Family School of Family Therapy. *In* "Developments in Family Therapy", (Walrond-Skinner, ed.), Routledge & Kegan Paul, London.

Lomas, P. (1973). "True and False Experience", Allen Lane, London.

Rycroft, C. (1968). "A Critical Dictionary of Psychoanalysis", Nelson, London.

Winnicott, D. W. (1971). "Playing and Reality", Tavistock, London.

─────── Chapter 11 ───────

The Treatment of
Marital and Sexual Problems
A Behavioural Approach

─────── M. Crowe ───────

I. INTRODUCTION

Behavioural marital and sexual therapy can be said to have been launched as a specialist area in 1969-1970, when Stuart (1969) and Liberman (1970) published their seminal papers on marital therapy, and Masters and Johnson (1970) published their now famous textbook on Human Sexual Inadequacy. The twelve years since that time have seen various developments in the two fields, which have brought to attention both the strengths and the limitations of the behavioural approach.

Recent accounts of behavioural marital therapy are given by Jacobson (1981) and by O'Leary and Turkewicz (1978), and both have tended to emphasize a kind of "package" of therapy including the various aspects of reciprocity, negotiation and communication training described below: but for the purpose of simplicity, I will be separating the two approaches in this chapter, and dealing in a third section with approaches to sexual dysfunction. However, this should not be taken as an indication that one should carry out the various types of therapy exclusively of each other. Indeed in most cases, they can be combined to deal with different aspects of the problem simultaneously.

A. Characteristics of Behavioural Approaches in General

Behavioural approaches in general have certain characteristics which distinguish them from dynamic and other forms of psychotherapy. They are characterized by

(1) Observation of behaviour as the raw material for interventions
(2) A concentration on problems complained of, as the goal for therapeutic endeavours
(3) A general reliance on principles of learning
(4) A general tendency to directiveness in interventions
(5) An empirical approach to innovation
(6) A preference for short-term, problem solving involvement and
(7) A commitment to objective evaluation of efficacy

Family Therapy
ISBN: 0-12-089355-X

B.   Behavioural Approaches with the Family

Behavioural approaches are distinguished from dynamic and more traditional
family systems-orientated approaches in the following ways:
  (1) They are not concerned with fantasy-life, with historical origins of
      problems, or with any metaphorical aspects of communication.
  (2) They use facts rather than feelings or intuition on the part of the therapist
      as criteria for intervention.
  (3) They are not concerned with the acquisition of insight.
  (4) They are not designed to produce "growth", although this may occur as a
      side-effect of improved interaction.
  (5) In assessing progress, the client's and therapist's feelings are given less
      weight than objective behaviour change.
More recent family systems-orientated approaches, however, have more in
common with behavioural approaches. For instance in structural therapy as in
behavioural therapy, actual observed behaviour in the treatment session is often
the starting-point for therapeutic intervention. In strategic therapy, task-setting
shares the directiveness of behavioural work. However, each of these approaches
uses the therapist's understanding of the "system" (often based on quite marked
speculation on motives and underlying emotions) in framing tasks, and thus
depart from the reliance on objective behavioural observation.
   Those aspects of behavioural marital therapy which are shared with almost all
forms of family and marital therapy include definition of the initial referral, the
acceptance by the couple of the interactional nature of the problem, an assessment of the history of the problem and the formation of a therapeutic alliance.
These principles might be termed the basic underpinning of the treatment of a
case. Problems can arise if inexperienced therapists simply attempt to apply the
methods detailed here as if from a recipe book without consideration of the infra-
structure of the problem.

II.   ELEMENTS OF A BEHAVIOURAL APPROACH

A.   Referral

Often the referral letter will talk of marital or relationship problems and ask the
therapist to see the couple, but in less favourable referrals, there is a tendency for
the referring agent to say something like "Mrs G has been depressed for many
years, and her long-suffering husband is now saying that he finds this difficult to
endure, and is thinking of separation". In the latter case, a good deal of groundwork will have to be done in order to re-align the couple's thinking from the
medical to the interactional perspective.

B.   Assessment and First Session

It is important to take a reasonably full history of the marriage, including its
strengths and weaknesses. A good question to ask is "What brought you together

in the first place?", and this will often lead to discussion of the residual positive attractions holding the couple together in spite of their present difficulties. In addition, an assessment should be made of the couple's willingness to stay together and work on the problem: difficulties may arise if one partner is seriously contemplating divorce, or having an affair, and the other is desperate to remain married. Their willingness to change is another important factor to be assessed in this initial stage. My own preference is to give couples in most cases the benefit of the doubt and to take them on for therapy, bearing in mind some of the factors mentioned above in the form of private reservations on the likely outcome.

C. Making a Therapeutic Alliance

As part of the first session, it is necessary to achieve sufficient co-operation from both partners to begin working on the relationship. It is therefore necessary to make both partners feel that the therapist understands what each wants of the therapy, and he should therefore make every effort to empathize with both partners in the first session.

Having achieved this (and it may be necessary to repeat the exercise from time to time during therapy), another necessary exercise is to shift the couple's thinking from the behaviour disorder/illness model to the interactional model. This may not be achieved quickly, and with some very rigid couples it may be necessary to "accommodate" to their way of thinking for quite some time before being able to work on changing the relationship. For example, a woman with a husband who was partially impotent was most unwilling to concede at the beginning of treatment that the marital relationship could possibly contribute to the problem. She was asked to enter the treatment situation "to help him with his problem", and was soon co-operating well in behavioural therapy.

D. Principles of Task Setting

Tasks in BMT should be essentially interactional in nature, having either something for each partner to do, some gain for each partner to achieve, or at least the necessity for one partner to praise or appreciate what the other partner has done. Tasks should always be simple and practicable (see below under reciprocity negotiation) and goals for the couples to reach between sessions should be well within their reach.

III. BEHAVIOURAL APPROACHES TO MARITAL AND SEXUAL PROBLEMS

These may be divided into three types:
  (a) *reciprocity negotiation* (also known as operant interpersonal or contract therapy),
  (b) *communication training* and
  (c) *sexual skills training combined with anxiety reduction.*

The three types of approach are not mutually exclusive, and can indeed be combined, not only with each other, but other approaches based on cognitive or systems considerations.

IV. RECIPROCITY NEGOTIATION

A. Introduction

This was the initial approach in the field, as described by Stuart (1969). The fundamental principle here is the hypothesis of Thibault and Kelley (1959) that in social interactions the participants are always striving to achieve maximum "rewards" for minimum "costs". Stuart's oversimplified view of marriage and marital problems is as follows:

(1) Of all the possible alternatives for habitual interaction between marriage partners, *the existing one is the most rewarding and the least costly in terms of effort.* Thus, if a man spends many hours in his study working in the evenings, that activity is by definition more rewarding than talking to his wife or doing chores around the house. If, in the same relationship, the wife spends most of her interaction time with her husband complaining about his solitary habits, that to her must be a relatively more rewarding behaviour than any alternative. This concept has a respectable pedigree from the literature of operant conditioning, in the so-called Premack principle, which states that behaviour frequently and spontaneously carried out must be rewarding, and the opportunity to carry out this behaviour can be used as a reinforcer to encourage an increase in a more infrequent piece of behaviour.

(2) Most married people expect a *fairly equal sharing of rewards and costs (or duties) between the partners.*

(3) In unsuccessful or problematic marriages, *this sharing has either reached a very low level, or is unequal.* Some workers have postulated a "balance-sheet" concept of marital interaction in which couples who are well adjusted can accept a negative piece of behaviour from the partner in the expectation that it will soon be outweighed by the more frequent positive behaviour which is expected to occur. In problematic marriages, such positive behaviour is infrequent, and the occurrence of a negative piece of behaviour elicits from the partner an instant complaint, leading to a vicious circle of negative interaction. Thus, in unsuccessful marriages, each partner has great difficulty in persuading the other to do what he or she wants. In the face of this difficulty, each partner resorts to negative control, the implication being "if you stop doing what I'm complaining of, I will stop complaining." However, it is a poor method of control because the partner who is complained of is unlikely to comply, and therefore a kind of escalation of complaint can occur on both sides, with one partner or other usually "leaving the field" by sulking, depression, leaving the room or initiating physical violence which leads the other to seek shelter. Some couples seem to have developed this escalation of complaint to a fine art, as in those marriages in which the major element of interaction is blaming, complaining, threats and

negative reinforcement (cf. Dicks' "symmetrical marriages" and Edward Albee's *Who's afraid of Virginia Woolf?*)

In the face of this situation, the prescription of Stuart, Lieberman and others is very simple. The therapist takes an approach based on the premise that instead of using punishment ("I am hurting you because you hurt me") or negative reinforcement ("When you stop doing what I object to, I will stop hurting you") the couple should use positive reinforcement ("If you do what I want, I will try to please you.") The approach may be dismissed as naïve or excessively optimistic, but outcome studies detailed in a later section have shown it to be more effective than control procedures.

B.   Basic Principles of Reciprocity Negotiation

The principles for the therapist to remember are few and simple:

(1) *Tasks for one partner* arise from stated wishes for changed behaviour by the other partner.

(2) If they express no wishes, but only complaints about each other's behaviour, these should be *translated by the therapist into wishes for positive behaviour.*

(3) Such behaviour should be:
   (a) *specific rather than general,*
   (b) *repeatable rather than once-and-for-all,*
   (c) *positive rather than negative,*
   (d) *acceptable to both rather than unrealistic.*

(4) If no wishes for positive behaviour can be extracted from the complaints, the therapist must devise a task which *substitutes a positive piece of behaviour which is incompatible with the negative behaviour complained of.*

By these simple principles, some 50% of marital problems can be significantly improved.

One or two examples will illustrate the approach. A husband may want his wife to show more affection. That is a positive goal, is repeatable and may be acceptable to both partners. However as stated thus, it is too non-specific. The wife has to know exactly how and when to show affection. The agreed task may be: "Kissing me when I go out in the morning and come home in the evenings", or "having a cuddle in bed before we go to sleep". The husband will judge whether it is being carried out.

A wife may want her husband to stop going out to the pub so often. That is a negative, repeatable but rather over-general goal. The task would have to be designed to be positive and incompatible with outings to the pub. A suitable compromise, acceptable to both parties, might be to arrange for the husband to go out to the pub only or two nights per week, and to arrange to do something involving the wife on the other nights (which might be to stay home with some cans of beer, or to go out as a couple). The new task is positive, specific, repeatable, and (if properly negotiated by the therapist) acceptable to both parties.

Another possible task for a wife whose husband objects to her nagging could be to "listen to what my husband says for a few minutes without criticizing". A husband who leaves too many chores for his wife to do could be asked to "spend half an hour between 8 and 9 p.m. helping with the washing up and clearing away". This last task has the advantage that the couple would be thrown together during the washing-up period; lack of time to talk together is often a complaint.

The examples above may seem naïve and irrelevant to the major underlying conflicts experienced by the couple. However, experience with the method shows that often the minimal improvement in relationship achieved by the use of reciprocity negotiation (probably the first such improvement achieved by the couple for many months) improves the whole atmosphere to the extent that more major conflict areas can be tackled.

C. Reciprocity Negotiation: Case Example

(1) A Combined Marital and Sexual Problem

This couple presented with a combined marital and sexual problem which they both saw as predominantly sexual in nature. The husband, aged 37, was in his second marriage, and he had in fact terminated the first marriage as a direct result of the present relationship. His wife, seven years younger, had not been married before; indeed he had been her first sexual partner. The problem was that, although the couple were having intercourse twice weekly, with mutual orgasm, the wife almost invariably refused sex and had to be persuaded into it, with more or less bitter arguments. The husband would have preferred to have intercourse more often, and could not understand his wife's "frigidity", especially as she enjoyed sex so much when it occurred. Six months before, the wife had taken a mild overdose of tablets because of continual tension in the marriage.

It appeared that there was a communication problem in that the husband was an eloquent and persuasive talker with an arts degree, whereas the wife was a quiet but competent woman who had little to say and a rather poor self-image. A straightforward explanatory approach was tried, explaining the power differences in the marriage and the way that I could see sex being used as a defensive weapon by the wife. This produced no improvement, and in the second session I suggested that if sex took place twice a week in any case, it would be better to create a timetable for themselves; they agreed to this. Every Thursday and Saturday they agreed would be the husband's days, and the wife would comply in any sexual activity he suggested. However, Sunday, Tuesday, Wednesday and Friday would be the wife's days, and on those days it would be the wife who decided absolutely what the couple did together: she thought that this would probably be cuddling and expressions of affection but not actual intercourse. Monday was left open because both were often unavailable on Mondays.

At the next session, both reported a great improvement. They had enjoyed sex on two days a week (with some interchange of days which had been amicably arranged), and the wife had greatly appreciated the lack of pressure on her days. There had been one dispute, over whether the husband had the right to insist what dress she should wear on his days, but this was settled in her favour without much negotiation. The improvement continued, and in the next session the wife requested that, as it seemed that I had created an unfair division of days, it would be best if Monday (the spare evening) could be designated another of his days, and it transpired that in the previous two weeks sex had been occurring on average three times a week. This increase in the husband's days was arranged, and although I was doubtful of the necessity for continuing the strict rota any longer, both said that it had transformed their marriage and requested for it to be continued indefinitely.

In the last session (the fourth), things were again going very well, with further improvements in their sexual satisfaction, and a considerable increase in harmony in the marriage. The remaining problem the husband defined as their lack of truly intimate communication leading to growth in the marriage: "We really should have no secret thoughts or opinions". While the wife agreed to this, I noticed considerable hesitation in her voice, and suggested that such growth, while desirable, should proceed at the pace of the slower member. Both agreed to work towards it, but recognized the need for the husband to avoid putting on pressure, a pitfall he had learned to avoid in the sexual area. At the follow-up of two months, they reported by telephone that the marriage remained very satisfactory, with continued improvement in sex and communication and no further depression on the wife's part.

The tasks suggested for this couple were in one sense behavioural, in that they ensured that both partners began to get what they wanted out of the relationship. However, the main task also had strategic respects, in that it took sexual relationships out of the area in which the partners were waging an undeclared power struggle, and enabled them to communicate freely in the secure knowledge that the rights of each were being respected.

(2) Extending from Reciprocity Negotiation

This case illustrates some of the points above, but the interventions were not exclusively "reciprocity negotiation" ones.

The couple were referred with a marital and sexual problem. The husband (aged 33) had developed a revulsion against sex with his wife (aged 27), and they also complained that the wife was irritable, depressed and unreasonable, while the husband was "shut in" and unemotional. The husband's parents were divorced, and his mother was described as manipulative, but the wife's family were unremarkable. The couple were professional ballroom dancers who worked together, and had decided at this stage not to have children.

The treatment began with some relaxation and sensate focus (see section on sex therapy), but it soon appeared that there were no technical sexual problems, and the main issue was to change the husband's motivation, which had prevented him in the first three weeks from initiating any sexual or petting activity. When asked what they wanted of each other, the wife said she wanted her husband to take initiatives and be assertive in daily life as well as in sex, and the husband said he wanted his wife to be less assertive, and more of a "little wife". These were specified as the husband initiating some kind of physical (non-sexual) contact each day, and the wife approaching him in a seductive rather than demanding way sexually.

The relationship improved considerably at this stage, and they succeeded in having intercourse once, but the husband did not ejaculate. They reported that the husband had become more assertive, and the wife more "soft and womanly".

A considerable amount of work was done on their communication at this point, and the husband expressed his resentment of the wife criticizing his function as host at a Christmas party: "He should have refilled the glasses more often". She objected to his paying too much attention and respect to his mother and neglecting his wife. I suggested at this point (not strictly behaviourally) that the wife should exaggerate her criticism of him by giving him points out of ten (as in a competition) for his public "performance". I also pointed out how the divided loyalty between wife and mother helped the husband not to be entirely committed to his wife, and that that seemed to be as he preferred it to be.

The relationship continued to improve, as did their dancing and teaching, but sex remained very infrequent, until following a session in which I expressed pessimism and wondered whether it would end in divorce, after a discussion with her mother-in-law, the wife decided to become a more conventional wife (see above) and to cook her husband breakfast each morning. The husband responded by reducing his masturbation and initiating sexual activity as a couple more often. When last seen, they had returned from a successful European tour and holiday, during which sexual intercourse had taken place three times each week, although this frequency had reduced on return. Their final suggestions were to take regular short holidays together, to interrupt their gruelling work routine (husband's idea) and to buy a new double bed (wife's suggestion).

In spite of some non-negotiating interventions, I feel that the main thrust of this therapy, and especially the wife's change of behaviour towards the end, was related closely to reciprocity negotiation.

V.   COMMUNICATION TRAINING

A.   Introduction

This approach was originated almost as early as Stuart's and Lieberman's Reciprocity Negotiation. For instance, Patterson and Hops (1972) described the training of couples in improving their negotiation patterns, substituting positive and constructive requests for negative and destructive criticism. A full description of the communication technique, which was written for the benefit of clients, but is extremely readable and useful for therapists, is "A Couple's Guide to Communication" by Gottman et al. (1976).

The approach shares with Reciprocity Negotiation the rather naïve idea that both partners wish to have a good and peaceful relationship, with logical and matter-of-fact communication, and that the only reason that this doesn't happen is that they are inefficient communicators. While the idea is clearly over-simplified, it does at least give the couple the "benefit of the doubt", and puts the therapist in a relatively unassailable position as someone who is on the side of good relationships and is seeing the best in both partners.

The therapist in this approach asks the couple to talk to each other, and is therefore doing a similar thing to what Minuchin (1974) describes as "de-centering". This is a particularly difficult role to play, especially for therapists who like to be active negotiators, but it is vital to the success of the method to be able to insist that the partners speak only to each other, and that neither of them involves the therapist in conversation until the therapist is ready to intervene with a comment or a re-phrase of what has been said.

B.   Examples of Destructive Communications

When the couple talk to each other, it is almost inevitable that one or other will make a comment that intrudes on the sensitivities of the other. Such comments may be of many types, for instance

(1) *Destructive criticism:* ("You're a real coward", or "You really like to hurt me").

(2) *Generalizations* which often amount to character assassination: ("You're always showing me up", or "That's typical of your immature attitude").

(3) *Mind-reading, or imputing destructive motives:* ("You say you're trying to help, but I know it's just to humiliate me").

(4) *Bringing up the past* (often combined with generalization): ("I've suffered this for 16 years and you're still doing it", or "I'll never forgive you for what you said to my mother").

(5) *Putting oneself in the right and partner in the wrong:* ("I've never started a row in the whole of our marriage", or "All I want is peace, and look at the way you treat me").

(6) *Using logical argument as a weapon:* ("All you have to do is to stop over-reacting", or "Be reasonable, can't you see that this is the only way?").

(7) *Raising the voice:* (a ploy that can easily be overlooked)

(8) *Using the sting in the tail:* ("You've stopped criticizing me, but now you've gone silent and that's worse", or "You are trying now, but why couldn't you have done so 5 years ago?")

C.   Interventions to Reduce Destructive Communications

This is a small sample of all the possible variety of ways in which couples can play on each other's sensitivities. In intervening in this kind of conversation, the therapist has to be able to stop the action without causing offence, and that is an art which has to be learned by trial and error. After stopping the action, it is important to say something which will enable the partners to get the same message across, but without the problem which emerged in the communication. Thus the therapist may have to point out the error in communication, while at the same time emphasizing the speaker's good intentions. This could take the form of asking the speaker to re-phrase what was said, or suggesting a new form of words more acceptable to the listener. Ideally, some teaching would also be included to help the speaker learn the principles of avoiding the same error in future discussions.

Here are some examples of the kind of feedback which can be given, both in terms of teaching of principles, and the actual suggestions for phraseology:

(1) *Use expression of one's own feelings* instead of imputing feelings to the other partner: ("You really like to hurt me" becomes "I felt very sad to hear you say that."). This example has three improvements: the speaker's feelings are expressed, no imputation of intent is made on the speaker's side, and the sentence applies to a specific and not a general situation.

(2) *Use specific examples:* ("You're always showing me up" becomes "I felt really embarrassed when you spoke about me to George last Friday").

(3) *Avoid mind-reading:* (Partners are requested to ask about motives rather than to insist that they know better than the other partner what he is thinking).

(4) *Stick to the point:* (this can mean not bringing up the past, and not generalizing to similar instances).

(5) Replace logical arguments with *expressions of one's own emotions:* ("All you have to do is to stop over-reacting" becomes "It makes me feel hurt when you raise your voice").

(6) Therapist can point to *non-verbal aspects* such as *body posture* or *eye contact* as something that raises sensitivities.

(7) Partners should be encouraged to *take responsibility for their own actions:* ("You always make me angry and then I get violent," becomes "I can't seem to control my temper.")

(8) Often *monologues* kill communication, and these can be politely discouraged, with a clear message that short-sharp comments are more desirable (note the phrasing of this sentence, with emphasis on the desirability of one rather than the undesirability of the other).

D. Communication Training: Case Example

This case, as the previous one reported, is not "pure" in its illustration of the communication training approach, but contains enough features of it to be of interest here.

(1) Presentation

The couple presented via another therapist, who had been treating them for the wife's problem of anorgasmia. This had been partially reversed, but she was still unable to achieve orgasm except with a vibrator. However, a more serious problem was that she seemed to be showing an obsessional jealousy of her husband's previous sexual partners.

He was 70 and his wife, 58. It was his third marriage (he was divorced from his first wife due to her infidelity, and from his second wife when she became chronically psychotic) and her second marriage (she had been widowed some years earlier). When the couple first got together, they lived in the village where the husband (then divorced) had been having an affair with a single woman living nearby, and after the marriage, this woman had made a good deal of trouble for the couple, with anonymous telephone calls, etc. This had coincided with the husband experiencing a short episode of impotence for which the wife was very helpful and considerate, but when she complained of not experiencing an orgasm, he replied "Well, none of the others have ever complained". This the wife found intolerable, especially in view of the behaviour of the neighbour, but she could never elicit an apology from the husband, and at the time of therapy, six years later, their communication was characterized by continual complaints by the wife of his previous insensitivity and lack of support, and stone-wall defence by the husband.

(2) Interventions
From the beginning, I asked the wife to write down many of her thoughts instead of bottling them up or talking to her husband about them, and this she did assiduously: I have some sixty typed sheets of her thoughts on the file. However, the pattern was still the same in their interaction, although a bit softer than before. I was very aware of the wife's great tendency to go into monologues, and I asked her to try and leave gaps every minute or so, until she received a reply from her husband. He was then able to reply, but I also had to ask her to avoid interrupting him and let him finish what he had to say. He said that although he knew sex was a sensitive subject, he wanted to say that in spite of the anorgasmia, sex with her was the best he had experienced. When she interrupted to say that he should have told her that 6 years before, I tried to impress on her that he should be rewarded and not punished for statements like that.

In spite of all the improvements, however, the wife was not satisfied with his account of the past, and needed reassurance about that period. The husband got as far as to say "I'm deeply distressed that you were so hurt at that time, but of course I had no intention of hurting you". I asked him to reword this so as to leave her with the reassurance at the end instead of the sting-in-the-tail (she tended to respond to his defensiveness instead of his apology). He did so, by simply reversing the order: "I had no intention of hurting you, but I'm deeply distressed that you were so hurt," and this proved much more acceptable to her, while being something that he could say sincerely.

On another occasion, she began talking about another couple, saying "I don't suppose she has any worries about her sexual relationship". He replied "That's a ridiculous thing to say", which made her very angry. Asked to replay his answer, he said, "It was rather imaginative of you, but I do understand", which she found partially acceptable. He then produced the most satisfactory answer: "I'm sorry that you haven't been satisfied sexually in the way you want". All along, I was careful to ensure acceptability on both sides for what was said, and after a traumatic session in which the husband rebelled and said it was 90% her fault, to the wife's great dismay and anger, they continued their progress until, at the end of therapy (12 sessions over 9 months), they were having a peaceful and less argumentative relationship, with few accusations from her and not much defence from him. The sexual relationship was as before, but both were accepting the use of the vibrator and reducing their unrealistic demands.

VI.   ADVANTAGES AND DISADVANTAGES OF BMT

The above account and case examples have, I hope, provided an understandable and usable framework for practising BMT. The approach has many advantages and some possible disadvantages, which will be outlined here.

A.   Advantages of BMT

The advantages are mainly related to its simplicity, its objectivity, its effectiveness and its clarity of goals.

(1) Simplicity
The approach *is simple to learn and put across to couples in treatment.* This particularly applies to the reciprocity negotiation approach, and in many couples, especially for the inexperienced therapist, this is a satisfactory way of initiating small but worthwhile changes in interaction. The communication training approach is more complicated, but can be introduced piecemeal while continuing to work with reciprocity.

(2) Objectivity
The approach *is based on objective criteria,* those of behaviour which may be observed by others besides the therapist, so that consensus of observation does not depend, as in more speculative systemic approaches, on agreement as to the underlying hypotheses used in therapy. Most outcome studies in the field use simple client-evaluation of improvement, or evaluation by independent assessor of improvement. An implication of this is that, in a broad sense, "the customer is right", and one cannot make statements such as "they say that interaction is worse, but that's just their resistance."

(3) Effectiveness
The approaches are of *proven effectiveness* as shown by the numerous controlled trials mentioned in a later section. This fact also highlights the susceptibility of the behavioural approaches to relatively uncomplicated assessment of effectiveness, an advantage which is not shared by the theoretically more complicated approaches such as strategic or dynamic family and marital therapy.

(4) Goal Directedness
The directive and goal-orientated nature of the BMT approach makes it highly compatible with the approaches to sexual dysfunction outlined in the next section. Since 60% of cases of sexual dysfunction appear to be associated with major marital problems, a marital therapy which combines easily with sexual therapy is an invaluable adjunct to the other techniques designed to improve sexual interaction as such.

B. Disadvantages of BMT

Obviously, the above advantages are not an unequivocal recommendation for Behavioural Marital Therapy and there are disadvantages.

(1) Over-simplistic
Behavioural Marital Therapy has been accused by Gurman and Knudson (1978) of being *over-simplistic*, and even Jacobson (1981) has not claimed that the perspective of reinforcement and positive communication can explain all the depths and subtlety of human interaction. Undoubtedly the BMT approach is over-simplistic, but it does not claim to be anything else: only to isolate the more easily manipulated factors for alteration, and to alter them successfully.

(2) Motivation can be poor
Poor motivation on one side or the other can indeed sabotage BMT, as when the agreed goals in reciprocity negotiation are not adhered to. This situation can result when either both partners appear to find the status quo more acceptable than the apparent risk involved in change which entails trust in the other partner: or when one partner is clearly in favour of improvement and the other is not willing to commit himself/herself to change. This last situation can arise, especially in the cases where there is an apparent psychiatric condition in one partner. I have been impressed in my experience of marital therapy that, while psychiatric illness does not render therapy impossible, it does increase the "rigidity" shown by the couple, and as such makes change, especially that induced by simple means, less likely to be achieved.

(3) Undermined by Conflict
Real internal or external conflict can render treatment less easy. *Internal conflicts* are those such as poor self-image or ambivalence about relationships, and are likely to be found in partners who would in other settings be said to suffer from personality disorder. In such couples, like those with psychiatric problems as such, simple resolution of conflict is likely to make only a small difference to the severe interpersonal problems. *External conflict* may be of many types, but one type commonly found is when one partner overtly wishes to terminate the marriage or cohabitation, and the other is keen to remain together. Such couples are perhaps more in need of "separation counselling", which leaves to them the decision of whether to separate, but concentrates on other issues such as deciding on trial separations, on reducing excessive closeness, etc.

(4) Ignoring Historical Issues
It is also objected, by Gurman amongst others, that BMT *ignores historical issues* such as relationship with families of origin, especially with the couple's parents. This is broadly true, and the only defence of this omission is that it seems in many cases to be possible to achieve satisfactory and *lasting* solutions (see below on outcome) without delving into painful areas such as parental influence.

VI. SEXUAL DYSFUNCTION AS A PRESENTING PROBLEM

A. Introduction

Cases of sexual dysfunction naturally divide themselves into two types, namely those with a technical problem ("I feel sexy but I can't have an erection", "I can't achieve an orgasm in sexual intercourse", or "I can't relax sufficiently to allow penetration"), and those with a more complicated relationship difficulty ("Somehow I just don't fancy my wife", or "I can't bear him to touch me, but I could be aroused by other men"). Analysis of cases presenting at a sexual dysfunction clinic (Crowe *et al.*, 1977) showed that cases of the second type outnumbered those of the first by about 3:2. Both have a sexual problem as defined, but the second type need considerable help with the relationship as well as with the sexual function as such.

Since the publication of *Human Sexual Inadequacy* by Masters and Johnson (1970) a great deal has been learned about the treatment of sexual dysfunction, both from a behavioural viewpoint (Bancroft and Coles, 1976; Annon, 1978; Crowe, 1978; Jehu, 1979; Heiman and Lo Piccolo, 1981) and from a more eclectic approach (Kaplan, 1974). In this section I shall be dealing mainly with behavioural approaches and mainly with couple therapy, although in practice the

Table I. Classification of sexual dysfunction

Problems presenting in the male partner:
Erectile impotence (primary: no successful intercourse ever)
Erectile impotence (secondary: successful intercourse in the past)
Premature ejaculation (may be associated with impotence after some years)
Retarded ejaculation (if totally absent may be called anorgasmia: prognosis better if
    ejaculation is possible in masturbation)
Retrograde ejaculation (orgasm present, but ejaculation occurs into bladder)
Painful ejaculation
Anaesthetic ejaculation (usually accompanied by hypochondriacal attitudes)

Problems presenting in the female partner:
Anorgasmia (total orgasm never experienced)
Anorgasmia (secondary: orgasm experienced in the past)
Anorgasmia (situational: orgasm achieved by manual or other stimulation but not in full
    intercourse)
Vaginismus (involuntary muscular resistance to penetration)
Dyspareunia (superficial: pain experienced in vulva and vagina)
Dyspareunia (deep: pain experienced in pelvis and abdomen)

Problems presenting in either or both partners:
Low sex-drive or reduced libido
Incompatible sex drives
Fear or phobia of sex
Dislike or refusal of sex

---

number of single people consulting therapists for impotence and other sexual dysfunctions appears to be increasing.

It would not be possible to discuss the treatment of sexual dysfunction without reference to the classification of types of problem and some of the contributory causes. These are given in Table I (classification), Table II (physical causes) and Tables III and IV (non-physical causes). In some conditions (e.g. premature ejaculation and anorgasmia), physical causes are very rare, and one may safely assume that the problem is, for the purposes of treatment, psychogenic. In other conditions, especially secondary impotence and dyspareunia, contributing factors of a physical nature are not unusual and should be investigated before proceeding with therapy. However, even in the most obviously "physical" cases such as impotence caused by diabetic neuropathy or multiple sclerosis, there is often an element of anxiety or marital communication disturbance which can be treated by psychological means with some success (see case No. 1, p.277).

As with marital therapy, there is a good deal of connection between the apparent aetiological factors and the therapeutic interventions used. Thus, in cases where marital communication seems reasonably good and the problem seems mainly related to anxiety, the therapeutic thrust will be towards anxiety reduction, and vice versa in cases of poor marital communication and low

Table II.   Physical factors predisposing to sexual dysfunction.

---

1. Endocrine: (a) oral contraception (?)
             (b) castration (accidents or surgery)
             (c) pituitary tumours, etc.

2. Neurological causes of impotence:
             (a) multiple sclerosis
             (b) spinal diseases and injury
             (c) diabetes with autonomic neuropathy
             (d) nerve compression (disc prolapse)

3. Vascular causes of impotence:
             (a) fistula joining corpora cavernosa and spongiosum

4. Pharmacological causes of impotence, delayed ejaculation and anorgasmia
             (a) anti-depressants
             (b) tranquillizers and hypnotics
             (c) anti-hypertensives and diuretics
             (d) most drugs of addiction (loss of libido)
             (e) alcohol (liver and nerve damage, loss of libido and other more general effects.)

5. Pelvic and vaginal causes of dyspareunia:
             (a) tumours and cysts
             (b) salpingitis and other infections
             (c) vaginitis (monilia, trichomonas, or post-menopausal)
             (d) herpes genitalis

6. Any debilitating physical illness, causing loss of libido.

Table III.   Individual non-physical determinants of sexual dysfunction.

Sexual attitudes (parental influences)
Level of sex drive
Experience of sex (ignorance)
Sexual deviations
Traumatic sexual events (rape, etc.)
Quality of self-image
Ageing
Psychiatric illness of all sorts
Anxiety and life stress
Performance anxiety (often in both partners)

Table IV.   Relationship factors contributing to sexual dysfunction.

1. *Distance and closeness*
   (a) excessive politeness and consideration
   (b) continual symmetrical hostility
   (c) disparate needs (jealousy or constant nagging)

2. *Power relationships*
   (a) threats and violence
   (b) withholding sex as a power gambit

3. *Excessive dependency and protection*
   (a) the "patient" and the therapeutic spouse
   (b) the "parent" and the "irresponsible child"

anxiety. The course of treatment may change from session to session, and the improvement of marital communication may reveal that, even in the presence of good communication, some interference with function is resulting from anxiety, and needs appropriate treatment.

It will be seen from Tables II to IV that there are many possible causative factors in any case of dysfunction, and the need for flexibility in approach should be obvious. In particular, it is often necessary to do simultaneous therapy on improving marital relationships and dealing with the more technical aspects of sexual function. However, it is also useful to have a framework of therapy in mind, and at least in the early stages, the approach modified from Masters and Johnson (1970) is still a very valuable standby.

B.   An Approach to Sexual Dysfunction

(1)   History taking
This is usually done seeing each partner separately, to elicit in a non-threatening way some of the factors contributing to the problem (Tables II and III).

In addition it is useful in the early conjoint sessions to enquire about marital history and stresses.

(2) Physical Examination

This is not necessary in all cases, but is especially useful in cases of secondary impotence to exclude physical causes (including testing for sugar in the urine, testicular pain sensation and reflexes). In cases of dyspareunia, consultation with a gynaecologist or experienced general practitioner is advisable to exclude physical disease. In cases of vaginismus, manual examination of the female partner can demonstrate the muscle tension which slowly relaxes: the male partner can insert his fingers afterwards as a prelude to the homework exercises in which he helps to produce relaxation in the vaginal muscles in the same way.

(3) Conjoint Interviews

All those subsequent to the history-taking are conjoint (or "round-table" in Masters and Johnson's phrase), and many general therapeutic measures are used. A good deal of *education* goes on, especially in shy and inexperienced couples. Permission-giving is another important facet: many people are obsessed with the "right way" of having sex, and need reassurance that their own preferred way is probably the best for them. The use of *humour* is extremely helpful: it provides for many couples a face-saving way of achieving change in attitudes, and removes some of the deadening seriousness with which some couples view their problem. *Empathy* is of course important, though it can be dangerous to "understand" one point of view too well, thus making an enemy of the other partner. Sometimes a *challenge* is necessary, as when couples make slow or negligible progress in treatment. All the *marital therapy* techniques mentioned in earlier sections can be extremely useful in dealing with relationship issues. *Bringing out of emotions* can be very beneficial, especially in couples who are inhibited in this area: a good approach is to ask them to make "I" statements about their immediate gut-feelings (Stanley, 1981).

(4) Relaxation

Although not supported by research findings, our experience is that many couples with sexual dysfunction find relaxation helpful (see Jacobson, 1981). Progressive relaxation of different muscle groups, preceded by tensing the muscles, moving systematically up the body from the feet, is accompanied by deep, slow breathing and mental imagery of something like a white flower. Particular attention is paid to the pelvic muscles, as relaxation and contraction of these (Kegel exercises) (Kegel, 1952) is helpful in many forms of dysfunction. Almost all couples in our clinic are given relaxation instructions in the early stages of therapy.

(5) Sensate Focus Techniques

These are a series of exercises practised by the couple at home, between sessions, often with the help of written instructions. The term "sensate focus" was introduced by Masters and Johnson (1970), but techniques have varied a good deal in the intervening 11 years. There is a ban on intercourse and on any touching of genital areas, of breasts or nipples. The couple should ensure that they are warm and comfortable (this may entail special heating of the bedroom during the English winter), and should undress and stroke or caress each other's bodies alternately, using body lotion or oil on the hands if desired. The emphasis is on physical communication through the hands of the active partner and the body of the recipient, and the couple are asked to use very little verbal communication. What they do say should be confined to reporting emotional states ("I feel good", "I feel sad" etc.), and to asking for a change in techniques (as before, this should be phrased as a positive request, such as "Could you press a little harder?", or "I'd rather you touched me on the leg just now"). The absence of the necessity for sexual intercourse often acts as a powerful anxiety-reducer, and may enable the dysfunctional partner to enjoy physical contact for the first time for months or years.

Not all couples are given sensate focus instructions. Some are not ready for it, as their marital relationship is too full of tension or hostility to make it likely that they will co-operate, and even if they do so, the technique is likely to be sabotaged. Others do not seem to need it, and may go straight on to the techniques to reduce premature ejaculation or vaginismus. Still others have "tried it all before" in therapy at other centres, and it would be counter-productive to attempt the same routine as before. However, for those who do co-operate and find the technique anxiety-reducing, it can be a very helpful step in the reversal of their dysfunction.

(6) Self-focussing

For many people, mostly women, who are afraid of their genital areas, who have been indoctrinated against touching themselves sexually, or have simply never experimented, it can be very helpful to encourage them to explore their own anatomy and responsiveness. The use of a hand-mirror can be included as part of the homework task, and it is often helpful to suggest this as an individual exercise, perhaps during a bath. As a later stage in self-focussing, both for men and women, the use of a vibrator can be recommended, which may be either a mains-operated body vibratory massager, or a milder battery-operated vibrator. Many women, in particular, can easily achieve orgasm with a vibrator when this is impossible using other means, and many experience their first climax in this way.

(7) Teasing Techniques

Particularly in cases of impotence and anorgasmia, the transition to mutual genital contact is a rather tricky one, and there is often a complaint at the session following this stage that introducing contact with the genital area reduced sexual excitement rather than increased it. It is particularly helpful here to recommend that the couple do not try to aim directly for an orgasm or for a hard erection: instead they should stimulate each other intermittently, with breaks or pauses whenever a partial erection or some sexual excitement is achieved. Apart from reducing "performance anxiety" in such cases, the pauses also act as a reassurance that it is possible to regain an erection or sexual excitement once it is lost, and this can be a very important factor in increasing confidence.

(8) Oral Sex
Oral stimulation can be recommended at this stage (but not imposed on couples who object to it) as a good transition between manual or vibrator stimulation and full intercourse.

(9) Control of Ejaculation
Control can best be achieved by the stop-start technique first introduced by Semans (1956). The squeeze technique of Masters and Johnson is similar in effect, but harder to teach and therefore less practicable. In the stop-start technique, the male partner is asked, as part of his homework, to stimulate his penis to erection and then to masturbate as if to produce an ejaculation. At the point when inevitability of ejaculation is about to be reached, he is asked to stop touching himself and allow the urge to go off, and to leave about 30 seconds before beginning stimulation again. This activity can be repeated several times, and we suggest carrying on for fifteen minutes before finally ejaculating. The next step is to carry out the same sequence using body oil on the hand (to increase sensitivity and make control more difficult). The man is then asked to carry out the same sequence, with his partner providing the stimulation, first with a dry hand and then an oily hand. Eventually control can be achieved by stopping and starting in the same way in oral sex and in full intercourse. The need to use the stop-start technique eventually diminishes as greater control is achieved.

(10) Ejaculation Failure
Where ejaculation is retarded or does not take place at all, the approach is somewhat similar to that for premature ejaculation, but the emphasis is on what Masters and Johnson called *super-stimulation*. In self-stimulation, in mutual genital stimulation and finally in intercourse, the emphasis is on short but intensive bursts of very rapid thrusting with pauses for rest: in the early stages the use of body-oil on the hand is recommended, to provide a more rapid and stimulating action. The use of vibrators is. sometimes very helpful for these patients.

(11) Vaginismus
The use of *dilators* or *finger dilation* is recommended. It is almost always possible to examine the women vaginally using one finger, and the homework following this examination usually entails the insertion by male or female partner of one, then two or three fingers into the vagina very slowly and carefully. Graded dilators can be used in a similar way, and eventual penetration with the erect penis usually follows the use of three fingers or the largest dilator (No.6.) preferably with very little interval so that the vaginal muscles do not have time to contract following the withdrawal of the dilator or fingers.

(12)   Use of Different Positions

In the processes of moving from genital teasing or the other special techniques to full intercourse, it is often a good idea to suggest a different position. The woman-above position is a very good one for many problems. If impotence is present, or ejaculation has to be controlled, these can both become problematic at the time of penetration, and it is easier in both situations for the man to be lying on his back, and for either him or his partner to be stimulating the penis just before penetration, which takes place with the female partner kneeling over him and penetrating in that position.

In cases of anorgasmia, a very good position is the one called the "feel free" position. The woman lies on her back with her knees raised, and the man lies on his side facing her with his legs bent under the arch made by her legs. The penis is in a good position for penetration, but both partners are comfortable if they want to go on with intercourse for a long time; also both partners have their hands free for access to the clitoris to stimulate this during intercourse. They can also use a vibrator at the same time as having full intercourse, and this may be a very valuable transitional stage to successful intercourse.

Other positions can help by providing variety of psychological stimulation, and getting away from the conventional position, associated as it is with failure and the expectation of failure.

(13)   Psychological Stimulation

Psychological stimulation can be provided in several ways, and can be an adjunct to therapy both in those with a low sex drive (male or female), and in those who have problems where deviant sexual urges are interfering with hetero-sexual drives towards the partner. In such cases, it may be helpful to suggest regular reading of mild pornography (Forum, Playboy, etc.), to go to explicitly sexual films in the cinema, or to orchestrate their sexual experience as a couple to include particular objects or activities (lights, fur, silk, feathers, mild degrees of bondage or domination, etc.). Whatever is agreed must be acceptable to both partners, but there is no doubt from research (Gillan and Gillan, 1976) that such stimulation can increase the frequency and enjoyment of sexual interaction.

In the cases where there is a deviant competing urge, the possibility of mastur-batory re-training may be considered, in which masturbation begins with the deviant fantasy and the patient switches to heterosexual fantasies at the point of orgasm.

(14)   Desensitization

This and similar anxiety reduction techniques can be used where there is a clearly phobic element to the sexual dysfunction, as in cases where the imminence of sexual activity causes an acute panic attack. Many workers in the past (e.g. O'Gorman, 1975; Friedman, 1971) have relied primarily on desensitization for sexual dysfunction problems in general, but most thera-pists would now favour the general conjoint approach outlined in the above sections.

(15)   The Time Scale of Therapy
The time scale is usually brief, i.e. weekly or fortnightly visits to the clinic over a period of 3-6 months; maximum of perhaps 10-12 visits. The initial visit is usually about 2½ hours in duration, but subsequent visits average about 45 minutes. In some couples, however, particularly those with low sex drive, non-consumation, or primary impotence, a *slower time scale*, with perhaps 15-20 visits spread over 18 months, may be preferable. In those cases, the problem may be to motivate the couple to interact sexually often enough to make therapy worthwhile, and other approaches such as regular letters from the couple to the therapist reporting activities between sessions can improve progress.

C.   Case Examples (Sexual Dysfunction)

(1)   Secondary Impotence with Diabetes and some Undeclared Marital Problems
The couple, who had one son, were both in their 40s, and presented with the problem of secondary impotence in the husband, which had been present about 3 years, and which was accompanied by a high sex drive on his part. The impotence had begun following his hospitalization for diabetes, and he was being treated with insulin for this, with good control. On examination, there was no evidence of neuropathy, and in particular his deep testicular pain sensation was preserved. There were some rather bitter arguments between husband and wife, which mainly centred on their sexual relationship. Both were musicians, but the wife was the more talented, and in other ways she was better than her husband: more intelligent and more competent socially: their friends were mostly hers before they were his. The husband was excessively tense and lacking in poise at interview, and his wife tended to be the spokesman and dominate the discussion, in a very natural and unassertive way.

Treatment began as usual with sensate focus and relaxation, and she ensured that the rules were kept during the first week, despite his wish to "go further" when he began to have good erections. It emerged in this second interview that the wife had very ambivalent feelings about sexual intercourse: she refused to be examined physically, and at first refused the genital sensate focus (manual genital stimulation). The therapist firmly took the husband's side on this occasion, saying that his wife must not be allowed to dominate him, and telling the wife that for the sake of her marriage she must sometimes give in to his wishes. On the third visit, they had made further progress, the husband had had good erections, and the wife had participated in genital sensate focus despite her misgivings. The therapist underlined the importance of the wife taking her husband's opinions and wishes seriously, and suggested to the husband that before coming to decisions about things involving the two of them, he should consult his wife. They were given instructions for penetration in the female superior position, and at the next visit they were having mutually satisfying sexual intercourse quite frequently.

During the next 3 months there were no appointments made, and at their follow-up appointment they reported that all was going well. They had had a setback to their sexual relationship 6 weeks before, when the husband had again lost his erection. However, they had recognized the problem, and had dealt with it by going back to non-genital sensate focus; within a week they had progressed again to having normal intercourse. There was an alteration in their interaction at the interview: the wife took less command of the situation and allowed the husband to be the spokesman on many occasions. At further follow-up 6 months after treatment, all the improvements were maintained.

(2) Primary Impotence and Non-consummation

The couple, in their early 30s, were referred by another clinic where they had had 3½ years of weekly marital therapy from a dynamic standpoint, with no improvement of the presenting problem of non-consummation, but with the acquisition of a good deal of self-understanding. They had been married 7 years, and were both technically virgins: the husband was a quiet and insecure professional translator, and the wife was a tense and active schoolteacher with a tendency to talk for both partners, and to take the initiative in discussing the problem at home. The husband masturbated approximately weekly, as did the wife, but when they attempted foreplay his erection was insufficient to penetrate, and the mutual sex play only rarely resulted in an orgasm for the wife: in any case, this activity had taken place less than once a month in recent times.

Both were keen to improve the situation, and followed the instructions for relaxation and sensate focus, with some sexual excitement on both sides. However, from the third visit onwards, some problems were obvious: they had had no time to practise genital teasing, both were feeling depressed, they had had some major rows and long periods of non-communication, and his masturbation was causing her to feel resentful. Some friendly fighting was suggested, which would hopefully improve their physical interaction and lead to more obvious sexual interaction. They responded well to this at first, and broke the leg of their bed, while he experienced some more sexual excitement, but they did not progress beyond mutual masturbation. Another period of inactivity followed, in which he became obsessed with physical fitness and began using a bullworker. In an attempt to undercut the couple's dependency on me and their passivity, I expressed impotence, and said that their problem was too strong for my limited abilities. Their next visit (the tenth), they reported that on the wife's return from playing badminton, he had met her in the kitchen, been excited by her flushed face and short white skirt, undressed her and achieved penetration for the first time, but without ejaculating. They continued to improve at a very slow pace with visits spaced perhaps a month or two apart, and at the time of writing, they are having regular weekly sexual activity with penetration and climaxes for her, but ejaculation still does not take place intra-vaginally, and they are contemplating AIH as a means of achieving pregnancy.

(3) Phobia of Intercourse in the Female Partner

This couple, in their early 50s, were referred from a sexual dysfunction clinic some 100 miles away, with a history of having had no sexual contact for some years. They presented as a very co-operative couple, the wife being a part-time hairdresser and the husband a British Rail driver. The wife reported that every time sex might be expected, she would become highly anxious to the point of breathless panic, and that although she could hold her husband's hand and they shared a bed, she could never allow him to touch any other part of her body. This situation had obtained for 16 years, and before that time she had passively accepted sex, discouraging foreplay and suffering in silence despite her panic, until eventually she had told her husband of her fears, whereupon he resolved not to trouble her any further for sex.

They were not ready for sensate focus, and so I embarked upon a very slow form of systematic desensitization, using her approach to his body as the first measure, and encouraging her both in the session and for homework to touch his leg and thigh, first through his trousers and then unclothed. A breakthrough occurred when she was able to touch his penis, albeit with much panic and some fears at first, and gradually he was able to touch her body (at first legs and arms, and later breasts and genital area) without her feeling panicky. Mutual orgasms were experienced in petting, which for her was a revelation, and led to a period euphoria in which she kept talking to her customers about sexual matters (a most uncharacteristic reaction). Over the next couple of sessions (Nos. 9 and 10), successful intercourse took place, the first time that they had both enjoyed this activity, and follow-up showed continued success both sexually and maritally.

D. Limitations of the Behavioural Approach to Sexual Dysfunction

As in the previous section describing behavioural marital therapy, it is clear that some cases of sexual dysfunction are more complicated and difficult to treat than others. Particular factors which have been shown to have an adverse effect on progress are the presence of severe marital problems and the co-existence of *psychiatric symptomatology* (Crowe *et al.*, 1977). Other features showing a more unfavourable prognosis are *poor motivation, internal or external conflicts* (see above) or *personality disorders* associated with impulsiveness and unpredictability. In cases of *alcohol abuse* associated with impotence, the prognosis depends on the ability of the patient to reduce alcohol intake, and this is of course not the easiest of tasks even in uncomplicated alcoholism. In cases where *depression* is a feature associated with sexual dysfunction, there is often a dilemma between improving the depression (and with it perhaps the libido) by antidepressant medication and the known propensity for many anti-depressants to reduce the ability to obtain erection in the male and orgasm in the female. In some cases where there are *organic factors* (e.g. diabetes or multiple sclerosis), progress can still be made by psychologically-orientated behavioural treatment, but the ultimate end-point of treatment is likely to be less favourable (e.g. partial erection and some need for prolonged sex-play or the use of vibrators) than in the uncomplicated case.

E. Alternative Courses of Action in cases where the Behavioural Approach is unsuccessful, in both Sexual and Marital Problems

It may be asked, in view of the limitations shown by both behavioural marital therapy and behavioural treatments in sexual dysfunction, whether other forms of intervention, such as dynamic, structural or strategic, would not achieve good results in precisely those cases for which the behavioural approach is of limited use, i.e. couples with psychiatric problems, personality disorders, alcoholic abuse, poor motivation, etc. In clinical practice, I tend to use a somewhat hierarchical system in this area. Initially I try to use a behavioural approach, either reciprocity negotiation or direct treatment of the Masters and Johnson type, as these are the simplest approaches, and involve a situation of complete frankness and overt helpfulness on the part of the therapist. If difficulties arise, I tend to involve a communication training, which also takes the couple into my confidence, but which involves a more dictatorial style, bringing in overt criticism of interactional style, and active side-taking on the part of the therapist.

Both of the above types of approach are, as shown in the section on research, of proven effectiveness in significant proportions of couples presenting with problems. However in more disturbed couples with motivational problems, clinical impressions suggest that the direct approaches are not so effective, and the next hierarchical step is to move to a structural approach, which has many features in common with communication training, but takes into account other factors such as boundaries, alliances and power within the relationship. A further step along the hierarchical ladder is to move to a strategic approach, in which tasks are set which take the therapist even further away from the "teaching" role and may include "prescribing the symptom" or directing the couple to fight or create tension in the marriage. I will not go into detail on either of these treatment approaches, but further reading could include Haley (1977), Minuchin (1974) and Sluzki (1978).

A word of caution is needed, however, in advocating the move to structural or strategic approaches in cases of unsuccessful behavioural therapy. These approaches require much skill and adequate understanding of systems concepts, and in any case, they have not been subjected to the same rigorous outcome research as the behavioural approaches. But the future of marital therapy, with more far-reaching outcome studies on structural and strategic approaches, and with more accurate identification of problems suitable for each approach, may reverse the situation.

VIII. OUTCOME STUDIES

This is not the place for an exhaustive review of outcome research in behavioural marital and sexual therapy. Numerous studies have now shown that both reciprocity negotiation and communication training are superior to no treatment in improving marital relationships (Azrin, 1973; Liberman et al., 1976; Baucom,

1981; Hahlweg *et al.*, 1981). One or two studies have included extra comparisons: Crowe (1978) showed that a package of treatment including reciprocity negotiation and some Masters and Johnson techniques was significantly superior to a control approach involving non-directive interventions, but that an interpretative systems-orientated approach was intermediate, and not significantly different from either BMT or the control group. These differences held up to 18 months' follow-up, and in this period, the interpretative approach showed some late increase in effectiveness compared with the control group. Emmelkamp *et al.* (1981), in three separate studies, showed that couples treated with a BMT approach and couples treated with a systems theory interpretative approach both improved significantly more than waiting-list couples. At follow-up of one month, there was a slight relapse in the systems theory-treated couples, but the BMT couples had maintained their improvement.

Bögner and Zielenbach-Coenen (1981) found that those couples given BMT in 15 weekly sessions, showed less extensive changes than couples given the same number of sessions given in two blocks with a five week gap in which there were brief telephone contacts with the couples (the "booster" treatment).

Jacobson (1978a) showed, in a single case design using multiple baseline measures, that six couples with severe marital distress significantly improved their marital interaction through the introduction of problem-solving therapy on one conflict area at a time. In another study, Jacobson (1978b) showed that couples treated in two behaviourally orientated treatment approaches involving problem-solving and communication training, performed significantly better on a behavioural post-test than control couples given non-directive interventions or untreated control couples. However, on marital satisfaction, all three treated groups including the non-directive group improved more than the untreated control couples.

In the area of sexual dysfunction, a large number of anecdotal studies are reported, but few controlled trials. Mathews *et al.* (1976) found, in a well controlled study, no differences in outcome between (1) Masters and Johnson therapy with two therapists, (2) Masters and Johnson therapy with one therapist, (3) systematic desensitization and (4) "postal" therapy with Masters and Johnson instructions and minimal therapist contact.

Everaerd (1977) found no significant advantage in conjoint therapy using a Masters and Johnson approach compared with systematic desensitization. Arentewicz (1978) found that there were no significant differences between one *vs* two therapists or intensive *vs* spaced treatment in sex therapy. Riley and Riley (1978) found that significantly more women presenting with primary anorgasmia became orgasmic in coitus with a programme involving the use of a vibrator, compared with a sensate focus and supportive approach, Kockoff (1976) found that, of patients previously treated with desensitization for impotence, a significant proportion of the unimproved patients benefited from a subsequent Masters and Johnson approach. In the previously quoted study by Crowe (1978), couples treated by Masters and Johnson and other behavioural approaches improved their sexual adjustment significantly more than couples treated with the control non-directive approach. Crowe *et al.* (1981) showed, similarly to

Mathews *et al.* (1976), that Masters and Johnson therapy was equal to contract marital therapy in the treatment of impotence and anorgasmia, and again that two therapists obtained no better results than one.

IX. CONCLUSIONS

In the eleven or twelve years since its inauguration, behavioural marital and sexual therapy has established a firm place in the range of techniques available to therapists. The approaches are easy to learn and to apply, although some general marital/family therapy skills are required, such as empathizing with each partner and focussing on the interaction. Reciprocity negotiation and communication training have been shown in numerous trials to be effective treatments for moderately disturbed couples, although in seriously disturbed or "psychiatric" couples, these techniques may not be clearly superior to alternative systems or dynamic approaches. In sexual dysfunction, marital therapy is an important component, but specific techniques are undoubtedly effective, especially in such conditions as vaginismus and premature ejaculation. All the approaches mentioned are best learned in supervised practice, and in all of them, the simplest interactional behaviours are used as the basis for change, with the undoubted advantage of such change being objectively assessed and, in many cases, quantified.

REFERENCES

Annon, J. S. (1978). "The Behavioural Treatment of Sexual Problems. Vols. 1 & 2", Harper & Row, New York.

Arentewicz, G. (1978). "Partner therapy with sexual dysfunctions: final report on a controlled study with 202 couples. Paper presented at III International Congress of Medical Sexology, Rome.

Azrin, N. H., Naster, B. J. and Jones, R. (1973). Reciprocity Counselling: a rapid learning-based procedure for marital counselling. *B.Res. & Th.* **11**, 365-382.

Bancroft, J. H. J. and Coles, L. (1976). Three Years' Experience in a Sexual Problems Clinic. *British Medical Journal* (i), 1575-1577.

Baucom, D. (1981). A Comparison of Behavioural Contracting and Problem-Solving Communications—Training in Behavioural Therapy. A controlled outcome investigation. Paper presented at international BMT conference, Tegernsee, W. Germany.

Bögner, I. and Zielenbach-Coenen, H. (1981). On maintaining change in behavioural marital therapy. Paper presented at international BMT conference, Tegernsee, W. Germany.

Crowe, M. J. (1978). Conjoint Marital Therapy: a controlled outcome study. *Psychological Medicine* **8**, 623-636.

Crowe, M. J., Czechowicz, H. and Gillan, P. (1977). The Treatment of Sexual Dysfunction: a report of 75 cases. Presentation at VI World Congress of Psychiatry, Honolulu.

Crowe, M. J., Gillan, P. and Golombok, S. (1981). Form and Content in the Conjoint Treatment of Sexual Dysfunction. A controlled study. *Beh. Res. and Therapy*, **19**, 47-54.

Dicks, H. V. (1967). "Marital Tensions", Routledge, London.

Emmelkamp, P., van der Helm, M., MacGillavry, D. and van Zanten, B. (1981). Marital Therapy with Clinically Distressed Couples: a comparative evaluation of system-theoretic, contingency contracting and communication skills approaches. Paper presented at international BMT conference, Tegernsee, W. Germany.

Everaerd, W. (1977). Comparative studies of short-term treatment methods for sexual inadequacies. *In* "Progress in Sexology", (W. Germond and C. C. Wheeler, eds), Plenum Press, New York and London.

Friedman, D. (1968). The treatment of impotence by Brietal relaxation therapy. *Beh. Res. & Therapy*, **6**, 257-261.

Gillan, P. and Gillan, R. (1976). "Sex Therapy Today", Open Books, London.

Gottman, J., Notarius, C., Gonso, J. and Markman, H. (1976). "A Couple's Guide to Communication", Research Press, Champaign, Illinois.

Gurman, A. S. and Knudson, R. M. (1978). Behavioural Marriage Therapy I. A Psycho-dynamic-Systems Analysis and Critique. *Fam.Process*, **17**, 121-138.

Hahlweg, K., Schindler, L. and Revensdorf, D. (1981). The Treatment of Marital Distress, Formats, Modalities and Prediction. Paper presented to international BMT conference, Tegernsee, W. Germany.

Haley, J. (1976). "Problem-solving therapy", Jossey-Bass, San Francisco.

Heiman, J. R., Lo Piccolo, L. and Lo Piccolo, J. (1981). The Treatment of Sexual Dysfunction. *In* "Handbook of Family Therapy", (A. S. Gurman and D. P. Kniskern, eds), Brunner/Mazel, New York.

Jacobson, E. (1938). "Progressive Relaxation", University of Chicago Press, Chicago.

Jacobson, N. S. (1978a). Problem solving and contingency contracting in the treatment of marital discord. *J. Consulting and Clinical Psychol.* **45**, 92-100.

Jacobson, N. S. (1978b). Increasing Positive Behaviour in Severely Distressed Marital Relationships: The Effects of Problem-Solving Training. *Behav. Ther.* **10**, 311-326.

Jacobson, N. S. (1981). Behavioural Marital Therapy. *In* "Handbook of Family Therapy", (A. S. Gurman and D. P. Kniskern, eds), Brunner/Mazel, New York.

Jehu, D. (1979). "Sexual Dysfunctions", John Wiley, Chichester.

Kaplan, H. (1974). "The New Sex Therapy", Brunner/Mazel, New York.

Kegel, A. H. (1952). Sexual function of the pubo-coccygeus musde. *Western J. of Surgery, Obstetrics & Gynaecology*, **60**, 521-524.

Liberman, R. (1970). Behavioural approaches in family and couple therapy. *American Journal of Orthopsychiatry.* **40**, 106.

Liberman, R. P., Levine, J., Wheeler, E., Sanders, N. and Wallace, C. J. (1976). Marital Therapy in Groups: a comparative evaluation of behavioural and interactional formats. *Acta.Psychiat.Scand.*, Suppl.266.

Masters, W. H. and Johnson, V. E. (1970). "Human Sexual Inadequacy", Churchill, London.

Matthews, A., Bancroft, J. *et al.* (1976). The Behavioural treatment of sexual inadequacy: a comparative study. *Beh.Res. & Ther.* **14**, 427-436.

Minuchin, S. (1974). "Families and Family Therapy", Tavistock Publications, London.

O'Gorman, E., Macallister, H., Quinn, J. T., Graham, P. J. and Harbison, J. J. M. (1975). Treatment of frigidity by group desensitization. *In* "Progress in Behaviour Therapy", (J. S. Brengelmann, ed.), Springer Verlag, Berlin.

O'Leary, K. D. and Turkewitz, H. (1978). Marital Therapy from a Behavioural Per-spective: *In* Marriage and Marital Therapy", (T. J. Paolino and B. S. McCrady, eds), Brunner/Mazel, New York.

Patterson, G. R. and Hops, H. (1972). Coercion, a game for two: Intervention techniques for marital conflict. *In* "The experimental analysis of social behaviour", (R. E. Ulrich and P. Mountjoy, eds), Appleton, New York.

Riley, A. and Riley, E. (1978). A controlled study to evaluate directed masturbation in the management of primary orgasmic failure in women. *Brit. J. Psychiat.* **133**, 404-409.

Semans, J. H. (1956). Premature ejaculation. *Southern Medical Journal*, **49**, 353-7.

Sluzki, C. E. (1978). Marital Therapy from a Systems Theory Perspective. *In* "Marriage and Marital Therapy", (T. J. Paolino and B. S. McCrady, eds), Brunner/Mazel, New York.

Stanley, E. (1981). Principles of Managing Sexual Problems. *Brit. Med. J.* **282**, 1200-1202.

Stuart, R. B. (1969). Operant-interpersonal treatment for marital discord. *Journal of Consulting and Clinical Psychology*, **33**, 675-682.

Thibaut, J. W. and Kelley, H. H. (1959). "The social psychology of groups", Wiley, New York.

Part III

Intrusions in the Life-Cycle and Family Breakdown

Chapter 12

Loss, Mourning and Grief

S. Lieberman and D. Black

I. INTRODUCTION

The loss through death of a spouse or immediate family member such as a child or parent is one of the most stressful events we as human beings must face, as well as being a major disruption in the organization of family life. Grieving such a loss is nature's way of attempting to heal the wound which has been sustained, as evidenced by the occurrence of mourning in all primates, most mammals and some birds. Morbid grief is the process of improper repair, mourning gone sour like curdled milk. A description of morbid grief and its effects is illustrated by the following short case history.

A. Case History: Miss K

Miss K, a 20-year-old secretary, lost her 25-year-old fiancé. They had known each other since childhood, and had been engaged for two years. They would have married three months before he died if it were not for his illness (carcinoma of the larynx). Neither of their families would discuss the illness, but they were overkind and protective towards Miss K. She resented the silent, passive way the families seemed to be reacting. Very little discussion of the future took place between herself and her fiancé.

Her fiancé spent his last six weeks in a terminal ward in a large general hospital. Miss K gave up her job and was allowed to take care of her fiancé. In the later stages of his illness, he refused to have anyone else do anything for him. He died on Christmas morning with only his girl-friend present. She was given a strong sedative and seemed to be in a daze. She attended the funeral, but did not cry. Afterwards she returned to her office job but continued to feel that everything was unreal. She became detached from the world. She longed to discuss her bereavement with her family but could not. Her family showered pity on her, and she felt that they kept protecting her emotionally. She visited the grave of her deceased boy-friend daily as she had to pass the cemetery on her way from work. Eventually she suffered severe weight loss, depression and withdrew from people. She spent all her time in bed. Her relatives were very concerned about her.

Losses and an individual's reactions to them are not solely rooted in the person visibly suffering the loss. Losses have repercussions in the family and its relationships which are equally profound. The nuclear and extended families' reactions to and acceptance of loss, mourning and grief can hinder or help each

Family Therapy
ISBN: 0-12-089355-X

individual family member. In this example, the nuclear family was unable to provide the correct emotional atmosphere, and it was fortuitous that a member of the extended family stepped in.

Miss K accepted an invitation to live with the family of her aunt. She spent the first week in tears and moods; eventually the crying became less, and long discussions took place about her fiancé's illness and death. These discussions occurred over and over again for at least 3 months. Almost daily there was a bout of crying. A great deal of resentment towards her parents was expressed, especially towards her father. Pictures of her dead boy-friend and his grave were displayed in her bedroom. She became brighter, more interested in life generally, and eventually took down the pictures in her bedroom and stopped wearing her engagement ring. After nine months, she met and became engaged to a new boy-friend.

At last contact, she felt that she had worked through the loss for her first fiancé, but knew that she would never forget her first love.

II. THE INDIVIDUAL'S REACTION TO LOSS

A. Stages of Feeling State and Behaviour

Before proceeding to discuss the effects of loss on a family relationship system, the effects of loss on the individuals who make up the systems will be reviewed. Mourning follows upon the loss of a loved one and is distinguished by changes in feeling state and behaviour which occur in stages. First, numbness and unfeeling shock intervene to provide a brief period of disbelief and unreality. Second, a stage of disorganization occurs during which physical symptoms such as "heartache", sighing, sleep disorders, palpitations and various digestive upsets may occur. These are accompanied by feelings of hostility, guilt, anger, despair and sorrow, which wash over an individual in waves or pangs of grief. Mental life becomes preoccupied with the deceased, and behaviour is disturbed by a loss of normal patterns of conduct, pining, searching behaviour and weeping. The third stage marks the resolution of the above disorganization, as the deceased ceases to occupy a central position in the mental life and new activities and behaviour fills the void.

Bowlby (1963) prefers to distinguish four stages:
(1) Shock
(2) Protest
(3) Despair
(4) Recovery

Parkes (1972) agrees with Bowlby that it is difficult to distinguish protest and despair as separate phases.

B. Morbid Grief Reactions

Morbid grief in the individual distorts or delays the normal grief process. In a clinical study of 19 patients suffering with morbid grief (Lieberman, 1978), the signs and symptoms were evaluated using a Morbid Grief Scale. The scale includes many of the most frequently observed reactions including: absence of expected reaction, delayed reaction, avoidance, panic attacks, anniversary reactions, overidealization, identification symptoms, recurrent nightmares, extreme anger, extreme guilt, prolonged grief and physical illness (Lindemann, 1944; Parkes, 1972).

Correlation of these items revealed three patterns. The first was an avoidance pattern in which avoidance of persons, places or things related to the deceased is combined with extreme guilt, extreme anger and the delayed onset of grief. The second pattern combined an absence of expected grief with idealizing the deceased and extreme anger directed towards others. The third pattern was the combination of prolonged grieving with recurrent nightmares and the development of a physical illness.

III. FAMILY REACTIONS TO LOSS

These individual reaction patterns cannot help but be reflected in the family system. The family system may operate like a tuning fork: vibrating in phase with the individual's pathology, or it may operate like a shock-absorber, damping down the pathological manifestations so that a loss may be properly mourned. When the family reacts to enhance or add to the pathology, a family system reaction to loss that parallels the behaviour of the individual occurs; avoidance, idealization and prolonged stressful grief patterns may be seen.

A.   Clinical Example: Family Avoidance Patterns

Family avoidance patterns developed in the family of a 54-year-old woman who suffered the death of her mother in 1973 with great fortitude, but became increasingly housebound. In 1974 her sister died, and with that death, the patient was unable to walk out of the house alone at all. She feared she was going insane as her sister had done (her sister developed senile dementia prior to death), and stated she had seen people she mistook for her mother and sister in the street, which had frightened her and kept her from leaving the house.

Her husband and two children went along with her wish not to mention her mother or sister. They tried to protect her by being with her constantly, hiding pictures of her dead relatives, and avoiding contact with other members of her extended family. They completely avoided travelling to the village where her mother was buried.

B.   Family Patterns of Idealization

Family patterns of idealization were evident in the family of a 64-year-old white retired widowed woman seen because of feelings of anxiety and depression and an inability to concentrate. Her husband had died 3 years before, and was described as "a wonderful man, a preacher who was very good and kind, a husband who was perfect in every way". Life without him had become very difficult, and she still missed him. Prior to his death, all had been well. She was bitter about her children's reactions to her and to her husband's death. She even blamed them for his last illness. When at last she was persuaded to invite her daughter to the office, the meaning of her morbid symptoms became clear. Her daughter was black, and for the first time she admitted that her husband was black and that her parents had disapproved of her marriage and disowned her. Later she admitted that she was pregnant when she married him, and that he had left her with very little livelihood when he died. Her children felt that their mother blamed them for their father's death, and they in turn felt angry towards her and idealized their father.

C. Family Patterns of Physical Illness

A third pattern occurred in the family of a woman whose daughter died. During the year following the death, she developed eczema and irritable colon. Her prolonged bouts of crying and nightmares about her daughter's leg amputation caused her son and husband to isolate her at home.

IV. AMPLIFICATIONS IN THE SYSTEM

Patterns of response to loss deriving from individual reactions are complemented by family system reactions to loss. Bowen (1976) describes one such reaction as the "emotional shock wave". This is a network of serious life events in the extended family occurring in proximity to the death of a significant family member. Paul and Grosser (1965) describe a second pattern of family response in the following terms:

the inability to cope with loss might be characteristic of a family pattern acquired in a milieu where other family members showed a similar failing. This inability was usually expressed through denial of its significance on an affective level. Although the original losses may have occurred as much as 50 years ago, the response to them exercises a lingering effect on the present. Such losses were usually suffered by one or the other parent often before the birth of the identified patient. Affects and attitudes towards the lost persons had remained essentially unchanged and recent losses evoked similar reaction patterns. The current style of family life appears permeated with varying degrees of denial or warding off of losses and disappointments. Major changes in family homeostasis, such as those which might result in separation or independence of its members are resisted.

Two other patterns exist which have been found to be manifested uniquely in family dynamics and interactions rather than more isolated in the individual.

A. Family Substitutions

The first and most striking observation is that family losses are often followed rapidly by family gains through marriages or births, as if in an attempt at restitution.

For example the Brown family, when paternal grandfather died, the following year saw the birth of five great-grandchildren and two marriages among the eleven grandchildren. The significance of the act of marriage or conception and birth lies in the replacement of those who have died. Replacements in a family can be conscious or unconscious, covert or obvious. The effect on the spouse or child who becomes the replacement may be negligible or catastrophic depending on the reality of their attributes, the strength of the projections, and the way in which the two match. Equally important is the conscious awareness of the container for the projections and the person seeking a replacement relationship.

The following is an example of the way in which the unconscious projection of a dearly loved but dead relative can affect the child who receives those projections. Miss S, a 17-year-old anorectic girl, was born 10 months after her paternal grandmother died. Her father had been very close to his mother as shown by their one enforced separation during the war. After the war he returned to the family home and remained there even after marriage. His wife became pregnant purposely in order to force him to move, a manoeuvre he never forgave her for. Shortly after the move and birth of his son, his mother became ill and died two years after. His daughter was born the year following her death. When she was born, he felt she looked exactly like his mother. She grew up with him treating her as if she were his mother and developed the same overclose relationship with her. When she became an adolescent, he stifled her independence while his wife was continuously angry and jealous of her daughter's closeness with her husband. She was unaware of the reasons for the growing tension at home, but when her body began to develop and it was clear that she would take after her mother's more voluptuous form, her father began to comment unfavourably. Her father's mother had been very thin all her life and she began to slim with her father's encouragement. The anorexic illness took over and she had to be admitted.

This example illustrates the unconscious use of a child as a container to be filled with the relationship patterns pre-established with a dead relative. Children who serve as replacements can face enormous difficulties related to their eventual growth into adulthood. Separation from parents is a particularly difficult task when the parent is projecting an unseparated dead relative onto the child.

B. The Destruction of Families

An unfortunate family pattern related to loss, is not an uncommon occurrence but tends to come to the notice of a family therapist too late. This is the destruction of families which can occur after a loss, either through further deaths, divorces, illnesses or separations. For example, Mr and Mrs D were happily married for three years until Mr D's father developed lung cancer. Mr D began to show jealousy, and became suspicious of his wife. He started drinking heavily. When his father died, he began to beat her. He started going out with other women. He rarely saw his mother or brother who lived nearby. His only sibling, an older brother also had several affairs, and his marriage was shaky.

Neither brother could discuss their father's death with their mother. Mr D denied that his father's death had any effect on his behaviour, although he also admitted that when his father became ill, he began to wonder for the first time in his life what life was all about.

When his wife threatened a divorce, he agreed to see his GP who referred them both for marital therapy. During the first meeting it became clear that Mr D was severely affected by the death of his father. He had shown a delayed response to the death (greater than two weeks) extreme excess anger, identification with personal traits present in the deceased's last illness and overidealization; four out of thirteen positive indicators of morbid grief. When discussing his father he began crying in the office, and his wife turned away. She was unable to support him when he showed his upset because of her own intense feelings of loss of her father-in-law. After this session, the couple decided to emigrate to Australia. They divorced after returning one year later.

V. FAMILY PATHOLOGY FOLLOWING LOSS

A. The Revealed Partner

Clinically, it is clear that family patterns of reaction to the loss of a loved one are present, but little systematic work has been attempted to discover the incidence of family pathology following loss. The work which has been done usually relates to widows or widowers only. There is an increased incidence of mortality of the remaining partner in the first year after bereavement estimated in studies to be 40 to 1200 times as great as in the general population (Parkes, 1972). Heart disease is particularly implicated as a constant factor. Other psychosomatic studies of the bereaved have established that they tend to consult their doctors more often, that 28% reported a marked deterioration in their health, that four times as many bereaved are admitted to hospital during the first year following bereavement, and that bereavement precipitates mental illness in a proportion of patients during the first year of bereavement.

There are important implications to draw from this work on the individual for the family system sustaining a loss. Not only must the family react to the loss itself, there is an implicit expectation after a loved one dies that further disasters are likely to occur in one or more close family members. In some families, this expectation leads to an overprotective stance in which fragile family members are given a cotton wool treatment which could prevent them from grieving normally. Other families react by increasing the tension and anxiety as they await further disasters while still others deny the loss either passively or actively.

B. Young Children and Their Reactions to Loss

(1) The Child's Conceptual Grasp of Loss
There is evidence that young children respond to the death of family members in a special way. Most of the evidence relates to the circumstances in which a child

loses one or both of his parents. About 1.6% of British children are orphaned of at least one parent (Finer, 1974), although the incidence is falling. The reaction of a child to the death of a parent depends on his stage of development, and on his previous and subsequent experience. A young child's understanding of death is limited by his difficulty in handling abstract concepts, by ignorance, and by lack of experience. There are only a few satisfactory studies of the growth of conceptualization about death (Anthony, 1940; Nagy, 1948). More recently, Koocher (1974) studied the development of the concept of death linking it with the Piagetian stages of cognitive development. These studies have their limitations, but there is general agreement that young children have difficulty in understanding the fact that death is final, and irreversible, and that the dead are different from the living or from objects which have never lived. They tend to think magically and to impute causation to events linked by time or to wishes. Their egocentric view of the world makes it likely that they will feel responsible for the death of someone for whom they harboured antagonistic or ambivalent feelings. They tend to concretize abstract concepts so that they have difficulty in understanding why, for example, Daddy does not return from heaven in time for dinner as he did when he went to Manchester. However, Bluebond-Langner (1978) has demonstrated that very young children with leukaemia can acquire the knowledge that they are going to die, suggesting that concept formation depends on experience. A child's bizarre ideas about death can be understood only by taking account of the limitations in his understanding and knowledge.

For example, a six-year-old was asked what happens to people when they die. "An angel comes down from heaven, cuts off their feet and puts the feet on a shelf in heaven to use for new people." This gruesome fantasy originated from an explanation about what happens to people's souls (soles) after death, which no doubt the adult concerned thought was understood!

(2) Family attitudes to the child

The attitudes of the family, parents, grandparents and siblings have profound influences on how a child integrates his experiences. The twentieth century taboo on death, coupled with a reduction in the incidence of premature death, has made it difficult for children to acquire either knowledge or experience. Parents and other family members may have to provide manageable experience of death through the keeping of pets and attendance at funerals of distant relations. Whether they can do this depends on their own attitudes to death. The widowed mother who told her young son that "Daddy has chosen to go to Baby Jesus in Heaven", unwittingly left him wondering about how one copes with such a powerful competitor. Pattison (1976) has suggested that "death has become pathogenic because sociocultural taboos prevent children and their families from appropriately coping with death". He suggests that children can cope with the experience of death, but not with the family myth and mystification process.

Bowlby (1963) has suggested that children are more prone to pathological reactions to bereavement. Miller (1971) reviewed the psychoanalytic literature and concludes "that children, in comparison to adults, do not pass through mourning . . .", further, she finds that there is wide agreement that a particular set of responses tends to occur in children who experience the death of one of their parents. These reactions include unconscious and sometimes conscious denial of the reality of the parents' death; rigid screening out of all affective responses connected with the parents' death; marked increase in identification with and idealization of the dead parent; decrease in self-esteem; feelings of guilt; and persistent unconscious fantasies of an ongoing relationship or reunion with the dead parent.

All the studies she quotes are of symptomatic children undergoing psycho-analytic therapy which stated either prior to or subsequent to the death of a parent, so no firm conclusions can be drawn. Nevertheless, there is an impressive body of evidence (Black, 1978) that psychiatric disorder is significantly more common in bereaved children, both during childhood and adult life.

C. Absence of Parenting

One family-related explanation for this morbidity is that children must be parented, and the absence of one parent inevitably distorts their experience and makes it harder for them to learn how to be a father/mother, husband/wife, and an adult man/woman. Birtchnell, (1971) found that having a sibling of the same sex as the dead parent was some protection against the development of later psychiatric disorder, but that *being* an older same-sex sibling predisposed one to mental ill health. Brown *et al.* (1977) found that women who lose their mother in childhood are predisposed to depressive illnesses which is in keeping with these results. Widowed mothers may have to guard against making their eldest son a parental child and thus breaching the generational boundaries (Minuchin, 1974), and of course similarly widowed fathers with their daughters. But whether this increased morbidity is a product of the child's difficulties with expressing and resolving grief, or his adverse family experiences subsequent to the bereavement such as changes in income, housing, schooling, or family structure, and dealing with the grief of a remaining parent cannot be definitely answered at present and must await the outcome of further research.

VI. FAMILY THERAPY WITH BEREAVED FAMILIES

A. Operational or Forced Mourning

Forced mourning is used in family therapy to deal with families pathologically entangled in a reaction to loss.

Operational mourning or forced mourning is a therapeutic manoeuvre in family therapy based on the presumption that a family pattern of grieving is morbid and has stifled the growth and development of the individuals within that family. The primary goal of forced mourning is the conversion of a morbid grief reaction to a more normal one which is then followed to its completion. Making real the loss requires active intervention by the therapist by directed enquiry. The sharing of the strong feelings generated is an important new family communication pattern which is used to strengthen new relationships within and without the family boundaries. The therapy proceeds in three phases, the first of which is the detailed enquiry into the major losses sustained by family members. This includes enquiring as to the timing of the loss and the subsequent reaction to it.

(1)   Clinical Example: Mr and Mrs H
For example, Mr and Mrs H had not mentioned the existence of a child, Michael, who had died early in their marriage. It is in the collection of this sort of history that the geneogram (Lieberman, 1979) is a valuable aid. Directed enquiry into the death of Michael revealed that he was the cause of their marriage. Mr H had been in the army and returned there after Michael's birth. Michael's death was borne by his mother alone while her husband was attempting to get emergency leave to join her. They had never shared any discussion of feelings about him, his death or their own marriage forced by a birth and possibly released by a death. Kevin's birth 4 years later exacerbated the bouts of depression Mrs H had been suffering.

(2)   Stimulating Blocked Painful Feelings
The second phase of operational mourning is an inexorable and pitiless attempt to stimulate the painful emotions which are blocked. Mr and Mrs H were asked to visit the grave, to relive the exact circumstances of the final illness, to verbalize feelings of the most negative sort directed at Michael and each other in conjoint sessions including Kevin and their young daughter at times. The therapist must be willing to tolerate and stimulate the painful feelings stored within the individuals in the family without rancour or reproach. The moment arrived when Mr H, having been involved in an angry argument with his wife who insisted that he hadn't cared about Michael, suddenly began to cry. It was then that he revealed his trips to a spiritualist to attempt contact with his dead son.

(3)   Resolution of Grief
The third phase of therapy involves the resolution of the grief and a change in relationship patterns within the family. This was evidenced by the ability of Mr H to leave his wife in one of their stormy scenes at home which was played out in front of both his and her mother. Mr H had never before dared to separate from his wife. His ability to do so stimulated within Mrs H a new awareness of the love she had for her husband. He had altered a dependent clinging relationship into a more mature awareness of their mutual needs. They are continuing at present in therapy, and have been able to share much of their work with their children. A picture of Michael now hangs in their living room along with that of the other children, although important further work is still continuing.

B.   Family Therapy with Bereaved Children

Children, even very young ones, can be aided to express grief and to mourn (see Furman, E., 1974; Miller, 1971; Reeves, 1973; Harris, 1973 for individual treatment; and Black, 1974, 1980; Evans, 1976; Tuters, 1974; Clark, 1972 for family therapy) with a subsequent improvement in functioning. It is likely that their reported difficulties are due to adult avoidance of the task rather than to children's inability to mourn. It is painful for adults to contemplate childhood bereavement; it does violence to our fantasy that childhood should be a happy and conflict-free period. This avoidance can happen even with experienced therapists. Reviewing recently a videotaped interview with a family of children who had lost both parents, one of us (DB) was fascinated to note that she and her co-therapist, as well as the older children had failed to listen to the tentative but clear questioning of the five-year-old, "My mummy is dead, isn't she?", so intent were we to deal with a problem raised by the oldest child.

Furman (1980) describes the sensitive yet painful way in which a three-year-old is helped to know about his father's suicide, "His mindsickness made him so mixed up that he made himself die. The doctors tried to help his mindsickness but they couldn't", he was heard later to tell his friends, demonstrating that he had incorporated this reality. His friends then say: "Your dad was a great swimmer, wasn't he?" "Yes, this is one of the trophies he won. He was a great swimmer."

(1) Clinical Example: Brian and his Family

Brian, aged 12, had been unable to express any grief for his mother, who had died suddenly. Instead he angrily criticized his foster parents who were caring for him and his younger sister. They were not dressing her as his mother would' have liked, not giving her the right schooling or the right religious upbringing. He thumped his chair angrily. His violence alarmed his social worker who tried to reason with him gently. But what was needed here was boldness (Parkes, 1977). "What you are really angry about is that you will never see your mother again", his therapist said. Abruptly the rage switched over to grief. He sobbed loudly, inviting what comfort the therapist could give. The loud protesting tears of grief came readily for the first time. When he recovered, he was able to relate more warmly to his foster parents and allow them to care for him instead of feeling he had to do all the parenting of himself and his sister.

Children learn their coping behaviour within their family (Paul and Grosser, 1965; Bowlby and Parkes, 1970). The effect of being brought up in families which suppress and avoid the expression of sad affects, is to produce a rigid family system in the next generation. The logical treatment for such dysfunctional systems is family therapy and this may need to involve three generations.

(2) Clinical Example: Katie and her Family

Katie, aged 8, was referred to one of us (DB) because the G.P. was concerned at the enmeshment of mother and daughter which he felt was impairing the child's development. The mother's concern was different. She wanted help for Katie's learning difficulties. The family consisted of mother (a part-time secretary) and Katie. Father had died when she was 2 years old. The referral had been asked for by father's mother, herself a widow, who was concerned about the damaging over-protectiveness of mother and the constriction in her social life. The three were seen together.

Mother was unsure that they needed a psychiatrist, and kept her at arm's length with a bright, brittle defensiveness which was felt to cover prolonged and unresolved grief. She was close to and dependent on P.G.M., having poor relationships with her own parents who had been unsupportive throughout the years of her widowhood, as indeed they had been in her childhood. Mother felt her own life was over; she only lived for Katie. She had no joy from her work, friends or family. Two men were courting her; she strung them both along but made it clear there was no question of remarriage or involvement. Katie was unsure about her father's death, as she was about most things. In talking about father, she often used the present tense: "Dad and I both like the same foods, don't we Grandma?" An emotionally immature girl, she had few friends and struggled hard but unsuccessfully to learn at school. Could mother's unresolved grief be affecting Katie's learning ability and her maturation? Using techniques of forced or operational mourning, mother was pushed boldly to consider her life together with her husband, and P.G.M. encouraged to review her life with her son. Both women began to cry and Katie was helped to understand why. P.G.M. was asked to continue to meet with mother and look over old photos with the aim of grieving for what they had lost. Mother was sceptical but agreed to participate.

At the next session 3 weeks later, mother looked very happy. "Do you notice anything different about me?" She announced that she had got engaged and was to be married soon. She and P.G.M. had carried out the task that was set and had had a sad time. Curiously she then felt happier and had allowed her boy-friend to get closer. She could commit herself to him, and for the first time contemplate remarriage. Katie was delighted at the prospect of a new father, and referred to her own father only in the past. Mother was able to begin to recognize P.G.M.'s need for companionship and reciprocate some of the support, thus making the relationship more symmetrical. Follow up one year later showed that Katie was performing at an age-adequate level at school, and was not considered a problem there or at home.

Children's communications can be difficult for parents to understand, and misperceptions and misunderstandings are common. A parent's grief may alarm a child by its vehemence and unfamiliarity, and the family therapist can interpret the mother's behaviour to the child (Black, 1981). Family therapy can therefore be prophylactic, and should be considered in bereavements where there is a high risk of pathological reactions. These would include the loss of a parent in childhood, the loss of a child, loss during pregnancy (Lewis, 1979), loss by suicide, two or more significant losses in close succession, and loss in adults where there was a previous childhood loss.

C. The Death of a Sibling including Stillbirths

Children are often left out of the rituals around the death of a member of the family. In the case of sibling death, they may have entertained ambivalent or frankly hostile feelings which go unrecognized. The parents too may displace their feelings of guilt and self-hatred on to one of the surviving children which may in extreme cases lead to child abuse (Tooley, 1975; Lewis, 1979). If a stillbirth occurs, mourning may be particularly difficult for the family (Lewis, 1976).

(1) June and her Family

June, aged 7, had never been heard to speak at school, although at home she spoke occasionally. Her birth and early history were normal, and by 2 years she was speaking in sentences. Shortly after starting school, her mother had a stillbirth. June, who had been told of the expected birth, saw her mother return from hospital without a baby. No one in the family told her what had happened. It seemed like a conspiracy of silence. June was diagnosed as having elective mutism. It was possible by family therapy to help the family to communicate about the loss, to help them grieve, and to work through June's fears that she had damaged or killed the missing baby by her wish, expressed during the pregnancy, but then forgotten, that her mother should not have a baby. That her wish had come true had shown her that words were damaging and therefore not to be used lightly. Perhaps it was safer not to speak. Her family had demonstrated this to her by not speaking about the baby. Once they understood her misconceptions, they were able to help her to recognize that she had not killed the baby and her speech became normal.

D. The Dying Child and his Family

We know of no family therapists who have treated families containing a dying child although individual psychotherapy with siblings has been reported (Rosenblatt, 1969) as was work with families containing a dying parent (Black, 1981). Dying children, especially in hospital, are isolated and cut off from their family, often feeling they have to protect and support their parents, and even their doctors (Bluebond-Langner, 1978; Howarth, 1974) rather than being able to count upon support for themselves.

(1) Clinical Example: Simon and his Family

Simon, a 16-year-old boy with progressive muscular dystrophy which had crippled him considerably, and for which he had been repeatedly hospitalized, talked to his psychotherapist about the burdens which he carried which he felt prevented him from growing-up. His father would not face the fact that Simon's illness would soon kill him, and the parents became unable to communicate about anything. Mother suddenly developed a fulminating breast cancer and predeceased Simon. Although father then accepted some social-work counselling himself, he refused to discuss with Simon the mother's death or Simon's own "burdens". In this case, family therapy was offered but refused.

The only child may have particular problems in coping with his position as the only product of his mother's womb to survive.

(2)   Clinical Example: Jacqueline and her Family

Jacqueline, 10, an only child was referred for abdominal pain which had no organic cause. At a family diagnostic session, a geneogram elicited an odd reaction. Jacquie could talk freely about her maternal grandparents, but hesitated when asked about her father's parents. She peered intently into father's face. She said she was worried to talk about paternal grandfather who had died 4 years ago in case it upset Dad. The latter was amazed, and later work revealed that Jacquie saw herself as a powerful person who could hurt her parents, cause them to separate, and blight her mother's fertility (there had been a series of miscarriages and a separation). Family therapy sessions focussed on helping the parents to "cut her down to size", and relieve her of the burden of omnipotence.

Few research studies, even when allegedly focussing on families with a terminally ill child, actually interview the siblings or consider their needs (see Black and Sturge, 1979 for review). Black and Sturge conclude that life experiences are likely to have their impact modified by the interaction between temperamental variables, and sibling and parental attitudes and relationships. The concept of role assignment within families (Toman, 1961) seems a fruitful one for understanding and intervening preventively in families containing a dying or dead member, where loss or impending loss is producing family dysfunction. The restructuring of the family involves the reallocation of roles hitherto held by that member, so that a sibling may have to take on the role of the "clever" one left behind by the dead child; the eldest boy must take on the dead father's role, etc. Family therapy is the only technique which is likely to do justice to the complexities raised by the need of a family to adjust to loss (Bowen, 1976).

VII.   CONCLUSION

Within family therapy sessions the importance of loss, mourning and grief must not be under-emphasized. The painful emotions and their resultant blocks to family growth and development require delicate but firm handling to carry through the therapeutic contract.

REFERENCES

Anthony, S. (1940). "The Childs Discovery of Death", Routledge & Kegan Paul, London.

Birtchnell, J. (1971). Early parent death in relation to size & constitution of sibship. *Acta. Psychiat. Scand.* **47**, 250-270.

Black, D. (1974). What happens to bereaved children? *Therapeutic Education*, **2**, 15-20.

Black, D. (1978). Annotation:— The bereaved child. *J.Chil. Psychol. Psychiat.* **19**, 187-292.

Black, D. and Sturge, C. (1979). The young child & his siblings. *In* "The Modern Psychiatry of Infancy", (J. Howells, ed.), Oliver & Boyd, Edinburgh.

Black, D. (1981). Mourning & the family. *In* "Developments in Family Therapy", (S. Walrond-Skinner, ed.), Routledge, London.

Bluebond-Langner, M. (1978). "The Private Worlds of Dying Children", Princeton Univ. Press, Princeton, N.J.

Bowen, M. (1976). Family reaction to death. *In* "Family Therapy", (P. Guerin, ed.), Gardner Press, N.Y.

Bowlby, J. (1963). Pathological mourning & childhood mourning. *J.Amer. psychoanal. Assn.* **11**, 500-541.

Bowlby, J. (1972). *Attachment & Loss* (3 vols.) Hogarth Press, London.

Bowlby, J. and Parkes, C. M. (1970). Separation & loss within the family. *In* "The Child in His Family", (C. J. Anthony & C. Koupernik, eds), John Wiley, New York.

Brown, C. W., Harris, T. and Copeland, J. R. (1977). Depression & loss. *Brit. J. Psychiat.* **130**, 1-18.

Clark, M. (1972). A therapeutic approach to treating a grieving 2½ year old. *J.Amer. Acad. Child Psychiat.* **11**, 705-711.

Evans, N. S. (1976). Mourning as a family secret. *J.Amer. Acad. Child Psychiatry*, **15**, 502-509.

Finer, M. (1974). "Report of the Committees on One-Parent Families", HMSO.

Furman, E. (1974). "A Child's Parent Dies", Yale University Press, Newhaven.

Furman, E. (1980). A case of bereavement. *Psychoanalytic Quarterly*, **49**, 554-556.

Harris, M. (1973). The complexity of mental pain seen in a six-year old child following sudden bereavement. *J.Child Psychotherapy*, **3:3**, 35-45.

Howarth, R. (1974). The psychiatric care of children with life-threatening illnesses. *In* "The Care of the Child Facing Death", (L. Burton, ed.), Routledge & Kegan Paul, London.

Koocher, G. P. (1974). Talking with children about death. *Amer.J. Orthopsychiat.* **44**, 404-11.

Lewis, E. (1976). The Management of stillbirth: coping with an unreality. *Lancet*, **2**, 619-20.

Lewis, E. (1979). Inhibition of mourning by pregnancy: psychopathology & management. *Brit.Med. J.* **2**, 27-28.

Lieberman, S. (1978). 19 cases of morbid grief. *Brit. J. Psychiat.* **132**, 159-170.

Lieberman, S. (1979). Transgenerational analysis: The geneogram as technique in family therapy. *Journal of Family Therapy*, **1**, 51-64.

Lindemann, E. (1944). The symptomatology and management of acute grief. *American Journal of Psychiatry*, **101**, 141-149.

Miller, J. B. M. (1971). Childrens reactions to the death of a parent: A review of the psychoanalytic literature. *J. Amer. Psychanalyt. Assn.* **19**, 697-719.

Minuchin, S. (1974). "Families & Family Therapy", Tavistock, London.

Nagy, M. (1948). The child's view of death. *J. Genetic Psychology*, **73**, 3-27.

Parkes, C. M. (1977). What becomes of redundant world models? *Brit. J. Med. Psychol.* **48**, 131-137.

Parkes, M. (1972). "Bereavement: Studies of Grief in Adult Life", Tavistock, London.

Pattison, E. M. (1976). The fatal myth of death in the family. *Am. J. Psychiatry*, **133**, 674-678.

Paul, N. L. and Grosser, G. H. (1965). Operational mourning & its role in conjoint family therapy. *Community Mental Health Journal*, **1**, 339-345.

Reeves, G. (1973). Real life trauma & its implications for therapy. Treatment of children following the death of a parent.*J. Child Psychotherapy*, **3**, 11-26.

Robertson, J. (1952). [Film] "A two year old goes to hospital", Tavistock Child Development Research Unit, London.

Rosenblatt, B. (1969). A young boy's reaction to the death of his sister. *J.Amer. Acad. Child Psychiat.* **8**, 321-325.

Toman, W. (1961). "Family Constellation: Theory & Practice of a Psychological Game", Springer, New York.

Tooley, K. (1975). The choice of a surviving sibling as "scapegoat" in some cases of maternal bereavement — a case report. *J. Child Psychol. Psychiat.* **16**, 331-339.

Tuters, E. (1974). Short term contracts: Brief focal intervention in family mourning. *Social Work Today*, **5**, 226-231.

Chapter 13

Reconstituted Families:
Some Implications for the Family Therapist

M. Robinson

I. INTRODUCTION

Most families bring up their own children in nuclear family groups consisting of parents and their natural children. But these numbers are slowly diminishing and there are now large numbers of "families" of "parents" and "children" who spend a good deal of their conjoint family lives in alternative groupings, some of which might hardly be considered as "families" at all. Nevertheless, society, through various social institutions and what passes for family policy (haphazard as it frequently is), exercises a good deal of normative pressure towards the maintenance of this nuclear family group. At this time, approximately 1 in 10 are single parent families, consisting of deserted, divorced or widowed parents who have to, or who choose to bring up their children alone. Some of these single parents remarry, forming new nuclear groups, and others voluntarily or involuntarily give their children up to become members of other alternative family groups. It is on these reformed reconstituted family groups which this chapter focusses.

Reconstituted families consist of those family units who, for one reason or another, have come together in an attempt to reform a nuclear family of parents and children who are not equally legally and biologically related in the sense of consisting of a marital couple with their natural children, as is the case with natural nuclear families. Most reconstituted families which are reconstructed in this way consist of the "core" of a former originating nuclear family system, which may or may not have been a complete family unit of itself, plus an extra member (or members) who have been added, thus making up an apparently new nuclear family of two parents plus children, not all of whom are biologically related to both the parents.

It will already be apparent that reconstituted families are even more complicated than natural nuclear families, and that each is in the process of becoming reconstituted following its own particular pattern, but also sharing some characteristics with other reconstituted families. It is possible to distinguish three main groupings, each with various sub-types which share some of the main characteristic variables. These three main groupings are adoptive, foster and step-families, who are all reconstituted families who reform with at least some intent to remain together as a nuclear family group for some length of time. (The possible exception to this is the temporary foster home, here differentiated from short-term fostering.) The main distinguishing features of each of the

Family Therapy
ISBN: 0-12-089355-X

three groupings will be described briefly, so that the similarities and differences can be considered.

II. VARIETIES OF RE-CONSTITUTED FAMILIES

A.   Adoptive Families

Adoptive families are those which have added a child who is not the natural child of either parent. Traditionally the perception of an adoptive family is one in which an infertile couple adopt a baby, and thus it is by the act of adoption that the marital partners change from being a couple into becoming a family. But traditions have changed, and nowadays such a stereotype is only one among numbers of recognizable adoptive families. Due to a shortage of babies for adoption, many childless couples are adopting older children. In doing so, they are attempting not only to develop a family unit of their own, but also trying to assimilate into this developing group a child who already has some experience of family life, perhaps in a natural nuclear family or also in a foster home.

Other natural nuclear families are adopting children in addition to their own natural children, and these adoptive children are now more likely to be older children, some even handicapped in one way or another, than they are to be illegitimate babies. (These are now most likely to be brought up in single parent families, who are often later assimilated into step-families.) A third sub-group of adoptive families are those who adopt children of a different racial origin from their own. Many of these children are in fact multi-racial, and in such adoptive families, the initial and outwardly distinguishing feature is that the child's colour is different from that of the rest of the family, which in itself has implications for the reconstituted family group. Adoptive families who add to their number children from a different ethnic culture also have to take this into account within the culture of their own reconstituted family unit.

B.   Foster Families

(1) Definition
Foster families are those families to which children who are not the natural children of the couple may be added, as a planned temporary measure (that is, short-term fostering), or for long-term fostering either with a view to adoption or for the duration of the rest of their childhood. Foster children may in fact be biologically related to the foster family, children in need of care being frequently fostered with aunts and uncles. But while there may be some familiarity of family culture, there may also be difficulties which stem from the history which lies within the family of origin (as was the case with Maria Colwell). Most foster families take in children who have already spent some part of their childhood in their natural nuclear family, and in the case of short-term fostering, it is expected that they will return to their own family at least in due course; but meanwhile the intent is that in some measure, they should become part of the foster family.

(2) Fostering Problems

This entails some degree of mutual accommodation within a reconstituted family group, even though the intention is often that the foster child should be regarded as a bird of passage, either retaining his or her personal identity as a member of another natural nuclear family group, or as a preparation for long-term fostering with a view to adoption. As well as the difficulties inherent in the issues of short-term or long-term fostering, and the capacities of the foster child and foster family to accommodate each other with a mutual sufficiency, there is also the vexed question of the relationships between the foster-child-in-the-foster-family, and the foster child in his own natural family. At the time that a child who has been subsequently fostered, was received into care, his or her own natural nuclear family must have been failing to care for the child adequately, although the reasons for such failure may have been temporary and remedial (see Bentovim Chapter 28). Two of the major problems for foster families are whether the foster family and the foster child are able to develop sufficient attachment for the fostering to be functional for all of them, and whether the child's attachment to his or her natural nuclear family (or more likely the residual members of such a family) can be maintained. This will be discussed further when capacity for attachment is being considered, but in the meantime Holman's (1975) concept of "inclusive" and "exclusive" fostering is a useful distinguishing feature.

(3) Inclusive Fostering

For a foster family where the foster child has considerable attachments to his or her own natural nuclear family, it is proposed that the fostering should be *inclusive* in that the child's relationships should be maintained with the original family. The implication is that there should be some kind of direct interaction between the foster-child-in-the-foster-family and the natural nuclear family.

(4) Exclusive Fostering

In the case of *exclusive* fostering, such contacts should not be required of the foster family, the decision being made according to the needs of the foster child. The implication here is that the more the foster child is absorbed into the reconstituted foster family, the less he or she remains attached to his or her original natural nuclear family. This question of whose needs should prevail is a moral dilemma in fostering, but also one in family therapy with reconstituted families, and will be discussed later.

C. Step-families

(1) Definition

Step-families are those families where the additional member of the family is an adult who is not the natural parent of the children and has not previously been related to the custodial parent. There are however, some step-families where the incoming step-parent already has some legally recognizable affinity with the family, as for instance when a widowed father marries his deceased wife's sister, who now becomes step-mother as well as aunt. Such situations, as with fostering children with relatives, have special familial features which have their roots in the parental families of origin. Some step-parents may already be natural parents in their own right, others may become an instant parent figure upon marriage and entry into the family. Some may bring into the family their own natural children from a previous family unit, others may leave behind them such children who remain in the custody of a previous partner. Thus the children in families where there are divorce chains, that is where both partners divorce and remarry, may find themselves concurrently members of two (or more) family units where, as is the case with inclusive fostering, the relationships between the family units may vary in quality.

(2) Legitimating Step-families
In the formation of a step-family unit, the fate of the original family group is an important factor. Some step-families are formed following the marriage of the single parent of an illegitimate child (or children) either to the child's natural parent or to another partner. I have elsewhere distinguished such step-families as *legitimating step-families*, although legally such a term only applied if the step-parent (usually a step-father) is either the natural father of the child, or an adoption order is made.

(3) Re-vitalized Step-families
Other step-families are those in which one of the natural parents has died and the widow or widower has remarried; I have described these as *revitalized step-families*.

(4) Reassembled Step-families
Step-families which are created following the divorce of the natural parents are increasing in numbers and in these *reassembled step-families* one of the natural parents (most often the natural mother) has the custody of the children who reside with him or her and the step-parent, while the non-custodial natural parent usually has access to the children, which may be exercised regularly or not at all.

(5) Combination Families
The final category of step-family, to which reference has already been made, is that of the *combination family* described by Schulman (1972), where each partner has natural children from a previous marriage who, whether they all live together or not, are in some degree of relationship with each other, as step-siblings to each other and step-children of their natural parent's new partner. In step-families where children are born following the remarriage, such children, while being the natural children of the new partnership, are half-siblings to those of the previous marriage or marriages.

III. THEORETICAL MODELS FOR FAMILY INTERACTION IN RE-CONSTITUTED FAMILIES

From a broad definition of the loose categories into which reconstituted families can be grouped, it will already be apparent to those engaged in family therapy that such families are by definition even more complex and confusing than natural nuclear families. Therefore, before commenting on some of the typical issues which underlie many of the difficulties in which reconstituted families find themselves, it is useful to distinguish a theoretical model which may be both clarifying and familiar. The one adopted here is the systems approach, which despite its many drawbacks, provides a model for differentiating family relationships and boundaries, and thereby creates a framework within which the therapist may focus and guide his intervention. What a systems approach fails to do is to provide an ideology of family treatment on which a therapist may base a therapeutic paradigm. For instance, one example of the ethical issues which occur again and again in family therapy with reconstituted families is that of a family situation where there is conflict between the needs of the parents and those of the children. The question of whose needs should prevail is always a difficult one, but where there are two (or more) sets of "parents" and children who have already been at risk, it is sometimes a situation where quick action must be taken, especially where family therapists have statutory responsibilities such as those in Social Service Departments and the Probation Service.

IV. THE SYSTEMS APPROACH

A. Here and Now*

Davies (1977) points out

> that all systems of living organisms are open systems and that characteristically an open system is defined as a system in an exchange of matter with its environment importing and exporting energy, building up and breaking down its component parts. Although stable, open systems are always changing, always evolving; although identifiable, classifiable, they present differences over time and in changing circumstances.

Walrond-Skinner (1976) writes of families as open systems.

> A system is not a random collection of components but an inter-dependent organisation in which the behaviour and expression of each component influences and is influenced by all the others . . .

She postulates that each family has

> a vital boundary which provides an interface both with its external environment and its own sub-systems and which circumscribes its identity in space and time.

---

*See Cooklin, Chapter 2

Perkins and Kahan (1979) develop this further. In discussing their comparative study of natural families *vs* step-families with step-fathers, and basing their thinking on the systems model of Kantor and Lehr (1976), they describe three systems that interact with each other and also the outside world.

> These three are the family unit system, the interpersonal subsystem and the personal subsystem. When two or more of these subsystems meet, each with its own boundaries and each with its own set of interrelated parts, they are said to be at an interface. The three subsystems of the family meet at interface both with each other and with the outside world.

Perkins and Kahan postulate that it is important for family system functioning that there is a congruence of perception between the interface of the interacting family subsystems where they meet both with each other and with the outside world. Their view is that interpersonal and intrapersonal problems develop where there is a lack of congruence at the interface. They suggest that in families where a family member is placed, or places himself or herself

> in the position of being inside the family perimeter, but outside the interpersonal subsystem, then he or she will have a different experiential domain from the other family members.

Such an experience will lead to the family member feeling dislocated and cut off from other members of the family.

In any family therefore, there is the family unit system, the interpersonal subsystem of parents and children, which incorporate further subsystems of parents as marriage partners and children as siblings. There are then the subsystems of each of the family members in their own right: a personal or intrapersonal subsystem. Miller and Gwynne (1972) draw attention to the intrapersonal subsystem, commenting that each individual

> has an inner world of thoughts and feelings that are derived from his biological inheritance and from what he had learnt and mislearnt from his lifetime and experience; he lives in an environment to which he has to relate himself in order to survive; and it is the function of the ego—the conscious thinking mind—to regulate transactions across the boundary between inside and outside.

B.   Systems: Over Time

The usefulness of the systems model for family functioning is that as well as distinguishing the three interlocking systems within the family, it is also possible to differentiate between the "inner life" of the family and the outside life as part of the social world. What Perkins and Kahan's model does not emphasize is the process through time which, together with systemic influences outside the family, can and often does bring about changes.

(1)   Bohannen's Approach

Bohannen's (1971) work is helpful here, in that he hypothesizes the occurrence of what he calls six stations in the process of divorce, all of which may be happening concurrently or consecutively in couples as they move from the initial estrangement to an ultimate regaining of personal autonomy. These six processes he describes as the emotional, the legal, the economic, the co-parental, the community, and the psychic divorces. It could be argued that many couples, particularly those whose children are still young, may not fully complete these processes for many years. It may not even be advantageous to themselves or their children that they do so, even though this may delay them gaining a new personal autonomy. There has been little research in the area of family breakdown and the capacity for investment in multiple family relationships.

(2) Wallerstein and Kelly
Recent work by Wallerstein and Kelly (1980) carried out with well motivated and previously intact families at the time of their divorce, and followed up at 18 months and 5 years after, indicates that it takes at least that long for family systems to restabilize. They also found that the children in their study could make room for a visiting non-custodial father and a step-father and custodial mother; and that step-father only became the psychological parent, when the children voluntarily chose to replace their father in this way.

The model described by Perkins and Kahan seems to describe families who are only some way along this process, and does not take into account the economic and community aspects of the divorced couple. Bohannen on the other hand, does not consider the *family* perspective in his model, though it might usefully be considered in relation to whole families.

V. APPLICATIONS OF A SYSTEMS APPROACH

A. Introduction

The systems model as developed by Perkins and Kahan is based on their research into step-families where there are step-fathers following a divorce in which the non-custodial natural fathers continued to have warm relationships with their children and a civilized relationship existed between the former spouses. Nevertheless, it is a useful model to attempt to adapt to other step-families, and to explore in relation to all reconstituted families; although of course further research is necessary.

If Perkins and Kahan's hypothesis is correct and family members in the position of being inside the family perimeter but outside the interpersonal subsystem of the family find themselves in a dislocated situation, then it is at least possible that there may be similar phenomena following the addition of an adoptive or foster child into a natural nuclear family. They consider that in many of their step-families the step-parents

are caught in the intraspace, inside the family perimeter, but outside the interpersonal subsystem, that of the children. Step-children too, may be caught in the intraspace, without access to the marital subsystem.

B.   Clinical Example: The J Family

The J family provide an illustration of this family situation. Mr and Mrs J married following his divorce from his second wife. Mr J's three children from each of his two previous marriages had strong bonds of loyalty to each other as the result of going through two divorces, the elder ones "teaching" the younger ones what to expect, and how to manage as the second divorce proceeded. The third Mrs J found herself in the role of wife to Mr J and cook/housekeeper to the children, who it might be said, regarded her as the next in a line of not very adequate "women in the house". They derided her cooking and complained that she talked down to them, and was really only interested in their father. She in turn felt overcrowded, pushed out, and much resented the hereditary burden of "expectations" that she had stepped into, wanting to create within the family a new and more co-equal sharing model for housekeeping.

C.   Application to Adoptive Families

In would-be *adoptive* families where the couple are childless, there is a lack of congruence at the interface between themselves as a marital couple who would like to become parents and the outside world's perception of them as a childless couple. Similarly in couples with children of their own who would like to adopt others, there may be a lack of congruence, not only at the family unit interface with the outside world, but also either as between the married couple and their natural children or at an intrapersonal level of one of the family members.

D.   Application to Foster Families

In *foster families* the situation is even more complicated, mainly because of the temporary nature of foster care (even long-term), and the concomitant effect of uncertainty on relationships between the foster child and foster family. Child care practice tends first to emphasize the possibility of congruence at the interface of the intrapersonal system of the foster mother and the possible foster child. Secondly, the emphasis is on congruence at the interface of the interpersonal subsystem of potential foster mother and foster father. The third important consideration is the congruence at the interface of the marital interpersonal subsystem and the intrapersonal subsystem of the potential foster child. It is relatively unusual for the family unit system to present a congruent interface to the outside world with regard to the advent of a foster child, or even to present a congruent interface between the whole interpersonal subsystem and the family unit system as regards the including of the foster child within the interpersonal subsystem. Often such congruence is not altogether achieved, and there remain two distinct interpersonal subsystems: one which includes the foster parents as natural parents and their own natural children.

VI. THE SOCIAL CONTEXT OF
RE-CONSTITUTED FAMILIES AND
PROFESSIONAL INTERVENTION

A. Introduction

The discussion so far has focussed only within the boundary of the family unit system, the interface between this and the other subsystems within it, and the interface between all three family systems and the outside world. It will be apparent that in reconstituted families the congruence between them and the outside world is a particularly important factor, and that society impinges on them in ways which are unusual in natural nuclear families. It is therefore necessary to discuss the social context in which reconstituted families are placed.

B. The Needs and Rights of Children

Statutory family policies have remained very chary of intervening directly in the inner family life, and many of the social institutions within which family policy has developed were originally created to maintain and support this privatized sanctity.

For instance, the whole structure of housing and income maintenance policies demonstrate at least the intention to give priority to families with young children, despite the haphazard nature of their growth and co-operation with other social institutions. A study of the development of the education and social service policies reveals a gradual shift from protection of the family unit against the ravages of the industrial revolution when children were considered the possessions of their parents, to present day policies which recognize the needs and rights of the child as an individual.

Statutory intervention in inner family life initially developed for the protection of children at risk from negative societal influences but also from inner family breakdown. Of course the two are intimately connected, and there is a continuous debate as to which has the greater responsibility. Nevertheless, it has long been recognized within family policy that it is necessary for some children to be removed from their families in order to rescue them from what has been proven to be an inner family life which is deleterious to their development. The whole question of the statutory removal of children is a highly controversial one which has many implications for the family therapy approach (see Bentovim, chapter 28).

It is however, important to recognize that in the case of all reconstituted families, with the possible exception of revitalized step-families, the state takes some interest in the provision of proper care for the children. Statutory intervention in the inner life of reconstituted families is haphazard and at times inconsistent, as will become evident later, but the possibility of such intervention is present, and serves socially to differentiate those reconstituted families from natural nuclear families. Such social differentiation inevitably reinforces the inner family experience of being different or even counterfeit, in that they are aspiring to acquire an inner family unit of systems so that they can pass as if they were a natural nuclear family.

C.   Adoption and Fostering Situations.

In the case of the addition of children by *adoption* or *fostering* the statutory intervention takes the form of some kind of assessment of the family unit system in order to see whether or not it "comes up to scratch". From the perception of the inner family, it is not always clear on what criteria such judgments are based; and many resent such intrusion, although they may not dare say so, feeling that this may go against them. The representative of statutory intervention in *adoptive* and *foster* families is usually a social worker, and it is he or she who will be working at the interface of the family unit system with the outside world. While the individual social worker has a particularized role and is part of the social service system which has prescribed policies for adoption and fostering, he or she also has an intrapersonal system in their own right. All these factors inevitably influence the shared task, which is to achieve some degree of congruence at the societal/family unit interface with regard to the possible adoption or fostering. Inevitably the social worker is perceived as a person of considerable power; in the case of a possible adoption, that of someone who can give or withhold the child which they want. It could be argued that for this reason, as well as to protect the needs of the child who is to be adopted, the state has devised the system of a further social worker (acting as guardian *ad litem* for the child) who also assesses the family unit system and makes a report to the court, where the ultimate decision is made regarding an adoption order. It will therefore be seen that in *adoptive* families, at least during the period of assessment and the granting of the adoption order, the social workers involved become very much part of the family unit system.

For *foster* families there is a similar period of assessment in which the social worker will be attempting to establish not only what kind of individual foster child could best be assimilated into the potential foster family, but also their capacity to make short- or long-term commitments. Here again, although not always, there are often two social workers, one aligned with the family unit system and endeavouring to understand their perceptions, and another who is aligned not only with the intrapersonal system of the potential foster child, but also with the remaining interpersonal system of the child's natural nuclear family. Certainly this is often the intended policy; it is not difficult to see why such a complex, important and painful procedure too often falls down. Where there are two social workers, each initially aligned with two separate and distinct family unit systems (or partial systems), then it will be clear that the congruence which can be achieved at the interface between the two social workers is a crucial factor in the process. It is also easy to see that in a situation where a foster child is in the family, any difficulties between the various foster family unit subsystems are likely to produce echoes which will resonate along the systems with which each of the social workers is aligned. This is unfortunately not always recognized.

Even more unfortunately, either one may carry out the whole process of assessing, matching and supporting the new unit of foster-child-within-the-foster-family, or one of the usually hard pressed social workers will diminish or terminate their contact with the foster family once an apparently successful placement has been achieved.

D. The Social Context of Step-families

It has already been indicated that it is in the creation of the step-family unit system that the inconsistencies of statutory intervention are fully revealed. Unless a family is already known to some care-giving agency, there is no statutory involvement in legitimated or revitalized step-families. It is only where the children concerned may have already been under the statutory supervision of the local authority, or perhaps on probation, that the state evinces any interest in the reconstitution of such families. Of course, because such incomplete families may be at risk, it is possible that they may be receiving the support of a social worker from a voluntary agency caring for the unmarried mother and her child, or from the medical social worker at the hospital caring for the dying natural parent, but it is unlikely that such workers will have the statutory powers which could lead to state intervention around the time of the remarriage.

In the case of reassembled or combination step-families, state intervention is, if anything, even more haphazard although again the children in such families may already be under some kind of statutory case.

E. Divorce and Professional Intervention

It is at the time of the divorce between the two natural parents, rather than on the occasion of the remarriage of either or both partners, that the possibility of statutory intervention is considered, albeit fleetingly. At the time of granting the decree nisi, the divorce court judge is required to consider the arrangements proposed for the minor children of the divorcing couple, and before the subsequent divorce absolute, he must issue a "certificate of satisfaction" stating either that these arrangements are satisfactory, that they are the best that can be made under the circumstances, or that it is not practical to make any arrangements for the children.

The judge may decide to interview the children himself within the privacy of his chambers, or he may ask the Court Welfare Officer to provide a report. Either of the divorcing partners may also request for such a report by the Court Welfare Officer, who would then attempt to make an assessment which would include, where practicable, the wishes of the children as well as those of the parents. Unless requested by the judge, involvement in conciliation procedures over custody and access of the children is a voluntary matter, and it is only when these arrangements are specifically set out by the court during the divorce proceedings that statutory intervention becomes a possibility.

In fact, Eekelaar et al.'s (1977) study of custody after divorce showed that of 652 cases in England and Wales, in only 11.3% was a Divorce Court Welfare

Officer's report available. A breakdown of figures in cases where custody was uncontested compared with those where it was contested, showed that a report was available in 8.2% of the former and 53% of the latter. Of course divorced couples may subsequently return to the divorce court to request that such custody or access orders may be made, and the number of such orders is quite small in relation to the large numbers of divorces and remarriages which involve children. The statutory involvement of the Court Welfare Officer (usually a probation officer) is limited to initial or subsequent requests for recommendations regarding custody, and although they may, and quite often do provide support during the period following the divorce or custody order, they are not statutorily required to do so. Murch's (1980) study of families in divorce proceedings found that a number of Court Welfare Officers went beyond providing a report for the court and provided casework help, and that this was appreciated by a sizeable minority of the parents who experienced it.

It will therefore be apparent that whereas in all *adoptive* and *foster* families the state impinges on the inner life of the family unit system, at least for a short crisis-oriented period when the reconstituted family group is initially attempting to become a family unit system, it is relatively unlikely that it will do so at the same stage of development for step-families. It is of course possible that newly reconstituted step-families are referred to statutory agencies but, not infrequently, the focus then has a partialized child-care orientation rather than a recognition of the particular needs of the step-family.

VII. COMMON AREAS OF DIFFICULTY

In the discussion of theoretical models, it has already been pointed out that individual family members may find themselves cut off from the rest of the family and, while remaining within the family unit system, are out of touch with some of the interpersonal subsystems within the family. The possibility of there being two distinctive interpersonal subsystems within the family has also been discussed. But such hypothetical models of dislocated family systems and the resultant possible manifestation of problems can only serve as informative guidelines within which the family therapist must focus with greater precision when it comes to therapeutic intervention. Family therapists also need to consider the phenomenological form in which these problems are likely to become manifest, and bearing this in mind, to select nodal points for actual interventions. There are two main areas in which many reconstituted families find themselves in difficulties. The first is the area of family loss, aspects of which are important to all families, but for reconstituted families there has been an actual loss within the lifetime, if not the cognitive living memory, of all the remaining family members. The second area is the capacity of family members for developing new attachments and here again this is of obvious importance for all families. Where reconstituted families differ is that within the lifetime of at least one of the individual family members a major loss has occurred, one which may well have been preceded by a series of traumatic experiences and one of such severity that the individual's capacity for developing mutual and trusting relationships has been impaired.

VIII.   LOSS

A.   General Aspects

Murray Parkes (1975) has written widely about the importance of mourning in adult life, basing the stages of mourning on his research findings in studies of widows and widowers. His work has been used as the basis from which much understanding has been developed in other areas of loss than that of the death of a loved person. He describes the process of mourning as a series of stages which individuals must go through, though in their own individual ways and time, so that personal autonomy can be ultimately regained and the capacity for making new attachments released. The mourning process is initially one of denial, or avoidance of the recognition that the loss has occurred. The work of the Robertsons most clearly demonstrated in their films of children who are separated from their families and hospitalized, this tendency to deny what is happening. As the realization of the loss begins to become more apparent, the bereaved person feels alarmed, and these feelings may be accompanied by the physiological accompaniments of fear. At this time there is often restless searching, in an attempt to seek out the lost person in some form.

Bereaved people at times apparently reproduce symptoms which are either similar to those of the deceased, or which replicate the manner of their death. The children with whom the Robertsons worked became protesting, clinging and whiney. At these times there are also often outbursts of both anger and guilt, frightening both because of their unpredictability and the intensity of the feelings aroused. These angry feelings may also be directed at the very people who are trying to help; adults for instance, may find themselves outraged at the hospital staff whereas before the death they had found them both caring and competent. Children may regress to earlier tantrums or hostile and withdrawn, sullen anger. The guilty feelings of reproach may lead to internal feelings of loss of self and phantasies of mutilation.

As the grieving begins to become apparent to the bereaved person, there is an intense sadness, which at times gives way to despair, a sadness which seems to occur suddenly and inexplicably at sudden reminders of the loss. Gradually, in a mourning process which is following its normal course, the periods between the bouts of sadness lengthen, and the bereaved person begins to find themselves forgetting for short periods in which they begin to regain a capacity for enjoyment, which they had felt was lost for ever. As they begin to recover and turn towards building a new life without the lost person, they experience feelings as if they were recovering from a serious illness which has been both physical and mental. On recovery, many people find they have acquired new characteristics and strengths they did not hitherto possess (see Lieberman and Black, Chapter 12).

B. Loss and Divorce

Many people in fact never fully recover from serious loss, but some significantly fail to grieve sufficiently, and this has serious repercussions for their future family life. In Pincus' (1976) account of her work with married couples, she points out that repressed mourning unresolved in childhood may become resurrected within the marital relationship, where the old failures to grieve lead to new problems. She writes

> Divorce, like death, means loss and bereavement. Marriages that ended in divorce may be regarded as failures, yet unless some new insight has been gained through the pain of this failure, here too the previously unhappy pattern of interaction may be almost compulsively re-enacted in a new marriage.

C. Loss in Divorce and its Effect on the Children

The recent work of Wallerstein and Kelly (1980) distinguishes various processes through which individual family members pass during divorce and its aftermath. Many of these are connected with the various losses experienced as part of this process, as for instance the reduced economic state which often leads to women going out to work; and the need to take on a new role as head of single parent household, plus major responsibilities for child care, which are onerous and exhausting. In almost every family there was one, if not two angry parents whose anger often spilled over into mutual vilification, either directly or via the children. For some of these parents which they describe as "embittered chaotic", the anger was apparently unabated 18 months or even 5 years later, and Wallerstein and Kelly hypothesized that this covered a severe depression. Emotional estrangements and sexual frustrations had characterized many of these marriages, and about half the men and a third of the women launched into new social rounds and sexual activity, some of it quite frenetic. Many of the parents were also quite evidently depressed, at least for a time. Depressed non-custodial fathers for instance, either avoided visiting altogether, or were driven by their guilt to visit with a flurry of intensity which they could not sustain. In general, there was a diminished capacity for parenting, particularly for the younger children, most of whom had been given no satisfactory explanation and had no adequate understanding as to why their parents were divorcing.

There were common experiences among all the children, and others which were age-specific. In general, the experience of the children seemed to be that divorce is a time of anger, fear, worry, sadness, loneliness, yearning for the departed parent, of conflicting loyalties and of feeling rejected. Most of the children did not feel guilty about their parents divorce, although almost all of them had phantasies of bringing them together again. As might be expected, children in the 3-5 age group also showed bewilderment, regressive behaviour, macabre phantasies, considerable emotional needs and attempts at mastery through play. Children of 6-8 showed fear sometimes amounting to disorganization and inhibition of aggression towards the departed parent, which was expressed openly towards the custodial parent. But the 9-12-year-old children, while apparently coping with poise, courage and clarity revealed underneath an anger which was divorce-specific and remained unaltered at the 18 month follow-up. Particularly vulnerable in this age group were the pre-adolescent boys, who had often been particularly close to their fathers and were also being neglected by their custodial mothers who characteristically gave their attention to the younger children and the girls. The 13–18-year-old age group showed characteristic anger, some of which was age-related, loyalty conflicts and mourning and particular worries about sex and marriage. Some of them were surprisingly realistic about money matters, and some dealt with their fluctuating perceptions by a strategic withdrawal from the family.

D. Loss in Adoption and Fostering

Even in *adoptive* families where the adopted child has been introduced into the family as a baby, there has been the loss of the natural mother, the effect of which remains as yet unknown. For children who are adopted later, or placed in long-term *foster* families, there may be not one, but a series of losses ranging from the original loss of one natural parent to the loss of a family unit, perhaps the privation of a family unit which never was complete, all of which may also include a cumulation of losses from children's homes or foster homes. For children who have experienced such serious and multiple losses, it may be impossible either to face or to work through the mourning processes, and they may remain damaged as personalities who cannot assimilate what for them have been disastrous experiences.

E. Loss in Adoption: Case Example

Jane, for example, was adopted at 4½ following abandonment by her natural mother and a series of foster and small group home placements. She was referred at 14 for violent fights with her adoptive mother. The social worker saw these as a response to current family tensions relating to the transitional pressures within a family which was attempting to contain a developing adolescent. The parents however, and especially the adoptive mother, continually, and in a concealed way, linked the difficulties back to Jane's origins and history prior to living with them. They had never told her very much about her history and were reluctant to do so, referring her back to the social worker for individual discussions. Following the referral, Jane's behaviour became so disturbed that she was briefly admitted to an adolescent unit. The family then firmly reorganized itself around the idea of Jane as a "damaged child" and refused to do any more work on how the adolescence as a whole might be handled, nor would they become involved in helping Jane to work on the loss of her previous "families". The parents' way of coping seemed to be to separate the two sets of familial experiences, thus cutting off to an extent Jane found intolerable.

Others, while remaining partially damaged by their experiences, can come to terms sufficiently with their loss experiences to risk once again attempting to form new attachments, even though they may remain transient and superficial.

F.   Loss in Step-families

In *step*-families, the loss situation is often extremely complicated. Where the natural parent has died, most people would expect the remaining partner to mourn the loss, as they probably would also the children who are older. But it is surprising how many people do not consider that young children also experience the death of a parent at a very basic level, and too often they deny the child the right to grieve by insisting that they are too young to remember or understand. In step-families which have been created following desertion and divorce, or even a planned and relatively civilized divorce, there is still mourning to be done. Each of the individual family members has to grieve at an intrapersonal level for what they have lost, and at the interpersonal subsystem, there may be different experiences of loss for the sibling subsystem which they do not feel able to share with the now remarried custodial parent. The custodial parent may find that, surprisingly, he or she is mourning for the lost family unit, and yet find this difficult to face or to share because of their guilt about their own part in breaking it up. They may even find themselves grieving for the loss of the marital subsystem or deeply concerned about their previous spouse; yet how can they share this with the new step-parent? Many of the early problems of step-families lie in their failure to acknowledge and share with each other their grieving for the loss of the former interpersonal subsystem and the resultant changes in the family unit; and if a sensitive and perceptive family therapist can find ways of opening the system out so that these feelings can be shared, the natural healing processes may be completed by the family themselves.

G.   Loss in Step-families: Case Example

For instance Mr G had married the widow of his great friend (who had committed suicide) thereby becoming step-father to two children with whom he already had good relationships. His own three children remained in the custody of his first wife. The second Mrs G had not been able to mourn the death of her first husband fully, nor to help her children to do so; moreover, she felt immense guilt in relation to the breakup of Mr G's first family. He, in turn had not expected to find himself so cut off from his own children, and had expected his new wife to become as close to them as he was to her children. This family, as the result of various individual, dyadic and family interviews, were able to face and to share at least to some extent, the grief and guilt they all felt, which thus openly acknowledged could begin to run its natural course.

IX.   CAPACITY FOR ATTACHMENT

A.   General Factors

By definition, reconstituted families are those where family members are in the process not only of developing attachments to the new member, but also of redefining the family unit system and the interpersonal subsystem within the family. Despite the immense amount of research in the area of child development, into the effects of separation from natural mothers, and of being brought up in institutional care, we know surprisingly little about the development of bonding processes *within the family*. Much of what is known about early *child* development remains the subject of controversy. However, a recent review and discussion of the state of research in this area by Pilling and Kellmer Pringle (1978) does yield some definitive facts. They consider that an infant's relationship to his or her care-giver begins very early and that the child's congenital characteristics do affect the interaction through their influence on the care-giver. They conclude that

> the infant becomes attached from about the third quarter of the first year to people who interact sufficiently with him and deeply attached to those who are sensitive to his signals and who provide the most social stimulations for him.

While other attachments follow soon after the first, there is no agreement as to whether the child has one major attachment (usually to the mother) and other subsidiary attachments, or is equally attached to two or three people. There have however, been insufficient longitudinal studies to be able to state with certainty that early attachments are linked with later behaviour.

B. Children who move from Institutions to Families

With regard to children who have been in institutional care, it is known to be beneficial to their adjustment if they can form a stable tie with an adult; but that frequent changes of care-giver may lead to difficulties in forming relationships with future care-givers. The quality of substitute care provided is also important. Adcock and White (1977) in writing of planning and decision-making for children in care, base their recommendations on Rutter's work, and stress the importance of the child's experiences before separation; the quality of experience in foster care; the transition from care to back home and the understanding given to him on return. In addition, it is important that the children are not further exposed to stresses and unhappy situations. Tizard's recent work (1977) on the *adoption* of older children throws some light on fostering. Although the number of *foster* children in her research were small, she is able to differentiate three distinct kinds of relationships between the foster child and foster parents, though nothing about their relationship with the natural children of the family. These relationships are described as those who "foster as a charitable act"; "fostering in the hope of adoption"; and "experienced foster parents". This last group sometimes make a deep mutual attachment to a particular child and effectively become a "pseudo adoptive family". She writes

> There was in fact an element of selflessness in the foster parents which one could not help admiring — they lavished the same devotion on quite disturbed children as did the adoptive parents, although these children were not and would probably never be 'their own'. In all these instances the children had no contact, or only minimal contact with their natural parents. Provided that the foster family could

be confident that the natural mother would not reclaim her child they were content not to push the issues of adoption.

Tizard's study of children was concerned with those children who had spent the early years of their lives in residential nurseries, compared to those who were adopted early (between 2 and 4) or late (between 4½ and 7) and those who were restored to their natural parent early or late. Her research shows that though there are often difficulties, and that for some parents there is lasting regret at missing the early years, determined, consistent, committed and sensitive parenting can lead to the development of mutual attachment in a significant proportion of *adoptive* families. Where the adoptive parents' motivation was sufficiently strong they were able to tolerate the limitations and degree of regression which older children seem to need in order to begin to make a mutual attachment. Tizard concluded that

> the subsequent development of the early institutionalised child depends very much on the environment to which he is moved. This seemed to be as true of attachment behaviour as of emotional problems . . . our evidence suggestions that what is more important is that he should be reared by parents, both of whom really want him, and are prepared to devote time, energy and thought to him.

C.   Attachment, Divorce and Step-families

Wallerstein and Kelly's five-year follow-up after divorce showed the important influence of the following components, various combinations of which seemed to have affected the outcome: the way the parents had been able to resolve their own conflicts and anger; the custodial parent's handling of the child and the quality of relationships within the home; the quality of the child's relationship with the "visiting" parent and the way this had kept pace with the child's developing needs. The age and sex of the child seemed less important in the outcome, but the child's strengths and deficits, his or her present resources such as intelligence, capacity for phantasy, social maturity, ability to turn to peers and adults, and the absence of continuing anger and depression all had some relevance; as did the pre-divorce history within the family, and the availability of a supportive human network. By this time, about half the children's parents had remarried, but the study seemed to reveal very little about the relationships within the reconstituted family.

Future research will need to find the answers to many questions about the development of attachment behaviour in *step-families*. If it is possible to assume that the individual capacity for attachment has sufficient potential for each of the reconstituted family members, then two key questions need to be answered. First what is the effect on the parenting capacities of the parental couple, where one of them chose to become the marital partner of the custodial parent, rather than to "foster the children with a view to adoption"? And secondly, how possible is it for children to develop and maintain sufficiently deep attachments for what and to whom? Wallerstein and Kelly's research seems to indicate that children can maintain sufficiently deep attachments to more than one set of parents. Indeed their findings disagree with those of Freud *et al.* (1973), and they recommend that wherever possible divorcing parents should be helped to shape post-divorce arrangements which allow for and encourage continuity in parent–child relationships.

X. SOME NODAL POINTS FOR INTERVENTION IN RE-CONSTITUTED FAMILIES

A. Introduction

In the previous discussion of models for family interaction and in considering the areas of possible difficulty, two key themes have been developed. First, the capacity of individual newly reconstituted families to recover from previous loss experiences sufficiently to develop new attachments is crucial. Secondly, it is essential that the newly developing family unit system must, almost from its inception, develop the ability to maintain open interactions with other family systems closely connected with it, as well as sufficient trust in interactions with social systems available for support. For those in the caring professions who come into contact with reconstituted families at this early and vulnerable stage, a family therapy approach may enable and reinforce the development of congruence at the boundaries of the family unit system and those of the outside world with whom open interactions are critical.

There are several nodal areas where therapists may gain entry to the inner life of the family unit system and which, in discussions with the family, may enable supportive help to be given. These nodal points may be revealed according to the pattern of interaction within any individual family and are not therefore discussed in any order of priority.

B. Names

First names and surnames are important in all families, but in reconstituted families, the names of individual members and also those which denote their relationships to each other are one of the ways in which they are differentiated from natural nuclear families. In *foster* families and *step*-families, the first names of the children have not been given them by both the parental couple, and frequently these names denote elements of the natural family history from which the children come. Even in *adoptive* families where the adopted children are very young, they have usually already been given a name, which has either been retained as a first or second name, or has been changed altogether. Surnames are another aspect of dissonance within the family relationships. It is only in *adoptive* families and *step-families with step-mothers* that the family will all have the same surname; and this fact is often of immediate and lasting embarrassment or even shame. Mrs G for instance, could not bring herself to wear a wedding ring, and continued to be known by her previous married surname, which was of course that borne by her own children. Many families in fact try to cover this difference by using the same surname, even though strictly speaking, this is not legal. Finally, there is the vexed question of the names which are given to the role relationship within the family. Most children can fairly quickly come to terms with the concept of foster, step or half brother or sister; it is the symbolic meanings which lie behind these terms which are more difficult. But the question of nomenclature for the foster, adoptive or step-parents often remains a long-lasting and thorny issue which is also exacerbated by the actual or psychological presence of the natural parents.

C. Access

(1) In Adoption
The *adoption* of a child is legally considered to have extinguished all previous natural relationships, and apart from Scotland, where adults who have been adopted as children have long had the right to find out about their natural parents, the question of access to natural parents has not arisen. However, recent legislation (1975 Children Act) has extended this opportunity to such adults over the age of 18 and subject to safeguarding counselling procedures. The numbers who pursue their inquiries about their natural parentage to the point of meeting their parents is small, but the anxieties around such a possibility now lend a shadow to the family life of adoptive families.

(2) Fostering and Access
As will be clear from the previous discussion, and particularly from the comment about inclusive or exclusive fostering, the question of access by natural parents is one of particular difficulty for *foster* parents. This is a matter over which they have little control, as what powers there are to constrain the access of natural parents to their children in foster care are in the hands of the social workers who, not surprisingly, are frequently reluctant to stop such visiting.

(3) Reassembled, Combination Families and Access
It is in reassembled and combination *step*-families that problems of access seem to cause the most difficulty, as even when the amount of access is laid down by the court, the custodial parent has to return to the court in order that access conditions, which are being abused or refused, are in fact carried out. But in the great majority of cases, conditions of access have not been laid down legally, but left to negotiations between the custodial and non-custodial parents and may continue to be an area of wrangles and disputes for the whole of the children's childhood as the following example shows:

(4) Case example: Susan and her Family
Susan lived with her mother and step-father following a very turbulent divorce between her parents when she was aged 3. The violence of feeling between her parents was so great that all communication was by letter, not even by the phone. Her father was only able to have access to her via "doorstep deliveries" with no

conversation. Negotiations about holidays took place between step-father and father. On one occasion when Susan was not delivered back, the mother and step-father sent the police round to collect her, preferring to do this than face the alternative violent scene they feared.

(5)   Access and the Extended Family

The question of visits by or to natural parents is not the only area of access which may cause difficulty for reconstituted families. By the very fact that there has been some previous breakdown in the natural family, it is often the case that other relatives, particularly grandparents or aunts and uncles, have been particularly involved and attached to the children in such families, in the period between the breakdown and the reconstitution of the family. These key relatives are often very important members of the extended family system, and their attitudes to the developing reconstituted family are often crucial in the early stages of attachment.

Access is an issue in which passions run high, and as has already been indicated, are apt to spill over in ways which are disadvantageous and distressing to all concerned. Murch (1980) in a discussion on cathartic listening comments

> Insofar as both solicitors and welfare officers are part of the legal machinery of divorce, it can be argued that through their agency the response of the law to parents in conflicts is emotionally appropriate. Legal machinery has within it powerful symbolic authority — particularly in the form of an independent judge and court, imposing their presence on the psychological background. It often seems to help people contain and yet not deny, powerful and aggressive feelings.

D.   Territory

(1)   Where is Home?

The question of which place is "home" is an initial problem for all reconstituted families, and there is some evidence of a hierarchy of attachment to particular places of residence. While it is obviously important that the reconstituted family have sufficient time to develop individual and familial attachments to the place in which they reside, it is also necessary for the member who is being incorporated to have sufficient personal physical space which they can consider their own. It is not only the question of the home and surrounding locality which is problematic, but also material belongings such as clothes and toys for the children, and furniture and furnishings for the adults.

E.   Possession

Arguments about material goods, hi-fi sets, casseroles, and things chosen and brought together may furnish much of the material of inter-family interviews. For children, even the temporary loss of a toy which symbolizes particularly strong attachment to their lost or left behind natural parent, can be deeply upsetting. Mother's determination that her child should not be beholden to a "previous" father for anything led to her refusal to say who had given her daughter the bicycle that "Santa Claus" had left for her. The child, no longer believing in such things, knew this to be a ploy to refuse her father even a limited place in their lives, and attacked her mother for her inability to buy her what she wanted and for not telling the truth, and this led to the daughter realizing that her mother had also been untruthful about a number of other issues. Helping mother to talk with her daughter about her own feelings regarding father's role in the new family enabled boundaries to be more clearly defined and he was less feared as a seducer of the child's loyalties.

For foster parents, multiple gifts of expensive toys or unnecessary additional clothing, the anger or competitiveness of the natural parent, may be apparent and difficult to manage. In the case of step-families, the constant reminder of a home previously occupied and furnished by the custodial parent with their previous spouse may lead to repeated pangs of jealousy.

F.   Example: the F family

An example from the F family shows how issues of unresolved attachment can reach strange proportions in terms of household arrangements. Mr F insisted on his younger second wife, Samantha, keeping the house exactly as his first wife had furnished it, even to including a cabinet case of "show" objects they had collected together on their holidays. He also insisted on Samantha being courteous and hospitable to his first wife who frequently dropped in for drinks and stayed for supper. One day Samantha threatened to leave unless all the things were removed; packed them up in several packing cases, and put them outside the front door, where they remained for three days. Now all are back in their "rightful" place.

G.   Financial position

While the question of financial circumstances is important in the case of *adoptive* families, there is not the opportunity for the development of financial tangles developing between the reconstituted family and the natural or extended family as there is in *foster* and *step*-families.

The matter of expensive gifts which may be considered unsuitable within the family life-style of the reconstituted family has already been mentioned, but there is also the question of payment for the care of the children and/or the upkeep of the home.

(1)   Foster Families

In *foster* families, there is the payment of a boarding out allowance, and for older children a pocket money allowance and sums of money for clothing. The natural parents of children in care are also expected to contribute to their keep, and this is assessed and payments made to the local authorities. These facts in themselves constitute grounds for the development of tensions between the reconstituted family unit system and those outside, but it may also be the case that the foster children may in fact have more money spent on them or available to them than the natural children of the foster family.

(2) Step-families
In *step*-families, the whole area of maintenance payments is one fraught with difficulty, as very few men can afford to maintain two families at the level to which the family members are accustomed to live. This usually means arguments or tensions over the amount of the maintenance payments for the mother and children (whether or not she has remarried), and often a failure to make regular contributions, even when these have been laid down by court order.

XI. THE USE OF A FAMILY THERAPY APPROACH

A.   Introduction: Gaining Therapeutic Access

How can those adopting the family approach use these nodal points in such a way as to gain therapeutic access to the family system? Here the agency setting within which the therapist is working is important, as much of the information concerned with these nodal points is an integral part of initial assessment procedures. In some reconstituted families, particularly those with a long history of involvement with care-giving agencies, there will be such information contained in the records, but this remains to be made available within the therapeutic relationship between the therapist and the family. One way of gaining access to these nodal points is for the therapist to construct a *geneogram* together with the family. In reconstituted families this is usually particularly complicated, involving as it does the interconnections of at least two family units with their own historical antecedents. But even more important, the construction of such a geneogram is a particularly delicate and sensitive activity, as it involves opening up areas of considerable pain, many of which have been repressed with considerable strength and for good reason. There are also likely to be gaps of knowledge and experience which cannot now be filled, and these too are the cause of grief and anger. Nevertheless, if the family members are interested and willing, the use of geneograms, built up sensitively and over a period of time, do allow a focus for the therapy.

It is only possible to give a brief example of the use of a family therapy approach with two kinds of reconstituted family.

B.   Family Therapy and the Adoptive Family

(1) Clinical Example: the D Family
This family, the D family, were referred to another therapist and myself for a private consultation by the adoption section of a local authority social services department. It has been written up more fully elsewhere (see Robinson, 1976 for complete details) but is useful to quote here, as we worked closely with the

adoption social workers who, of course, had the power to make the recommendation to adopt.

The Ds had been approved as potential adopters but had a long wait, during which Mrs D became more and more preoccupied inwardly with the coming baby, and Mr D felt more and more pushed out of what had been a close marital relationship. He had an affair, more by way of an SOS than because he was particularly involved with the lady, and on discovering this his wife returned to her family for a few days to think things out. Unfortunately, during this time the baby for whom they had waited so long became available to be placed, and the rift in the marital relationship was apparent to the adoption worker, so that they lost the opportunity to adopt this baby.

(2) Initial Work with the D Family
The therapists saw the couple together and agreed with them that the focus of the therapy should be a marital one, though the question of the possibility of adoption could be reconsidered later. Initially the therapists worked individually with the couple, the wife's therapist working with her disappointment at her infertility and the loss of the available baby. The husband's therapist worked with his ambivalence about wanting to have a child at all, and in particular with his resentment at having to be assessed as fit for parenthood.

(3) Later Work with the D Family
After three or four separate interviews, the therapists worked with the couple as a foursome, exploring and reinforcing the strengths within the marriage and reconsidering the possibility of parenthood, for a further five sessions. The therapists considered that their own criteria for successful parenthood should be made explicit to the D's, and when they felt confident enough to be honest with them about this, this provided a further focus for therapeutic work. Finally, at the request of the Ds, they were reassessed for adoption, accepted by the local authority, and eventually a baby was made available to them. As they both liked it, they decided to retain the name given to her by her natural mother. The therapists remained in touch with the Ds after the adoption, although less intensively and more informally than in the previous therapeutic work. About a year after the apparently successful establishment of an adoptive family, Mrs D had what appeared to be a very self-destructive and short lived affair which seemed to be related to her resentment at the amount of commitment which mothering entails, but also her resentment at her husband's attachment to the baby, a girl, which was certainly excessive. After a further period of work, particularly with Mr D, the couple resumed their attempts to become a family, and at this stage moved away.

(4) Comment: the D Family
It will be seen that in the D family, the therapists first of all worked at the interface of the intrapersonal system of the individual marital partners, later and with their agreement, shifting the focus, working with them together towards the achievement of congruence at this interface. It was only in the final stages of the

first period of treatment that the therapists worked with the focus on their potential development as a parental subsystem. It may be that this stage of the work was not particularly successful, although the second period of therapy seemed to indicate that sufficient strength had developed within the family unit system for the interpersonal system to survive the destructive vicissitudes which both partners appeared to have brought from their families of origins and which appeared to have been reinforced by their infertility.

C. A Family Therapy Approach to Step-families

(1) Clinical Example: the B Family
Work with the step-family B was first commenced in the child guidance clinic to which the son, S, was referred at the age of six, only a few weeks after his father and step-mother had married following the death by suicide of his natural mother. It was S who discovered her body, and as he appeared to demonstrate no feeling about this event, but was having destructive temper tantrums, the parents were worried. The family were seen by two therapists, in fact it was one of the early families which they saw together, and one of them worked with S, the other working individually or together with the father and step-mother. Both the therapists had occasional interviews with the whole family.

(2) Initial Work with the B Family
At the time, the clinic accepted the family's definition of S as the identified patient, and the work with the parents was consistently child-focussed. The case was closed after about two years of weekly treatment, during which S was apparently able to work through the death of his mother. The father and step-mother were able to work through their guilt and at some later stage, perhaps in adolescence, S should be told of his mother's suicide following their affair. After a chance meeting with step-mother in the street, the author was invited to have social drinks with the B family and met S, now a young man of 18, and their own child, T. All seemed to be going well, although the parents revealed that the mother's suicide had still not been discussed with S though they felt he might know. S remembered little of his therapy except how angry he had been; he was now planning to go to University and working hard.

(3) Later Events and Work with the B Family
Some 18 months later, step-mother managed to trace me, and begged me to see her again as the marriage was in difficulties. After an initial meeting in which we agreed to work on her marital difficulties and whether or not she wished to continue the marriage, we have continued to meet weekly. Father refused all further offers of help, though clearly he had never come to terms with his own feelings about the death of his first wife, though through step-mother's support and insistence, he did discuss this with S. Step-mother left father and set up home with T, eventually joined by maternal grandmother, a foreigner who lived abroad and had recently divorced her second husband.

Again at step-mother's insistence, father maintained paternal contact with T, and S had his own room and a base in each of the two homes. There have been no legal proceedings to date; father maintains T (Mrs B is a successful career woman in her own right) and access to T, achieved by mutual negotiation, is now fairly regular. Mrs B prided herself on the civility and maturity with which she felt the separation had been conducted, and was dismayed and disconcerted to find herself demonstrating intense aspects of a grief reaction some 6 months after she had left father. She was momentarily jealous of discovering he was having an affair with a much younger woman, despite embarking herself on a sequential series of affairs (always making sure another man was "in the wings" before she terminated the previous one), in which for the first time, she discovered her own potential as a sexual woman.

S went to college, but on each visit home in the vacation, he and step-mother have a series of bitter rows followed by reconciliations in which they appear able to face the strength of their feelings for each other, both positive and negative, as well as being able to share their feelings about mother's suicide. Step-mother has been able to support T in her own grief over the break-up of her parents' marriage, but in doing so, has found herself trapped in single parent motherhood in which she feels deeply inadequate and guilty. This, together with her recent concern about her ability to have a lasting and mutually-fulfilling relationship with a man, is our current area of work.

(4) Comment on the B Family

When first seen, the therapists adopted a child-centred approach to the therapy, although this was within the context of the family unit. With hindsight it was clearly a mistake not to find ways in which the father and step-mother could have informed S about the suicide of his mother, as the guilt and grief around this area has festered throughout the family life of this reconstituted family. While current therapeutic work is being conducted mainly at the intrapersonal system level with Mrs B, the experience of the earlier, more family-oriented therapy has enabled the therapist to adopt an approach which recognizes the importance of paying attention to the intrapersonal and interpersonal systems within the whole family unit system. Mrs B herself recognizes this now, and considers that this was the reason why she sought me out when she realized she needed further help, as she felt that I had helped her to take on the step-parent role, and would understand how things were for her now.

It is too soon to make any judgment about what the future holds for this reconstituted family, which came together in destructive circumstances, now revealed to have their roots in the family history of both Mr and Mrs B, but at least it seems possible that S will be able to seek further help at University, and that Mrs B is struggling to achieve some kind of family security for herself and T.

REFERENCES

Adcock, M. and Robinson, M. (1976). Brief Marital Counselling and Adoption, *Child Adoption*, **83**, no. 1.

Adcock, M. and White, R. (1977). Assumption of Parental Rights and Duties. A.B.A.F.A. London.

Bohannen, P. (1971). "Divorce and After", Doubleday Anchor, London.

Davies, M. (1977). "Support Systems in Social Work", Routledge & Kegan Paul, London.

Eekelaar, J. and Clive, E. with Clarke, K. and Raikes, S. (1977). "Custody After Divorce", Centre for Socio-Legal Studies, Wolfson College, Oxford.

Goldstein, J., Freud, A. and Solnit, A. (1973). "Beyond the Best Interests of the Child", Free Press, Glencoe.

Holman, R. (1975). The Place of Fostering in Social Work. *British Journal of Social Work*, **5**, 8-10.

Kantor, D. and Lehr, W. (1975). "Inside the Family", Jossey Bass, San Francisco.

Miller, E. and Gwynne, G. (1972). "A Life Apart", Tavistock, London.

Murch, M. (1980). "Justice and Welfare in Divorce", Sweet and Maxwell, London.

Murray Parkes, C. (1975). "Bereavement: Studies of Grief in Adult Life", Penguin, Harmondsworth, Middlesex.

Perkins, T. and Kahan, J. (1979). An Empirical Comparison of Natural-Father and Step-Father Systems. *Family Process*, **18**, 176-181.

Pilling, D. and Kellmer Pringle, M. (1978). "Controversial Issues in Child Development" Paul Elek, London.

Pincus, L. (1976). "Death and the Family", Faber, London.

Robinson, M. (1980). Step-Families: A Reconstituted Family System. *Journal of Family Therapy*, **2**, 45-70.

Robinson, M. (unpublished). "What's in a Name".

Robinson, M. and Adcock, M. (1976). Brief Marital Counselling and Adoption. *Child Adoption*, **83**, 49-53.

Schulman, G. (1972). Myths that intrude on the adaptation of the step-family. *Social Casework*, **53**, 135-137.

Tizard, B. (1977). "Adoption: A Second Chance", Open Books, London.

Wallerstein, J. and Kelly, J. (1980). "Surviving the Breakup: How Children and Parents Cope with Divorce", Grant McIntyre, New York.

Walrond-Skinner, S. (1976). "Family Therapy: The Treatment of Natural Systems", Routledge & Kegan Paul, London.

Chapter 14

Handicap and Family Therapy

D. Black

I. INTRODUCTION

What does "handicap" mean? What provision should a caring society make for people with handicaps? What contribution can the family therapist make to the well-being of handicapped people and their families?

In this chapter I will briefly review the literature on handicap with special reference to children, examine the relevant concepts developed by family theorists, and assess the contributions that family therapists can make to the total provision for families with a handicapped member.

II. SOME BASIC ASSUMPTIONS ABOUT HANDICAP

A. Definition

The various definitions of handicap (see Younghusband *et al.*, 1970; Pless and Pinkerton, 1975; Rutter *et al.*, 1970) all emphasize the concept of handicap as something to be applied to functioning rather than people. The same disability may handicap different people to different degrees. Thus one of the effects produced by arthritis is limitation of movement. This disability, even if slight would severely handicap a violinist, but might be negligible in a telephonist. Someone who is handicapped in some of his functioning, is not necessarily handicapped generally. Pless and Pinkerton (1975) stress that the notion of generalized handicap imposed by a specific disease is unjustified and has unfortunate psychosocial consequences. Both the disabled person and the non-disabled may view the former as more limited than he is. They point out that this phenomenon of "spread" (Wright, 1960), i.e. a generalized devaluation of body function and even of self, can be more handicapping than the original impairment itself, and that a "marginal" disability, because it keeps the individual in the community, may be harder to adjust to than a severe one which forces him to come to terms with his limitations.

Rutter and his colleagues (Rutter *et al.*, 1970) examined the prevalence of handicapping disorders in 10-11-year-olds under four headings: intellectual, educational, physical and psychiatric; and used strict criteria which included the concepts of severity and duration. "Handicap for most of the children studied meant a considerable interference with their ability to lead a normal life." (p. 351).

Family Therapy
ISBN: 0-12-089355-X

295

A handicapped individual therefore is one whose functioning in one or more areas of his life is retarded, impaired or distorted by a disorder which is permanent or present for a substantial period. Handicapping disorders may be physical, intellectual, psychiatric or educational. Commonly there may be a combination of handicapping disorders. A person with a disability interacts with his environment. His family is the most important matrix in which he is embedded and is the most important determinant of outcome in terms of adjustment. The concepts developed by family theorists are very relevant to our understanding of the effects of disability on individual and family functioning, but have rarely been applied to the study of people with handicaps and their families.

Is it true, as Sheridan (1965) suggests, that "in the background of every individual handicapped child there is always a handicapped family", or when we find such a handicapped family, could more skilful or plentiful services have prevented or mitigated their disabilities?

B.   Prevalence of Handicap

The most comprehensive epidemiological study of childhood disorders (Rutter *et al.*, 1970) found that one in every six children between 9 and 11 years had a chronic or recurrent handicap, physical, intellectual, educational or psychiatric. A quarter of the handicapped children had at least two handicaps; 90% of the intellectually retarded children and 29% of the physically handicapped children had other handicaps as well. In over half the children, the disorder was associated with some disorganization of family routine. In some there were impaired family relationships, and over half the parents expressed some dissatisfaction with the services available to them. These figures can be regarded as minimal population estimates and reveal the widespread existence of handicap in a developed society, and the relative inadequacy of health, education and social services to meet the needs of the families. Educational help was insufficient, and while the strictly medical aspects of treatment were fairly adequate,

> parents felt they needed more guidance in the individual management of the handicapped child; more moral support and advice in coping with the disturbed family situation and relationships sometimes associated with the handicap . . . , and more tangible help to relieve them of the mental, physical and financial burden of caring for and living with severely handicapped children. (Rutter *et al.*, 1970, p.356)

C.   Services for Handicapped Children

Improvements in medical care and other social measures have brought benefits to children's health and physical well-being in the last half-century, and have thrown into relief the problems of handicap. While the aim of society must be to prevent handicapping disorders wherever possible, the role of health, educational and social services in diagnosis, support, advice and treatment and other services to the handicapped and their families has only recently received systematic attention (see Kellmer-Pringle, 1964; Dinnage, 1970, 1972; Pilling, 1973; Court, 1976 for summaries of research). The establishment of comprehensive Paediatric Assessment Centres in Great Britain, staffed by professionals from many disciplines, has improved the ascertainment of handicapped children, and in the best centres (e.g. Brimblecombe, 1974; Goddard and Rubissow, 1977) a continuing treatment, support and education service to families is offered which is already reducing the need for permanent hospital beds for handicapped children.

A major problem in the field of handicap is the misuse of costly resources by parents peddling their child round from hospital to hospital in the hope of finding a cure. The causes of this phenomenon are complex: failure of communication on the part of the professionals involved in the diagnosis; lack of an ongoing treatment and management plan which is comprehensible to the parents, and a failure to help the family in their task of mourning the loss of the normal child they expected.

D.   Case Example: Florence

(1)   Basic Facts

Florence was 3½ years-old when she was referred by the consultant paediatrician because of several behaviour problems. He wondered if she was autistic. Severely retarded in speech and language, she had no symbolic play, was waking several times a night and screaming, was negativistic in behaviour and would scream when her 1-year-old sister was present. She did not play with other children, and there were temper tantrums on mild frustration.

The family were from Ireland, and father was a bus conductor. Neither parent was bright, and they had few family supports here. They were caring parents, but father coped by getting very angry if people didn't do what he wanted. Mother seemed very depressed. An incredible number of people had become involved with this family (see Fig. 1).

They had seen all these people frequently, but seemed confused and unable to tell us what was wrong with Florence. Susan (1 year) seemed developmentally normal. Seen as a family, the following sequence became apparent. Father or mother would ask Florence to do something. She did not respond. Father's voice would grow gradually louder, to a shout. Florence, seeming anxious, would throw a toy at her sister, who would run to mother and cry. Florence would get a smack for being "bold", an Irishism for "naughty". She would cry and try to go to mother; Susan would push her away; she would hit Susan and in return be hit and shouted at by mother.

Father's exasperation made him look ill; he shouted that no one would tell him what was wrong with Florence. Most of the confusion was semantic. He had been told she was slow and backwards, but understood that to mean a delay in development which would eventually disappear. "Why couldn't she have some schooling now, so by the time she was five she would have caught up?", he asked. What was the *reason* for her backwardness, is what he meant by "what was wrong", and it was clear that they did not know.

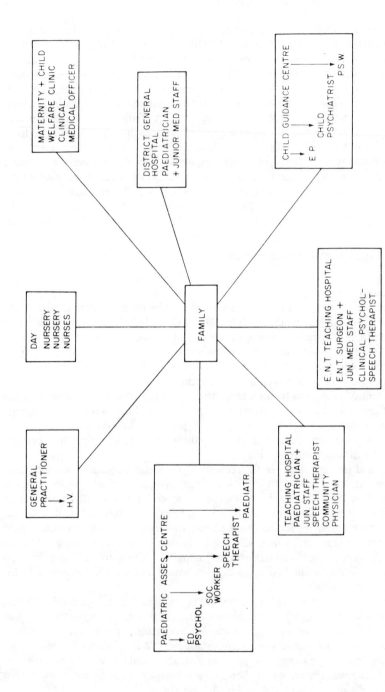

Fig. 1. Florence's professional network.

(2)   The Therapist's Tasks

There were two tasks here: to establish a diagnosis, and then to help the parents to understand its implications. Could Florence understand gesture? We got the parents to communicate their wishes silently. Florence was eager to please. She carried toys from mother, to Susan, to us, when she understood father's instructions given by gesture alone. The parents could experience at first hand the way in which Florence was locked into herself because of limited understanding. With help from other specialists, a diagnosis of specific severe speech and language disorder in a mildly retarded girl was made, and a contract for four family therapy sessions made. These sessions enabled us to work on communication within the family and with the professional network; on specific disordered behaviours (such as sleep disturbances) which were remediable, and to facilitate the expression of the parent's grief when they finally understood that they had a child with a severe handicap.

When last seen by us one year after referral, Florence was understanding four or five words with meaning, making good social contact, and was able to play with her sister and peers. Her parents had stopped peddling her round to several hospitals, and although they were under considerable strain, family life appeared happier. The problems of coping with this severely handicapped child will of course be lifelong, but it seemed as if the family therapy had been able to convert the aggressiveness and blaming into grief, and then into understanding and acceptance, so that they no longer attacked or rejected Florence or their advisors, but could tackle their problems in a more adaptive way. The family continues to receive much professional support.

In this case, there were communication problems between Florence and her family, between the parents, and between them and the many doctors they had seen. Family assessment helped to establish the diagnosis, and family therapy was needed to maximise communication within the family and with their advisors. The establishment of a firm diagnosis, with its implications, provoked an appropriate grief reaction in the parents, which could be worked through, releasing more adaptive behaviour.

(3)   Implications for Services

Services for handicapped children like Florence and their families should be comprehensive and long-term. There are advantages to the families and to the professionals in the establishment of a centre from which all the services needed can function so that there can be an association of the different relevant disciplines over time, and an opportunity for the cross-fertilization of ideas. Services must start with the diagnosis and ascertainment of handicapped individuals, and will therefore involve hospital and community paediatricians and other hopsital specialists, and will also involve in counselling (including genetic counselling), treatment and support some or all of the following: medical, psychiatric and local authority social workers, health visitors, general practitioners, hospital and community nurses, physiotherapists, occupational therapists, speech therapists, clinical and educational psychologists, psychotherapists, and consultants in paediatrics, neurology, child psychiatry, mental handicap, and genetics, as well as junior medical staff. Such a team should be headed by a consultant paediatrician with a special interest in handicapped children, and children and their families, once registered with the service should be able to use it as needed. The provision of short stay "respite" accommodation, of more permanent residential care which is child-centred (Tizard *et al.*, 1975), of information about benefits available (such as mobility and attendance allowances, and grants for house adaptation), and about the availability and suitability of day and residential schools and pre-school play-groups, nursery schools and day nurseries, is essential if severely handicapped children are to develop their full potential without impoverishing or exhausting their families.

Unfortunately, few districts can boast a comprehensive service, but if the recommendations of the Court Committee to establish district handicap teams is implemented, the prospect for the handicapped and their families should improve.

III. IMPACT OF HANDICAP ON CHILD, FAMILY AND COMMUNITY

A. General Effects of Disability

The extensive literature on the effects of handicap can only be briefly summarized here. Interested readers are referred to reviews by Barker *et al.* (1953), Pless and Pinkerton (1975), Dinnage (1970, 1972), Pilling (1973) and Kellmer-Pringle (1964). The literature on sibling reactions to handicap is reviewed by Black and Sturge (1980). The psychological problems in physically ill and handicapped children are reviewed by Fox (1977) and Steinhauer *et al.* (1974). The problems of adolescents are reviewed by Freeman (1970) and Dorner (1976), and there are numerous studies of the families of children with single handicapping conditions, of which Jan *et al.* (1977) on visual impairment, Hewitt *et al.* (1970) on cerebral palsy, Burton (1975) on cystic fibrosis, and Gath (1978) on Down's Syndrome may serve as excellent examples.

B. Effects on Parents

The parents attitude to their child's handicap has been found to be the most important factor in the family's successful adaptation. Parental attitudes are of course influenced by many factors. Table I attempts to summarize the research findings.

Significantly high rates of both physical and mental ill-health have been found in parents of handicapped children, especially those with other adversities, (financial, housing, employment etc.). The good marriage may be strengthened by the stress of a handicapped child, but the strain on a weak marriage may be too great. Handicapped children may also keep a bad marriage going. These factors may be equally balanced, and there is little hard data showing an increased rate of marital breakdown.

Table I. Summary of research findings.

Factors affecting adjustment to handicap.

(1)   Large families more tolerant of handicap.
(2)   Catholics less guilty than Protestants.
(3)   Parents more accepting of handicap when child is young than later.
(4)   Parents more affected by handicap in boys than girls.
(5)   Adjustment better when good counselling available early and practical help given.
(6)   Younger siblings are more affected by parental absences in hospital.
(7)   The following ameliorate the adverse effects of handicap:
    (a)   mildness of handicap.
    (b)   large age gap between handicapped sibling and the rest.
    (c)   moderate family size.
    (d)   a good marriage.
    (e)   good financial and community support.
(8)   Life-threatening diseases increase family vulnerability.

C.   Effects on Siblings

The effect of handicap on siblings are similarly balanced. The development of beneficial traits such as tenderness, compassion, generosity and protectiveness tending to occur as often as adverse traits and symptoms. A child may imitate or identify with his disabled sibling, to the extent that it impairs his development. This may be an attempt to gain more parental attention, or a genuine empathy with the sibling (Black and Sturge, 1980). Diseases which are familial or life-threatening appear to affect siblings adversely. Certain handicapping conditions may even affect the size of the family itself, parents limiting their families after the birth of a handicapped child.

D.   Effects on Others

The effect of handicap on grandparents appear to have been studied rarely, if at all. The effect on the community has not been systematically described. The myth of the accepting and tolerant primitive community is belied by the tradition of exposing handicapped infants, and the high rates of infanticide and abandonment right up to the present century. The allocation of public funds nicely illustrates public attitudes. The mentally and physically handicapped have always had the crumbs from the table of the acutely ill, and the recent public outcry at the exposures of the inadequacies of Britain's Health Service in caring for the mentally handicapped (e.g. the Normansfield Enquiry 1978) was a muted and short-lived one.

The effects on physicians and other professionals of handicap are interesting. The priorities have always been with the acute illnesses. The concept of a continuing role for paediatricians and others in the care of the handicapped has really only developed in the last 10-15 years, as the acute diseases have receded.

E. Effects of School

One section of the community needs special consideration: children spend much of their early life at school. What is the interaction between them, their non-handicapped peers and their teachers? Facial deformities have been shown to render children unpopular (Richardson, 1971; Lansdown, 1975), and so has obesity, which is often the consequence of the immobility imposed by some physical handicap. Strong arguments exist for and against segregation of the severely handicapped in special schools (see Anderson, 1973, for the "anti" arguments, and Fox (1976) for the "pro" ones.) If children are in special schools, they rarely meet non-handicapped children. Teachers and children in ordinary schools do not have the opportunity to become familiar with the problems in living that face the handicapped child, or to develop desirable attitudes to the disabled. It is more difficult to provide a wide enough range of educational facilities for young adolescents with physical handicaps at a special school. Furthermore, the regular withdrawal from lessons for the physical treatment of the handicap may deprive the handicapped child of the education he needs if he is to have a chance of independent adult life.

F. Effects on the Child

Summarizing the research findings, we can say that the effects on the child himself depend to some extent on the age of onset and the nature and severity of the handicap, but much more on the quality of parental and professional (including educational) care. A disability can prevent or disrupt the early formation of bonds which we believe to be essential to emotional health (Bowlby, 1969), either because of separation because of treatment needs (admission to special care units, removal to specialist hospitals etc.) or because of parental rejection, or depression. The disability itself may handicap the development of relationships, either by producing in the parents a "too perfect" adaptation to the child's needs (Bentovim, 1972), or in the case of children with sensory impairment or brain damage, especially, behaviour problems stemming from poor impulse control, frustration and insecurity which the parent can find no way of mitigating. The child thus becomes unrewarding to the parents and is relatively neglected or rejected.

The problems of frequent hospitalization are the same for the handicapped as for the normal child, and may produce an anxious, clinging and phobic child, who is passive and dependent with a constricted, fearful personality. The effect of frequent pain and of limitations in movement imposed by some diseases, can also cripple personality development and produce a demanding and querulous child.

That 29% of physically handicapped children are educationally retarded too may indicate the difficulties that both parents and teachers have in providing a rich and varied experience for them. Their educational failure serves further to lower the child's feelings of self-worth already damaged by increasing awareness of his disability.

Some parents over-protect their handicapped child, which impairs the development of autonomy, and prevents normal sibling interaction. The sibling may not be free to resent, fight with or compete with his handicapped brother or sister (Jan *et al.*, 1977), and the disabled child then cannot give up his fantasies of omnipotence, a necessary step in the development of social relationships.

The social isolation that the family finds imposed on it, or that it imposes on itself because of rejection, guilt, depression or over-protection (so that for example the parents never go out because they cannot trust a baby-sitter), further limits the child's opportunities for the development of social skills.

The rates of psychiatric disorder are raised in mentally, physically and educationally handicapped children. Children with chronic physical handicap in the Isle of Wight study (Rutter *et al.*, 1970) showed a rate of psychiatric disorder nearly twice (11.6%) that of the general population. If the handicap affected the brain (e.g. epilepsy, cerebral palsy etc.), the rate of psychiatric disorder was 3-4 times that of the general population. However there was no specific association between the type of psychiatric disorder and the physical handicap, nor was there an association between the severity of the handicap and the incidence of psychiatric disorder. Only 10% of children with handicapping psychiatric disorder were in fact receiving any psychiatric treatment.

G. Adolescence and Handicap

The cognitive changes associated with puberty, bring the possibility of increases in disturbance in the handicapped youngster, especially the physically handicapped. He begins to face the implications of his disability. Can he support himself, will he be attractive to the opposite sex, can he marry, have children, become independent of his parents, like his non-handicapped peers? Since the rate of psychiatric disorder is raised in adolescence in the general population, and epidemiological studies of the handicapped adolescent are not available, there is no clear evidence for an increase in problems in the handicapped adolescent specifically. Pless and Pinkerton (1975) suggest that there is limited evidence that suicide and suicidal intent is more common in physically ill adolescents, but that there is little evidence for a specific increase in problems of the handicapped at adolescence, greater than in the general population. We urgently need good studies in this area.

Freeman (1970) indicates the problems that physically handicapped young people have to face. There may be an actual deterioration in their physical conditions, they have to give up fantasies of a cure, social isolation may increase at a time when sexual maturation brings problems of impulse control, which heightens family and neighbourhood concern. Indiscriminate affection is no longer acceptable. The problems of leaving school and finding work, difficult as they are in themselves, bring with them the changeover of professional staff as well. Probably the majority of adolescents with handicaps and their families, would benefit from skilled counselling at this time.

H.   Handicap and Adulthood

So far, we have focussed on the handicapped child and his family, as indeed do most of the research studies. Marriage rates are lower in the handicapped, rates of psychiatric disorder and unemployment higher, and the handicapped are more likely to be in low-level jobs (see Pless and Pinkerton, 1975 for a review). The effect on children of parental handicap and chronic illness was studied by Rutter (1966), who found a significantly increased rate of chronic or recurrent parental illness in psychiatrically disturbed children. The mechanism of the association is probably through the stresses on family and marriage imposed by the disorder (finance, job difficulties, separations, personality disorders arising from chronic handicap, and death). Disabled parents are more likely to die during their children's childhood with all the implications for the children that carries (see Chapter 20, Loss, Mourning and Grief). The quality of affectional relationships seems to be the best predictor of whether the children will be affected by the parent's disability.

Adult handicap may be accentuated to maintain a bad marriage, or to bind families together in ways that can be dysfunctional. Changing practices in the treatment of psychiatric patients by adult psychiatrists can affect family functioning, and those professionals working with children and their families must liase more with the adult services.

I.   Specific Effects of Disability

So far, we have described the effects of handicap in general terms. There are consequences specific to certain diseases and to certain phases of the family life-cycle to which brief attention must be paid, although it is beyond the scope of this chapter to describe the consequences of each individual disorder. Travis (1976) has summarized the problems for children and their families of each of the major chronic illness, and Gath's (1978) account of the effects of Down's Syndrome has applications to most of the mentally handicapped.

IV.   CRISIS INTERVENTION AND
FAMILY INTERVENTION

A.   Crisis Periods and Handicap in the Family Life-Cycle

All families are vulnerable at times of crisis, and Caplan has suggested (1964) that they are also more open to change. He distinguished times of potential crisis in the life of each individual as "normal crises" at times of transition e.g. marriage, birth of the first child, going to school, leaving home, starting work, retirement, death of parents; and the crises which are not common at all, such as the birth of a handicapped child, the death of a spouse or child, marital break-up, loss of job or house, etc.

Dare (1979) has taken these concepts further by suggesting that the more there are family members at important critical transitions or phases in their lives, the more likely it is that the family will be encountering stresses and need for adjustment and change that springs largely from the fact of the multiplicity of individual crises.

The work of Rappoport (1963) in identifying phases in the life-cycle of families is relevant to an understanding of crisis in families.

The special potential crisis periods for families of a handicapped child are:

(i) At diagnosis.

(ii) When the parents realize the implications of the impairment for the child and family.

(iii) When a decision about placement has to be made (hospital, school etc.)

(iv) When a decision about future pregnancies has to be made.

(v) During subsequent pregnancies.

(vi) When the prospect of promotion or job change involves moving away from family, neighbourhood and professional supports.

(vii) When the handicapped child goes to primary school, and when he would have changed to senior school, had he not been handicapped.

(viii) If there is a significant deterioration in the disorder, so that it becomes life-threatening or terminal.

(ix) If the child dies.

(x) When the child fails to negotiate a normal developmental stage (talking, walking, reading etc.)

(xi) If another child in the family develops the same or another disorder.

(xii) At the onset of puberty.

(xiii) When leaving school and starting work (or not starting work).

(xiv) If the child requires operation(s).

(xv) If the child goes into residential care.

At all these times, it may be possible to intervene briefly to make a positive contribution to the welfare of the family. All these potential crisis periods are additional to those normally experienced by every family and the likelihood of two or more hazardous times concurring is high.

B.   Family Therapy and Crisis Intervention

The family therapist who is part of the handicap team is well placed to intervene swiftly with a family in crisis who is known to the centre. The child psychiatrist, social worker, psychotherapist and psychologist may have acquired family therapy skills, and others (health visitors, general practitioners and physiotherapists in particular) are recognizing the advantages of learning these therapeutic techniques to help their patients.

(1)   Case Example: Douglas and his Family

Douglas, aged 8 was referred to a child guidance clinic because of enuresis, and behaviour difficulties at school. There was a strong family history of Huntington's Chorea, a familial disorder affecting 50% of the children of victims. It causes involuntary movements of the body, personality deterioration, psychosis, eventual dementia and death (Fig. 2). The paternal sister had first developed the disease, and mother was convinced her husband was showing early signs. Unspoken was the concern that Douglas was the next victim. The marriage was an unhappy one, but mother was caught in a bind: she could not confront her husband honestly about her unhappiness if he was a sick man. His tense

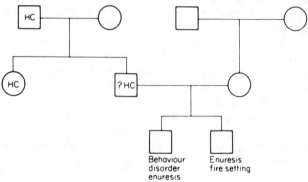

Fig. 2. Douglas' geneogram.

constricted personality, the result of much suffering in childhood at the hands of a deteriorating irascible father, led him to avoid emotional commitment to his wife and family, and he denied that he had any worry about inheriting the family disease. The complaints about Douglas were ill-formulated, and the parents spent the whole time talking about the marriage so that he seemed to be being offered as a passport to marital therapy which was what was offered. During the course of six sessions, the parents began to face together the implications of the family disease and to plan appropriately. Father had a vasectomy and made realistic plans with his wife for that eventuality. Freed from the unspoken dread, they turned to getting some enjoyment from each other: mother was clearly impressed by the caring way father had made his plans and could relinquish her ambivalent protectiveness which had of course been patronizing, and make demands on him for a reciprocal relationship. Douglas was no longer a cause for concern, and his mild symptoms improved.

The crisis of hospital admission, especially for operation can cause a temporary period of individual or family malfunctioning even in the most stable families. In the following case, two crises, i.e. father's unemployment, and Dennis's admission, coincided.

(2) Case Example: Dennis and his Family

Dennis, aged 9, was referred by his cardiologist having developed somatic symptoms of anxiety while awaiting an operation to improve his chronic valvular heart disease, which had stunted his growth and prevented normal activities. He had had 16 previous admissions. The middle of three children, father was unemployed and expressed great fury at the referral: his son was not mad, and anyway why drag the whole family an expensive 70-mile journey? However they could be engaged by the offer to do some rehearsal for the operations which were clearly a realistic worry for them all.

In the course of these sessions, each member of the family was asked to role-play Dennis and then his own role in the family system during the forthcoming hospitalization for surgery. Dennis was strikingly passive, and could not even indicate where his heart was. His drawing (Fig. 3) indicated a view of himself as isolated and deformed. The role-play enabled others to voice for him the common fears—of injections, pain, abandonment, and death which he could not articulate. All the family had some personal experience of hospitals, and it relieved them to be able to express anxiety and know it was accepted and considered normal by the therapists. Dennis had a successful operation and his behaviour was normal. His mother in a letter acknowledged that the family sessions had enabled Dennis to "sail through his time in hospital".

Fig. 3.

Dennis's symptoms were due to anxiety with which his parents and medical and nursing staff could not help. We intervened by short-term family therapy, and also by some counselling on the ward so that Dennis had oral premedication and mother accompanied him to the anaesthetic room and stayed with him till he was unconscious. In family sessions we explored areas of anxiety in Dennis and his family, and helped them all to find roles for themselves in his "scene", and thus gain mastery over their fears and helpless feelings. The forthcoming operation was rehearsed, and time was spent helping them to anticipate what would happen and prepare themselves.

The use of a family approach at times of crisis may prevent the development of secondary disability in children and their families. It is possible that Dennis might have added a psychiatric disability to his chronic cardiac disorder and that in the former example, Douglas's mild developmental delay could have led to educational disability and a conduct disorder had not family therapy tackled the underlying anxieties and tensions.

V.   FAMILY THEORY AND THERAPY WITH HANDICAP

A.   The Place of Family Theory and Therapy

The treatment needs of handicapped children and their families are as complex and diverse as the disorders from which they suffer. No attempt will be made here to consider the full range of resources, physical, psychological, educational or social, needed, but to look specifically at the contribution of family therapy. It must be emphasized that such therapy is but a small contribution to the overall treatment provision, but may be effective in enabling a family to free itself from blocks to its development and improve family functioning.

In the previous section we looked at the effects of handicap on individual family members, but family theory has much to contribute to our understanding of the effects of handicap on the family system, for example, the concept of role assignation (Toman, 1961). In a handicapped family, the eldest girl is assigned the role of caring for the other siblings, and has been shown to be at greater psychiatric risk (Farber, 1959; Gath, 1974). A non-handicapped child may be appointed by the family to achieve all the parental aspirations, and may feel himself to be "special", or have a messianic mission. This overvaluing of one child throws particular stresses on the child and on the homeostasis of the system. The family assignment of the role of "handicapped" or "stupid" to the child with a disability may lead to an exaggeration or "spread" of his disability so that the child becomes handicapped more severely or in more spheres than he need be. The handicapped child himself may receive the "special" label either overtly or by implication, and is not submitted to the normal rough and tumble of family life. In Minuchin's words, the sibling subsystem is,

> the first social laboratory in which children can experiment with peer relationships. Within this context children support, isolate, scapegoat and learn from each other. In the sibling world children learn how to negotiate, co-operate and compete. They learn how to make friends and allies, how to save face while submitting and how to achieve recognition of their skills. They may take different positions in their jockeying with one another and those positions, taken early in the sibling subgroup, can be significant in the subsequent course of their lives. (Minuchin, 1974, p. 59)

If the role assignment becomes rigidified by attitudes to handicap, the flexibility necessary for the development of social skills is not present in either the handicapped or the non-handicapped sibling.

Non-handicapped children, especially older ones, may cross the generational boundary to become a parental child (see Sandra below), with the ensuing dangers of skewing the marital relationship and forcing premature and distorted maturation of the child so affected.

B. Effects of Particular Handicaps

Sensory handicaps in particular may produce enormous problems of communication within the family. Shapiro and Harris (1976) describe the use of family therapy with deaf patients. A deaf and hearing co-therapy team treated a family containing a suicidal adolescent girl who was deaf. Individual therapy had been unsuccessful and because of the intrusiveness of other family members, a family evaluation was made. Although the girl had been deaf since infancy, the parents had never learned to communicate with their daughter. The authors suggest that the girl was scapegoated in order to mask the guilt and anger provoked by her handicap, and to detour the marital conflict. The girl misinterpreted family laughter as directed at her, and her resultant distress was misconstrued by the family as bad behaviour. The role of the therapist in patiently unravelling these distortions of communication is described, as are the considerable difficulties of communicating with deaf patients.

Communication problems may occur because of retarded development, or because of cultural or language differences between parents and/or between the family and their advisors.

C. Family Therapy and genetically inherited Handicap

An important use of family therapy with genetically inherited handicaps is to aid the family to explore the implications of the familial disease. Martindale and Bottomley (1980) give a detailed description of their work with one of these families, in which they were able to involve the extended family and help them to help the next generation to understand and cope with the effects on the family of a disorder which causes personality deterioration, psychosis, severe physical disablement, and eventually death (Huntington's Chorea). The outcome of such sensitive work might be, they suggest, that afflicted families would choose to eliminate the disease (which affects 50% of a sufferer's children) by adopting children rather than conceiving their own. They demonstrate the reluctance of professionals to counsel families adequately, and in particular the difficulty that everyone has in believing that young children could have any real understanding of the implications of the disease. Yet it was the youngest children in the family they describe who were the first to talk about their fears of developing the disease, and the first to reveal their plans for coping as parents: by adopting a child. In view of Rutter and his colleagues' (1970) finding that children with hereditary disorders are more vulnerable to psychiatric disorders, and Atkin's (1974) poignant description of the agony that siblings and their parents suffer when they observe the first signs of the familial disease affecting the second child in the family, family therapists should be developing their work further to help such families.

One aim of all those who are involved in helping the handicapped, is to prevent secondary handicaps.

Family attitudes to handicap may be determined by their experience of it in their families of origin. The use of geneograms (Guerin, 1976; Lieberman, 1979) to explore the meaning for each family of having a handicapped member is illustrated in the following case.

D.   Case Example: Michael and his Family

(1)   Presentation of the Family

Michael, aged 9, was referred by the educational psychologist because of odd behaviour in his ESN (M) school where he had been placed at the age of 5. He made no social contact, and was "nervy, jumpy", and over-active. He couldn't concentrate or settle to anything.

He was a non-identical twin, and his brother Martin was of superior intelligence. The parents were highly intelligent: both working full time in professional occupations, so that Martin assumed the care of Michael after school until mother came home one hour later. Father had a physical handicap. A diagnosis of infantile autism was established. Mother broke down into tears when we offered a diagnosis, expressing guilt and relief in equal measure. There seemed· little communication between the parents.

We noted that the mother treated father as if he were also a child, and that she related more to Martin as a spouse. For example she always insisted on going with father to his specialist because "he wouldn't ask the right questions". He had never learned to drive, assuming that his handicap would prevent it. When we queried this, she said that he would only take lessons if she arranged it.

We were concerned about Martin who seemed to be a parental child. He did not play with the toys, appearing as a too serious unjoyful, responsible older brother although they were in fact the same age. The family were immigrants and had few family supports. Mother's parents had disapproved of the marriage which was to a man of lower social class and she had had to wait a long time for her father's permission to marry. Father's family were stigmatized by other handicaps; Michael was said to be like him, Martin like mother.

(2)   Family Therapy Process

We offered a contract of family therapy sessions with the goals of improving the parental relationship and alliance, relieving Martin of the burden of parenting Michael, helping the parents to accept Michael's handicap, and giving specific help with the management of Michael's behaviour. I can only illustrate some of the highlights of this family's treatment which included drugs and behavioural techniques, all in a family setting.

For example, they wanted to work on Michael's long-standing tendency to scribble over everything including important papers brought home from work. We explained the difficulty Michael had in distinguishing important paper from drawing paper, and suggested a behaviour therapy programme in which he was given pink paper and encouraged to scribble on that, but a firm "no" was always given to any other paper he tried to use. He was rewarded at first when using pink paper. This behaviour improved in a few days. The problem of Martin's parentification was tackled obliquely by strengthening the parental alliance.

The male therapist agreed to take the lead, and model more assertive behaviour with me, the older and more senior therapist. My acceptance of his leadership we felt might then enable mother to accept father's tentative attempts to lead which had hitherto been squashed by her.

The male therapist encouraged father to explore the possibility of learning to drive: to "help his wife" with the chauffeuring. She offered to find out about driving schools for the handicapped, but was firmly blocked by the therapist. By the next session father had begun driving lessons which he had arranged himself.

(3) Use of Geneograms

We then used geneograms to examine the concept of handicap in the family. Geneograms are an elaborate form of family tree in which the family are invited to draw parallels between people through the generations on the basis of shared characteristics, either actual or fantasied. In this way family myths can be exposed and challenged. In Michael's father's family, there had been handicapped people in three or four generations, and the tradition in their country of origin was that the siblings had to care for them at the expense of their own happiness. Caring for father, disabled as a child, had caused father's eldest brother to neglect his wife who had left him. Martin was being moulded into the same role as a caretaker for Michael.

The family worked hard on their geneogram, enjoyed the exploration of their family history and retelling it to the boys; even Michael realized that something important was happening, and sat still without his usual stereotypies (Fig. 4).

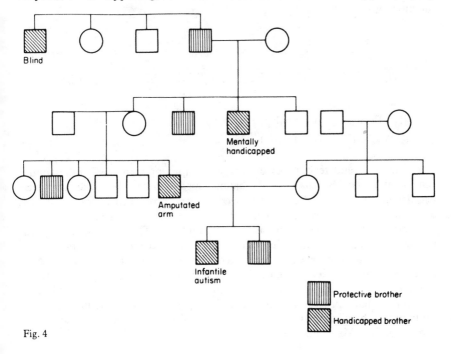

Fig. 4

Father had lost his arm at 15 because of a bone infection and was considered too handicapped to live independently. Paternal grandfather had detailed the oldest son to have him live with him and his new wife. The brother had lavished inappropriate and overprotective care on father, and his wife had become jealous and left him. Father had felt it to be his fault, and seemed condemned to repeat the family history with his own sons. He had chosen a wife who had perpetuated his brother's care but who also exacted a price for it: an unhappy, dominating woman whose alliance with Martin pushed father into the handicapped child subsystem with Michael. The genograms made the parents aware of how much they had followed the family tradition. But their courtship had in fact been a rebellion against the traditions of their culture, and they recognized that it was their guilt about this rebellion that had bound them to perpetuate the other tradition. After working on this myth, the parents were able to make better caretaking arrangements which relieved Martin of his parenting role.

We were delighted when he began to use our toys in an age-appropriate way and with evident enjoyment. Michael made considerable strides during this time in his social behaviour and his ability to concentrate and learn at school.

Why had it taken so long for Michael's autism to be recognized and referral to a child psychiatrist arranged? Could the passivity of the parents, based on their fatalism derived from their own cultural and family traditions have infected their professional advisors too? Certainly, even with this severely handicapped boy, it was possible using a family approach to improve family and individual functioning.

VI. ASPECTS OF FAMILY THERAPY WITH HANDICAP

A. The Process of Family Therapy in Handicapped Families

The principles and techniques of family therapy apply to the families under consideration no less than to non-handicapped families. What distinguishes handicapped families is the repeated need to work through their grief at the loss of the normal child they expected, and this need may recur again and again as another hoped for achievement has to be relinquished. Thus parents may appear to have accepted their child's limitations, only to grieve anew when the onset of puberty, or adult life, reveals how limited he will be. Families continue to hope for physical and intellectual normality while they experience progress, however slow. When the ceiling is reached, renewed mourning may have to be facilitated. The other major process which is found frequently in dysfunctional families containing a handicapped member is the use of a disabled child to diffuse or detour conflict (Minuchin, 1974).

B.   Case Example: Sandra and her Family

(1)   The Family

Sandra, an adopted child, was 4½ when she was referred to the school psychological service by her middle-class parents because of long-standing severe temper tantrums and backwardness in speech and social development. At that time, the educational psychologist and social worker were involved, and after psychological assessment had revealed mild intellectual handicap, the social worker saw the mother regularly over the next 2 years for counselling and advice about management. Sandra's learning difficulties increased when she entered junior school, and eventually at 9 years, she was transferred to a school for mildly educationally subnormal children. (At this time, her intelligence quotient on the Wechsler Intelligence Scale for Children verbal scale = 72, Performance scale = 61. Full scale IQ = 64.) She settled well there, but when she was 11 years, the school doctor referred her to the child psychiatrist because of behaviour difficulties at home which were increasing. She shouted and screamed unbearably when she couldn't get her own way, and was persecuting the cat by squeezing his neck.

A family diagnostic interview was offered and accepted. The parents were in their 50s, and had an older, adopted boy of 14, Tony, who was very bright. The adoptive mother was obese and in poor health. The father was a quiet man who seemed calm and placatory. Tony was clearly a parental child. This extract is from the fourth family session. In the previous sessions, a behaviour programme had been set up to reward Sandra for not shouting, which had been successful, so that the family life was happier.

(2)   Extract from Fourth Session (15 minutes from end)

Tony: The main problem is that I try to stop Sandra from making mummy angry. But if I do, Dad gets cross with me and tells me off: sends me to my room, so Dad and I quarrel. I'm good at stopping Sandra from getting Mum cross: better than Mum is.

Dad: [to Tony] I don't want Sandra not to like you—I don't want you to have a bad relationship. I know that when you boss her, Sandra dislikes you.

Mum: I know I shouldn't do it, but I really invite Tony to help and appreciate it when he does. When Sandra is angry and attacks me I can't cope: she is quite big now.

Dr Black: Can you describe the sequence of events. What are you doing when Sandra gets angry?

Mum: I am lying down in my room watching TV. Sandra comes in for a cuddle. At first things are O.K. We're both enjoying it, then Sandra starts to get silly, tries to turn off the TV, or starts nagging or mucking around and I get angry. At first my anger mounts slowly, but eventually I am screaming at Sandra, but she won't obey me or take any notice.

Tony: When I hear Mum screaming I get worried because of her heart.

Dr Black: What's that?

Mum: I had a heart attack and get blood pressure. I've been told I mustn't get excited. Anyway I'm in a terrible state after one of these shouting matches. I know I shouldn't shout and lose my temper, but it is almost impossible. I need Tony to help.

(Dad says nothing. Sandra has been very quiet, looks from face to face, seems anxious.)

Dr Black: It seems to me that Sandra's not the only handicapped member of the family. Mum is handicapped in the control of her temper, Dad is handicapped in coming to her aid, Tony is handicapped in not knowing what he should do. Can you, Mum and Dad talk together about how to change things?

Dad: Maybe I'm not the ideal man.

Mum: [to Dad] I know that you think I really should control my temper.

Dad: Yes. I think you should. You're an adult and you should be able to control your temper and control Sandra.

Tony: [attempts to join parental subsystem] I would like to have Dad's permission to go and help Mum, because I can control Sandra, I can get her out of the bedroom. (Dad is silent).

Dr Black: [redraws the generational boundary to exclude Tony] I guess this is something that Mum and Dad will have to discuss together and decide how they would like it to be dealt with. If Dad and Mum make the decision that Tony should be involved, then Tony would obviously be glad to help, but I feel it would need to be the parents who decide that. In the meantime Tony, I guess you'll have to see whether being a child in this family has any compensations.

(3) The Next Session

The next session with the parents alone had been planned some time before, because they were bothered about Sandra's burgeoning sexuality and wondered if she could be sterilized, as they felt she might easily be seduced and violated. During this exposition father had sat with his back to mother and I asked why. Father admitted that he had felt agonized after our last session because of the realization of the burden they had put on Tony to be grown up before his time because they couldn't control Sandra. They had in fact been able to talk about this, and had given Tony clearer instructions which were working well. For the first time Sandra had controlled a temper herself. Mother turned to me to tell me how embarrassed she had been all her married life because of father's social incompetence. He refused to make any small talk and so she rushed in, talking nineteen to the dozen, when they had company. Really she was at heart a quiet person, and she resented being forced to be loud and loquacious. She felt she was a very incompetent parent. She could only talk to children as if they were adults. Father was much better at coming down to their level. She realized that she was really making Tony into a parent for herself, and she felt awful about this. Father seemed surprised at this outpouring, and turned around to face her. With some encouragement they began a dialogue in which their tender feelings for each other could be recaptured.

(4) Comment

Although individual casework had helped mother to come to terms with her infertility and with the fact of Sandra's handicap, father and the children had been excluded from the treatment. The generational boundaries had not been firmly established because of the intellectual discrepancy between Tony and his parents on the one hand, and Sandra on the other. Mother's unhappiness in her marriage and her ill health had led her to put pressure on Tony to husband and parent her. The system had always been a vulnerable one, but it was probable that what precipitated the breakdown in family functioning was the onset of puberty in both children which reactivated incest fears, rivalry between father and son, and envy in mother of father's close relationship with Sandra.

What would restore system stability was an improvement in the marital functioning. In fact Sandra was being used to detour marital conflict. Some improvement in her behaviour, using behavioural techniques forced the parents to look at their own relationship. The will to work on what they found was fortunately present. In the past, early attempts by therapists to redefine a problem identified by parents as in the child, as a marital problem has resulted in their losing the family. In this case, the improvement in the marital relationship was achieved by using family therapy. This resulted in generally improved family functioning and a diminution in the symptoms of the identified patient. The anxiety about Sandra's sexual development reflected the dysfunctioning in the marital subsystem, and subsided once attention was paid to the marriage.

In this case the process of family therapy enabled a long-standing marital problem to be exposed and helped. Individual therapy previously had not revealed the problem.

VII. CONCLUSION

Family therapists working in this field need perhaps more than those working with other families, to have a good family and professional support system, and to spend only part of their professional day in such taxing work, if they are to bring to it an enthusiasm tempered with compassion and reality. Living with a severely handicapped child is a constant and unremitting strain for parents, and although we can use our skills to improve family functioning, it is imperative that we remember the burdens these families bear. They have much to teach us about courage and endurance, and about how to find pleasure in the almost imperceptible development of the most handicapped children. In the words of Bentovim (1972)

> physical or mental impairment should not handicap the future emotional adjustment and development of the child.

Children with handicaps need not produce handicapped families.

REFERENCES

Anderson, E. M. (1973). "The Disabled Schoolchild: A Study of Integration in Primary Schools", Methuen, London.

Atkin, M. (1974). The "doomed family" — observations on the lives of parents and children facing repeated child mortality. *In* "Care of The Child Facing Death", (L. Burton, ed.), Routledge & Kegan Paul, London.

Barker, R. G., Wright, B. A., Myerson, L. and Gonick, M. R. (1953). "Adjustment to Physical Handicap and Illness: A Survey of the Social Psychology of Physique and Disability", Social Science Research Council, New York.

Bentovim, A. (1972). Handicapped pre-school children and their families — effects on child's early emotional development. *British Medical Journal*, **3**, 634-637.

Black, D. and Sturge, C. (1980). The young child and his siblings. *In* "Modern Perspectives in the Psychiatry of Infancy", (J. Howells, ed.), Oliver & Boyd, Edinburgh and London.

Brimblecombe, F. S. W. (1974). Exeter project for handicapped children. *Brit. Med. J.*, **74**, 4, 706-709.

Burton, L. (1975). "The Family Life of Sick Children", Routledge & Kegan Paul, London.

Caplan, G. (1964). "Principles of Preventative Psychiatry", Tavistock, London.

Court, S. D. M. (1976). "Fit for the Future. Report of the Committee on Child Health Services", H.M.S.O., London.

Dare, C. (1979). Psychoanalysis and Systems in family therapy. *Journal of Family Therapy*, **1**, 137-151.

Dinnage, R. (1970). "The Handicapped Child: Research Review. Vol. 1. Neurological Handicap". Longman in association with National Childrens Bureau. London.

Dinnage, R. (1972). "The Handicapped Child; Research Review. Vol. 2. Physical and Sensory Handicap", Longman in association with National Childrens Bureau, London.

Dorner, S. (1976). Adolescents with spina bifida. *Archives disease childhood*, **51**, 439-444.

Farber, B. (1959). Effects of severely mentally retarded children on family integration. *Monographs of the Society for Research in Child Development*, **24**, 2.

Fox, A. M. (1976). Special educational needs of physically handicapped children. *Childcare, Health and Development*. **2**, 45-71.

Fox, A. M. (1977). Psychological problems of physically handicapped children. *British Journal Hospital Medicine*, **22**, 479-490.

Freeman, R. D. (1970). Psychiatric problems in Adolescents with Cerebral Palsy. *Developmental Medicine and Child Neurology*, **12**, 64-70.

Gath, A. (1974). Sibling reactions to mental handicap; a comparison of the brothers and sisters of mongol children. *Journal of Child Psychology and Psychiatry*, **15**, 187-198.

Gath, A. (1978). "Downs Syndrome and the Family", Academic Press, London and New York.

Goddard, J. and Rubissow, J. (1977). Meeting the needs of handicapped children and their families. The evolution of Honeylands. *Childcare, Health and Development*, **3**, 261-273.

Guerin, P. J. (1976). "Family Therapy — Theory and Practice", Gardner Press, New York.

Harris, J. (1980). Personal communication.

Hewitt, S., Newson, J. and Newson, E. (1970). "The Family and the Handicapped Child", Allen and Unwin, London.

Jan, J. E., Freeman, R. D. and Scott, E. P. (1977). "Visual Impairment in Children and Adolescents", Grune and Stratton, New York.

Kellmer-Pringle, M. L. (1964). "The Emotional and Social Adjustment of Physically Handicapped Children", National Foundation for Educational Research, London.

Lansdown, R. and Polak, L. (1975). A study of the psychological effects of facial deformity in children. *Childcare, Health and Development,* 1, 85-91.

Lieberman, S. (1979). Transgenerational analysis: The geneogram as a technique in family therapy. *Journal of Family Therapy,* 1, 51-64.

Martindale, B. and Bottomley, V. (1980). The management of families with Huntington's Chorea. *J. of Child Psychology & Psychiatry,* 21, 343-351.

Minuchin, S. (1974). "Families and Family Therapy", Tavistock, London.

Normansfield Inquiry (1978). Committee Report. H.M.S.O., London.

Pless, I. P. and Pinkerton, P. (1975). "Chronic Childhood Disorder: Promoting Patterns of Adjustment", Henry Kimpton, London.

Pilling, D. (1973). "The Handicapped Child; Research Review. Vol. 3. Mental Handicap", Longman in association with National Childrens Bureau, London.

Rappoport, R. (1963). Normal crises, family structure and mental health. *Family Process,* 2, 68-80.

Richardson, S. A. (1971). Children's values and friendships: A study of physical disability. *Journal of Health and Social Behaviour.* 12, 253-258.

Rutter, M. (1966). "Children of Sick Parents", Oxford University Press, London.

Rutter, M., Tizard, J. and Whitmore, K. (eds) (1970). Education, Health and Behaviour. Longman, London.

Shapiro, R. J. and Harris, R. I. (1976). Family therapy in the treatment of the deaf: a case report. *Family Process,* 15, 83-96.

Sheridan, M. (1965). *The Handicapped Child and his Home.* National Childrens Homes, London.

Steinhauer, P. D., Mushin, D. N. and Rae-Grant, Q. (1974). Psychological aspects of chronic illness. *Pediatric Clinics of North America,* 21, 825-840.

Tizard, J., Sinclair, I. and Clarke, R. V. G. (1975). "Varieties of Residential Experience", Routledge & Kegan Paul, London.

Toman, W. (1961). "Family Constellation: Theory and Practice of a Psychological Game", Springer Publishing Co., New York.

Travis, M. (1976). "Chronic Illness in Children", Stanford University Press. California.

Wright, B. (1960). "Physical Disability: A Psychological Approach", Harper & Row, New York.

Younghusband, E., Birchall, D., Davie, R. and Kellmer-Pringle, M. L. (eds) (1970). "Living with Handicap: A Report of a Working Party on Children with special needs", National Bureau for Co-operation in Child Care, London.

Chapter 15

Physical Illness, the Family and the Setting

B. Lask

I. INTRODUCTION

Physical illness may affect all families, our own included, at any time. It is a rare family that has not been so affected. The family therapist must be aware of both the impact that such an intrusion may have on the family, and the role of the family in the cause, aggravation and maintenance of physical illness. This is true of all illness whether it be "purely organic", psychological or psychosomatic. (Such terms are best avoided, as any distinction is arbitrary and potentially misleading. Organic, psychological and social factors require due consideration in all illness.) Following a review of the literature, I propose a conceptual model of interaction between illness and the family in which I show how physical symptoms or illness play an integral part in family homeostasis. Some case examples are provided to illustrate the clinical application.

II. REVIEW OF THE LITERATURE: INDIVIDUAL VIEWPOINT

Few would dispute that psychological factors are relevant in the precipitation and maintenance of a wide range of physical illness. The evidence for this has been comprehensively documented (Lipowski et al., 1977). Until recently, most emphasis has been placed on the roles of stress and specific personality characteristics. These linear views state that stressful events create emotional arousal which disrupts the endocrine and autonomic nervous systems with resultant physiological changes. Further, specific personality characteristics predispose individuals exposed to stress to specific illnesses (Alexander et al., 1968).

Grolnick (1972) states that the vast majority of stressful events are interpersonal and involve significant relationships, most commonly in the family. He criticizes the hypothesis linking personality-type to specific illness by pointing out that there are many more illnesses than specific personality profiles, and that "it is fallacious to assume a linear correlation between events at the levels of physiological and psychological integration".

III. REVIEW OF LITERATURE: INTERACTIONAL VIEWPOINT

In the last few years, much more consideration has been given to the interactional model (e.g. Watzlawick and Weakland, 1978). Most illness is of

Family Therapy
ISBN: 0-12-089355-X

multifactorial origin. Asthma, for example, results from an interaction between stress, infection and allergy on a labile bronchus. Even the common sore throat conceals subtle processes. Mayer and Zaggerty (1962) have shown that a major determining factor as to whether or not a child who has acquired a streptococcal infection in his throat becomes ill, is the presence of acute or chronic family stress. Thus instead of asking whether a sore throat is due to streptococcal infection we should ask "If this is a streptococcal sore throat, why has this child become ill at this time?"

The literature on illness and interpersonal interaction concentrates upon both dyadic and family interaction (Meissner, 1966; Grolnick, 1972).

IV. DYADIC INTERACTION

A. Parent-Child Dyads

The purported findings are at best unconvincing and often absurd. For example, patients with *tonsillitis* are "overly dependent upon their mothers" (Schellack, 1957) while *hyperthyroid* patients are also "over dependent upon their mothers, but deny this because of their ambivalence" (Alexander, 1961). Alexander also found that children with *arthritis* have "aggressive and demanding mothers", and a year later Finch and Hess (1962) reported that children with *ulcerative colitis* have "aggressive and dominating mothers". The fathers of children with *ulcerative colitis* are "passive and ineffectual", and the fathers of children with *rheumatoid arthritis* are "gentle and inconsistent" (Finch and Hess, 1962). The relationship between children with *ulcerative colitis* and their mothers is "nearly symbiotic and tremendously ambivalent" (Titchener *et al.*, 1960). *Cancer* patients have "an unresolved emotional attachment to their mother" (Perrin and Pearce, 1959), and *asthmatic* patients have "dominating and narcissistic mothers" (Bastiaans and Groen, 1955). The reverse side of the coin has also been examined: *arthritic* mothers "tend to dominate their children" (Alexander, 1961).

The majority of these studies lack elementary scientific precautions such as clearly defined terms, blind assessment and control groups. There are only three published studies of parent-child relationships in physical illness that warrant detailed consideration.

Block (1969) has questioned many of the deeply entrenched myths regarding the psychopathology of parents of asthmatic and schizophrenic children. She compared the parents of
(1) schizophrenic children, with those of
(2) neurotic children, and found no differences between them.
Further, she compared the parents of
(3) asthmatic children, with those of
(4) congenitally ill children,
and was unable to find any distinguishing characteristics.

In a study of the parents of 100 asthmatic and 100 physically disabled children, Fitzelle (1959) found no quantitative or qualitative differences in psychopathology between the two groups. Williams (1975) compared two groups of asthmatic children, of differing severity, and matched them with two control groups, one of normal children and the other containing children with a chronic chest disease (cystic fibrosis). Using carefully defined terms, and reliable and valid tests, he found that asthmatic children had "an excessive dependence–independence conflict with an intensive mother–child bond, and core anxiety around the threat of separation". He concluded that these themes were specific to asthma regardless of severity.

It is difficult to know what to conclude from all these studies. Certainly there is no evidence whatsoever to suggest specific personality types of modes of interaction between parent and child in physical illness. It is just possible however, that asthmatic children experience more separation anxiety than others.

B. Object Loss

The literature is well-endowed with reports of the loss or the threat of the loss of significant relationships shortly preceding the onset or exacerbation of physical illness. Grolnick (1972) quotes reports of object loss associated with ulcerative colitis, rheumatoid arthritis, leukaemia and various "psychosomatic conditions". Meissner's earlier but more fruitful review (1966) quotes references to object loss being important in tuberculosis, anaemia, arthritis, hypertension, duodenal ulcer, ulcerative colitis, leukaemia and cancer. Paulley (1976) considers object loss central in multiple sclerosis.

For such reports to have meaning we need to know the incidence of object loss in other physical disorders not mentioned, as well as in psychiatric disturbance, and in the general population. The absence of control data and the wide range of pathological processes included render most of the above reports suspect. The findings of Stein and Charles (1971) are more credible. They discovered that diabetic adolescents had a significantly higher incidence of loss than did a matched non-diabetic control group. They advanced the hypothesis that juvenile diabetes occurs as a consequence of psychological stress in a physiologically susceptible individual.

C. Husband-Wife Dyads

The spouse dyad literature is more helpful in that the methodology is generally more satisfactory; no claims for specificity are made, and the findings have practical value. Researchers have concentrated on the relationship between the illness and marital equilibrium.

Kellner (1963) reported that a wife's illness followed a husband's almost twice as often as vice-versa. Witkin (1965) suggested that it is more common for one spouse to manifest psychosomatic symptoms at any one time than for both to do so, while Kreitman (1964) has shown that the spouses of psychiatric patients had more physical symptoms than those of a control population. Similarly, Cobb (1972) found in a study of 49 couples in which the wife had rheumatoid arthritis and the husband had a peptic ulcer, that the wife's controlling behaviour dovetailed with the husband's need to be controlled.

Hoebel (1977) has shown that the efforts of the wives of heart-attack patients to modify the latter's type A, high-risk behaviour (Friedman and Rosenman, 1974) often play a role in maintaining that behaviour (see also p. 447). Significant and possibly life-saving changes can be brought out by effecting a change in the wife's problem-solving behaviour. Wikran *et al.* (1978) compared the patterns of communication of the parents of children with asthma with those of children with congenital heart disease using an experimentally-induced communication conflict. The heart-disease parents had a very efficient communication as did two-thirds of the asthma parents. However, one-third of the latter group had an extremely inefficient communication.

The complexities of such studies have been commented upon by Stewart (1962) who, using a similar experimental design, found no difference in communication patterns between the parents of children with "psychosomatic" disorders and the parents of other clinic-attenders.

V. FAMILY INTERACTION

The reports on family interaction may be grouped as follows:
(a) Affective style,
(b) Typology,
(c) Homeostasis,
(d) Contagion,
(e) Reaction to illness,
although there is considerable overlap between them.

A. Affective Style

For many years, individuals with psychosomatic disorders have been described as unable to express negative affect, and the same has now happened to families. Goldberg (1957) has described families with a psychosomatic member as using mechanisms which contribute to family cohesion, but oppose the expression of negative or dysphoric feeling. Jackson and Yalom (1966) studied eight families of children with ulcerative colitis, and concluded that they were restricted. Gehre and Kirschenbaum (1967) have described "repressive families" giving rise to "repressive symptoms" such as headaches, enuresis, stomach disorders and phobias, while Looff (1970) stated that families containing children with psycho-physiological reactions had particular difficulty in the verbal expression of affect.

B. Typology

With so much written on individual and dyad typology, it is inevitable that the family typology bandwagon should roll. The study referred to above by Jackson and Yalom was biased in its selection of families, did not include controls for chronic illness and had small numbers, but the findings are similar to many clinical reports. The families were severely socially-restricted, and restricting of each other in the range of permissible behaviour. They had a feeling of sameness that seemed almost like solidarity (Wynn's pseudomutuality). Jackson and Yalom's report was unusual in this area in that it contained a detailed critique of the research design and a caution about the validity of the findings.

Lask and Kirk (1979) did not find any specific typology or common patterns of interaction in their study of asthmatic families. Indeed although the families were matched for social background, pathology, severity and length of asthma, directly opposing patterns of interaction were found. Rees (1964) and Pinkerton (1967) have reported similar findings.

Minuchin *et al.* (1978) and their colleagues at the Philadelphia Child Guidance Clinic have done as much as any group to advance our understanding of family interaction and physical illness. They have described a general type of family constellation that encourages somatization of emotional conflict. Three factors in conjunction are considered necessary for the development of severe childhood psychosomatic illness:
(1) a physiologically-vulnerable child;
(2) an enmeshed, overprotective and rigid family who are unable to resolve conflict;
(3) the ill child plays an important role in the family's conflict-avoidance.

Detailed clinical observations are provided to support the hypothesis, and the work is considerably strengthened by the inclusion of some remarkable biochemical studies. The level of free fatty acids (FFA) in the blood is an indicator of stress, and Minuchin and his colleagues studied these levels in groups of children with labile and well-controlled diabetes, during stressful and non-stressful phases of family interviews. The parents' FFA levels were also recorded. Raised FFA levels in diabetes are early precursors of diabetic coma. FFA levels were significantly higher in the labile children during stress, and took significantly longer to return to normal. This finding could not be replicated for stressful events outside the family interview where there was no difference between the groups. Further, when a parent's FFA level was raised, and he or she brought the child into the conflict, the parent's level dropped to normal, while the child's rose and failed to return to normal during the recovery period. Hence the emotional arousal related to family conflict in labile diabetic children produced a significant physiological change. Parental arousal can be alleviated at the expense of the child. This pattern may well account for the lability of the diabetes.

As the authors state, the significance of these findings cannot be over-emphasized. There is a clear parallel between family interaction and physiological events. It is therefore all the more frustrating that details of the methodology for rating family interaction are not available. References are made to the analysis of the family diagnostic interview and family tasks, but until such important work can be fully evaluated and replicated, the findings relating to the family characteristics remain unproven.

Despite these criticisms Minuchin and his colleagues have clearly demonstrated the relationship between family conflict-avoidance and labile diabetes. It is of interest that these findings could not be replicated in asthma or anorexia nervosa, although the authors state the "therapeutic observations of such patients have validated the generalisability of their hypotheses, as have the strikingly successful therapeutic results."

Loader et al. (1979) have tested the Minuchin "enmeshment hypothesis" and the "affective hypothesis" (see p. 322 *Affective Style*) for families with eczematous children. Using carefully-defined terms and reliable and valid measures, they found that most but not all families fitted in with one or other or both of the proposed interactional patterns, but that the hypothesis of a specific family, "the psychosomatogenic family", was not supported. Their findings complement the studies of individuals where specificity hypotheses have proved to be over-simplified.

C. Homeostasis

This term refers to the *balance* of forces within a family: disturbance of one part affects the whole and sets in motion compensatory events to re-establish equilibrium (Hopkins, 1959). The idea that physical illness plays a major part in the homeostatic equilibrium of a family is not new (e.g. Richardson, 1948), but it has yet to be fully researched. The phenomenon has been described by Jackson and Yalom (1966) in ulcerative colitis; Lask and Kirk (1979) in childhood asthma; and Minuchin et al. (1978) in childhood anorexia nervosa, labile diabetes, and recurrent abdominal pain.

D. Contagion

Linked to the homeostatic idea is the commonly-reported phenomenon of illness contagion. Illness in one member produces illness in another (Dunbar, 1954; Hopkins, 1959; Kellner, 1963; Peachey, 1963).

E. Family Reaction

Contagion is but one of many possible reactions to illness. Apley et al. (1978) have reviewed the effects on the family of acute and chronic childhood illness, while Schonfeld (1966) has described the effects of having a handicapped child, and Gath (1978) has studied in depth the effect on families of the birth of a child with Down's syndrome (mongolism). One of her most important findings is that the quality of the marriage is a major determining factor in the family's adaption, and that marital breakdown is less frequent where there has been an early therapeutic intervention.

Reddihough and her colleagues (1977) interviewed 43 asthmatic children and their parents, and found that there were basic misconceptions about the disease and its therapy. Fears and anxieties were expressed about death and permanent damage to the heart and lungs. The disease caused a burden to all members of the family, especially the mother. The child was not able to discuss adequately his asthma with the doctor. (This last finding should really be phrased: "the doctor was unable to discuss adequately the asthma with the child," for any failure in communication between doctor and patient is a failure on the doctor's part.) The authors conclude that treatment should include more time spent with the child and family to relieve many of their anxieties.

Gath (1977) has drawn attention to the effect on the siblings of the birth of a child with Down's syndrome. Lask and Kirk (1979) have noted that the siblings may be more adversely affected psychologically than the asthmatic child, and Crain et al. (1966) reached a similar conclusion about diabetic families. Lavigue and Ryan (1978) have shown a high rate of sibling disturbance when examining children with chronic illness, dependent to some extent upon sex and age.

VI. THERAPY AND ITS EFFECTIVENESS

Despite the massive literature, credible and otherwise, on the relationship between illness and the family, and the obvious importance of therapy, there are relatively few reports of techniques or outcome studies.

The Philadelphia team have described in detail the family treatment of asthma (Liebman et al., 1974a), anorexia nervosa (Liebman et al., 1974b) and psychogenic abdominal pain (Liebman et al., 1976). They claim spectacular results for their therapy, but the details are not available. Hughes and Zimin (1978) have also described the family treatment of psychogenic abdominal pain, while Tomm et al. (1977) have outlined their approach to the family treatment of childhood diabetes.

Bingley and her colleagues (1980) have described the use of a family approach to all children with primary and secondary emotional problems on a general paediatric ward. During a one-year period, 96 children were so treated, and two-thirds of these had improved at a one to two-year follow-up.

The only controlled trial of family therapy for physical illness is that reported by Lask and Matthew (1979) in which the effectiveness of family therapy as an adjunct to standard medical management for childhood asthma was evaluated. At a one-year follow-up, the treatment group showed a significant improvement on various parameters when compared with a control group. The therapy was relatively short (a total of 4½ hours in 4 months) compared with the Philadelphia approach of about 75 hours during one year, but the authors concluded that this approach is of value in selected cases of childhood asthma.

VII. CONCEPTUAL MODEL OF INTERACTION BETWEEN ILLNESS AND THE FAMILY

There is a complex interplay between the individual, his illness, the family and extrafamilial factors, which may be conceptualized as an open system. Within

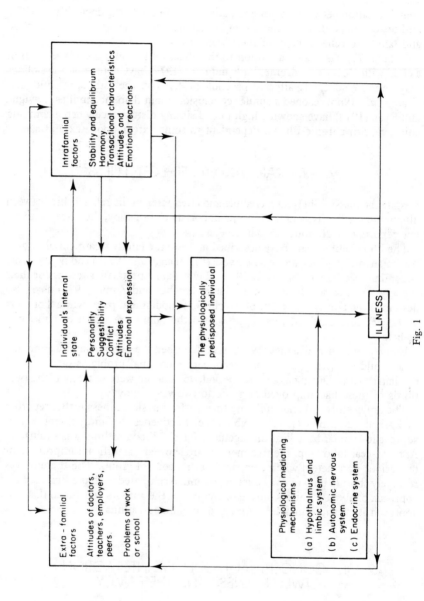

Fig. 1

this system there is no specific causal factor, and due consideration is given to the relative contribution of each of the elements identified in the circular process (Fig. 1). As I have discussed this model in detail elsewhere (Lask, 1980), I shall only summarize it in this chapter.

A. The Physiologically Vulnerable Individual

Stress of any nature is a potent trigger for a wide range of psychophysiological responses (Fig. 2). Most people have a "target-system" or "target-organ" (part of the body already primed to respond to stress in a pathological way, e.g. the labile bronchus of an asthmatic, the labile cranial arteries of the migraine sufferer) or an already diseased system or organ e.g. narrowing of the coronary arteries. Prolonged or severe stress, whether it be physical or psychological, may thus precipitate an attack of asthma, migraine, angina or other symptoms. An elegant illustration has been provided by Tal and Miklich (1976), who demonstrated how the bronchospasm of an asthmatic may be induced by instructing the subject to concentrate on the recall of an incident associated with intense anger or fear.

B. The Individual's Psychological State

Various aspects require consideration:

(1) Personality Typology
There is very little evidence linking specific illness to personality-type despite considerable effort to do so (e.g. Alexander *et al.*, 1968).

However, the personality-type may precipitate or aggravate a problem in an individual who is already predisposed to a specific illness. Friedman and Rosenman (1974) have shown that high-risk coronary-prone behaviour pattern (Type A) can be distinguished from low-risk (Type B) behaviour. Type A individuals are aggressive, competitive, ambitious, restless and experience a profound sense of urgency. Type B individuals are free of these characteristics.

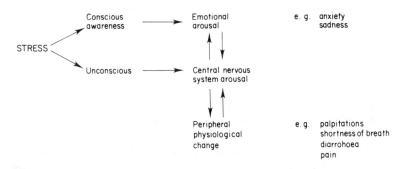

Fig. 2

It should be noted that not all Type A individuals suffer coronary thrombosis. For this to occur there is required an *interaction* between the presence of arterio-sclerosis. Type A behaviour, and possibly one or more other factors such as smoking, unhealthy diet and lack of exercise.

(2) Emotional Expression

Psychosomatic theory has long held that those individuals who suffer psychogenic physical symptoms are unable to express negative affect (e.g. Nemiah and Sifneos, 1970). One of the few convincing studies in this area is that of Stewart (1962), who was able to show that "delinquent" youths, who seldom suppress discordant affect, are spared psychosomatic illness. Unfortunately much of the research in this area is methodologically suspect, and there is no evidence for such views as that of Pincus and Dare (1978), who consider asthma to be "the literal suffocation of the anger which cannot be expressed". It is true that many asthmatics have difficulty expressing anger, as do many non-asthmatics, but a large number are well able to give vent to their anger.

(3) Suggestibility

The degree of suggestibility of any person plays a part in determining the course of his illness and the response to treatment. This concept comprehensively reviewed by Rachman and Philips (1978) applies particularly to symptoms such as pain, disorders like asthma, and the use of symptomatic treatments.

(4) Attitudes

The "patient" may respond to his illness with a wide range of attitudes to not only his illness, but also the doctor and his treatment. This attitude-spectrum is outlined in Fig. 3. Either extreme represents an unhealthy adjustment, and is likely to be part of a pathological process within the system. The concept of the attitude-spectrum and its associated emotional responses such as anger, guilt, despair, fear or resentment has been comprehensively described by Pless and Pinkerton (1975).

Fig. 3

(5) Conflict

There is no doubt that conflict is a central feature of our everyday lives. Among the many "defence mechanisms" for coping with conflict is that of "somatization". This term was first used by William Stekel, and later Freud (1905) when referring to what we now describe as hysterical conversion. I use it to describe the process by which distress is expressed in physical terms. Between 50% and 70% of a general population consult their doctors with functional (non-organic) somatic complaints (Langner and Michael, 1963), and the persistent somatizer has received full recognition (Lowy, 1977). The significance of somatized conflict in the interaction between illness and the family has been fully documented by Minuchin et al. (1978).

C. Extrafamilial Factors

The attitude-spectrum (Fig. 3) applies also to important persons outside the family such as employers and teachers, peers and friends, and doctors and nurses. Any of these may be overaccepting and overprotective, or rejecting or denying. Further the "patient" may become overdependent on, or rejecting of the doctor and the treatment (Lask and Kirk, 1979).

Consideration must also be given to other relevant extrafamilial factors such as examinations, interviews and changes of job, school or housing.

D. Intrafamilial Factors

There is only limited practical difference between the consideration of a family with physical illness, and one without illness. A careful assessment of the family is required with attention being paid to all the relevant aspects of its structure and function, including its stability, harmony, equilibrium and transactional characteristics. The illness requires due consideration in the same way as any other aspect of the family system. Note will be made of the role of the illness in the family, the attitudes and reactions to it, its effects on family life, and its relevance to family homeostasis.

E. Comment

It will be seen from the case illustrations below that using the conceptual model described, there is no requirement for specificity in terms of attitudes, personality-types, family constellations or transactional characteristics. The wide range of each of these is recognized, and the interaction between the various components is emphasized.

VIII. CLINICAL APPLICATION

The family therapist's approach to illness in the family should be the same whatever the reason for the family being seen, whether the illness is seemingly incidental, or it is taking its toll on the family life or because there is doubt as to its cause. Although the significance of the environment in the precipitation and maintenance of the disorder may vary, the physical manifestation is genuine, and of intense importance to the "patient" and his family. The therapist can use discussion of the illness as a method of observing the mode of function of the family system.

A. The Differing Role of Illness

The first three examples illustrate the differing role of illness in the family and the range of reactions to it.

(1) Clinical Examples: The A's "Denial Patterns"

A middle-class professional couple, the A's, had adopted two children after failing to have children of their own. When these children were 7 and 5 respectively, Mrs A developed multiple sclerosis. The illness ran a typically fluctuant course with periods of normality and other times when Mrs A was confined to a wheelchair. Neither parent could admit to the severity of the illness or to the effect it was having on the children. For example, Mr A would allow his wife to take the children on holiday to remote areas of the countryside despite her considerable difficulties. Any suggestion of weakness or vulnerability in any member of the family was suppressed, and perfection was demanded.

As the elder child, Jim, approached adolescence and started seeking some autonomy, his age-appropriate behaviour was forbidden, and his mother increasingly infantilized him in an attempt to keeping him as a "perfect" and conforming child. His reactive protests increased in severity until eventually he ran away and committed a variety of offences. There was an immediate relapse of the multiple sclerosis with subsequent return of the wayward son to the family fold, and renewed promises of good behaviour. This repetitive pattern led ultimately to Jim being taken into care.

This extreme denial of the severity of the illness was an unhealthy adaption to a handicapping condition, and it was linked to the unrealistic and impossible demand for perfection which forced one of the children into a delinquent mode of behaviour. His delinquency coincided with relapses of the disease, which remitted on his return. A close interaction can be seen between multiple sclerosis, the denial, the demands for perfection and the delinquency. The opposite extreme to denial, overacceptance and overprotection plays a major part in the next example.

(2) Exploring the Interaction between Illness and Family Functioning

The second example demonstrates how important it is to understand the interaction between illness and family functioning.

A 35-year-old teacher, Mrs R, divorced her husband two years after he had developed a crisis of identity which he was unable to resolve. His behaviour included having temper tantrums, lying in bed for days on end, and then joining a hippy cult. She had chosen as her second husband a man who was ambitious, competitive and keen to please, completely the opposite in character to her first. The reconstituted family consisted of Mr and Mrs R, Christine 10, and Sean 8. Christine had been referred because of a long history of defiance, rudeness and temper tantrums, particularly in relation to her stepfather. Mr R was wary of showing his feelings for fear of being compared with Christine's father. Supported in this by his wife, he failed to express any of his own distress or anger at the situation. In addition, Mrs R discouraged him from taking disciplinary action against Christine, feeling that as her mother she was the only person who should do this. Mr R had a heart-attack within three months of their marriage.

Individual, analytically-orientated psychotherapy, aimed at helping Christine see that through her behaviour she was both expressing her identification with her real father and displacing her anger and hurt feelings from him to her stepfather, had little effect. Mr and Mrs R asked for further help. The therapist insisted on family meetings, which were dominated by Christine's rude and defiant behaviour. When Mr R made unconvincing and unsuccessful attempts to control Christine, his wife would protect her, but when this was pointed out, both parents rationalized their actions and returned the focus to Christine who happily accepted it.

An important point in the therapy occurred during the third session.

Mrs R: Christine can be really odious at times.

Christine: No I'm not, you two are odious.

Mr R: If only you weren't so rude we would all get on much better and . . .

Mrs R: But you do provoke her by telling her off so much . . .

Christine: [to Mr R] Yes it's your fault, you silly fool.

Mr. R: You see you're doing it again.

Therapist: I think you're all doing it again: you, Mrs R, make a comment about Christine; Christine responds aggressively; you, Mr R, attack Christine; and you, Mrs R, then defend her.

Mrs R: Yes that's right, she gets between us, what can we do?

Christine: Go off and stuff yourselves.

Sean: Christine gets all the attention, you never talk about me.

Mr R: Yes well let's talk about you. Why don't you do your homework?

Sean: I do.

Mr R: No you don't, you sit around watching television and finding all sorts of excuses for not doing it.

Mrs R: But he's only 8, you can't expect him to do much homework.

Therapist: It seems like Sean comes between you as well.

Mrs R: Well I have to protect Sean from David's criticism; he does go on at him a lot.

Mr R: I don't think protect is the right word, it's more like seeing his point of view.

Therapist: Hold it . . . the same thing's happening now with Sean. Either Sean or Christine is the focus of attention, the two of you as parents disagree, and you Mrs R side with one of them, I point this out, and you then philosophize about it: "protect" or "point of view". I think you're avoiding something between the two of you, some sort of conflict.

Mr R: No you've got it wrong—we don't have any conflict, sometimes we disagree, and other times we . . .

Therapist: Okay, not a conflict. Sometimes you have a problem working effectively as a couple.

Mr R: Yes that's right. I feel like an undermined policeman. I'm expected to control the children, but when I tell them off, I get told off myself.

Mrs R: But it's when you pick on them, especially Christine. You're always picking on her, and I know you don't like her, but I just don't know what to do about that.

Therapist: There are times when you feel really angry with each other, like now, but it never gets sorted out.

Mrs R: But I don't know what will happen if I have it out with David. I don't know if he'll get upset and feel hurt, or go quiet and sulky, or take it out on the children more, or what.

Therapist: Or even have another heart-attack.

Mrs R: Yes . . . [cries]

Therapist: You can't really have it out with David because you're frightened he'll have another heart-attack, so you snipe at him instead, through the children, and things never get sorted out.

Mrs R: That makes sense.

Mr R: So what do we do?

The therapist's offer of a couple of sessions just for the parents was eagerly accepted.

They started the next session by saying they did not need marital therapy, did not think Christine was caught up in any disagreement, and they simply wanted advice on management. The therapist asked for an example of an incident over which they had had difficulty, and the parents gave a perfect description of how they had disagreed over management. Christine had defied her stepfather's request to do something and had sworn at him. Mrs R, feeling angry with her husband for making an unreasonable demand but not wishing to hurt him by expressing this, had invited Christine to join him doing something else.

The therapist encouraged Mr and Mrs R to work out an alternative response for a similar situation, and in so doing, considerable pent-up feeling was expressed. Afterwards Mr R said to his wife "and you needn't worry. I haven't got angina". In succeeding sessions, they shared their previously covert fears of further serious illness. Gradually they learned to confront and support each other. This model of discussing and resolving disagreement helped Christine find a more acceptable way of expressing her own feelings, and Mr R remained well himself.

In this example, there was a circular interaction between an inability to cope with conflict, a serious illness, and fear of recurrence of the illness. The successful intervention was based on an understanding of this interaction, after an attempt to help one individual with her intrapsychic distress had failed.

IX.   FAMILY THERAPY IN PAEDIATRIC SETTINGS

In North America, collaborative work between paediatricians and family therapists seems commonplace. Carey and Sibinga (1972) consider the illness, the child, the family and the paediatrician as separate-but-interacting participants. Sack (1978), having analysed the child psychiatry consultations in a paediatric hospital concludes that paediatric hospitals can serve as a disguised mental health facility for a sizeable number of children and their families. Schneidermann *et al.* (1976) always assess the families of children with fatal lipid-storage disease. Tomm *et al.* (1977) have described the treatment of juvenile diabetes using family therapy, as have Hughes and Zimin (1978) for childhood abdominal pain. Minuchin *et al.* (1978) and Minuchin and Fishman (1979) have outlined the family approach to the treatment of a number of psychosomatic disorders. Russak and Friedman (1970) consider the involvement of the paediatric resident in family interviewing to be an essential part of his training. Allmond *et al.*, paediatricians in California, have described their own use of family therapy in their practice (1979).

It is not all sweetness and light, however, in North America. Bolian (1971) has described situations where parents initiated and demanded psychiatric consultations over the objections of the attending physician, and others where he has been asked to see a child surreptitiously so that the objecting parents would not know.

Paediatricians in Britain have long preceded child psychiatrists in calling for a family approach to childhood illness. They have commented on the complex interplay of family and illness (Miller *et al.*, 1970), and the relationship between family patterning and childhood disorder (Apley, 1963). This attitude is best summarized by another paediatrician, Weller (1975), who, when referring to childhood illness, stated:

> By failing to see the whole family as a collective patient, we run the risk of adding to the burden on the community. Not only may the child have to be re-admitted, but the damage to the family may mean more calls on the general practitioner and the social services, both now and in the future, as the stresses wreak havoc on the personalities of the next generation.

The problems of linking the practice of family therapy to the organization and philosophy of a paediatric or general hospital can be enormous. Clearly, there will be many differences between in- and outpatient work. Working in the latter, more self-contained setting, the therapist not only has to contend with structural problems such as space and time, but is aware also that the attitudes of the referring paediatrician as well as the family are often influential. Churven (1978) has investigated the attitudes of families referred to a Child Psychiatry Department of a general hospital to the idea of family assessment and treatment and on the whole found them to be favourable.

A. Initiating Family Therapy on a Paediatric Ward

A *sine qua non* for the successful use of family therapy in a paediatric setting is a multi-disciplinary team. The joint philosophies of such combined team-work, and the family approach have to be integrated into those of the ward. Successful therapy is dependent upon a mutually trusting relationship in which the family therapist, whatever his or her professional training, is considered an equal with a specific contribution to make to the welfare of the child and his family. Such a relationship can only be built up over a period of time in the context of frequent, regular meetings in which there is an open sharing of views between the family therapist and the medical and nursing staff.

B. Principles to Facilitate a Family Therapy Approach

(1) The early involvement of the family therapist in the management of the case is essential. If the parents know from the first day of the hospital admission that an interest is taken in not just part of the child but the whole child, and not just one member of the family but the whole family, and that this is a normal and natural part of the process, then the required transitions are more easily achieved.

The family therapist should meet the family with a paediatrician within a few days of admission. This meeting may be used both to convey the results of observations and investigations, and to continue the process of helping the family in their transition from perceiving their child as physically ill to understanding that they all have a vital part to play in their child's recovery. When necessary, further explanations are offered of the mechanism by which emotional arousal can precipitate physical symptoms. Exploration of family relationships continues (the paediatrician admitting the child will have already discussed this issue with the parents).

This phase of assessment and conversion may be brief or prolonged. As soon as possible, however, the therapist should prepare a formulation and decide on the aims of therapy, and who shall be involved in the treatment. There are good reasons for the continuing involvement of the paediatrician during the hospitalization.

(2) The use of the paediatrician as co-therapist provides an important bridge for the families. Within the security of a medical nexus, a family finds it easier to look at the different strands involved in illness. The paediatrician's presence in sessions assists the therapist to cope more effectively with the tendency of families to seek organic explanations. The combination of paediatrician and family therapist can help the family at a symbolic level to appreciate the interaction between physical symptoms and family relationships. The paediatrician may be able to add relevant observations about events affecting the family on the ward between sessions. Finally, he gains from the experience of assessment and treatment of family problems. Although an overall family perspective is retained, other modes of therapy may be incorporated, either as complementary to or an alternative to family therapy.

X. WHEN SHOULD FAMILY THERAPY BE OFFERED?

A. Indications and Contraindications

In the light of present knowledge, and in the absence of appropriate research, no one can say with any certainty what the indications and contraindications are for family therapy. In general, I agree with Bloch and La Perrière (1973) who use family therapy for all conditions where some form of psychotherapy is indicated, unless a specific contraindication can be found. It is worth remembering Haley's point (1970) that any form of intervention is an intervention in the family. In the context of this chapter, contraindications include practical considerations such as the refusal or inability of a key member to attend sessions, or problems related to travelling long distances. Even so, I have treated families who travel 200 miles each way once a week for treatment. Such families invariably seem to do well! The only families I have found unsuitable are those containing severely paranoid individuals. I do not agree with Bloch and La Perrière (1973), Martin (1977) or Elton (1979) who all consider serious illness as a contraindication to family therapy. Satir (1978) recommends family therapy whatever the diagnosis. Stewart and Johansen (1976) use such an approach for end-stage renal disease and Cohen and Wellisch (1978) have described the treatment of families in which one person has cancer. Minuchin, Rosman and Baker (1978) and Lask and Matthew (1979) have described replicable studies which claim to show that family therapy can improve the outcome of serious illness.

B.   Particular Indications

I have found family therapy in a paediatric setting to be of particular value for the following problems:

(1) the presenting symptoms are physical, but psychological factors are of major importance in the aetiology and maintenance of the condition,

(2) adjustment to physical illness or handicap,

(3) adjustment to mental retardation and developmental delay,

(4) relationship difficulties between parents and pre-school children as manifested by screaming, tantrums, sleeping and feeding disorders, and failure to thrive,

(5) specific problems arising from such aspects of hospitalization as separation, special investigations, and painful and immobilizing treatments.

XI.   CRISIS INTERVENTION

Central to the use of family therapy is the element of crisis, created by the hospital admission, i.e. period of disequilibrium overpowering the family's homeostatic mechanisms. The family in such a state of crisis has a unique potential for change, for it is faced with a new problem that requires novel solutions (Spiegel, 1957 p. 15).

A.   Case Example: Rachel and her Family

Rachel, 5, the eldest of four children, was referred to the psychiatrist and paediatrician jointly by a local psychiatrist who had been unable, on an outpatient basis, to help the family deal with her compulsive over-eating, sullenness and temper-tantrums. On the ward, Rachel was well-behaved and happy, with no over-eating, except at the times her family visited, when she became miserable and demanding. The family meeting was initially chaotic with all the children shouting, crying and making demands. The parents responded inconsistently, and their only predictable response was either to neglect or discipline Rachel. At the next family meeting, the psychiatrist instructed the parents to control the children and divide their attention equally. At the third meeting, Rachel's parents stated, much to the psychiatrist's surprise, that they had been missing Rachel while she was in hospital, felt they had been giving too much attention to the other children, neglecting her and then resenting her reaction (a perfect formulation). During the course of a couple of weekends at home, they seemed to be able to adjust their handling of her, and she lost some weight. At three months' follow-up she had not gained any appreciable weight, and was obviously happier. Her parents said that everything was better.

Such a positive use of hospital admission is also valuable in helping children with chronic or handicapping conditions and their families to adjust their responses to the problem. Similarly, this approach can be used to involve the extended family who so often profoundly affect the nuclear family's reaction to illness, and who can in other situations be significantly inaccessible.

B.   Chloe and her Family

Chloe S, aged 2, was admitted for the investigation of her failure to thrive, severe sleep disturbance and tantrums. Her parents had married against the wishes of their own parents when they were both 17. Chloe's father was unemployed and her mother was studying at a local art college. The maternal grandparents lived in the same area, and the grandmother would visit her daughter every day. She denigrated the attempts of Mr and Mrs S to be parents, and imposed her own views on child-rearing. The young couple were increasingly undermined, and eventually lost any confidence they had. Their inability to cope reinforced Chloe's behaviour problems.

The medical social worker and a paediatrician-in-training arranged a series of meetings, initially for Chloe and all four adults, and later separate sessions for the parents and grandparents. The aims of this treatment were to (a) distinguish between the parental and grandparental roles, (b) increase parental confidence and autonomy, (c) establish and consolidate the appropriate nuclear family, and (d) enhance the relationship between the grandparents to offset the loss of their parenting role.

The nursing staff taught Chloe's parents how to manage her behaviour problems, and particularly her sleep disturbance. They pointedly discouraged the grandparents from usurping and undermining the parents, while encouraging them to play with Chloe and take her for trips to the park.

Chloe gradually improved, and was soon able to go home with her parents for a night at a time, and later for weekends. Six weeks after admission she was discharged, having gained a considerable amount of weight and lost her behaviour problems. The first three aims of treatment had been achieved, but the grandparents continued to need help with their "loss".

An unexpected and additional effect of this treatment was that the paediatrician, impressed with this approach, decided to undertake a training as a child psychiatrist.

XII. PITFALLS OF FAMILY THERAPY IN PAEDIATRIC SETTINGS

A. Pace of Work

It is essential to work at the family's own pace in the development of their understanding of the problem. Such families may not anticipate or accept the relevance of a family approach to their child's problems. Admission to hospital may imply considerable difficulties in unravelling the problem in the outpatients' department, or difficulty for the paediatrician in conveying the psychological aspects of the diagnosis of the child's problem. Often the family have a strong need to perceive the problem as based in the child's illness. Such high levels of resistance have sometimes been compounded by previous experiences in which a psychological explanation might have been offered in a ham-fisted way. Such families can cling to a medical model with tenacity and determination.

Resistant and disturbed families can increase the already numerous stresses experienced by ward staff. Regular team discussions are essential to support the staff involved and enable them to continue to work effectively. Without these, there are the risks of unconstructive overlap and professional rivalry in the contacts with the family.

The father of a 13-year-old girl who had been admitted for investigation of weight-loss and subsequently diagnosed by the psychiatrist as depressed, brought in presents for all the nursing and medical staff, but not for the psychiatrist who had successfully treated the family!

B. Over-identification with Children and Parents

Less experienced staff need support and advice to avoid over-identification with or judgment of families. They have to learn to be not only caring and uncritical, but also able to cope with criticism and hostility from parents. In parent–child relationship problems especially, often young and immature parents may themselves require parenting and lessons in new ways of managing their children. That this may be provided by nurses younger than themselves can create resentment and bewilderment.

Joan, aged 3, the youngest of three children, had a six-month history of recurrent vomiting, extensively investigated without success elsewhere. She was admitted obviously ill and seriously dehydrated. Further assessment confirmed our initial suspicion that she had cyclical (psychogenic) vomiting. Her parents reacted to this diagnosis with disbelief and resentment, feeling that their parenting skills were being questioned. They reminded us that their elder children had no problems. Their resentment was accentuated by Joan's improvement in their absence. They embarked upon a systematic campaign of criticism of and complaint about every aspect of Joan's management. Many nurses were reduced to tears, and one of the doctors repeated overt expressions of anger at the parents. Several staff meetings were necessary to help everyone understand what had happened, and how to respond.

XIII.   ILLUSTRATIONS FROM THE T FAMILY

This case illustrates the significance of many points made previously, and in particular emphasizes the combined roles of the paediatrician and the family therapist, the problems relating to the necessary conceptual changes both for the family and the staff, the effective use of a crisis, the support necessary for nursing staff, and the use of additional modes of therapy.

A.   The Family Constellation

Caroline, 13, had been admitted with a six-month history of anorexia nervosa. Her parents had separated six years previously, and her mother had remarried three years later. The reconstituted family consisted of the stepfather, Mr T, a businessman in his late 40s; Caroline's mother, Mrs T, an ex-secretary in her mid-40s; Pauline, 18; and Andrea, 17; the daughters of Mr T's first marriage; and Marilyn 17; Caroline, 13; and Fiona, 9, the daughters of Mrs T's first marriage. The stepfather was an overweight intellectualizer, who tended to sit back, puff his pipe and avoid important issues. Mrs T was the opposite, intensively and dramatically involved, highly loquacious. She was receiving treatment for alcoholism, but currently "dry". All the girls were upset and bewildered by what was happening. A series of meetings with the reconstituted family and one with Caroline and her biological parents allowed the following formulation. Caroline played a central role in the family, being caught up in unresolved conflicts between:
  (1) her mother and stepfather,
  (2) her father and stepfather,
  (3) her biological parents
as well as being the person her mother leant on during drinking bouts. The family pointed to her central position by all agreeing that they felt safer when Caroline was at home. There were unclear boundaries between the two families, with much unexpressed and unrecognized anger and sadness, and the three youngest children all felt personally responsible for the disharmony.

B.   The Family Therapy Contract

A contract was made for weekly family meetings with the social worker and paediatrician as co-therapists, and a behavioural programme instituted to help Caroline gain weight. For the first month there was no appreciable change, after which Caroline dramatically deteriorated until she was only half her expected weight. In the family meetings much of the conflict had come into the open, the sessions became increasingly distressing, but the family resisted change, persistently denying the severity of their distress, and "covering-up" at the start of each session. The parents particularly insisted that this was a problem within Caroline and not to do with them.

C. Initial Work

Caroline complained of her humiliation related to the behavioural programme and pleaded for more autonomy. She begged to be allowed a weekend at home where she lost yet more weight. The therapists concerned by her progressive deterioration offered her a choice between stricter behavioural controls and tube-feeding. Despite her mother's plea to the contrary, Caroline chose tube-feeds and accused her mother of wanting her to die, for why else would she oppose tube-feeding? The nursing staff were split in their reactions, some feeling resentful of Caroline's verbal abuse at them, others feeling sorry for her, and angry with the doctors for "force-feeding" her, and so upsetting her in the family meeting.

After two weeks of tube-feeding, Caroline had regained all the weight lost while in hospital. The therapists used this critical period to emphasize the severity of the problem, and challenge some of the defences.

D. Extract of Session

The following extract illustrates the family's tendency to deny and detour conflict, to accommodate and intellectualize.

Mrs T: I suppose the real problem is that I have always leaned on Caroline especially when I'm drinking. You see I've always felt closest to her, we have an understanding of each other, and a sort of respect. This must be difficult for you to understand though I suppose you might have seen families like us before. No, I don't think that's likely. Anyhow I don't think the rest of the family appreciate how it feels for us and . . .

Therapist: Caroline, can you respond to what your mum's saying?

Caroline: Well, yes, you see I love Mummy so much . . .

Therapist: I wonder why your wife can't lean on you, Mr T.

Mrs T: I lean on everyone, on Richard, on the girls, not just Caroline. You see being an alcoholic is like . . .

Therapist: I asked your husband.

Mr T: I become unsympathetic after a time. I can stand so much, but there's a limit. I attend Al-Anon, and there we're told what makes alcoholics do the things. You see my wife's a special case, and I have to not let her lean on me too much. But anyhow this really hasn't anything to do with Caroline . . .

Mrs T: Oh yes, oh yes it has, Richard. It has everything to do with Caroline. You see so much has happened to both of us even before you came to the scene, and when you get angry we're closer together . . .

Mr T: But don't you think Doctor that the anorexia arises from within Caroline;
it hasn't anything to do with the family and Jean's drinking? In fact I read an
article about it and it said that there are all sorts of hormonal changes and
that these take away the appetite.

Therapist: Look, I think if we start discussing hormones we'll be avoiding more
important issues. I'd like to hear how you react, Mrs T, to your husband's
lack of sympathy and his describing you as a case.

Caroline: It's not Daddy's fault, he tries very hard; it's not Mummy's either. It's
all my fault because I don't eat. If only I ate everyone would be very
happy.

Mrs T: I don't blame Richard or Caroline. Richard's right to get angry with me.
I am really impossible . . .

Therapist: Yes but sometimes I guess he could help you.

Mrs T: Only by not shouting and bullying us when . . .

Mr T: Shout? Me? I'm amazingly good-tempered.

Mrs T: Oh, Richard, you know we're always arguing, we've argued since the day
we married. Someone said it was a marriage of convenience and they were
right, you just don't want to see it.

Caroline: Oh, shut up.

Mr T: So what's wrong with a marriage of convenience?

Therapist: Why did Caroline say "shut up"?

Caroline: I can't stand Mummy's way of speaking when she speaks like that. It
goes right through me. I can't stand it. I wish you'd shut up.

Mrs T. What is it about how I speak?

Therapist: How can we help Caroline and the others not to rescue the two of you
when you're trying to work something out between you?

Mrs T: Well we're okay really. The girls understand, and they just go out of the
room if Richard and I want to discuss something.

Caroline: Then you shout at us for always going out.

Mr T: No Caroline, only at meal-times when you should be eating with us. You
see it really all comes back to her not eating [!]

Therapist: I think we'll make more progress if we ban discussion of Caroline's not
eating. This may sound odd to you, but Caroline has a life-threatening illness. You've come to us for help, and you're going to have to accept our
advice.

E. Response to Work

After several weeks, the conflict between Mr and Mrs T became the central
focus. Caroline continued to gain weight both in hospital and at home during
weekends, until she was discharged having reached the third percentile.
Family therapy continued on a long-term basis after Caroline's discharge. The
family continued to use a number of defences but slowly changed. Despite many
periods of concern and threats to withdraw from treatment, the situation slowly
improved, and Caroline had maintained a most satisfactory weight-gain one year
after discharge.

F. The Paediatrician's Role

Throughout Caroline's hospital admission, there was realistic concern about her physical state, which required constant monitoring. At one stage, day-to-day decisions were necessary regarding life-saving measures. The family's understandable concern often intruded upon treatment, but the use of a paediatrician as co-therapist proved particularly opportune in that it was possible for the therapists to deal with anxieties at a factual level at the start of each session. Practical decisions could be made by the paediatrician while the social worker, as the experienced therapist, controlled the rest of the session.

XIV. CONCLUSIONS

The successful application of family therapy in physical illness and in hospital settings is dependent upon the attitudes and co-operation of such staff as paediatricians and nurses. They start from a similar position to that of the client, expecting an organic, didactic and individual approach to childhood psychological and psychosomatic problems. Their bewilderment at a family approach may parallel that experienced by the family therapist who discovers that a colleague whom he expected to treat a family had in fact not seen the parents at all, and had prescribed a tranquillizer for the child.

The family therapist must understand the other's position, put himself into his colleague's conceptual framework and educate from that point. Education, like therapy, is a two-way process, and discussion and explanation are essential components. Repetition of points may be as necessary an education as is the repetitive challenging of rigidity or enmeshment.

The essence of such work is the use of a multi-disciplinary team which meets regularly and is able to discuss freely its difference and reach some resolution — just like any functional family.

Acknowledgements to Liza Bingley for teaching me so much about liaison.

REFERENCES

Alexander, F. (1961). "The Scope of Psychoanalysis", Basic Books, New York.

Alexander, F., French, T. and Pollock, G. (1968). "Psychosomatic Specificity", University of Chicago Press, Chicago.

Allmond, B., Buchman, W. and Gofman, H. (1979). "The Family is the Patient", C. V. Mosby Co. London.

Apley, J. (1963). Family patterning and childhood illness. *Lancet* Jan. 12, 67–70.

Apley, J., McKeith, R. and Meadow, R. (1978). "The Child and His Symptoms", Third edition. Blackwell, London.

Bastiaans, J. and Groen J. (1955). Psychogenesis and Psychotherapy of Bronchial Asthma. *In* "Modern Trends in Psychosomatic Medicine", (D. O'Neill, ed.), Hoeber, New York.

Bingley, L., Leonard, J., Hensman, S., Lask, B. and Wolff, O. (1980). The comprehensive management of children on a paediatric ward—a family approach. *Arch. Dis. Child.* **55**, 555-561.

Bloch, D. A. and La Perrière, K. (1973). *In* "Techniques of Family Therapy—A Conceptual Framework", (D. A. Bloch, ed.), Grune and Stratton, New York.

Block, J. (1969). Parents of schizophrenic, neurotic, asthmatic and congenitally ill children. *Arch. Gen. Psych.*, **20**, 650-674.

Bolian, G. (1971). Psychiatric consultation within a community of sick children. *J. Amer. Acad. Child Psych.* **10**, 2, 293-307.

Carey, W. and Sibinga, M. (1972). Avoiding paediatric pathogenesis in the management of acute minor illness. *Paediatrics* **49**, 4, 553-562.

Chassin, L., Perelman, M. and Weinberger, G. (1974). Psychotherapy: theory. *Research and Practice* **11**, 4, 387-399.

Churven, P. (1978). Families: parental attitudes to family assessment in a child psychiatry setting. *Journal of Child Psychol. and Psychiat.* **19**, 1, 33-42.

Cobb, S. (1972), "The intrafamilial transmission of rheumatoid arthritis", *J. Chronic Diseases*, **25**, 193-225.

Cohen, M. and Wellisch, D. (1978). Living in Limbo—psychosocial interventions in families with a cancer patient. *Amer. J. of Psychotherapy* **32**, 4, 561-571.

Crain, A., Sussman, M. and Weill, W. (1966). Family interaction, diabetes and sibling relationships. *Int. J. Soc. Psychiatry*, **11**, 35-43.

Dunbar, H. (1954). "Emotions and Bodily Changes", Fourth edition. Columbia University Press, New York.

Elton, A. (1979). Indications for selecting family or individual therapy. *J. of Family Therapy*, **I**, 193-201.

Finch, S. and Hess, J. (1962). Ulcerative colitis in children. *Amer. J. Psychiatry*, **118**, 819-826.

Fitzelle, G. (1959). Personality factors and certain attitudes towards child rearing practises among parents of asthmatic children. *Psychosomatic Medicine*, **28**, 323-332.

Friedman, M. and Rosenman, R. (1974). "Type A Behaviour and your Heart", Alfred A. Knopf, New York.

Freud, S. (1905). "Fragment of a Case of Hysteria", (Standard edition 7:41) Hogarth Press 1953, London.

Gath, A. (1978). "Down's Syndrome and the Family: The Early Years", Academic Press, London and New York.

Gehre, S. and Kirschenbaum, M. (1967). Survival patterns in conjoint family therapy. *Fam. Proc.*, **6**, 65-80.

Goldberg, E. (1958). "Family Influences and Psychosomatic Illness", Tavistock Publications, London.

Grolnick, L. (1972). "A family perspective of psychosomatic factors in illness", *Fam. Proc.*, **11**, 457-486.

Haley, J. (1970). Family Therapy. *International Journal of Psychiatry* **9**, 233-242.

Harkin, H. (1979). A family-orientated psychiatric in-patient unit. *Family Process* **18**, 3, 281-292.

Hoebel, F. (1977). Coronary Artery Disease and Family Interaction: A Study of Risk Factor Modification. *In* "The International View", (P. Watzlawick and J. Weakland, eds), Norton Press, New York.

Hopkins, P. (1959). Health, happiness and the family. *Brit. J. Clin. Practice*, **13**, 311-313.

Hughes, M. and Zimin, R. (1978). Children with psychogenic abdominal pain and their families. *Clinical Paediatrics*, **17**, 560-573.

Jackson, D. and Yalom, I. (1966). Family research on the problems of ulcerative colitis. *Arch. Gen. Psych.*, **15**, 410-418.

Johnson, A., Shapiro, L. and Alexander, F. (1947). Study of rheumatoid arthritis. *Psychosomatic Medicine*, **9**, 295-304.

Kellner, R. (1963). "An Investigation in General Practice", Tavistock Publications, London.

Kreitman, N. (1964). The patient's spouse. *Brit. J. Psychiatry*, **110**, 159-170.

Langner, T. and Michael, S. (1963). "The Mid-Town Manhattan Study: Life Stress and Mental Health", Vol. 2 McGraw Hill, New York.

Lask, B. (1980). Illness in the Family: A Conceptual Model. *In* "Family Therapy: Collected Papers", (S. Walrond-Skinner, ed.), Routledge & Kegan Paul, London.

Lask, B. and Matthew, D. (1979). Childhood asthma: a controlled trial of family psychotherapy. *Arch. Dis. Childhood*, **54**, 116-119.

Lavigne, J. and Ryan, M. (1979). Psychological adjustment of siblings of children with chronic illness. *Paediatrics*, **63**, 616-627.

Liebman, R., Honig, P. and Berger, H. (1976). An integrated treatment programme for psychogenic abdominal pain. *Family Process*, **15**, 397-406.

Liebman, R., Minuchin, S. and Baker, L. (1974a). The use of structural family therapy in the treatment of intractable asthma. *Amer. J. Psychiatry*, **131**, 432-436.

Liebman, R., Minuchin, S. and Baker, L. (1974b). The role of the family in the treatment of anorexia nervosa. *Amer. J. Acad. Child Psychiatry*, **13**, 264-274.

Lipowski, L. (1968). Review of consultation psychiatry and psychosomatic medicine. *Psychosomatic Medicine*, **30**, 395-422.

Lipowski, Z., Lipsitt, D. and Whybrow, P. (1977). (eds), "Psychosomatic Medicine — Current Trends and Clinical Application", Oxford University Press, New York.

Lowy, F. (1977). Management of the Persistent Somatiser. *In* "Psychosomatic Medicine", (Z. Lipowski, D. Lipsitt and P. Whybrow, eds), Oxford University Press, New York.

Martin, F. (1977). Some implications from the theory and practice of family therapy for individual therapy and vice-versa. *British J. of Medical Psychology*, **50**, 53-64.

Mechanic, D. (1977). Illness behaviour, adaptation and illness. *J. Nerv. and Mental Disease*, **165**, 83.

Meissner, W. (1966). Family dynamics and psychosomatic process. *Family Process*, **5**, 142-161.

Meyer, R. and Zaggerty, R. (1962). Streptococcal infections in families. *Paediatrics*, 539-549.

Miller, F., Court, S. Walton, W. and Knox, E. (1960). "Growing Up in Newcastle-upon-Tyne", Oxford University Press, London.

Minuchin, S., Rosman, B. and Baker, L. (1978). "Psychosomatic Families", Harvard Press, New York.

Minuchin, S. and Fishman, H. (1979). The psychosomatic family in child psychiatry. *J. of Amer. Acad. of Child Psychiatry* **18**, 1, 76-90.

Nemiah, J. and Sifneos, P. (1970). Affect and Fantasy in Patients with Psychosomatic Disorders. *In* "Modern Trends in Psychosomatic Medicine", Vol. 2. (O. W. Hill, ed.), Butterworth, London.

Paulley, J. (1976, 1977). Psychological management of multiple sclerosis. *Psychotherapy and Psychosomatics*, **27**, 26-40.

Peachey, R. (1963). Family patterns of stress. *General Practitioner*, **27**, 82-87.

Perrin, G. and Pierce, I. (1959). Psychosomatic aspects of cancer — a review. *Psychosomatic Medicine*, **21**, 397-421.

Pincus, L. and Dare, C. (1978). "Secrets in the Family", Faber and Faber, London.

Pinkerton, P. (1967). Correlating physiologic with psychodynamic data in the study and management of childhood asthma. *Journal of Psychosomatic Research*, **11**, 11-25.

Pless, I. and Pinkerton, P. (1975). "Chronic Childhood Disorders", Kimpton Publications, London.

Rachman, J. and Phillips, C. (1978). "Psychology and Medicine", Penguin, London.

Reddihough, D., Landau, L., Jones, J. and Richards, W. (1977). Family anxieties in childhood asthma. *Australian Paediatric Journal*, **13**, 295-298.

Rees, L. (1963). The significance of parental attitudes in asthma. *Journal of Psychosomatic Research*, **7**, 181-190.

Russak, S. and Friedman, D. (1970). Family interviewing and paediatric training. *Clinical Paediatrics*, **9**, 10, 594-598.

Sack, W. (1978). Making the second diagnosis. *Clinical Paediatrics*, **17**, 7, 548-550.

Satir, V. (1978). "Conjoint Family Therapy", Souvenir Press, London.

Schneidermann, G., Lowden, J. and Rae-Grant, Q. (1976). Family reactions, physician responses and management issues in fatal lipid storage diseases. *Clinical Paediatrics* **15**, 10, 887-790.

Schonfeld, W. (1966). Body image disturbances in adolescence. *Arch. Gen. Psych.* **15**, 16-23.

Shellack, D. (1957). Neurosenpsychologischke Faktoren in der Aetiologie und Pathogenese der Tonsillitis. I. *Z. Psychosoma. Med.* **3**, 265-276.

Spiegel, J. (1957). The resolution of role conflict within the family. *Psychiatry*, **20**, 1-15.

Stein, S. and Charles, E. (1971). Emotional factors in juvenile diabetes mellitus. *Amer. J. Psychiat.*, **128**, 56-60.

Stewart, L. (1962). Social and Emotional Adjustment during Adolescence as related to Development of Psychosomatic Illness in Adulthood. *Psychol. Monogr.*, **65**, 175-215.

Stewart, S. and Johansen, R. (1976). *Psychotherapy and Psychosomatics*, **27**, 86-92.

Tal, A. and Miklich, D. (1976). Emotional induced decreases in peak flow rate in asthmatic children. *Psychosomatic Medicine*, **38**, 190-200.

Titchener, J., Riskin, J. and Emerson, R. (1960). The family in psychosomatic process. *Psychosomatic Medicine*, **22**, 127-142.

Tomm, C., McArthur, R. and Leahey, M. (1977). Psychologic management of children with diabetes mellitus. *Clinical Paediatrics*. **16**, 1151-55.

Tomm, K., McArthur, R. and Leahey, M. (1977). Psychologic management of children with diabetes mellitus. *Clinical Paediatrics*, **16**, 12, 1151-1155.

Weller, S. (1975). The patient is the family. *World Medicine*. Nov. 19, 36-38.

Wikran, R., Faleide, A. and Blakar, R. (1978). Communication in the family of the asthmatic child. *Acta. Psychiat. Scand.* **57**, 11-26.

Williams, J. (1975). Aspects of dependence-independence conflict in children with asthma. *J. Child Psychol. and Psychiat.* **16**, 199-218.

Witkin, H. (1965). Psychological differentiation and forms of pathology. *J. Abnormal Psychology*, **70**, 317-324.

Chapter 16

Family Work in a Secure Unit

— T. Bruce —

I. INTRODUCTION

The following is an account of my work and that of my colleagues with families in a Youth Treatment Centre (St. Charles at Brentwood). St. Charles was the first of two Youth Treatment Centres (the second, Glenthorn, was opened in 1977 in Birmingham), and was set-up by the Department of Health and Social Security (DHSS) in 1971 to provide care, control and treatment in conditions of security for children between the ages of 13 and 19. These were children who had been found uncontainable (usually because of violent behaviour) in other institutions (such as community homes, observation and assessment centres and adolescent psychiatric units). Some of the St. Charles children attend under Section 53 of the 1933 Children and Young Persons Act. These are children who have committed a crime such as murder or arson, and who are either detained during Her Majesty's Pleasure or given a definite sentence of imprisonment. Although most of the children at St. Charles are the responsibility of the DHSS, the Section 53 children remain under the care of the Home Office.

The Centre does not have perimeter security. It is divided into three houses, one of which is especially secure, and it is to this house that children usually go for the first 10 months of their stay in St. Charles. As a rule, they usually then transfer to either House 2 or House 3 where they are given what, in the Centre, is called "extra mobility". On average, the children stay in the Centre for between two to three years. Following their stay, a few return to their own homes, a few set up their own homes, but the majority go either into "living in" work, or into local authority hostels. The Centre is staffed by "group workers" who share the tasks of teaching, care and treatment of the children. The group workers are in the main recruited from the social work, teaching and nursing professions. There is a supporting staff consisting of a Psychiatrist, a Social Worker and a Clinical Psychologist.

II. WORK WITH FAMILIES OF ORIGIN

Systematic work with families at St. Charles started in 1976. It is worth saying at the outset that the results of three years of work suggest that the majority of the children who come to St. Charles are the products of family systems which are so disturbed or disrupted that there is little hope of mending them. One of the main tasks for the St. Charles staff is therefore to provide substitute parenting for the

Family Therapy
ISBN: 0-12-089355-X

children in their care. If this substitute parenting is good enough, it enables the child to give up fantasies (both good and bad) which he has of his family and which are interfering with his adjustment to reality. The St. Charles experience is that process can occur most rapidly and thoroughly if, while receiving substitute parenting, the child is kept in contact with his family of origin (or put into contact with it where contact has been lost). Our experience is in line with that of Colon (1978), who, writing from personal experience and from professional experience with the children of divorced parents, has written:

> Persons who experience emotional cut-offs from significant others are persons at higher risk emotionally and psychologically than those who have resolved such cut-offs . . . A determined effort must be made to connect the child to an absent parent . . . Even if unsuccessful—the fact of the attempt is meaningful.

Colon's work on divorced parents is particularly relevant to the St. Charles system, not only because most of the St. Charles children are the products of broken families, but also because the St. Charles staff in their role as substitute parents tend in many ways to function like the parent of a divorced couple who has custody. Using Weisfeld and Laser's terminology (1977), they are the "in-parents", while the family of origin becomes the parent without custody, the "out-parent".

A.   The Roles of "In-parents" and "Out-parents"

As an example of the "in-parent"/"out-parent" phenomenon in St. Charles, I have chosen the case of a boy, Brian, aged 14, who came to the centre because of several offences involving arson. In his fire-raising (he had burnt down his school, and had also tried to set fire to the approved school he was in before coming to St. Charles), he had displayed what appeared to be a totally ruthless disregard for other people's life and property. He had been adopted at the age of two by a childless couple. They were hard working professional people who had taken Brian on even though the first two years of his life had been spent in children's homes and in hospital because of an intestinal complaint. One of his adoptive mother's earliest memories of him was of his stepping over the Christmas presents they had put outside his bedroom door without giving them so much as a glance. The parents had been excitedly waiting and watching to see his reaction. There were some quite serious sexual difficulties between the parents, but on the whole they got on well enough together.

Brian treated them with total contempt. On one occasion when he ran away from the centre with two other boys, he broke into his parents' house and did a certain amount of damage, including defaecating on the sitting-room carpet. After many initial difficulties in the centre, Brian settled down to a considerable degree, and became very attached to his host worker, Ian. It was felt however that the split between Ian as the "in-parent", and Brian's own parents as "out-parents", was a problem which had to be worked on, and Ian, Brian and his parents were seen for a series of family sessions. At first Brian's mother presented as hard and embittered. As the sessions advanced she became more relaxed, until eventually in one session (a session which in retrospect had a profound effect on Brian), she was able to weep, and to talk about her feelings of guilt and failure.

Following this session Brian was able to begin to return for weekends to his family, and at the time of writing this chapter, he has been discharged from the centre, and is living at home.

I think it should be emphasized that family work on its own would not have been enough to have altered Brian's behaviour. He was able to forgive his adoptive mother only because he had had a good enough experience in relation to his "in-parent", Ian.

The St. Charles view follows that of Colon, and is in contrast to that of Goldstein *et al.* (1980), who have written of the children of divorced couples:

> A visiting parent has little chance to serve as a true object for love, trust and identi-fication since this role is based on his being available on an uninterrupted day to day basis.

Our experience has been that a child cannot become free to love, trust and form satisfactory identifications with the St. Charles staff unless the visiting parent is kept in the picture. If the parent, however unsatisfactory, is not kept in contact, the child is forever (in fantasy and, frequently, in fact) chasing after his family of origin. Even if a parent is in prison or in mental hospital, or thoroughly unreliable or malicious, it has been our experience that the child is better off having contact, although of course under controlled conditions, than not. Cutting a child off from the pain of relating to unsatisfactory parents may in Colon's words: "give temporary relief from conflict but only at the cost of burying that conflict".

B.   "In-parents" and "Out-parents": how they relate

It is impossible to generalize about the families of the children in St. Charles. They present as wide a variation of dynamics and pathology as families encountered in day to day child guidance work. These families do, however, have one feature in common, a profound suspicion of, and at worst a hatred of, authority as represented by the St. Charles staff, whom the families perceive as not only having taken over parental rights, but also as having consigned their child to virtual imprisonment. Even those families which start off by being non-resentful of authority become so following the massive intervention in their family life which the commitment of one of their children to a Youth Treatment Centre involves. There is no way that the St. Charles staff can duck the authority which society has invested in them. The great disadvantage to being perceived as a revenging authority is that the child can be manipulated often quite unconsciously by the family to undermine the authority of the St. Charles staff. One boy, for example, with a history of performing reckless electrical and chemical experiments was allowed by his parents (after a weekend at home) to return to the Centre with a chemical fertilizer which he very nearly succeeded in incorporating into an explosive device before being discovered.

Another example is that of Diana who was aged thirteen when she came to the centre. She had been utterly out of the control of her mother and stepfather, and was consorting with such unsavoury people that her life was feared for. On several occasions, Diana ran away from the centre and was harboured by a man with whom her mother had lived for a number of years and who had to some extent been like a father to Diana. There was some discussion whether to prosecute this man for failing to inform the centre and the police about Diana's whereabouts, but it was decided to try to involve him in family work instead. He had seen the centre as treating Diana very badly, and he was angry with Diana's mother for having, as he saw it, acquiesced to her being placed there. Once he had been included in the family work, he came to identify with the aims of the centre, and Diana also felt happier and more safely contained. Since then, she has done quite well for herself in the pop music industry. One of the great advantages of family work is that it can cut down the incidence of such acting out on the part of parents and relations.

III. DIFFICULTIES IN SETTING UP FAMILY THERAPY IN AN INSTITUTION

A. Liaison with Network

Although provision was made in the setting up of St. Charles for work to be done with families, and a full-time social worker was employed for this purpose, it was envisaged that the social worker's main function would be to act as liaison between the Centre and the local authority social workers. It was imagined that the latter would carry out most of the family work because most of the children would be coming from places far distant from Brentwood. This system did not work well for the following reasons:

(1) Once the child, who had been a thorn in the flesh of the local authority social work department, had gained admission to St. Charles, there was a tendency for the local authority social worker to withdraw interest from the case. Most local authority social workers found that other commitments made it very difficult for them to visit the child in the Centre more frequently than the quarterly reviews. In addition, the two-to-three year stay for most children in St. Charles usually meant that the social worker who had arranged their admission had moved on within a year or so. It was difficult for another social worker taking over the case to feel the same urgency once the family crisis centring around the admission of the child to St. Charles had passed.

(2) Because most of the St. Charles families live at some distance from the Centre, a great deal of fetching and carrying, either of the family to the Centre or of the child to the home, is necessary if family work is to take place. Few local authority social workers had the motivation to initiate such a programme.

(3) Local authority social workers vary very much in their training, overall experience, and in particular in their experience of family therapy.

(4) It is quite common for families to try to play the local authority social workers off against the Centre.

Because of the above difficulties, what is needed is a therapist who is in a position to work with a system which includes the local authority social worker. The "minimal sufficient network" (Skynner, 1971) consists of the St. Charles child (the designated patient), his host worker, his parents, his siblings (depending upon their availability), and the local authority social worker. At St. Charles, the only people who are in a position to act as therapists to this network are the Centre Social Worker, the Clinical Psychologist, and the Consultant Psychiatrist. For the Consultant Psychiatrist and the Clinical Psychologist, there were technical difficulties in adopting this role because it blurred with other roles. The Consultant Psychiatrist led staff support groups, while the Clinical Psychologist was responsible for staff training. By far the best-placed person to undertake the role of family therapist was the Centre Social Worker. To provide a service for thirty families, our experience was that a minimum of three social workers would be needed.

B.   Institutional Difficulties

In general, difficulties in setting up family therapy in an institution like St. Charles stem from two main sources.

(1)   General Resistance to Change

The first of these is the general resistance of any institution to change. This is particularly true of an institution which has to design its institutional structures to cope with frightening situations (Menzies, 1960). Hospitals, prisons and the armed forces have in common a relatively rigid hierarchy in which everyone knows his or her place and function. Such a system enables the institution to keep going when staff anxiety is high and when everybody is under pressure. At times of course this clarity of role can become rigidified, and the maintenance of a hierarchy becomes an end in itself. Using Schon's terminology (1973), the "Theory" of the institution then takes over from its function, as for example, in the last war in the United States Navy, where the introduction of a more efficient gun was held up because it would make particular naval gunnery ranks redundant. The staff in St. Charles, like those in hospitals, prisons and the armed forces, have to have clearly defined roles and lines of responsibility if the institution is to survive when under threat from very violent young people. Family therapy, however, to some extent cuts across hierarchical lines, and may be resisted because it does so. Haley has described similar resistance in a Mental Health Clinic (Haley, 1975).

Problems of cutting across an established hierarchy may be lessened (and this happened at St. Charles) by providing staff with some training in family therapy, and by helping them to get in touch with the difficulties which they bring from their own family of origin, using such techniques as sculpting and the geneogram. It is wise to include the director of an institution in such a pro- gramme if family therapy is to become firmly rooted. In our experience, it was particularly important to convey to staff the notion of complementarity in family systems. It is easy for staff, and indeed with very great justification, to see the St.

Charles type of child as a victim of appalling parental behaviour, and to feel extremely critical of the family of origin (Ekstein *et al.*, 1969). It can be a considerable wrench for staff to have to see, instead, the role which the child and his behaviour have in the overall structure and dynamics of his family, a system in which everyone may be the victim.

(2)   Difficulties with Substitute Parenting Functions

The second difficulty in introducing family therapy to an institution is related to the first, and concerns the substitute parenting function of the staff in an institution like St. Charles. Inevitably, this function introduces an element of rivalry between the natural parents and the staff which the children may be quick to exploit. Once family therapy is established, it is easier for these rivalries to be looked at, but it means that staff have to be prepared to look at their own feelings about neglectful parents. A few residential staff quite specifically come into such work because of their own experience of an unhappy childhood, and it can be especially painful and difficult for them to take part in network meetings with the parents of the child in their care.

IV.   THE SYSTEM OF FAMILY WORK
IN USE AT ST. CHARLES

A.   A System of "Family Care"

Before talking in more detail about family therapy at St. Charles, it is first necessary to say something about the overall system of care and treatment in use in the Centre.

(1)   Admissions and Early Phases.

Admissions to St. Charles Youth Treatment Centre are decided by an admissions panel which meets at the DHSS and which is attended by the Director of the Centre. Approximately 20% of the children referred are admitted. Once a child has been selected for admission, a visit is arranged to the institution where the child is being held (most commonly a closed observation and assessment centre, a remand centre, or a prison), and the social worker responsible for the child will bring the parents too, so that they can meet staff from the Centre. At that meeting, the parents are told that they will be expected to work closely with the Centre in its attempts to help their child. In particular, they are told that although the Centre is a secure institution, its overall aim is to try to understand and work with factors in the child's disturbance. As a rule, no child is admitted to the Centre until a discussion of this sort has taken place. In accordance with the principles stated above, even where a parent is in prison or in mental hospital, an attempt is made to include them in the admission plans.

  As a rule, once a child has been admitted to the Centre, he will not make any visits home for some months. The aim of this initial period is to make the child's environment as simple and as predictable as possible. Children who are referred to St. Charles have usually been through a bewildering barrage of experiences at all stages in their life. None of them have had an experience of parents able to provide an effective filter system to stimuli, screening out potentially overwhelming situations (most of the children have experienced severe parental discord, violence and separations). The initial stage of treatment at St. Charles is therefore directed towards giving the children an experience of consistency. The children's day is ordered almost from minute to minute; in some ways, the children are treated like toddlers: for example, they have an afternoon siesta. The guiding principle here is that of Abraham Maslow's need hierarchy (1976), in which lower-order needs have to be fulfilled before the child can make use of provision for higher order needs. There is little point in trying to provide formal psychotherapy for a child who has not yet learnt to trust the continued existence from day to day of the people who are caring for him.

(2) Regular Parental Contact

As part of the attempt to provide consistency for the child, parental contact is put onto as regular a basis as possible. With a few of the St. Charles families, this is relatively easily done. The great majority, however, fall into two main categories: the disengaged and the enmeshed. Mrs W's relationship to her son was an example of a disengaged family system at work. It was obvious that in many ways she cared very greatly about her son, but because of her own childhood in children's homes, and in approved school, she was utterly unable to sustain consistent contact with him. Having promised to turn up on a particular day, she would disappear for months; at other times she would arrive unannounced. From time to time she would disappear completely from where she was living. During these periods, her son would become utterly distraught and would attack staff and other children. Staff initially adopted a policy of trying to help Mrs W's son to come to terms with his mother's inconsistency. This however resulted in his becoming more rather than less upset, and it was finally decided that the staff and the local authority social worker should make every possible effort at the very least to keep the boy informed about where his mother was living. This involved the local authority social worker in what amounted to private detective work, but it resulted in a considerable alleviation of the boy's distress.

By way of contrast, Mrs M's relationship with her daughter was an example of over-enmeshment (neither she nor Mrs W were living with one man for any length of time). Mrs M could never accept that her daughter was in the least responsible for the difficulties that had brought her to St. Charles. Continuing problems while in the Centre resulted in Mrs M's complaining to the DHSS and her own solicitor that the child was being victimized. Mrs M's attitude clearly had a very disturbing effect on her daughter, and matters came to a head when the daughter, while on a gardening expedition, threw a pair of shears at another child's back. There was a considerable amelioration of the situation once Mrs M had been issued with a timetable regulating contact with her daughter.

B.   The Use of the Geneogram

(1)   Initial Construction of the Geneogram
During the first weeks of a child's stay in St. Charles, a family geneogram is set out using information from the parents and the local authority social worker. Very frequently with the St. Charles children, these geneograms are complicated, and include a large number of people who have had brief but, from the child's point of view, unsatisfactory contact with the St. Charles child.

In the initial meeting between the St. Charles staff and the family social worker, a family tree is set out using all the information available to the social worker who will also say what she knows of the St. Charles child's contact with the people in the family tree. A decision is then made as to whom to invite to the first family meeting. Unfortunately, it is the rule rather than the exception that various members of the family system are so much at daggers drawn that they absolutely refuse to meet all together. Usually, therefore, they have to be met piecemeal. In addition, as the family work proceeds, it is common to find that people have been left out who have been very significant in the child's development.

(2)   Clinical Example: the Mott Family
As an example of this sort of process I have chosen the Mott family. John Mott came to the centre at the age of fourteen because he had been uncontrollable in an adolescent psychiatric unit. He was felt to be potentially a very dangerous boy, and on one occasion tried to poison his brother. Initially, work was done with John and his brother (who is older) together with John's father and John's stepmother. John's host worker was included in all the family meetings. It soon became clear, however, that the main power in the family lay in the hands of John's great aunt (a woman of eighty) who held sway over the family because of relative wealth. Because of the sickliness of his own mother, Mr Mott had been brought up by the aunt. He had in many ways been quite unable to separate from her, and in both his marriages had been unable to exert any real authority. Both his wives had felt quite unsupported by him, and his childishness was indulged by his aunt. At one time, she had also had the care of John during the break up of Mr Mott's first marriage. As a result of the aunt's having been included in the family work, Mr Mott was better able to assert himself and to disengage from his aunt. It was at this stage that we felt able to turn back the family clock and look at Mr Mott's first marriage. Mr Mott's first wife had not seen him or John for a number of years. She had in fact walked out of the house on Christmas day when John was aged three and a half. Her main reason was that John and his older brother had opened some of their Christmas presents before they were supposed to, but behind this lay profound discontentment with the marriage. John's mother had not visited him in St. Charles although she had heard that he was in some sort of children's home. Since her divorce from Mr Mott she had remarried and had another child. She was visited at home on a number of occasions, and her second husband finally agreed that she should meet Mr Mott together with

John and his older brother. This was the first time that the original family members had met for about ten years. One of the main aims of the meeting was to enable John and his brother actually to hear their parents talking about the difficulties that led to the separation, rather than being left in the grip of fantasy about the causes of the family break-up.

(3)   The Family Meeting: the Motts

At this family meeting and in subsequent meetings, it soon became very clear that neither member of the couple had really been able to work through their separation. It was as though all their resentments and bitter hatred of each other had become encapsulated in their children. In fact, it was almost as though John's murderous attack on his brother mirrored the still active murderous feeling between his parents. This sort of family archaeology, in which old and apparently buried conflicts may find expression in later generations, has been particularly described by Murray Bowen (1975). As a result of the family work, John's mother has settled down considerably, and although at the time of writing he is in jail for a relatively minor offence, he has become a much less dangerous and sinister boy to live with.

C.   What is the Family Boundary?

The St. Charles families seem to have enormous difficulty in forming a stable boundary around themselves: individuals are recruited to the system and expelled from it with bewildering rapidity. This is perhaps a process akin to that described by Rowley (1977) in his paper *Two's Company and three's a Crowd!* Early on (as in the Mott family) a decision has to be made about which people are to be included in the minimal sufficient network. In these families, there is a tendency for members of the network who have been cut off for years to become activated (like moles in an espionage network) when other members have become engaged in family work. An example of this phenomenon, Vanessa, had not met her father for eleven years (she was aged fourteen when admitted to St. Charles). But within months of family work being initiated between Vanessa and her mother, her father reappeared, engineered her absconsion from the Centre, and harboured her for six weeks. Although it never became entirely clear, it is probable that Vanessa contacted him herself. With hindsight, it is obvious that we should have made contact with him at the same time as working with Vanessa's mother.

V.   THERAPEUTIC WORK WITH THE FAMILIES: SETTING AND STRUCTURE

The family therapists at St. Charles were the social worker, the psychiatrist and the psychologist, working either singly or in pairs. Family meetings were set up either throughout the whole of a child's stay in St. Charles, in which case they would be held at intervals of a month or of six weeks or when family meetings were more frequent (this was usually a matter of geography: families living closer to the Centre had more frequent meetings), the family work was arranged in "terms", with a break of a few months between each term of work. As far as possible, for each term a definite focus of work was set.

A. The Use of the Family Maisonette

A particular feature of the St. Charles work is the use of the family maisonette. This is attached to one of the houses and is particularly used for any of the families coming from a long distance. The experience at St. Charles is that any secure institution with a far-flung catchment area needs such accommodation for its families, and that it has to be jealously guarded against administrators who want to use it for such things as staff accommodation. For some of the St. Charles families, a stay in the maisonette is their only chance of having a holiday. While in the maisonette, a programme is organized, somewhat akin to McGregor's (1969) multiple therapy. Families may take part in the daily house meetings in order to reduce their sense of alienation from the work of the house. Their child is also allowed to stay with them in the maisonette, and tensions arising from the re-uniting of the family in this way, and from the whole family going out on trips together, can be examined in daily meetings with the family. For particularly inarticulate families, special techniques such as sculpting may be used. Meetings are also arranged between the family and the director of the Centre to discuss future plans for the child.

VI. SOME EXAMPLES OF FAMILY WORK AT ST. CHARLES

The following are examples of work done with families at St. Charles, chosen to illustrate both the limitations and the great potential of such work. The first two of these examples are of families in which "cut-offs" had occurred.

A. Families in which the Child has Experienced a "Cut-off"

(1) Calum
Calum, aged fifteen, was a boy of superior intelligence who had been sent to St. Charles because he had committed a large number of burglaries, some of them involving considerable destruction of property. The burglaries were meticulously planned, and Calum planted a number of clues to mislead the police. For example, he would leave footprints while wearing an army boot on one foot and a carpet slipper on the other. While he was on the job, he usually wore pyjamas so that, if caught, he could claim that he had been sleep walking. He was so successful in misleading the police, that in the end he was reduced to giving himself up. His father was a successful business man who, in court, requested

that his son be taught a lesson. This so enraged Calum that there and then he tried to assault his father. Calum's mother had walked out of the house when Calum was nine years old, and he had not seen her since. Calum was described by the psychiatrist who saw him before his court appearance as being "calculating, cunning and devious". It is noteworthy that Calum's father, in describing his ex-wife, talked of her as being "a devious, cunning woman". It seemed that in many ways Calum was identifying with his father's picture of the missing wife, and that in this way, the family (there were six other children besides Calum) was able to behave as though the mother was still present.

When we started work with Calum's family, there had been little contact between him and his father for about a year. Contact was initiated with a series of home visits to the father's house, followed by meetings at the Centre, in the course of which Calum came to understand his father's difficulties and point of view. From having seen his father as "really awful", he came to see that the split-up in his parent's marriage had as much to do with his mother as his father. Following the reconciliation with his father, however, all Calum's longing for his mother came to the fore, and he began to spin fantasies about how he had contacted her when in fact he was on leave from the Centre to go to football matches. In addition, he developed a passionate attachment to one of the female members of the staff. Calum did very well in the Centre, and was able to be discharged; and at the time of writing he is working for father. Following his discharge, however, he did make contact with his mother, and stayed with her for a short time. In retrospect, as in Vanessa's case (outlined above), Calum's mother should have been contacted at the same time that work started with his father.

(2) Colin

As a contrast to this is the case of Colin, who at the age of thirteen was admitted to the Centre because of violent delinquency and gross cruelty to animals. When work started with his mother, Colin was also put in touch with his father, whom he had not seen since the split-up of the marriage when Colin was about three. Colin's father had remarried, and in addition to one of Colin's full siblings, he had a number of children by his second marriage. This whole branch of the family was completely unknown to Colin, but he was welcomed by them, and said delightedly after the first meeting with them, "I didn't know I had so many relations". In fact, following his discharge from St. Charles, Colin went to stay with his father. In a case like this, we did not insist that the divorced parents should meet together, but on those occasions when this has been possible, by virtue of hearing parents talk about their difficulties at the time of separation, the child is enabled to begin to modify omnipotent fantasies about his own destructiveness.

B. Families which are "unsuitable" for Therapy

The next three examples are of children from families which would not normally be thought of as being good candidates for family work (using, for example,

Bloch and La Perrière's (1973) criteria). Family contact in these cases, however, proved to be very productive for the children.

(1) Tony

A boy, Tony, aged fourteen, was referred to St. Charles because of two attacks on women. He had been in care from the age of eight and was in the middle of three siblings, none of whom were living at home. Tony was preoccupied with violence, and festooned his walls with posters such as that advertising the *Texas Chainsaw Massacre*. His mother had put him into care because she had separated from her husband and had nowhere to live. She herself had a history of violence. She had had very little contact with Tony from the time of his going into care until his admission to St. Charles. She had remarried, had two more children, and had divorced her second husband. Within a month of Tony's admission to the Centre, his mother was invited to stay in the maisonette together with the two children of her second marriage. Tony's younger full sister was living in a local authority hostel and did not want to come to the family meetings. His older full brother was in Borstal. During Tony's stay in the Centre, it was possible for his mother to come to the maisonette on a number of occasions, and in the course of her meetings with Tony, she was able to talk about her own life. She herself had come from a home in which there had been a good deal of violence. At the age of ten, she had had to go into a sanatorium because of tuberculosis. Although she stayed there for about three years, she was not visited once by her family during this time, and shortly after her discharge, her mother died. These insights into his mother's history, enabled Tony to begin to understand and forgive her. His rage with women began to abate, and he was able to begin to use the substitute mothering available to him at the Centre. He was particularly attached to a middle-aged woman with whom he felt especially safe because he felt that she was not frightened of him. Contact was also made with Tony's father, and for a short time after he left the Centre Tony went to live with him.

(2) "Caring" for the Parents

It should be emphasized that in cases like this where one is dealing with very deprived parents, it has been our experience that very great care has to go into making the parents feel welcome and comfortable when they come to the Centre. Usually the child's host worker would be asked to ensure that the maisonette was ready and stocked with basic foodstuffs. As a rule, the programme of family meetings and of social contacts with the staff of the Centre would be very carefully planned before the arrival of the family. As with the programme for the children at St. Charles, their families' lower order needs have to receive as much attention as the higher order needs catered for by formal family therapy. Even with families not staying in the maisonette, it was the custom during family therapy sessions to provide tea and biscuits.

The parents of the children at St. Charles have as a rule been unable in their own childhood to take for granted the basic necessities of life: food, a roof over their heads, parents whose presence can be relied upon. To expect such families to engage in formal family therapy without first going through a phase of helping them to feel secure within the Centre is like giving a starving child a lecture on vitamins.

(3) Susan

The next example is of a girl, Susan, aged sixteen, who had been found guilty of infanticide. Susan was the only child of a schizophrenic mother (her father had died when she was six). Although Susan's mother lived at home, she was capable of only the simplest domestic chores, and had to rely heavily on the local authority social worker when Susan came to St. Charles. In a series of meetings between Susan and her mother, Susan was very greatly helped by our attempt to sort out the extremely convoluted way in which her mother communicated.

The following are brief extracts from two meetings with Susan and her mother, Mrs Mitchell. The extracts are presented in the form of transcripts of the meetings, and these are followed by the transcripts of the meetings (that is, the family therapist's attempt to convey something of the metacommunications that were occurring in the meetings).

Session A: Susan and her Mother

I (Dr B) am talking to Mrs Mitchell about the way in which she never trusts people with her thoughts. She agrees with me. I then turn to Susan and ask whether the sort of picture that I have been getting of Mrs Mitchell (and as I have been describing it to Mrs Mitchell) is a picture that is recognizable to Susan.

Susan: [addressed to Dr B] Well, it's sometimes difficult for me to know what Mum's thinking.

Mrs Mitchell: Has that woman upstairs gone?

Susan: Yes, she's gone.

Mrs Mitchell: Well, that's got rid of that menace then, hasn't it?

Dr B: [to Mrs Mitchell] Hey, just a minute, I was talking to Susan about how she sees you, and then you suddenly ask her about the woman upstairs. What was that about?

Mrs Mitchell: I don't know.

Dr B: Look, I've got an idea that the menace was really that Susan was talking about how she sees you.

Mrs Mitchell: [to Susan] So we won't see her again?

Susan: No.

Dr B: [to Mrs Mitchell] You did it again! And you (to Susan) fitted in with it. You could have said something like "that's not what we're talking about Mum".

Transcript A (The metacommunications or meaning behind the words)

Susan: Yes, I am beginning to get a more objective picture of Mum.

Mrs Mitchell: Don't you dare start to move away from me.

Susan: Oh God, all right, I won't move away from you.

Mrs Mitchell: Thank you, just as long as we've got that straight.

Dr B: I feel lost: what are you two up to?

Mrs Mitchell: Just keep out of this Dr Bruce!

Dr B: Mrs Mitchell, you are furious because Susan is beginning to move away from you.

Mrs Mitchell: You're not moving away from me are you? Please don't do that. Let's show him that he can't split us.

Susan: All right Mum, we'll stick together.

Dr B: O.K., you two win, but it's not going to do either of you any good to carry on in this way. But I've had enough for today; I can't carry on with this much longer.

Session B: Susan and her Mother

(Two months later)

Mrs Mitchell has talked about her boy friends. Susan has tried to butt in on one or two occasions, but has been stopped from doing so; for the past few minutes, however, Susan has been talking about her relations with men.

Susan: [to Dr B] You know the workmen who are working over there?

Dr B: Yes.

Susan: One of them fancies me.

Dr B: What?

Susan: One of them fancies me.

Dr B: Yes?

Susan: I try to ignore him. Cheek, isn't it?

Mrs Mitchell: Can't help it can you? [laughs]

Susan: [to Dr B] I hate him. I don't say a bloody word to him; that's the point. You know I went over to get a light? I rang the door bell, and he's whistling at me.

Mrs Mitchell: Ask him if he wants a kitten.

Susan: Are you still offering for a cat?

Mrs Mitchell: No [laughs] I'm not.

Susan: Do you still want to get rid of one?

Mrs Mitchell: No.

Susan: Yes or No? 'Cause I could find someone easy.

Mrs Mitchell: No.

Susan: You don't, right.

Silence

Mrs Mitchell: [to Dr B] ? Got two kittens at home.

Transcript B: Susan and her Mother

Susan: I can attract men very easily, you included!

Dr B: Yes, you are a pretty girl.

Susan: One of the workmen fancies me.

Dr B: How dare he, without my knowledge or permission!

Susan: I don't have to ask your permission.

Dr B: I suppose not.

Susan: I can't help it, I'm just attractive to men.

Mrs Mitchell: No. You can't help it. You're just attractive to men. Exciting isn't it? But don't leave me out of it. What are you and Dr B up to?

Susan: Ignore her!

Mrs Mitchell: Susan, please listen to me. Don't leave me out. I'll do and say anything to get you back.

Susan: Please be quiet Mum. You're being embarrassing.

Mrs Mitchell: Susan, what do you mean?

Susan: You're embarrassing me Mum. Please be quiet I find it difficult to say, but you've always embarrassed me.

Mrs Mitchell: Dr Bruce, do you see what you've done now? Please help me. Are you going to leave me with only my cats for company?

Repeated attempts to unscramble Mrs Mitchell's communications in a series of sessions lasting over a year gradually helped Susan to disengage from her mother and to become less panic-stricken. Following her discharge from St. Charles, Susan married and had another baby. Four years after the interviews reported above, she and her child remain well and her marriage is relatively stable.

(4) James

The third case concerns a boy, James, aged thirteen. When he was admitted to the Centre, he had been involved in burglary, wilful damage and actual bodily harm. He had also soiled very severely from the age of eight. He came from an intact but extremely disorganized family. His father had done a two-year stretch in prison because of incest with one of James' older sisters. There were five children besides James. James' mother was of low intelligence. A series of family meetings was arranged, some in James' own home, and some in the Centre. James' father managed to come to only one of these meetings, and this was perhaps understandable in view of the history of incest.

The family meetings were extremely painful because although James got some support from his siblings, he was constantly belittled by his mother, who brushed aside his pitiful attempts to gain her approval. For example, an offer to change an electric plug was rewarded with "You can't do anything"; a Christmas present was received with derision. Painful though these episodes were for James, they enabled him to begin to contemplate not returning home after leaving the Centre, and in fact following his discharge, he went to live in a hostel. If we had not worked with his family in this way, James would certainly not have been able to give up his hopeless longing that his mother could turn out to be different, and he would have returned home only to get into further trouble when his longing for his mother's approbation was frustrated.

C. A "Clinic" Family

Following these three cases I have chosen one to illustrate the fact that even in secure institutions, there are children from families whose problems are not very greatly different from those encountered in child-guidance work, where children can be helped by the standard methods of family therapy. Kate, aged fourteen, had been admitted to the Centre because she had kidnapped two babies whom she had cared for very well. The babies had been kidnapped shortly after Kate's younger sister had been killed by a car when Kate was out walking with her. In a letter to her mother about the accident, Kate wrote, "I really hate myself for what I did. Please forgive me this time. I really loved her and will never forget her ever". In spite of the tone of this letter, there was not a shred of evidence that Kate had been at all responsible for her sister's death. She said that she stole the babies because she "felt like looking after someone".

A series of family sessions including mother, father, Kate and her two siblings were organized, and meetings were held over a period of about eighteen months with breaks in between. The crisis point of these meetings occurred after about five months when the family, which had clearly been blocking its mourning of the young sister, began to open up their defences. In their account of this session, the therapists wrote:

> The details of the accident, the little girl's appearance, the rush to hospital and the panic which drove each member of the family to the scene were described with painful clarity, and obviously this was the first occasion in which the details of the day of the death had been brought out. It was clear that each member of the family had erected a defensive isolation to ward off grief and the need to acknowledge the difficulty they experience as a family in sharing and communicating.

Until the family could get in touch with the feelings described in the session, Kate had been the carrier of these feelings, and had stolen the babies in an attempt to make reparation. At the time of writing, Kate has been discharged from the Centre, is working in an office where she is doing well, and is living at home. She recently said of her parents: "They're awful, but they'll do and I love them".

D.   Children who have murdered and their Families

Finally, there should be some mention of the families of children who have murdered. Such children can be very depressing for staff to work with, because as a rule most of them will have to go on to other penal establishments after their stay in the Centre. Even so, it is thoroughly worthwhile to work with these children's families because the great majority will eventually return home, and will still be relatively young when they do so. It is of vital importance to keep them in touch with their families, and their families with them. In addition, there is an important area of research here. It is a common experience in secure institutions that children who have murdered are, paradoxically, less difficult to control and less prone to violent outbursts than children who have committed less serious crimes. In addition, some of the child murderers come from families which, on the surface at least, appear to be in no way different from families whose children do perfectly well in life. Where the difference lies remains a mystery.

VII.   CONCLUSION

Secure accommodation for children is notoriously expensive in terms both of money and of emotional distress in staff. It is the experience at St. Charles that the systematic involvement of the children's families in treatment can maximize the institution's therapeutic effectiveness and make the task of caring for the children very much easier.

Where possible, provision for family therapy should be made in the planning of a secure institution. It is much more difficult to graft family therapy on to an established institution, especially a secure one in which staff hierarchy and institutional structures have to be relatively rigid. It is the experience in St. Charles that the social work staff in a secure institution are best placed to run a family therapy programme, and that they should be in a ratio of one social worker to about twelve families.

Family therapy is particularly important in closed institutions because of its civilizing effect in keeping such institutions in touch with the outside world, and with the need to re-integrate their inmates with society. But perhaps the most civilizing influence of all is the way in which family therapy cuts across the institutional hierarchies and institutional structures which, although necessary in closed institutions, can become rigid, barren, and at worst, brutal.

REFERENCES

Bloch, D. and La Perrière, K. (1973). Techniques of family therapy: a conceptual framework. *In* "Techniques of Family Psychotherapy", Grune and Stratton, New York.

Bowen, M. (1975). "Family Therapy After twenty years. American Handbook of Psychiatry V", Basic Books, New York.

Colon, F. (1978). Family Ties and Child Placement. *Family Process*, **17**, 289-312.

Ekstein, R., Friedman, S., Caruth, E. and Cooper, B. (1969). Reflections on the need for a working alliance with environmental support systems. *Reiss-Davis Clinic Bulletin*, **6**, 111-120.

Goldstein, J., Freud, A. and Solnit, A. J. (1980). "Beyond the Best Interests of the Child", Burnett Books Ltd., London.

Haley, J. (1975). Why a Mental Health Clinic Should Avoid Family Therapy. *Journal of Marriage & Family counselling*, (January) pp. 3-13.

Maslow, A. (1976). "The Farther Reaches of Human Nature". Penguin Books, Harmondsworth.

MacGregor, R. *et al.* (1964). "Multiple Impact therapy with families", McGraw Hill, New York.

Menzies, I. (1970). "A Case Study in the functioning of Social Systems as a defence against anxiety", Tavistock pamphlet No 3, T.I.H.R., London.

Rowley, J. L. (1972). Two's company — Three's a crowd: some notes on human interaction. *B.J.Med. Psychol.* **45**, 115-126.

Schon, D. A. (1973). "Beyond the Stable State", Penguin Books, Harmondsworth.

Skynner, A. C. R. (1971). The Minimum Sufficient Network. *Social Work Today*, **2**, 3.

Weisfeld, D. and Laser, M. (1977). Divorced Parents in Family Therapy in a residential treatment setting. *Family Process*, **16**, 229-236.

─────────── Chapter 17 ───────────

A Family Therapy Approach
to Making Decisions
in Child Care Cases

─────────── A. Bentovim ───────────

I. INTRODUCTION

This chapter represents a development of an earlier paper (Bentovim and
Gilmour, 1981), where we attempted to describe a particular approach adopted
when difficult decisions had to be made in cases of child care, access and
custody. The approach developed tried to maintain a balance between the needs
of the individual child in terms of his future care and the needs of the family
unit. Thus it is concerned with providing a therapeutic experience for the
family while considering the actual break-up of the family unit if it cannot be
helped to become a place in which the child can thrive. Decision-making in this
area is vital, given a belief that a family, even if not his family of origin, is the
optimal context for a child to grow up in. Currently 120 000 children are in
local authority care, 50 000 for more than three years, and 3 out of 4 in care
until aged 18. Therefore an assessment using a family therapy frame has to be
concerned with how far the family system can stretch and change to meet an
individual's needs If that fails, then the task is to both find an alternate family,
and to ensure that transitions are successful for all involved despite gains or losses
(see Robinson, Chapter 13).

II. REFERRAL SOURCES

The context for the work is a psychiatric department in a post-graduate
children's hospital. The team is being asked to assess and give an opinion in
situations where decision-making as to a child's future is exceedingly
problematic, yet usually there is some urgency that the "best" solution be
found as soon as possible. Such decisions may be about whether children at risk
should or should not be rehabilitated with their families, about children in care
whose present placement is breaking down or is not suitable, about the
advisability of placing disturbed older children for adoption, or about infants
being removed into care at birth. We are also asked to help over the question
of access of children to their natural parents, when termination of access is
being considered and, in divorce situations, over custody and access issues where

Family Therapy
ISBN: 0-12-089355-X

there is a dispute between the parents. Such situations are brought to our notice by Social Services Departments, the Official Solicitor to the High Court, "private advocates" (solicitors acting for the parties), families and parents themselves, or other medical practitioners.

III. EXPLICIT CHILD-CARE VALUES

A. Child Care in a Family Therapy Setting

When trying to put together the basic elements of our approach, we realized that we had an articulated series of child-care values and beliefs which were more or less explicit in our practice. Although our basic orientation was a family systems one in the sense of seeing the logic of the interactional view of behaviour, nevertheless we have found a number of principles of use, particularly in communicating about the needs of the children and families we were seeing. What follows is based on the notion that whatever role children play within the family system, they are basically vulnerable through their developmental immaturity. This means that the family may induct society into its system through its destructive interaction and family breakdown; social agencies may then be forced to intervene to protect the child even though that child may be playing an active part in its own disqualification. A family therapy approach expects that the rigidity of family dysfunction be tested to explore any possibility for change, but the following principles as far as the child is concerned always have to be borne in mind.

B. Least Detrimental Form of Care for the Child

Primarily, we are committed to the importance of the *least detrimental alternative care* principle as described by Goldstein *et al.* (1973). This enunciates the principle of doing least harm when a decision about a child's care has to be made, and also indicates that there is no perfect solution, only the *least detrimental* one. The following factors have to be borne in mind:
(1) Decisions need to be made in relation to the age of the child.
(2) The capacity of the child to become attached to new parent figures must be recognized (see Robinson, Chapter 13).
(3) The time span of child *vs* adult must be recognized.
(4) Good enough parenting and continuity must be supported, whoever is providing it.
(5) Secure psychological parenting may have to be supported over "failed" biological parenting or improved parenting capacity when it is reached "too late".
Although we agree that short-term separations need not be detrimental, longer-term reactions and negative interactional patterns can be triggered or potentiated, and represent a risk in the long-term for the child well-attached to alternative parents if moved. We believe that infants are sensitive to separation

from the earliest period of life, and that the notion of a period of invulnerability to separation early on is to be seriously questioned (Bentovim, 1979).

Late fostering and adoption can be successful (Tizard, 1977), and is preferable to "institutional" parenting, but the later the placement, the more problems that are likely to evolve. "Late" return to a parent can be equivalent to a late adoption, yet it can be *more* problematic than placement with a "new" family. Adoption is preferable to long-term fostering because the latter inevitably creates insecurity for all concerned due to the uncertain legal status.

Adopted and fostered children have the right to have some kind of *access to their families of origin*, with information (in the form of a "life book") being the minimum needed to help the child and his new family in their task as a reconstituted group.

In "later" fostering or adoptive situations where attachments to families of origin exist, direct access may be appropriate *provided* that the loss of parent, child and family has been acknowledged, that the new/reconstituted family is a going concern and a "distant relative" role is accepted by the child and natural parents. This is a very major demand, however. Information giving can be a start to the process which needs careful monitoring, and a good deal of work has to be done with all concerned if it is to be successful.

The purpose of access must be clearly defined, access with a view to resume *care* being different to access which provides *information* to the child. This applies to situations of parenting breakdown and divorce, as well as to those of children in care. Children should be able to have direct access channels created before the age of 18.

Access strain which threatens the nurturing capacity of the "good enough" primary caretaker and the security of the child, may be detrimental and may need to be "thinned" and re-negotiated, or changed from direct contact to indirect information only (Bentovim, 1980).

The denial of *access* through information or contact with a "potential" alternative parent (e.g. in divorce) may be against a child's best interests.

Although we see the importance of the custodial parent having some power of controlling access, we favour joint custody, mediation and conciliation in divorce wherever possible, rather than the use of adversarial processes.

We feel "painful" conclusions need direct feedback, and any reports submitted to Court must be available to all parties concerned.

IV. FAMILY THERAPY PRINCIPLES

A. Focal Notions

In the process of developing a brief form of family therapy the notion of *the focus* has been used in an attempt to bring together a large number of disparate and apparently unrelated family phenomena (Kinston and Bentovim, 1981). A model has been described which is well suited to the sorts of cases which we are considering here. A model such as structural family therapy, which is concerned mainly with the family here and now, cannot in our view always encompass the devastating histories that these children and families have experienced and which may be encapsulated in the present (Parkes, 1971). Although structural family therapy methods may be absolutely essential to work with such families as described so powerfully in *Families of the Slums* (Minuchin *et al.*, 1967), in our view, a model is required for *assessment* where historical events can be incorporated from the beginning.

The model described by Kinston and Bentovim (1981) is basically a stress response model. The generally well accepted idea has been reinforced that, for a family to be healthy, there needs to be attempts at acceptance, integration, resolution and working through of the stressful life-events and circumstances which affected the parents of the present-day family, both when they were children and as adults. To say that stressful events have been worked through implies that they have been made sense of by the individuals who have experienced them, and they have an appropriate place in their world of meanings. The reading of meaning and the making sense of the pattern of events is a routine part of family life from the moment of birth, and to be a human being is to experience one's situation in terms of the meanings we give our lives.

B. Common Meanings and Intersubjective Meanings

(1) Common Meanings
Common meanings were defined as meanings which are rooted in the psychic lives of the individual family member. Each member has his own unique experience, much of which remains unconscious or private and is relevant to the concerns of other family members or the family therapist.

However, there are certain core meanings which are shared at the time of marriage and which develop in common afterwards; when children appear they assimilate and contribute to these. Such common meanings are exchanged and shared unconsciously, by example and instruction, and include beliefs, views, guiding principles, fears and expectations. They are the roots of belonging, loyalty and cohesion within the family. Common meanings are essential for comfortable communication, pleasureable participation in interests, and tolerance of each other's pain. They are the basis for consensus and easy conflict resolution, and a coherent response to the environment. When a member leaves the family he can take these meanings with him without disrupting the family, and use them in the creation of a new family.

(2) Intersubjective Meanings
Intersubjective meanings by contrast are not the property of any single member, but are rooted in the family life, and are part of the self-definition of the family-as-a-whole as a "multi-facetted organism" (Minuchin and Fishman, 1981). Powerful common meanings lead to the development of a web of intersubjective meaning. A number of concepts refer to such notions, such as shared inter-personal reality, family matrix or family identity. The idea of a family myth,

or culture (see Byng-Hall, Chapter 8 and Cooklin, Chapter 2) clearly expresses the notion that the family has its own reality. Such a family reality can of course have an obscuring effect on member's own psychic reality.

C. Healthy Families

In a family functioning healthily, we assume they have a set of common and intersubjective meanings which enable creative responses to occur to life crises and individual needs. When we meet the family, what we see and observe is a healthy *surface action* or family interaction pattern where communications are meaningful and supportive: alliances occur appropriately within generations rather than across generations. A variety of feeling states can be expressed and integrated, parenting and family operations provide for the needs of children and adults in terms of physical protection, stimulation, emotional support, and maintain the integrity of personal and intergenerational boundaries. Individuals are nurtured, socialized and supported (Loader *et al.*, 1981).

D. Unhealthy Families

Unhealthy family functioning, by contrast, presents to the observer a surface action with interactions which are repetitive, destructive, and develop a compulsive circular dominating quality which cannot be stopped on request, despite obvious harmful consequences. In families whose surface action leads to rejection or injury of children, alternative forms of care must be considered. We see a variety of dysfunctional patterns:

(1) Communication being apparently absent, confusing, or full of angry disqualifications, through a lack of mutual listening.

(2) Severe disagreements and lack of resolution of conflict.

(3) A family atmosphere which may be chaotic or panicky and convey a quality of danger and unpleasantness.

(4) Attack, criticism, rejection and denigration or disorganization may overwhelm and a pervading sense of dissatisfaction be present.

(5) Boundaries may be severely intruded upon, such as excessive reaction between individuals, infantilization of parents or parentification of children, or so rigid that there is absence of meaningful interchange.

(6) Family operations and parenting results in lack of sufficient care, accidents or neglect, physical and emotional.

When we examine the salient stressful events and circumstances in the families of origin, or procreation in these families, we find an extraordinary weight of personal and shared experiences of loss and distress. Here, punishing and rejecting attitudes are expected and evoked, and an excess of painful events have occurred. Yet, what to the observer is moving, painful and sad, can be emptied of meaning by the family. Alternately, they appear to share an anticipation that such events will recur endlessly. A belief seems to be held that there is no way of escaping from the loyalty of being the same sort of parent as one's parents, or that children in turn will reject. Professionals in "parenting" relations will be expected and provoked to leave abruptly and cause more of the same pain. Family patterns are recreated, and what was right for the parent will be felt to be right for the child in the face of similar provocative behaviour.

Other families seem perpetually to be attempting to reverse or overturn the meaning of events; deprivation experienced has to be reversed by constantly seeking for objects or new people to be close to, children to be given to so that they can give back in turn. Alternately, someone else has to be found as the cause of all bad things, particularly professionals who are drawn in to try to help, then in turn are seen as the deprivers, the rejectors and the parent who beats. Thus the family homeostasis is maintained and the pathological common and inter-subjective meanings circumscribe the family and prevent creative response.

V.   ASSESSMENT MODEL

Ideally, an assessment model will:
(1) define the surface action of the family and the professional system who are attempting to work with that family, and assess the degree of dysfunction of both family and capacity of the therapeutic system;
(2) pinpoint the relevant site of stresses and the way that they have been handled and remain represented in the current family system, influencing surface action;
(3) predict what would be a healthy surface action for this particular family in relationship to the child's needs, and what changes are necessary for that family to become functional, and to assess what therapeutic work might be necessary to achieve this;
(4) make a formulation which connects the events that this particular family has had to accept and integrate, the way in which the family characteristically handles such stresses, the major beliefs and meanings they hold and the surface action which results;
(5) decide what decision needs to be taken in the child's best interests in the light of the formulation of the family.
What is the least detrimental alternative given such factors?

VI.   THE ASSESSMENT PROCESS

The assessment process itself requires that we:
 (i) hear the individual's, family's, professional's report of self, others, episodes and history;
(ii) elicit and observe characteristic interaction so as to be able to define the family in action.

A.   Clinic Team and Setting

We find that a clinic family representing and reflecting the ecosystem of professionals and family who are consulting us is a helpful model in this field.

We need to hold within our own family both the overall interactional view of the ecosystem and the individual needs in that particular context. We find that a psychiatrist or social worker provides the medical and social work backup essential for communication with the professional and legal system. We also find it helpful to have a child psychotherapist on the team who is able to focus on the child's needs and communications *per se*, since the child, as the least physically powerful member of the system, has the quietest voice, yet the whole plan is to do with his needs. Having the whole panoply of one-way screens and video is helpful so that we can maintain a position both "inside" and "outside" the process.

Access to psychologists and paediatricians are also essential in the task of defining both individual needs and capacities, as well as the system as a whole. There are certain advantages of a central hospital or clinic setting which is separate from the localities of those concerned with the case. This enables a clear physical boundary to be established, separating the assessment team from local politicians and media pressures. Having a clearly defined authority role as a supra-regional Hospital clinic helps the clinic team to remain "meta" or at a different level to the system of the professionals and the family. There is a pressure cooker effect in such a consultation which can increase intensity and facilitate decision making. However, there is the disadvantage that family and professionals are having to operate in a strange context, and stress can distort the situation.

B.   Who Are Seen?

We see *together* all family members and significant professionals who have "living together" relationships, "responsibility and authority" relationships or access relationships. The "ecosystem" may include parents, foster/adoptive parents, grandparents, new co-habitees, other children, social workers, solicitors, or other professionals.

We also see family or system members in a variety of combinations, depending on the natural, recreated, therapeutic, decision making or significant past systems, but we do not bring together those who have no contact. Thus we would not see children with a parent where there is no current access, unless as part of the therapeutic plan. We would, on occasions, see older children alone, but would try to make it clear that we did not expect loyalty to be breached, and also that we would respect issues of confidentiality. Children must not feel they have *adult* powers of decision making. Seeing everybody in one session or sequentially gives multiple impact on the therapist. This can take several hours and is often very stressful! Tensions are often high and feelings fraught.

C.   What Techniques are Used?

(1)   Exploring and elaborating the Surface Action
In order to see the system as a whole and also the various subsystems, we need to foster interactions. All members of the group are asked to describe to the others

"the problem" as they see it, and to define the decision which needs to be made. On my part, I use techniques of joining by connoting destructive behaviour as "helpful", allowing individuals to negatively connote their own behaviour rather than having others do it. In many situations, there is considerable conflict between social workers and natural parents, and the latter feel judged and blamed, a state compounded by the fact that Court cases are often pending. In this way I attempt to keep myself "meta" to the system rather than creating alliances, i.e. I attempt to maintain a neutral position (e.g. Palazzoli *et al.*, 1980).

(2) Interactional Tasks
To prevent myself from being bombarded by a family who often feel they need to attempt to convince me of their view, I find interactional tasks helpful.
  (a) With infants, I ask the caretakers or potential caretakers to demonstrate their parenting skills, e.g. feeding, changing, comforting, stimulating, etc.
  (b) With toddlers, we provide and encourage care and play situations, setting of limits, separations, reunions, stranger reactions, etc.
  (c) With older children, I ask the various adults involved to talk to the children about the situation and about their life history as well as establishing them (the children) to express their wishes and opinions.
Throughout all, I am keen to assess attachment behaviour (Bentovim, 1979), the nature of relationships, as well as parental competence and insight.

(3) Observations of non-verbal Behaviour-play
While the adults are involved in their communications to each other or to us, the children are often involved in a range of play therapy material, and one or other of the interviewers is usually giving attention to this. If there is more than one child, then as well as noting their separate behaviours, it is important to observe their interaction with each other. The other non-verbal communications between all members of the system are readily enacted before us during the process of the interview so that we can assess the atmosphere, mood and operations of the group.

(4) Exploring the Surface Action of the Whole System
The interviewer needs to take note of the patterns of *dyadic* and *triadic* relationships, to observe circularities of interactions, the repetitive interacion patterns leading back on themselves. I may use structural approaches, e.g. "discuss this with him/her and we'll listen", or "change places" etc., or triangular questions: "which of the children would say they most want to be with you, which with a foster parent" etc. In these various ways, the surface action mapped.

(5) Depth Structure Exploration
The longitudinal process is very important, and through listening to the history of events in the families of origin and procreation, and through observing the *ways* of telling and the *meanings* attached thereto, it is possible to identify the meanings held in *common* and also the *lack* of common meanings which result in conflict (e.g. the role of biological parents as seen by substitute families and

vice versa). Therefore, the variation of meanings in the different subsystems can be endless, but are fundamental, and can be seen to be repeated continuously.

(6) Use of Geneograms, etc.

Compiling geneograms can be a useful addition to ways of gathering and conveying information, but, being so time consuming, are only of value in a few situations. However, we frequently advocate the need for a *life book* for any child who has a complicated life history involving separations and changes of caretaker. Such a book gives a year by year account of the child's life, with all important events and details recorded. It includes photos of the child, and of the people who have or have had an important role in his life, as well as photos of significant places where he may have lived. Details of a child's early life before he came into care are, sadly, often not available for the older child, and of course frequent changes of personnel during a child's life in care may also result in a lamentable lack of information for that period too. Where natural parents, with help, are able to relinquish their hold on the fantasy that their child ought to return home (e.g. in situations where a child has been in a substitute home for some years and may well be adopted eventually, and whose natural parents have been on the periphery), the compiling of a life book of the period when the child lived at home with them can be a therapeutic task. It can be seen as a gift to the child and therefore as a reparative gesture by the parents who are able to absolve themselves of some of the awful burden of guilt which most of these parents feel.

Parents have asked to present these books directly to the foster/adoptive parents so that they can explain the details face to face with the people who will be interpreting them to the child when the time comes for him to want to know about his real parents. It is conceivable that this could be a helpful occasion to all concerned, but implies that work has to be done with both the natural and the substitute parents. The life book can provide information for the child which can act as background context to give meaning to bewildering life events, and a secure base to explore from.

(7) Use of Family Doll Figures to convey History

In our assessment interview, we use doll family figures, small pipe-cleaner clothed dolls, to represent parents, grandparents, children, babies and any other significant people in the child's life. These can be used by the adults and the child as aids to the telling of the story. These figures help the older child (over three) to be an active participant in the process, and to demonstrate his attachments often in quite a remarkable way, and can be recreated with the "real" people in the room by seeing whose lap the child would sit on to watch T.V. or whose arms to be comforted in if he falls.

VI. CASE ILLUSTRATION

The following case illustration demonstrates the application in practice of these principles. The P family have been described briefly in Bentovim (1980), but the issues are so clear that it seems an excellent example to describe in more detail here.

Angelina P was referred as a 2½-year-old by a social services department, having been in care since 3 months of age with an experienced foster-family following a severe abusive episode. Her parents had been of considerable concern even before her birth because of poor marital relationships, marital violence, very poor financial and social coping. Loretta, the mother, had been at a school for slow learning children, and had met her husband when he was ill in the hospital where she was working as a ward orderly.

Angelina had recovered quite remarkably from the abuse, and there was no permanent injury. Her parents had separated when the father was imprisoned, and both returned to their families of origin where they did not resume their former relationship. Neither parent visited Angelina. Loretta had a brief relationship with another man, an abortion, and some six months before the consultation (i.e. after a 20-month gap), started to visit Angelina regularly with her parents' encouragement. The issue to be decided was whether it was in Angelina's interest to be rehabilitated with her own mother now that she was "ready", mother having divorced Angelina's father who had no wish for further contact. Alternately, should Angelina remain with the foster-parents who wanted her to stay with them? Angelina saw her mother one day a week, and was confused about who was who. Because of the intensity of pressure on the foster parents to support Angelina's return, the grandparents were stopped from seeing her to create some sort of boundary and space for decision making.

VII. THE PROCESS OF INTERVIEWING

A. Initial Contact

To have any opportunity of remaining being seen as separate from the local agencies involved, it was felt that it would be best to ask Loretta and her parents to come and "give their story" and be heard first. Accusations of being influenced by the social workers could then be avoided, and they would see that their "meanings" to the events would be heard before anyone else's.

The surface action of this particular family (Loretta herself was the youngest of three children) became evident. The step-grandfather, a quiet, placating man soon took a back seat, while his wife spoke for her daughter.

Therapist: What do you understand as the purpose of this meeting?

Step-grandfather: [a quietly spoken diplomatic man] We understand we are meeting together to see whether in your view, my daughter, or our daughter, has the ability to know how to cope with Angelina if consideration is given to her return. We would like to satisfy ourselves.

Loretta: [talks slowly and hesitatingly] To get something sorted out — to have her back.

Grandmother: [an awkward, jerky, angular lady with jerky movements and a rapid flow of talk] She wants her daughter, doctor, that's all she's asking for; it's not right, she's been punished for what her husband did, she should have her daughter, it's only right. We've been month after month fighting the case through the courts. There's been a change of personality. Speaking as a mother I worry about my daughter: what you don't learn with one, you learn with the next. I don't care how much book knowledge you have, it takes 20 years to know . . .

As described previously, we are interested not only in the salient events of the family's experience, but the way they have been "digested" by the family, and the web of meanings that these events have for the family, and therefore how the present decision is viewed.

B. The Telling of the Histories

Loretta clearly had little voice of her own, and in getting her to tell her story a good deal of boundary making was necessary. Her loyalty to her own mother's view of events, and the meaning she attributed was such that there was no independent view expressed. Instead of grandparents and a parent, there was a mother, a peripheral father and a child not of 20 but of about 11 years.

C. Loretta's Story

Therapist: How have things got to a position—how long is it, 2 years, since she was in hospital and has not been in your care. How did it come about?

Step-grandfather and grandmother: Do you want us to speak?

Therapist: I think Loretta should speak.

Loretta: When she first went into hospital . . .

Therapist: Could you take us back further.

Loretta: I don't know. He used to be out of work; he hit me around; I became pregnant, didn't know until 5 months, he hit me around, went to hit me in the stomach, threatened to kill her. I had her for 6 weeks. He was in and out of jobs like a yoyo. He hit her, she went into hospital. He went inside. The main thing I could do was get a job to pay bills he owed—gas bills, electricity—I went to work . . .

Therapist: How did you get involved with your ex-husband?

Loretta: I was working as a domestic assistant; he was a patient.

Therapist: How did you all get on at first?

Grandmother: [interrupting] He was the sort of fellow who could hide; a terrible liar. His grandfather told us to be wary, a fine time to tell us: at the wedding. He was spendthrift, exaggerates. I said he seems alright, a good family, all part of growing up.

Loretta: He had no end of jobs. He was telling everyone else what to do; gave him notice.

Therapist: You've learned the hard way . . .

Grandmother: May I interrupt, she was battered about but she tried to hold her marriage together like any wife; no one wants to be a failure. Like my first marriage, I was battered about; I tried to hold it together. Loretta was loyal to him, but according to his doctor he was a psychopath and "they will lock him away" the doctor said. I said "At least that's something . . ."

A shared agreement immediately emerges as the ex-husband as the source of all bad things. Loretta tells her story impassively, briefly, with little feelings, as if the whole thing has been emptied of any meaning except that there was nothing Loretta could do, nor her parents, except blame the "psychopathic" husband.

D. The Grandmother's Story

Therapist: [pulled in by the grandmother] Did you make the same mistake as your daughter?

Grandmother: [introducing a second belief that being in a foster home leads to pain and long-standing damage] I've gone through what the baby went through; I was brought up by somebody—you can ask my husband—I ask myself to this day, "Did my mother love me?" I wonder if it was a case like Angelina's—we didn't call it fostering—there was no such thing as fostering in those days was there doctor? I remembered children telling me and it left a scar.

Therapist: What happened in your marriage?

Grandmother: I was alone for 10½ years.

Therapist: Loretta was 4 when he left you?

Grandmother: No, older than that, about 6.

Therapist: Would she have known, do you remember?

Loretta: No.

Grandmother: She would have been too young.

Therapist: [pursuing] There would have been quite an atmosphere.

Grandmother: No, I reassured them and said "Daddy's gone away". I kept the photo on the dresser; he loved the children.

Therapist: What about before he went?

Grandmother: [jerking furiously] Oh . . . Yes—I would have to—it was dreadful—there was another woman on the scene—it was dreadful—I never blamed him, he was a weak man to go—I always blame the woman—I always do.

Therapist: But it was a pretty violent time.

Grandmother: I had to shield them, send them into the front room, watch the T.V. Daddy's coming back for dinner. He would start—the only vicious time was when he picked up the T.V. and threw it on the floor. That frightened them—it would. Then he threw a boiling cup of tea at me. I said "He's upset—he doesn't know what he's doing . . ."

Therapist: It sounds very distressing.

Grandmother: No, it never upset them, you can check with my doctor. I reassured them every day—the picture was on the dresser until they learnt for themselves when they grew up.

A pattern is thus revealed that despite trying to empty and deny the significance and meaning of very painful life events, rejection and violence still pervade marital choice and child-rearing. At the same time, fostering is seen as damaging, and once violent men are excluded, satisfactory partners (e.g. step-grandfather) are found; "Natural" mothers are seen as the best and return of the "natural" child the only solution.

E. Meeting with Angelina, Foster-parents and Social Worker

The next section of the interview involved bringing in Angelina, her foster-parents, and their social workers so that Angelina's relationships with the adults could be observed, and the relationship of the professionals to the families enacted, rather than just be talked about.

Angelina stayed very close to her foster-mother, facing ourselves and her own family. Loretta offered her sweets, and we saw the familiar pattern of the well-attached 2½-year-old who went to each person in the room but returned back on each occasion to her foster-mother for "re-fuelling". It was clear that her foster-mother was her primary attachment figure. Although she *knew* and recognized her natural mother and grandparents, her response was as to a group of strangers, and her principal attachment figures, primary and alternatives, were all in the foster-family.

The "pattern", surface action, between the adults was clearly one where two powerful women, the foster-mother and grandmother, were battling for control, both disqualifying each other and "triangling" in Loretta to back each other up. The social worker, a man, was locked into the "ineffective" father role together with step-grandfather and foster-father. The therapist similarly found himself inducted into the system and a response he recognized of talking continuously to try and stay out of the system followed, quite ineffectively.

Therapist: How does she get on when she goes with her mother?

Foster-mother: Well, she used to be irate, but they have been getting better. Yesterday was exceptional, she was very good.

Loretta: She played, got a small nursery book and pulled me down with her, sat on my lap, or she's even taken my hand to play in the garden (of children's home) or go up and down the stairs.

Therapist: Her development.

Foster-mother: [taking over] Talks in sentences and answers questions, draws and recognizes things in books.

Therapist: [following] Is she attached to you and your husband?

Foster-mother: I am afraid so.

Therapist: Why do you say "afraid"?

Foster-mother [holding Angelina in front of her] I feel it's natural; I feel for grandmother; I know she doesn't believe me, but she's living with us as a family member. It clashes when her own family wants to be the same. I try, you can ask Loretta, to understand but I am tied by what the (social work) office says. We are fond of her, had her since she was 14½ weeks, but it is very difficult all round, all the situation — it is difficult.

Therapist: [to grandparents and Loretta] It is difficult: you want Angelina to be truly loved. For her sake, you wouldn't want her to be in a place where she's not loved, and yet you want to love her and it is hard to hold . . .

Grandmother: [disqualifying] We've said to Mrs S many a time, she cries for her baby, she cries all the time.

Foster-mother [disqualifying] This is the difficulty. I've told her many times, doctor, she's been desperately upset in the house, and when she's been like this, I've wanted a social worker to see her. The conversation that came up last week—and I hope you'll bear me out, Loretta—was that I have had her since she was tiny and to be honest I would like to keep her, but I said I know I can't; it's not my position to say what happens to the baby. You said —tell me if I am lying—if you couldn't have her home you wouldn't want her moved from me. Is that how the conversation went?

Loretta: Of course I want her home.

Foster-mother: We were talking about placements elsewhere; I could accept her coming home, but not moved to another foster home.

Grandmother: [breaking in and disqualifying] I think a lot of these children who are fostered, doctor, and I'm speaking of experience again, and a lot of them are mixed up mentally.

Therapist: Can I stop you for a minute. Look, Loretta, you are in a difficult position in this room at the minute: you are trying to relate to the person who is mothering your child and your own mother, and it's hard; she's doing a good job. [Loretta sobbing]

Grandmother: So would Loretta if she was given a chance.

Therapist: [trying to make an alliance with Loretta] May I please? [to silence grandmother] The fact is you have a 2-year-old who was injured at 6 weeks and almost died, and she was in your and your husband's care at the time. You would want her to be cared for, and you want to care for her, and you're clearly caught between the messages you hear from the foster home and your own home; wanting to see her grow up well. The chances were high that she could be mentally handicapped; it's a credit to her foster family that she's not. You are all very attached to her as families and with yourselves, and want her to grow up in the right place; the question is now what are Angelina's needs; she's the main person here, what are her interests?

F.   Interview between Loretta and Angelina

We had been informed that to help Loretta separate from her mother, she had regularly attended a woman's refuge, worked with the children for some months, and had developed a reasonable degree of competence. So we tested this by seeing them together and giving Loretta the task of playing with Angelina. What we saw was as follows.

Loretta chose to play with the small miniature railway, circular track, engine and trucks. What was striking was seeing Loretta wheel the train around, making the appropriate noises, with Angelina standing by watching. Angelina fingered and touched the table and reached across to touch the train, to which Loretta said "You'll get your finger caught—yes you will", and proceeded to push the train around herself. "Put the animals in there" [the centre of the track] was Loretta's next suggestion. "What about all the others", and again Loretta proceeded to do it herself—"Put it on the table". When Loretta was distracted by us asking her something, Angelina immediately took up the game of putting objects in the centre of the track and showed more capacity for actual play.

A phone bell rang in the distance. Angelina looked sharply around and said quite distinctly to us "I want my mummy". Loretta's immediate response was "Do you want to go to the toilet, do you want to go to wee?" The therapist tried to interject that maybe she was suddenly aware of foster-mother's absence, but Loretta ignored it, felt her nappies and took her to the lavatory saying she was wet.

What we were seeing was two sisters rather than a mother and child, and although Loretta showed more independence alone, she failed to "facilitate" Angelina's play, and played herself. She failed to pick up the cue that Angelina wanted her mother (her foster-mother), but was acting in the inter-subjective belief that the meaning to be given to her behaviour was that, despite absence and separation, she was still part of *their* family and not the foster family.

G. Our Formulation and Advice

We saw this as a situation where Angelina was clearly well attached and was thriving with her foster family, and that her own family was locked into a repetitive pattern of maintaining powerful infantilizing relationships between mothers and daughters by excluding violent men, and so needed to restore Angelina to the family. Thus, they gave no meaning to her real position in the foster-family which we felt needed formalizing through adoption if necessary. However painful, Loretta's family must accept a shared responsibility for events, and to see that Loretta had a future and potential to be a good mother, but not for Angelina who was now part of the foster-family. Despite improvements on mother's part, they risked major disturbance if she was moved, due to disruption of attachments, and there could be a danger of recreation of rejection and even abuse.

We would advise lessening contact drastically and a life book for information to be created, going to court to dispense with family permission for adoption if necessary, maintenance of occasional contact could continue providing the family had worked through the losses and could take a more distant relative role, thus enriching Angelina's extended family network. *Realities* could then be shared rather than perpetuate the myth of Angelina being a "live" part of their family essential to its operation.

H. Feedback Process

We had a series of meetings with family, foster-family and workers to share this view and to start the process of painful working through. The grandmother's response was predictable, to attempt to label and exclude the therapist who, in making the formulation above, inevitably moved out of a meta position to one in which he was aligned with the perceived best interests of the child. He was seen as "violently" attacking Loretta, the family and Angelina, and she threatened to leave coffins outside the hospital, put a curse on him, and wished every evil on him.

The violence of her response led the social work department to say that they were not going to return Angelina but instead of holding on to Angelina's needs for continuity, they said that Loretta was too much enmeshed in her own family, and had not proved her independence, and therefore rehabilitation could not be considered then. Furthermore, they did not take the action to get adoption through dispensation of parental consent, but used the power of the court order, giving the authorities care and control and parental authority to regulate contact which was reduced to fortnightly. Therefore, Angelina remained without a clear unequivocal family to call her own, and there was sufficient contact, despite lowering its frequency, to create a conflict of loyalties. This maintained the confusion for Angelina over subsequent years, and the lack of a truly *clear* message to say that Angelina would *never* be able to return to her family of origin.

With hindsight, it was clear that there was a "denied" yet powerful alliance between the *biological* family and the *senior* management of the social services department. They shared the common meaning that "biological" families are "true" families, and there can never be a true divorce, unless the family agree to it. This is a common inter-subjective meaning and myth.

I. Follow-up

Two and a half years later there was a further consultation requested — Angelina was now 5 years of age and the question was the same: should rehabilitation with the biological family be considered? The statement made about rehabilitation of Angelina not being possible while *Loretta* was living and enmeshed with her own family was taken, as so often, as a challenge. Although the agency meant it as a "never to return", it was heard and acted as a statement of "You'll never do it". Inevitably, the reversal occurred. Loretta married a childhood sweetheart who agreed absolutely with the maternal grandparents; he married into their family.

They had a baby who was cared for beautifully; Angelina stayed for two weekends every month and was skilfully addressing all by their correct titles and in the right place, was becoming very attached to the new baby, and cried when she had to leave. The foster-mother was withdrawing; Angelina was about to start school, and her family felt that surely this was the right time to return to the family. This situation is one that occurs inevitably, and represents a failure to take decisive action earlier, and our failure to see where "change" had to occur for Angelina to gain a "real" family and not be in a limbo. She is now in danger of detaching herself from the family she lives with and live a "fantasy" life with the family she spends weekends with. This can seem to be truly perfect, and can result in an adolescent with no "real" family and literally living in a family in her head. Fortunately, we had a second chance, and so could ensure that the previous work could be brought to a more successful conclusion: e.g. to change the social services policy to ensure that a "real" family is created no matter how painful.

J. Conclusions

Angelina's story reveals many of the issues outlined in the earlier sections of this chapter: the characteristic surface action and depth structure of a complex ecostructure, and the approach to interviewing and assessment of the total system. Also the issues of the individuals, particularly the dependent child who is a member of so many competing and conflicting systems, and the needs for a view on that child's behalf. But this view needs to be meta to the whole system as well as keeping the families in mind. The relationship with the professional system also has to be carefully assessed, and the point of leverage needs to be discovered if the least detrimental form of care is to be found for the child. Then she can have an opportunity to grow up in a family, and yet know who her extended family are, and who she is.

REFERENCES

Bentovim, A. (1979). Child development research findings and psychoanalytic theory: an integrative critique. *In* "The First Year of Life", (D. Shaffer and J. Dunn, eds.), London, Wiley.

Bentovim, A. (1980). "Psychiatric Aspects in Terminating Parental Contact". *In* BAAF discussion series, no. 2.

Bentovim, A. and Gilmour, L. (1981). A family therapy interactional approach to decision making in child care, access and custody cases. *Journal of Family Therapy*, **3**, 65-78.

Goldstein, J., Freud, A. and Solnit, A. J. (1973). "Beyond the Best Interests of the Child", Free Press, New York.

Kinston, W. and Bentovim, A. (1981). Creating a focus for brief marital and family therapy. *In* "Forms of Brief Therapy", (S. H. Budman, ed.), Guildford Press, New York.

Loader, P., Burck, C., Kinston, W. and Bentovim, A. (1981). Method for Organising the Clinical Description of Family Interaction: The Family Interaction Summary Format. *Aust. J. Fam. Ther.*, **2**, 131-141.

Minuchin, S., Montalvo, B., Guerney, B. G., Rosman, B. L. and Schumer, F. (1967). "Families of the Slums", Basic Books, New York.

Minuchin, S. and Fishman, H. C. (1981). "Techniques of Family Therapy", Harvard University Press, Cambridge, Mass.

Palazzoli, M. S., Boscolo, L., Cecchin, G. and Prata, G. (1980). Hypothesising-circularity-neutrality: three guidelines for the conductor of the session. *Family Process*, **19**, 3-12.

Parkes, C. M. (1971). Psychosocial Transitions: A Field of Study. *Soc. Science & Med.*, **5**, 101-115.

Rowe, J., Hundleby, M., Paul, H. and Keane, A. (1980). Long-term fostering and the Children's Act 1975. *Adoption and Fostering*, **102**, 11-16.

Tizard, B. (1977). "Adoption — A Second Chance", Open Books, London.

INDEX

abdominal pain, 324, 325

access: in adoption, 286, 365; control of, 365; decision-making in, 363-4; in fostering 286, 365; and reconstituted families 286-7, 365; therapeutic 289; *see also* custody

acute illness, 324

adolescence: fantasy, 378; and handicap 303; patterns 52-3; sexuality in, 14-15

adoptive families, 267, 268, 274; access, 286, 365; finance, 288; life books, 365, 371; and loss, 281; names 285-6; of older children, 283-4, 365; state intervention, 276, 278; therapy with, 289-91, 346-7

adulthood: and handicap, 304; new, 15-16

agencies, *see* social services

alcohol abuse, 243, 338-41

alliances, *see* coalitions

alternatives, illusion of, 179, 180, 184-5, 187

analogic communication, 24-5, 27, 44, 50

animals, and communications, 25

anorexia nervosa, 324; therapy for, 49, 78-9, 352, 338-41

anorgasmia, therapy for, 230, 238, 239, 245-6

anticipation and pattern, 109, 112

apprenticeship training, 210, 211, 219

arthritis, 320, 321

Ashby's Homeostat, 51-52

assessment case study, 371-79; of ecosystem, 368-9; for local authority care, 366, 368-71; for marital therapy, 222-3; model, 368; process, 368-71; techniques, 369-71

asthma, 320-21, 322, 323, 324-5, 327, 328

attachment: in fostering, 275, 277; and reconstituted families, 282-5, 287-8

attachment behaviour, assessment, 370, 375, 377

attachment theory: and control processes, 53; and systems theory, 103-4

authority: parental, 28-9, 32, 162, 168-9; state, 347; therapist's, 161-2

autism, infantile, 310-2

avoidance patterns and loss, 253

babies, *see* infants

balancing, affective, 76-7, 84

beginnings: problem-focussed, 149-51; successful, 137

behaviour: change in, 101; classes of, 101, 104; and feelings, 40

behavioural therapy, 163, 223-4; advantages, 232; alternatives to, 244; disadvantages, 233; family approach, 222; limitations of, 243; marital and sexual, 221, 223-46; outcome studies, 244-6

belief systems, 38

bereavement, *see* loss

body language, 24-5, 44, 81, 370

boundaries: 4; definition, 8; dysfunction in, 164, 168; establishment, 201; flexibility, 76-7; homeostatic, 76; of human systems, 7-8; and infant, 10-11; marking, 76, 78; parental, 11-12, 60, 77, 201; therapist's role, 78-9

Byng family myth, 43, 180-9, 190, 191

cancer, 320

care, local authority, 275; assessment for, 366, 368-371; case study, 371-79; decision-making, 363-79; family therapy and, 364; least detrimental, 364-5

case histories, taking, 236-7, 373-5

catastrophe, double-ended, 181-2

catastrophe theory, 55

causality: circular, 5-6, 102, 160; linear, 5, 40-1, 42, 102

change: attitude to, 33; and family myth, 190-1; in here-and-now systems, 37, 38-9, 48, 50, 55, 58-9, 60, 63, 71, 202; and insight, 19, 21; levels of learning, 113; in medium-term sequences, 55-8, 63-70; and positive feedback, 5; resistance to, 158-61; in systems over time, 37, 39, 58-9, 60, 64, 71; theories of, 37, 39-41, 55, 101, 113-15, 145

381